GW00372091

A PUZZLED EXISTENCE

A 60 YEAR

AUTOBIOGRAPHICAL

PORTRAIT

BY THE ARTIST

JASON

COPYRIGHT 2012 BY:

JASON P. GOODMAN

a.k.a. ALCHEMY STUDIO, LLC

All rights reserved. No part of this book, in both paper and digital format, may be reproduced or used in any form, nor may this material be downloaded into any form of information storage and retrieval system without the written permission of the author.

Printed in the United States of America

First Edition

ISBN # 978-0-615-56793-8

Front cover design, rear cover photograph and complete manuscript design, e.g. fonts chosen and complete manuscript feel are by: ALCHEMY STUDIO LLC

DEDICATION

I can honestly say that I have only experienced true love once in my life, why she stays with me I will never understand, so I don't press the issue and just continue to walk around with the same stupid grin on my face.

ALSO BY JASON GOODMAN

POETRY

Simple Reflections…on a frozen surface (Dedicated to my fallen comrades, Riverine Forces, Mekong River, Vietnam: 1970)
Nervous Reader

STAGE PRODUCTIONS

Mental Perspectives

PERIODICALS

Art Voices Magazine- Palm Beach, supplemental.
The Atlantic Owl- Boca Raton, Weekly column.
Solares Hill Magazine- Key West, regular contributor, articles & page art

TECHNICAL INFORMATION

Sculpture Curriculum designed explicitly for Australian Secondary Schools. 273 pages of materials & illustrations, teaching advanced sculpture Curriculum in Australian secondary schools. 348 pages written commentary with parallel color 35mm slide projection- 89 pages with 72 slides. Subject: A maximum security prison, both physical & mental, from inside

The Impact of Adult Education on individuals and their communities, Melbourne, Australia and Boyton Beach, Florida. Complete curriculum for sculpture. 108 pages with pen & ink illustrations

Advertising copy: Multi-media; print, radio and television. Write, produce and direct 15, 30 and 60 second television commercial spots; book sound studio time and professional musicians to create unique, 'one off' sound beds for background music in both radio and television advertising; total time in this business- 7 years. ALCHEMY STUDIO LLC was the agency, no hired help.

FICTION

Blood on my hands and a knife in my back

PREFACE

To my reader; for more years than I care to admit, I have been told to keep a journal of my experiences in life. At the age of sixty, with a professional career as an artist spanning 40 years, I decided it was time to write one. Please realize that this is not a travel manual, a cook book nor a self-help book. It is a complete, brutally honest look at a man and his career.

In the composition of this text, I made every effort to keep everything in chronological order with the use of letters, calendars, newspaper clippings and automobiles. You will notice that the car will be mentioned, this was a way for me to determine the exact year I was writing about. As a young man, I was involved with many forms of automobile racing that left an indelible mark on my appreciation of cars and the excitement of the competition.

To protect identities, I have used very few names throughout the book, and names mentioned are actual people. The reason for this is both gallant in protecting someone's good character; and practical, to avoid any major legal action.

To write an unabashed and purely raw autobiography, I had to include many areas of my life that I am not very proud of. My involvement in combat during the Vietnam War left an impact that haunts me to this very day; both mentally and physically. Due to injuries sustained under fire, I have endured many major surgical interventions. Many of which dealt with neuropathy of my left side; and I am a left handed artist. The possibility is real that my long and prolific career may be coming to an end due to lack of feeling in my arms and left hand; another valid reason for penning this text. I have made every effort to be truthful and precise with the entire contents of this book. There are many parts of my story that I did not want to introduce, I did anyway to give you the most comprehensive autobiography possible. I sincerely hope my efforts will meet with your satisfaction and provide a "good read."

INTRODUCTION

Jason Goodman is quite a character, but A PUZZLED EXISTENCE is not a work of fiction. It is the autobiography of a man who has lived more deeply and experienced more broadly than a character in speculative fiction. Jason would never have been born were it not for a car crash between a refined woman who graduated from MIT and an uncultured man who barely made it out of the sixth grade. The unlikely love and the unresolved fault of the fender bender ultimately produced a child who was equal parts sensitive artist and brutish thug. Indeed, I have always been struck by how the serenity of Jason's paintings gives no clue to the turbulent interior of the artist. Yin and Yang coexist and interpenetrate one another in Jason, and whether Yin or Yang will reveal itself and dominate is unpredictable in his escapades.

A PUZZLED EXISTENCE tells the story of a journey from innocence to experience, from life in a Pennsylvania coal-mining town in the 1950's, to the heady days of the 1960's in New York, to the jungles of Vietnam and to the long road home again. On the way, Jason takes us on a tour of the depths of despair, but does not leave us there. A testimony to the power of the human spirit, Jason shows us the way out, taking us to the heights of love and hope.

I am happy to call Jason my friend and proud to say that several of his paintings hang in my private collection. For Jason's friends, A PUZZLED EXISTENCE is a treasure trove of the stories we have urged him to preserve in print. For readers who have not had the good fortune to know Jason personally, it is an opportunity to become acquainted with a unique individual. For the academic, A PUZZLED EXISTENCE is a valuable work of cultural history.

Dr. William Irwin
Professor of Philosophy
Kings College
Wilkes-Barre, Pa.

INTRODUCTION

If you look in the dictionary for the word Renaissance man it may very well be defined as Michelangelo, or Jason.

His story is so varied and complex it is hard to believe it is one man's life, lived in a mere 60 years. He pulls and pushes you through the pages like back streets in a strange city and will have you amused, titillated, perplexed, shocked or terrorized. From his humble beginnings, through his 'toil and trouble' teens you become aware of him as an intelligent, creative person, too advanced for a dirty depressing coal town. He unknowingly enlisted for a war as a young man and is thrown into a cauldron of insanity and death. His sensitivity becomes almost frozen and his deeds there will be carried to haunt him for the rest of his life. Jason's relentless energy, ambition, talent and hard work deserve honor and respect. He defined the term multitasking before it had reached another person's lips.

A PUZZLED EXISTENCE will fill your every moment with humor, intelligence, frankness and adventure, though be wary of turning the page too quickly as it could prove to be a 'choking hazard'.

As a published author myself, having researched a family's story based on fact, it is difficult to open up your life for everyone to see. Jason does this with complete, uncompromising honesty; the good, bad and ugly are all tossed about and exposed. The reader cannot walk away from this book and never think of it again. It is a story of such a full life it will have you reflecting on your own. So sit back and watch the puzzle pieces fall, even though the 'image may vary', I still found it 'suitable for framing'.

Teresa Marie Fee
Artist and Author of IRELANDS MAGDALEN

HOURS OF WHOLESOME FAMILY FUN

It was a one lane dirt road at best. During the hot, dry months clouds of dust rose from the surface and coated everything in grit. When the rains came, certain sections would wash out creating crevices that were up to three feet deep, depending on the strength and duration of the deluge. Then came winter, well, you were on your own, though the basement contained a stock of canned foods. By canned, I mean the Mason jars filled with everything from peaches to rabbit and 'ring neck' stew complete with occasional buckshot pellets. Winter also meant that you would have to heat a kettle of water on the 'Pittston' coal stove and use it to defrost the well pump head and handle. There was a special spout cast into the well head for this purpose. If it was particularly cold, which it always seemed to be when it was my turn to 'fetch' the water, the process would have to be repeated with the two kettles of water in quick succession. Every time I hear that line from a Bob Dylan song "the pump don't work 'cause the vandals took the handles" I think about that pump.

Bathing was another interesting event. There were two ways of doing it. The first was the way you did until you were about six years old. Have you ever seen those large copper tubs which were rounded on both ends, about 16" deep and 30" long with two wooden handles, one at each end? They were designed to rest atop a large cast iron kitchen coal stove and used to heat large amounts of water, bath water, which I duly carried in from the well outside. A round, galvanized tub was placed on the floor and you, the under six year old, would sit in it while hot water was dumped on your head. Even here there was a technique, you had to place your head between your knees and wrap your arms around like a flesh ball, or a piece of modern sculpture, this way water wasn't wasted. The reason it was either hot or cold was simple, coal. It cost a lot of coal to heat a large caldron of water and there were usually three brothers waiting in line for their bath, for which the water was not changed, so it paid to be the first.

Please understand, besides coal, water was a precious commodity, especially in the dead of winter. Wells were only 30 to 50 feet deep, hand dug and rock walled to the surface. The old hand pumps could only raise water about 40 feet and the winter was a perfect time for the wells to run dry. Anyway, back to bathing. After you were six years old you used a porcelain basin in the sink, the kitchen sink that is. There wasn't any running water, but there was a sink! You washed yourself using a slightly different technique, homemade lye soap made from fat, a wash cloth, which everyone used, just as with the towels. Again consider wash day; well pump, coal, hot water to wash and hot water to rinse. Not to mention the frozen fabrics when they came in off the clothes line.

We called them 'butt' towels, this may strike some as being a bit gross, but it was the way of life at that time. If you were the unfortunate last person in the bath chain of command, the towel smelled like someone's ass, except for certain corners which were reserved for one's face. There was only one towel for six people and two of those were our parents. Naturally, my thoughtful Father was always number one. I will explain that protocol a little later.

OUT OF THE BODY FUNCTIONS:

We had an outhouse, which, for rather practical purposes was located about 75 feet from the house, just past the raspberry patch and clothes lines. It was a 'two holer' as they were called, one hole being larger than the other, to be quite honest, I never measured them. When you thought you had reached manhood, you would carefully sit on the left side. If you were too hasty you could drop into the abyss up to your knees, unless, of course, your ass was manly and a double wide.

My Mother placed wallpaper on the inside walls, much to my father's constant ridicule. It wasn't all of the same pattern, but there were these tiny roses with little leaves, thousands of them, though they did nothing for the atmosphere we breathe in, that was dealt with by a bucket of 'sweet' lime,

4

which only my father was allowed to administer.

Our toilet tissue consisted of old telephone books or, most importantly, the Sears & Roebuck catalog. In the 50's Sears used newsprint for their catalog and that was the deciding issue. There weren't too many colored, glossy, photographic reproductions back then, nor would you want that sort of paper anyway. But, from time to time my Mother would receive her cherished Sears 'epistle' in the mail. It could take six months for it to make it the 75 foot journey to the 'house of convenience'. Another reason this catalog was so important, besides the obvious usage, was simple, sex. The Sears catalog in the outhouse was our sexual study-group session; it was responsible for my early sex education, unless that is, someone got to it first. The most sought after, and cherished pages, the pages that dealt with ladies undergarments, the pages full of black and white (more like a tan color) illustrations of brassieres, corsets and panties shown on the female body would be missing, never to be seen again. Also there was a secret code of silence; no one ever asked openly what became of those pages. Class would not convene for at least another six months, an eternity without knowing the most basic of female forms and their anatomy, As I sit here in Puerto Vallarta writing this, a man of 60 years, it just occurred to me why those particular pages were not removed from the catalog before its placement in the rose covered outhouse. Was this my parents attempt at teaching their four boys about women? Because not a word of that subject was ever mentioned in the house while we were growing up, but I will never know except for this nagging conjecture.

My Mother grew up in Newark, New Jersey, more will be explained in latter pages, but, her mother, my 'Jersey' Grandmother would visit us about every other light year and she was a smoker of cigarettes. My father on the other hand, disliked my grandmother and despised smoking of any kind. So, consequently when my grandmother would visit she would use the outhouse for her private smoking pleasure. Unfortunately, one day she threw her lighted cigarette butt (no pun intended) down into the bowels of the outhouse, then proceeded to return to New Jersey. After some time her cigarette caught fire to all those pages from the sears catalog showing women in different types of lingerie and nearly burned the outhouse down to its foundation. It was my Fathers fury, use of foul language and buckets of water from a rain barrel which saved our house of convenience from total destruction. And I'm not positive it was insured.

Needless to say, we heard about this sheer act of sabotage from my Father for at least 30 years, or whenever the subject somehow presented itself in idle conversation.

The truth of the matter is this, when my Grandmother heard about this, she laughed her dyed red hair off; she never cared too much for my Father anyway, and was the type that didn't keep her thoughts to herself. One thing I failed to mention was when she came into town, my Mother actually bought real toilet paper, which also made my Father go insane.

Our parents had four boys; we were all spaced approximately two years apart. Being a son of my father was not exactly correct, indentured servant or slave would be more appropriate.

My Mother, or Mary T, as I grew to call her, was a highly educated, sophisticated and cultured person. She was born in Newark, but spent most of her time in New York City. The woman drove a roadster with a rumble seat, belonged to the Polar Bear Club, studied art at the then renowned Fawcett School of Art and went on to become the first female student at M.I.T. in pursuit of mechanical drafting. With the onslaught of World War II, she worked at Grumman Aircraft and helped design critical components of the "Hellcat" fighter aircraft, a plane used extensively by the US Navy in the Pacific theater of war.

Allow me to revert for a moment, at age 19, Mary T won a full scholarship to study art at the Louvre in Paris, but, being the time period that it was, her father refused to allow her to go because a proper young, and rather good looking young woman should not be traipsing around Paris, France alone. My Father, aka "the Duke", in contrast, never completed the third grade, leaving school to work in the coal mines as a 'breaker boy'. This job entailed sitting on a plank over a fast moving conveyer belt and picking out rocks from the unprepared coal. He worked his way up to be a full-fledged coal miner. In the coal mines, a coal miner was like being in middle management, he had a crew of about 15 men working under him and he was the only one who could load the face hole with explosives and detonate them.

When the war broke out, he enlisted in the Coast Guard and served at a base in Baltimore. I will be addressing this later in a rather non-complimentary context, though for now, it is the beginning of my parent's story.

Mary T and the Duke had a minor traffic accident in Baltimore. It was never really established as to who was responsible for this fateful event, but we do know that the Duke had to stop by Mary T's house with $30 dollars to have her fender repaired and that was when he first asked her out on a date.

Practically to the day they died, my brothers and I could start the argument at any time by just asking the simple question, who ran into who?

My Father was somewhat of a ladies man, I gather that he was well endowed in the mid-section which might explain why he was a big prick.

Bill and Mary T went out and soon my brother Bill was conceived, out of wedlock, as they used to say. This tidbit of information was effectively concealed from us until 2004 when my brother Bill and I were putting our Mothers papers in order prior to her death. When we did the math, the months did not add up to nine, from the wedding date to his birth. Now that I think about this I have a feeling that it had more of an impact on my brother than he cared to admit. Here is where the dichotomy begins, Mary T made us listen

7

to classical music, read books, and introduced Amy Vanderbilt's social graces into our lives. In her mind, she was preparing four young men to become gentlemen and scholars.

Whereas, our father put a shovel into our hand and a pick in the other, scratched his scrotum, pointed at the ground and said "dig". He told us to keep digging until he personally said we could stop, that sentence was never spoken in my lifetime; the word stop that is.

Don't ask me where it came from, but in our yard, on one of the flat spots (we grew up on the side of a mountain) rested one half of a B-17 rubber gas tank. I think it came from the wing section because it had a porthole in it, a small round window with dozen of nuts and bolts holding it in place. Our illustrious father would occasionally rig up a set of old pipes when the creek was running, and fill this huge piece of rubber and 'viola' we had an above ground swimming pool, which you couldn't swim in, for one thing the fine steel mesh embedded in the rubber where it was cut in half would shred your underarms if you were not aware of the danger. It was even worse if it happened to your crotch. There are not too many dirt poor families that can boast about having a B-17 swimming pool in their yard. Just think a flying fortress gas tank that was prepared for our personal enjoyment, but that would not be the actual truth. Do I need to tell you who this pool was for during the August dog days? Let's just say it was usually dark before we were allowed to do a few laps.

'Volare' was playing on the radio, it was a popular AM hit at that time; my father was lying in his hammock, an old Coast Guard piece of ordinance which he had liberated from the base in Baltimore. I was reading a Reader's Digest in the cellar, where it was cooler, and ran across one of those 'Humor in these United States' columns. The article was about a man in boxer shorts, wearing an Army helmet and holding a bayonet, when an attractive woman from across the hall came by to borrow a cup of sugar, maybe it was semen, I was only about nine years old at the time and that subject did not appear in the Sears Catalog. For some reason I found this story to be outrageously funny which in turn prompted me to do the most logical thing and that was to share it with my parents in the front yard. Especially my father who we all sought favor from for various reasons, like staying alive.

I burst out of the cellar door telling this story and laughing like crazy when a back hand caught me across the face which sent me and the Readers Digest to the ground. Then he picked me up by my shirt and pants and threw me into the forsythia bush. All the while Al Martino belted out verses of that song "Volare, oh, oh, la la..."

In the 50's there was not a definition, let alone a word, for child abuse. It was more like child USE, which applied to me and my brothers. Remember the good book said, spare the rod and spoil the child. Can't say he ever committed that to memory, he never read many books, let alone that one.

The problem was multifaceted for me. First of all my oldest brother had paid his dues. My youngest brother was a 'baby', and the next oldest to me had suffered a bout with rheumatic fever, so he was pampered and happened to be my father's favorite.

Then to complicate the situation even more, besides the fact that I was normal and in good health, I, according to my father, "took" after my Mother. This was a real problem because our mother would talk back to my father and he would slap her around. I had a habit of doing the same thing, only my crime was asking too many questions. My dear dad did not like to be questioned about anything, so consequently, when excessive force and the legal use thereof was in order, your Dante became the most sought after object of rage release. Let's face it; a few ice cubes can stop any nose bleed, provided all of the ice cubes were not in the Dukes ice tea glass.

To be quite honest I have never been comfortable with the term "father". I mean, I'd walk before I bought a used car from this man. I promise I will grow up as quickly as possible as the pages of this book turn and take complete responsibility for my own life. But I must tell you a little more about the "Duke", aka, my father.

He adopted that nickname after someone seeing him for the first time mentioned that he looked a little like John Wayne. Well pilgrim, you could not have bestowed knighthood any better as he was a big fan of John Wayne, also known as the Duke. That is one of those moments in history that it is best to shovel the dirt back into the hole after the discovery.
As mentioned, he was a coal miner, and one of his jobs was to blast. The wall of coal at the end of a tunnel was called the face. The men tunneled in, and with wooden props, supported about 1000 feet of the earth above them. They would place wooden match sticks on top of the props as an early warning system that would let them know they would shortly be dead, if the match stick broke. After the tunnel was secure, pneumatic drills were used to drill predetermined holes into the coal. The Duke would then come along with his box of dynamite and pack the holes with a special tool that had a brass head with a small groove in it. The brass was to assure that no sparks would set off the dynamite and the groove was for the blasting cap wire, the last explosive device placed in the hole.
Once a safe distance was placed between them, the Duke would turn his little handle on the detonator and do two things; one would be to blow a big hole in the earth, and the other was to make some bastard richer than he already was. A set of railroad tracks quickly were laid, this was done before the dust settled because you were paid by tonnage. It was all about the number of cars that came to the surface full of coal. So as soon as the tracks were in place, the cars were pushed in and filled with coal, each one holding about 12 tons. They were loaded by hand with nothing but a shovel and brute force for the larger chunks.
After many years of doing this, the Duke, who was 6'4" tall

and almost as wide in the shoulders, had no trouble at all throwing his son Jason into his wife's pussy willow bush. Where I was tossed was not a random gesture, it was usually into something that Mary T had planted, thus adding a bit more drama to the incident.

Most people have heard the term "Coal Cracker", well I am going to explain exactly what that means in time.
The Duke was always on the make, you could say. If it could make a buck and wasn't anchored in concrete, it would find its way to the back of his pick-up truck. Coal was always king, he would always come home with a pile of coal in his truck, which we boys had to unload while he went into the house to yell and slap our mother around, usually about money, or his "lazy" sons.
This was one of those gestalts, he would beat the hell out of us for stealing and rant and rave about how much he hated anyone who stole things, yet he was a thief. Sometimes it would be dark by the time he got home. We couldn't have dinner because he would have to be there first for every meal. So we waited until he backed in, then went out and cleaned out the truck of its booty! After dinner we would have to go back out and crack coal, usually brother Bill and me, because of the baby and the walking wounded. To crack coal you sit on a piece of log with a large rock in front of you. First, one of us would smash the larger pieces with a sledge hammer, and then we'd sit down and grab a piece of coal and start cracking. That is hitting it with a smaller hammer until it was the correct size. It had to be "chestnut" size, or just plain nut size. After you had formed a pile around your rock with a ballpeen hammer, you would carefully shovel the nut size coal into its own pile, being careful not to get the real small stuff with it. We did this every night after our other chores, one of which was splitting wood for the fireplace. We had two coal stoves and a fireplace, the only heat in the house. But the coal we carefully cracked to the correct size was really for resale. On Friday night, we would unload the chunks and reload the

'nut' coal so the Duke could sell it Saturday morning. He would then come back for another ton and sell it on Saturday afternoon. One of us would have to go with him so we could unload the coal so he could stand around and talk. Money would change hands, but we never saw any of it. My father was always quick to point out that we were allowed to go to school and we got 'three hot's and a cot' each day, what more did we need? He sold about 6 to 8 tons of cracked coal a week, so my brother and I worked our ass's off and it wasn't fun. Coal was sharp as hell and could fly up and stick in your face. Plus you could only wear one glove as your hammer hand had to be without one so the hammer would not slip out of your hand.

As for the wood, we would go down by the coal company and take the old props that they had used in the mine. It was usually all hardwood; it had to be, to support the earthen weight. We would cut these up and then use steel chisels, sledge hammers and axe's to split them in four.

Eleven years old, that was my age around this time and I remember that because I asked the plumbers if our "indoor" convenience would be finished by my 12th birthday in January. With the extra money that the coal business was making and its low overhead for experienced labor, my mother forced my father to start adding onto the house. One of the first items was an indoor bathroom.

My brothers and I were sharing one room, with four bunk beds. Bill and I were delegated to the bottom beds, Mark and my youngest brother were on top. I was directly below the 'baby' of the family and he knew how to pack away the groceries at the dinner table. Consequently his weight started to increase quite dramatically. Combine that with the fact that he did not have to work as hard as we did, produced a huge mound of flesh that would climb the wooden ladder and flop into bed. Meanwhile, with one eye opened, I got to watch the pine slats and plywood create this enormous bulge directly above MY body, and then there were the creaking sounds like a ship at sea. I knew one night they would find me as flat as a bug, and there would be no warning, no match stick like the one in the coal mines.

One day the Duke decided to become a chicken farmer. Let's face it, he had 3 and ½ indentured servants at his beckon call, we were more like permanent migrant workers. The chicken coops were there on flat ground, which on the side of a mountain is at a premium, so we fixed and painted one of these buildings. I actually was pretty young when this undertaking began. My job, as a 5 or 6 year old, was to be the 'gofer', meaning one who was sent for things over and over. These edifices to stench were located behind our house, and up the side of the hill about 100 yards. There was a small path that made its way up hill to the site. This, of course, meant that every pound of material, including water during the dry season, had to be carried up hill. These were not the chickens that Colonel Saunders or Mr. Perdue made their fortunes on; they were mainly 'laying' hens. We were to be in the egg business. Allow me to tell you a few things about chickens; first of all you have to have a few roosters hanging around for the sexual enlightenment of the hens. Roosters are not very nice and they have sharp claws, sometimes they would fly up and try to tear up your face, but you couldn't just grab the thing and start twisting its neck because 'laying' hens are very sensitive ladies! For example, if a fox or feral cat got into the chicken house, they wouldn't lay any eggs for a week until they settled down.

If you wondered where the feral cats came from, it was right down the road. People would drive up, throw the cat out and speed away. The cat would then become feral, unless it fell into the sights of the Dukes M-1 carbine rifle, another liberated item from the U.S. Coast Guard.
Eggs are usually found under the mother chicken, so a lot of time you would have to go in there and remove them. This, of course, the hen did not appreciate at all and she would also draw blood with her claws. Chickens may be stupid, but they are masters at pecking, clawing and generally

13

destroying human flesh. I grew up with these things for about 3 or 4 years; lugging bags of feed and buckets of water up that hill. Cleaning out the coups of their copious amounts of fecal matter, which was a chore to fight over. You would think that we had plenty of chicken to eat, but that wasn't the case. Each of those birds was worth money as long as they produced eggs and sperm. On a rare occasion, when a hen reached retirement age, the Duke would remove its head with a hatchet, and then hand the carcass to one of us to remove the feathers. My Mother made clothes from the chickens feed bags, mainly pajamas for us boys. The bags were of cotton fabric with floral prints on them. You could blend into the walls of the outhouse rather easily, provided you didn't have a picture of a bra from the catalog in your hand.

The venture of getting rich by cornering the world egg market wouldn't last. Not that my opinion was requested, but I was sick of headless chickens running around spurting blood as they went. Mary T was also happy not to have to sit for hours at the foot powered sewing machine, making flannel pajamas.

As with many things in our house, almost overnight the chickens disappeared. I actually walked up there to feed the bastards and they were gone. My father never felt he had to tell us of his intensions regarding anything, that wasn't his style. With the money he got for the chickens he went out and bought a coal truck. I celebrated prematurely.

Before I go into this next facet, allow me to relate a few little stories that involve the chicken coops. One day the Duke told Mark and I to go up and cut the weeds down around the coops and along the path so he could have a clear range of fire (fox and feral cats). Our tools consisted of the type the grim reaper is always shown with; a sickle and a scythe. Naturally I was the scythe operator because it required two hands and a lot of work. As we worked away, I started to smell something burning. When I turned around, half of the hill was on fire. It seems that my next oldest brother Mark set

14

fire to the underbrush. The problem was the wind, the lack of rain and the fact that 300 chickens were in the direct line of the blaze, and they weren't scheduled to be barbequed that day.

Fire on the mountain was a very real threat and could turn into a full blown forest fire in short order. Everyone in the family came out with picks, shovels, old blankets, etc., to fight the blaze. After a few hours, we managed to extinguish the fire and then came the moment of truth. Who started it? Across the road from our house was a weird bush that grew into hundreds of dead straight, small branches. The Duke would bring you down to the bush and make you stand there while he picked out the perfect 'switch'. He would then take his pen knife and trim off the little leaves, stopping once in a while to bend it to check its resilience. Meanwhile your life is passing in front of you. When he was finally ready, he would take the switch and beat the crap out of you, or me in this case. It left long red welts on your skin, which hurt for weeks. I ended up in front of the bush for the near destruction of his entire chicken empire by fire; Nero laying eggs while the coops burned. But the real problem was that I could not exact my retribution on my brother who made the false claim. If I did so, that would warrant another trip to the beating bush, as he was, for years, so sickly and always at deaths door.

Now it is time for the second feature that centers on the defunct chicken houses. A bunkhouse! I was getting a little older now, maybe nine or ten, when the chicken coops became vacant. My brothers and I had to have a bunkhouse it was a rite of passage.

We already had some electricity because of the heaters that ran in the winter for the hens, plus we had lights. We began to clean up one of the buildings that seemed in the best condition. First we fixed the roof. Then we installed a window, a set of bunk beds, a pot belly stove and a telephone. When I say telephone, I mean one that came out of a coal mine. One end was a nice wooden cabinet with a crank and a typical "Untouchables" era mouth piece and ear horn. The other end was similar in design but was encased in a steel cabinet and weighed a ton. We bolted this end onto the wall inside so our mother could check up on us. We dug a shallow trench for the cable so our 'enemies' couldn't cut our communication line. Who our supposed rivals were is a matter of conjecture. We built a lookout tower complete with a siren, another item that was set free from the coal company. Freedom contains the word "free".

This being my first attempt at building, I gathered a pile of lumber and harvested some from the other coops and set about adding a sitting room to our bunk. The outside walls were covered with black felt paper and we found a large glass window somewhere which was placed in the front, affording a great view of the entire valley below where Wilkes-Barre was located. I attached some hinges on one of the windows so it could be opened on nice days. We used to sleep out there, on the side of the mountain above our house. Mary T would ring us up to say hello, or check on us. There was a guy around Marks age named Eddie who lived up the other dirt road below our house. Mary was convinced that Eddie was going to grow up to be a serial killer because he stole his Dad's cigarettes and actually smoked them. The age of the bunkhouse didn't last too long, maybe two years or so, though it provided a welcome respite from our father and his 'warpath' episodes.

It is early, and I am sitting on my balcony overlooking the entire Bandaras Bay; 25 miles wide from the northern mountain range to the one in the south. A Camel cigarette burns in my hand; it is a Mexican Lite, called Camel 6. If I smoke any lighter a cigarette, I'll be paying just to breathe the air. Naturally there is a large mug of really superb Altura coffee that is actually an extension of my right arm. I had a blue porcelain mug surgically attached to my hand. Looking over 25 miles of the Pacific Ocean is a far cry from delivering a ton of "pea" or "nut" coal in the middle of January. That is what the high lift truck was for, delivering coal to houses for heat and getting paid for it. There aren't any illusions; the Duke was about the acquisition of money in any way possible. If it had a dollar value, he was right there loading it into his truck.

Before I go into the detail of the life of a coal man, allow me to explain something about coal mines. In 1959, there was the "Knox Mine Disaster". What this amounted to in simple terms was greed. The miners were told to dig coal directly under the huge river that runs through Wilkes-Barre. Well, they dug a little too far up and the river stopped running down stream and simply ran into the hole in its bottom. It did this for weeks and in the process ruined the deep mine coal industry in Wyoming Valley forever. That is when they turned to that wonderful process they call 'strip' mining. But as the tunnels flooded, my father somehow knew how to pull out the huge rubber and lead covered copper wires that supplied power to Hades. He also began to acquire these heavy brass valves that were used on the water lines. Most of this stuff was removed quickly and under the cover of darkness.

So, we went from cracking 'hot' coal, to chopping up copper wires, which wasn't an easy task. First you had to straddle this black snake about 5 inches thick, and use an axe to chop through the black rubber and lead coating. The lead was then folded up into a neat package which went to the scrap yard. We would then coil the copper wire in a large pile and burn off all the grease and other undesirable material which would reduce the scrapyard price. After the funeral pyre, we would have to cut the wire into 3 foot pieces, as per the scrapyard instructions. Some of this wire was three stranded copper, each over an inch thick, so there was a lot of hack sawing to go around. This work replaced our other evening and Saturday activities. When the scrapyard closed, the Duke would take his sagging pick-up truck with the canvas cover on the back, over the mountain to his buddy's junkyard and large sums of cash changed hands.

We would receive our $1.00 per hour. After all those years we worked for food and shelter, he finally broke down and began paying us; one dollar an hour for work done six and a half days a week. On Sunday, around 4 PM the Duke would say, "You boys take the rest of the day off".
Well enough of that, now back to the coal delivery business. Coal came in a variety of different sizes; each having a specific purpose. The largest was called 'boat' coal, because it was used on boats and consisted of large chunks. Then there was 'stove' coal, it was about 4 inches across. The most popular sizes were 'chestnut' and 'pea, the type used in the old kitchen stoves. Then came 'rice' that was a new size used in the automatic coal furnaces, called 'stokers', because they fed themselves.
The high lift truck had a unique scissor type lifting system operated by one hydraulic piston buried in the frame of the vehicle. First it would tilt the 'box', which could contain anywhere from 3 to 6 tons of coal, divided into one ton compartments. This allowed more control over the number and type of coal delivered, depending on what the customer ordered. After the tilt, the entire box would raise into the air to a rather descent height of about 12 feet at the rear chute. Beer trucks and coal trucks were allowed to block one lane of a street for no longer than 15 minutes, so as soon as we arrived, it was all business. As the truck backed up, the 'helper' would be pulling out the aluminum coal chutes and as soon as the tilt came he dropped the metal ladder which allowed access to the coal in the truck. By now we are into the early 60's and I am at least 12 years old, old enough to be a 'helper'. After just a few years, we had over 300 customers and two trucks on the road. We were paid for haulage only which was $1.50 per ton, so speed was everything. The more tonnage we moved in a day (and into the night), the more money we made for the Duke.
Our father had a bad habit of taking on customers that lived on the side of a hill, which meant that we had to 'block' the lower tires to level the truck. These blocks were wood and

had metal handles; they were hung on the side of the truck's frame. The driver, usually an older brother, raised the lift, gunning the engine to make it go up faster. If the truck was full and we were on the side of a hill it would sway back and forth, calling for one of us to climb the metal ladder I mentioned, to even out the weight. Just that added body weight made the difference of a successful coal delivery or a catastrophe. It was similar to racing sailboats; on second thought, it was the farthest thing from it, as there was no fun in being a coalman.

A small chute about 4 feet long was placed at the opening in the house cellar. The main truck chutes were telescopic in design, and slid out as the box was being lifted in the air. As soon as the pitch was right, the guy hanging off the truck would open the trap door and the coal came rushing out. While this was going on, the driver was sitting in the truck preparing the bill so that as soon as the last drop of coal was in their basement, he was at the door with the bill in his hand. Speed, it was all about speed.

In the summer, some people would fill their coal bins because the price was cheaper. There were times the helper had to go into the basement, climb into the coal bin, and shout to the driver, to 'let 'er rip', then proceed to shovel the onrush of coal onto the back corners of the nearly full bin. At times you would be on your stomach shoveling that stuff. After the delivery, the process would reverse itself, except for the cursory cleanup of any spilled coal on the lawn or street. Elapsed time for 2 tons of coal was about 9 minutes from start to finish; total profit for 2 men and a truck, $3.00. To make any money at all we had to really hustle, by that I mean by hauling 12 to 16 loads a day; each one weighing about 4 tons.

The protocol was simple, Bill, the oldest, got his driver's license at 16. He was then the designated driver and either Mark or I was the chosen helper. When Mark turned 16, we added a second truck in earnest and the wheel just kept turning.

19

There were other guys hauling coal and we would see them at the breakers. One guy, named Larry, would show up wearing makeup! Turns out he was working on becoming a male model, so he delivered coal in between his modeling shoots. It was his father's truck also and I thought no less of the guy, it seemed that some of us dreamed of getting out of that godless town and its Black Blood Diamonds.

Coal is dirty and wet, but you probably didn't know that it came in colors. Silver and blue, they were trademarks for Sterling Coal and Blue Coal. After you were loaded under the coal breaker, you pulled the truck up to a special platform and the coal was spray painted, just to cover the top layer. I can still smell that odor; it was an oil based paint that got all over your clothes, hair, face and any other exposed areas.

The winter time was the worse; the coal would freeze in the truck, about 6 inches down from the top layer. And if you were loaded with the big chunks, it was a real chore to work with.

The Goodman Brothers had the dubious reputation for being the first and last to get a load of coal. We were usually the first trucks at the breaker, 6:30 AM, and be the last to fill up at 5 minutes to 5, when they closed, and they hated us for it. The longest haul of the day was saved for the last trip and that meant you were the last truck at the breaker. That delivery could be a 30 to 45 minute drive, one way. My brother Bill and I always seemed to get the last haul, our consolation was that the 4 ton truck had an AM radio in it. We would listen to "splish, splash, I was taking a bath", etc. By the time we got home it was after 7PM. We would walk in the house with our pants frozen to the knees and our hands one notch below frostbite, not to mention the silver hair or that lovely shade of blue. When we finally got to sit down for warmed over dinner we'd get comments like, "what took you guys so long?"

Mary T would write up the orders the night before, using maps and a series of triangulations. This was to assure the most effective routes to use so that we could make as many tons of coal deliveries as possible, and the pace was relentless. For food, Mark would pull up in front of a small store and I would run in and grab two quarts of chocolate milk and a pile of 'Tastykakes' and dash out into the truck. Before I shut the door we were moving, riding down the road slugging milk out of the containers and stuffing down cupcakes, mainly for the sugar buzz.

'On tick', meant that you would not get paid that day for a delivery. Usually the Duke would wait until Friday, just before suppertime to collect. There were two reasons for this, most important: it was payday for most working men, and secondly, before supper they didn't have time to clean up and head down to some gin mill and drink themselves into a coma.

There was one customer that always caused a debate when it came to going for the money. She was an older lady who owned a corner bar, and always came to the door in a see-through negligée. She would insist on serving you a cup of tea or coffee before her purse would come out. She'd make a point of scurrying around the kitchen while putting the cup together and always had to reach directly in front of you for something or other. Mrs. Kinney's breasts could have comfortably tucked into her waistline if she wore a belt. Profit margins and competition was so intense we HAD to be courteous at all times to every customer or feel the Dukes wrath if something got back to him, or a customer went to another coalman. So, I sat there at her kitchen table, looking or trying not to look at what was definitely not in our sex education manual. Finally payment was made, and she gave you a small tip, then after about 50 'thanks' she would open the door, which she had been standing in front of. Now that I think of it, she was one in four of our 300 customers who actually tipped us, normally no one would.

During this dialogue, or diatribe, you may have wondered about school, when did we go to school? We were allowed to leave classes early every day so we could jump onto the coal trucks we had filled earlier that morning before coming to school. They were parked, just waiting to go at 2:30 when we got home and changed into our coal wear. Occasionally the Duke would drive us to school in a coal truck. I found this to be mortifying, especially if the girls were out in front with their 8000 page copies of Exodus under their arm.

To add a bit of history here, it was around 1963 that my father's business really took off.   Because of the onslaught of strip mining, trucks were needed to haul the unprepared coal to the breakers, and the strip mines were everywhere. Somehow the Duke, a man of German descent, became quite friendly with an entire cadre of Italian men, who I choose not to name, but I will say this, they were photographed often from across the street! The Italians always had an affinity for the trucking business so generally were the people you discussed that business with. Obviously the Duke did just that, because within a month we not only had a fleet of trucks, we also acquired an old coal mine operation, complete with buildings and land: the 'Boston Coal Company'. The property consisted of a set of buildings, one red brick, built in 1869, and a newer cinderblock building that was big enough to place three truck bays in it. There were also over 3 acres of land with a lot of dirt from the strip mines on the rear boundary. That dirt would come in handy later on. Our fleet consisted of 12 trucks and my father hired 12 drivers. They were paid $7.00 an hour, not bad at that time.   My job was to keep them running. So every day after school, I went to the shop, and serviced 12 vehicles, sometimes receiving help from my brother Bill. I was around 14 years old at this time. We sons had worked our way up to $1.50 an hour, but were still tied to that expression, "three hot's and a cot". Plus he added a new one, "go on strike and get struck". Not an idle gesture I may add, though much of the physical abuse had passed, he still used other methods to keep us under his thumb.

Recently, I was talking to a friend of mine and we were comparing our 'family life' while growing up. I told him I never, and I am serious, never, heard the term "I love you" in my entire 60 years. He could not believe it and asked about my Mother, the reply was the same, never. We were German and talked about business most of the time; the other percentage was probably filled with silence. I will touch on this again later on.

Back to business! After a few years our drivers started making a lot of noise about their pay scale; even though they robbed us weekly of motor oil and gasoline, etc.
The Duke went to the office of the Blue Coal Corporation and met with a guy named Durkin, who was the big cheese, to discuss money. Blue Coal said they would pay $9.00 per hour for a truck and driver; our drivers wanted $8.00, so that meant we made $1.00 an hour for the use of our trucks and fuel. The Duke and Durkin had to be separated by office workers before it came to blows. That was on Thursday. On Monday all the trucks were gone. In his typical 'need to know' style, when asked where our trucks went, his only comment was that he sold them, end of conversation.
That year the Duke bought his first bulldozer, a D-3 Caterpillar, and a piece of crap. But it was the beginning of another metamorphosis; from trucking to the heavy equipment industry.
 All of this time we still had one high lift coal truck working. I ended up with it and hired a friend of mine to work as a helper. One day he and I were filling up a basement and I was outside. I knew the coal bin of this house, so I kept stopping the coal and yelling down, "Are you all right down there"? He would assure me that all was fine so I ran the rest of the coal in, but he did not come out. I went to the basement and there was my friend buried up to his chest in coal, laughing his head off. I had to pull off the bin doors and let the coal run onto the floor just to get him out, then shovel everything back in and mop the painted basement floor. When we got back into the truck I asked what had

gone awry, he told me he was just getting off on being buried in coal. Smoking hashish and delivering coal is not something I would recommend. Soon after that we phased out that business also because my father's Italian friends told him to buy two brand new bigger trucks, naturally we had to buy them from a Ford dealership with Italian ancestry.

There were to be no more hired help in our organization from that day on, it had to do with bureaucracy.
Speaking of which, for the past several days I have been in a rather precarious position. Due to my combat experience in Vietnam, which I will explore in autobiographical time, I have some serious health issues which require certain 'sensitive' medications. I had requested my sister-in-law, who was monitoring our mail, to overnight them to me here in Mexico. After two weeks of numerous e-mails, phone calls, errors and mistakes, my doctor in Puerto Vallarta told me they were shipped back to the United States! Not legal here, but the never made it back to my home, somewhere in route they just disappeared. Except for the empty package, which had been stamped at every post office from here to eternity? I suppose they made it to the 'street'.

I really have a thing about bureaucracy, and I know where that came from, the Duke hated it with a passion, as well as Unions. He would keep up to $30,000.00 in cash pinned inside a drape in the master bedroom. His policy was to take half of the business money and give Mary T the other half to pay bills. He felt entitled to this and felt no remorse, even when Mary had problems paying for everything.
The Duke would shove a roll of money in my face and say "this is the real measure of a man, and you, boy, will never amount to a pile of shit". Well, thanks Pa for the heart to heart talk.
Many years later when I became quite successful, I pulled out a roll of C-notes and said, "Do you see this? A guy once told me it was a measure of a man, do you want some?" He went crazy, calling me a big shot and a bastard for coming in

and saying that to him. I thought about laughing at him, and had conjured up a speech about WHO that guy was, but instead I put the cash back in my pocket and walked out. It was his birthday and it had been my intention to give him a few hundred dollars. As I left I thought of all those years that I wasn't a man, now I was just a well off pile of crap. Note: Personally I dislike the 'S' word.

As a post script, my father's aversion to bureaucracy cost my brothers a lot of money in IRS fines, penalties and interest when they took over the family business. Also, his social security check was minimal because he "didn't believe in it". Mary T had managed to pay into it for 5 years without his knowledge. Around this time our business was even listed on Dun & Bradstreet; which made my mother proud, and my father more arrogant, everything was his!

My Grandfather on my father's side was a true renaissance man. There wasn't much that he could not do, from blacksmithing to wine making, and he did not touch a drop. He had an original WWII Willy's Jeep. You could see the outline of the star under the green paint. We would go berry picking way out in the boondocks and once we hit the dirt road, I was allowed to drive. The old Jeep had a three speed gearbox in the typical 'H' pattern, reverse in the upper left hand corner. Back then and well into the 60's standard transmissions were not 'synchronized', which meant gear grinding, double clutching and listening to the engine was the norm. The trouble with Pop's Jeep was that to shift from 1st to 2nd had to be a perfect 90 degree motion or the transmission would jam between gears. This led to a diatribe of civil curse words and removal of the top of the transmission to unlock the 'forks' as they were called. This required all of 15 minutes, but could cost you your driving lesson for the day. This is where and how I learned to drive at 8 years old.

The berry picking was another matter. Once we arrived at the 'swamp berry' patch, he would hand you a 10 quart pail;

one of about six that were in the back of the Jeep. He expected all those pails to be filled before we went home. It was a lot of work. 'Huckleberries' were worse, they were smaller and close to the ground; it would take a toll on one's back. Your fingers would be stained purple too, and it did not wash off, it had to wear off. I got to drive though, if my 'H' was right, which made it worthwhile.

My uncle was the manager of the 'A&P' market, which was a meal ticket for my Grandfather. He would go there after hours and pick up 'day old' cakes, fruit which was 'going off', and a huge bag of coffee beans. At home he had one of those square wooden coffee mills with the little drawer at the bottom and a metal crank on top. I would get the word to walk to his house, a little further down the mountain, and he would have everything laid out; the beans, the grinder and a huge glass container that could hold a small lake. I would sit under the grape arbor and grind my little ass off until that glass jug was full. He would come along and bang on the bench to compact it and I would grind some more. I started chewing on the beans while I worked; my present heavy coffee drinking is probably due to that.

When he did Blacksmith work, he'd have me turn the forge. It was a science, too fast, and the steel got too hot, too slow and it was cold. I would turn at his command while he split square rod steel and twisted it to make mantles for fireplace utensils. He could make and fix all kinds of stuff and people paid him for his trouble.

Unlike my father, my Grandfather was a man of few words. He rarely talked; everything was in sign language or a swift kick in the rear. But he never would degrade me like my father would. Pop was a good man and he taught me a lot about things, nature and life. He died when I was going on 11 years old. I can still smell that grape arbor and the coffee grounds. "She's real fine my 409..." Actually that was a Chevy engine and I came from a Ford family. I read somewhere that when the rock group did that song they did not have the faintest idea what a 409 was.

26

This is not a technical manual for prospective auto technicians, but I may add that a 409 refers to the cubic inches of the engine output in terms of power and by today's standards gasoline consumption.

By age 14 I bought my first car, it was a 1952 Ford sedan with a Flathead engine in it (never mind) anyway I found two deuces(carburetors) for it and installed them, ripped out the entire interior and removed all of the glass, I then installed and old kitchen chair as a driver's seat. Next, the exhaust system and the installation of a special gasoline tank which only held a few gallons. I paid $38 dollars for this car and was in the process of preparing it for racing on an oval dirt track. All of the chrome was ripped off and anything else that added weight or junk, then two large pieces of steel had to be welded on for bumpers. The finishing touch was painting "Mr. Lucky" on the side of the car, both sides, super imposed over a set of 4 aces. Naturally Mary T was going crazy but these were her boys and we were raised with motor oil instead of breast milk.

Every Saturday they held the oval 'stock car' races at the "mud flats". The track was down by the river and had to be bulldozed in every spring because the river washed it away. We paid an entry fee and spectators paid a gate fee, there were cash prizes for three winners at the end of the day, it was getting to the end of the day that was the problem. The surface of the track was simply topsoil and when it was dry the dust was like talc powder. They would run around with a water truck between the 'heats' but it didn't matter, after a few turns with 20 cars going as fast as they could, the water was gone and the dust came back. It was so thick you couldn't see through it and just followed the bumper in front of you until a breeze came along and you passed if you could.

In those days I was called a greaser, Madras was the fabric of the Peter, Paul and Mary crew. For me it was black leather and 'Brylcream' the mousse of its day. My hair was done with jelly rolls and a DA in the back, better known as a

'Ducks Ass.' Girls like us death defying bad boys until we got to the bra snaps, then it was home or bone. Most of our types carried two things, a comb and a pack of 2 for .25 cent rubbers; it was the circle in the leather of the wallet that was impressive.

About half of that season I raced "Mr. Lucky" and gave it up after a few good wrecks and near rollovers, it was sheer suicide racing around a dirt track in a wall of dust at break neck speeds. I sold the car to another greaser and after the second 'heat' the engine exploded. My brother Mark and I bought a 52' Hudson Hornet with a super six engine. Now this car had an interesting story. The old man that owned it was one of our coal customers, more importantly he invented an oil filter system where you never changed the oil, ever, just the filters. Of course the oil companies offered him a fortune for its patent but he wouldn't sell it, he said that he knew what they do, so do we. His intention was to market it and make his money on filters. The guy actually sent his son to Penn State to get a degree in chemistry to work with him. When we bought that car it had about 90.000 miles on it, and back in those days that was incredible given the engine technology. Naturally, the original oil filter was on the car when we came to pick it up. The outcome of the story; Big oil just buried this guy in legal suits and anything else they knew he couldn't afford a lawyer for, but they didn't get his patent, it went to the grave with him.

Mark and I ripped the thing apart and prepped it for the track.
The car was shaped like a big turtle and was the Lexus of its day. Below our house was a huge dirt mining road a.k.a. stripping road. One day we had taken the "Green Hornet" and went like hell trying to get the thing to rollover and it just would not comply, perfect for our needs. The worst problem came when my brother, roaring up the mountain to our house blew one of the pistons right out of the engine, we

found it lying next to the steering box. Will wonders never cease, we disconnected the spark plug wire for that cylinder and ran up and down the mountain like the speed freaks we were and that engine would not blow up, in fact we drove it to the scrap yard.

Because of my relationship with my father and my own independence, I refused to accept the customary 'first' car he bought for my other brothers. A more practical reason was the car, it turned out to be a 4 door non-descript sedan whereas my brothers received really cool cars. So I went out and purchased an 1955 Ford Crown Victoria. Today this car would be worth a small fortune due to its design and the number that had been produced. It had a slush box in it and that was grease ball talk for an automatic transmission, it had to go. I had just turned 15 years old and wanted this to be ready for my sixteenth birthday, driving age. I found a big "Police Interceptor" 312 engine and all of the parts needed to put a floor shift and stick (manual) transmission in it. You will have to excuse me for the journey down memory lane; guys like us remember our first hot car like our first blow job, so please stay with me and I promise to keep the grease monkey lingo at a minimum.

The entire car was painted jet black and had "The Bounty" painted across the rear bumper. It was not unusual to name a car in those days. The reason I called it what I did was twofold, one, it was a mutiny from Captain Blight (the Duke) and the other had to do with the street racing money I intended to earn because this thing was fast.
At 16 I was on the street with my big Ford, cruising burger joints looking for women of course but also looking for a challenge. The technique was to drive around slowly with your arm out of the window holding a $50 dollar bill in it tapping the door. It was code for let's get it on girls and boys. I raced a lot of Chevy cars and they would jump out ahead of me on the starting line until that big Ford V8 found its pace, when I speed shifted 2nd gear it was over for the

Chevy and I was $50 dollars richer. Street racing was a few persons, one to hold the money and one to wave the start, roughly a quarter mile was established and that was the track, a straight line as fast as you could go. If the police showed up, we just kept on going and met at the "Stop n' Go" burger place, it was before McDonalds came to town, and I would pick up my loot. Because I drove a truck every day with two shift sticks and 20 gears, I got damn good on the shifting which could mean all the difference in the world whether you won or lost. I would take on guys with bigger engines than mine and beat them due to my speed shifting. After the race came the comb to fix the jelly rolls. There was a guy from my high school who had a Chevy that was nowhere near my league, and yet he insisted on racing me to the burger joint at lunch time. I never understood this guy and used to say to him why don't you give up the ghost already or beef up your ride, it didn't matter.

One night about 11:00 pm he had to race me up Washington avenue, so rather than lose face I ran him and was going about 80 mph when I passed the Larksville Police, I kept going thinking that by the time they finished the donut they would nail my counterpart. They didn't and followed me home and read me the riot act in the driveway of our house. I didn't know my old man was standing in the window of the master bedroom in his boxer shorts taking it all in. Finally, when the cop said: "If you weren't Billy Goodman's' boy we would haul you off to jail but we are going to let you go with a warning." With that they drove away and I thought I dodged a bullet. When I reached the rear screen door and opened it a fist hit me square in the face and knocked me over the patio furniture. There was the Duke standing there in his boxer shorts pointing at me saying, "Tomorrow you sell that car and you only drive truck", notice how he qualified that? This wasn't the only time he made me sell something that I bought with my own money. A few years earlier I saved up and bought a guitar from Sears, it was a beauty. I started to take lessons and came to realize that I wanted to be a bass player. I announced that I was going to get a bass guitar and he told me I couldn't, his comment was to learn to play the one that I had first. Of course I was on the fast track and felt that was a waste of time, so I parked the guitar in the living room on a window seat for years until the neck finally broke. You will hear about the bass guitar a few times before this book is finished. To this day I watch the bass players in any musical group, except "Spanky and the Coalminers"; a polka band, and wish it was me.

"Son you're gonna' to drive me to drinkin' if you don't stop drivin' that hot...rod...Lincoln." My brothers and I got together and bought an 1934 Plymouth with a huge Lincoln Flat head engine, it had 4 deuces on it and was designated an H Gas race car. This thing would pull the wheels off of the ground when you took off down the race track.

The space inside the car was so narrow that we had to place the gas pedal on the extreme right side and the floor shift was between your legs. If you slammed third gear to hard, your victory cup was full of pain in a certain anatomical part of the male body, cod piece anyone?

We would increase the horsepower of anything, give us a lawn mower and I guarantee that it would be the fastest on the block. My brothers and I worked nights, tuning engines, changing things and getting ready for Sunday at the drag strip. Our 'safety' equipment consisted of a small fire extinguisher, a seat belt lifted from the scrap yard (interesting to note that Ford actually installed seat belts in the 50's,) and a football helmet. We also had to gut the interior and place a piece of steel plate over the clutch area. If the clutch assembly exploded the parts would cut your legs off at the knees. If I am not mistaken, we used a piece of the B-17 gas tank/ swimming pool for our clutch guard to save weight. One day, right in front of our garage on the public street, I was doing what are called ' hole shots' and these consisted of revving the engine until it screamed then popping the clutch, I blew the engine up so bad that we literally used a broom and shovel to pick up most of the parts. That marked the end of our drag racing career. Anyway, it didn't matter; my oldest brother had been taking flying lessons and planned to buy a small airplane. After he got proficient, he let me fly it quite a bit.

It has occurred to me that I never completed the story of my run in with both the cops and the Dukes right fist. I sold the car to my brothers' boozer buddy who lived at the end of an alley with two stone walls enclosing it, within a few weeks both sides were all busted up and scrapped of any paint. I in turn, bought a little red Chevy 'Nova' convertible with a small engine in it, as fate would have it, it turned out that the girls at junior college loved it!

During this entire period of time a lot more was happening than what I have been making a fool of myself about.

Mary T. had enrolled me at the age of nine with an Italian portrait painter called Niccolo Cortiglia. He had studied at the Academy of Rome and was quite famous. For 3 years I attended his charcoal class once a week, drawing from plaster casts of noses, lips, eyes, ears and any other exposed part of a human body. I worked on a large newsprint pad and used sticks of charcoal that looked like they came from a Boy Scout camp fire. In the back room were the advanced students who had colors in the form of pastels, I asked almost every week if I could go in there and work and he would just laugh in Italian and call me something that had the word stupid in it. It was a frustrating exercise; I would spend a lot of time on a nose cast trying to get it just so. He would come along and take his thumb and just make a large arch through it and tell me to start again. Three years of this with Mary T. a very impatient listener to my complaints and my father's constant complaining about the money. But what came from that was the beginning of a formal art training.
It may be interesting to note, while my wife was spell

checking she came upon Niccolo Cortiglia in the Smithsonian museum, and it was the same guy because his thumb was black from charcoal.

My name for the place was Saint Basketball, others referred to it as Saint Vincent's School. It was a private school and my mother somehow managed to come up with the tuition money for all four of us to go there. We were by no means 'Catholic' and if my father had any religion at all it had dead presidents on the cover.

The school was staffed by the 'Sisters of Mercy' which was a complete misnomer at best. These broads in their penguin suits of black and white starch did not possess a modicum of mercy. Their weapon of choice was an oak ruler about an inch thick, in 12 years I never saw one break, I know that for a painful fact, let me just say I never felt one break. It was bad enough that we were not brainwashed at the Vatican, I had two brothers ahead of me who laid my future behavior. If the nuns could not beat something out of you, they sent you to the dreaded Father Gallagher, rumored to have been a heavy weight boxer. God must have KO'ed him in the seventh round; I just wonder who God put his money on? The padre had a technique of knowing exactly where to punch you for maximum effect with minimum damage. These were real man size punches too not just some love taps. I don't know about any sexual abuse, we heathens could not be altar boys; but I can attest to a sore mid-section on more than one occasion.

Mary T. really disliked the Catholic Church, but during her bid for the school board in our hometown, she was quoted as saying that; "…I would not send my dog to Larksville High School." End of quote and any chance of going to school there. Actually, she wanted us to have the best academic education that there was to be offered and she could afford at the time, this was it. I must admit that we did receive an excellent education, a bit bloody and brutal, but isn't that the papal way?

33

I was always being expelled for something. One Summer I read Darwin's "Origin of the Species," soon after I started my freshman year. One day in biology, the nun was rambling on about that Garden of Eden crap, Adam and Eve being stark naked with a piece of fruit and a snake. I shot my hand up and interjected my recent enlightenment about the primal soup with noodles when the oak ruler came out. First I was beaten senseless, and then sent to the principal's office from which I was duly expelled. The unfortunate thing about this entire story is that it is the honest truth.

Mary T. went ballistic and there was a lively exchange behind closed doors, finally a compromise was hammered out. I was never to mention Darwin in biology class for the duration, but I was back in. On another occasion, during " penmanship" class the nun beat my knuckles on my left hand so bad they were bleeding onto the floor, she claimed that it was the 'Devils hand' and that I would write with my right hand or else. Again, Mary T. caught on fire this time, when she saw my hand she went bonkers and the next day there was shouting in the principal's office. I am still left handed to this day.

St. Vincent's had an awarding basketball career; they were state champions. Only one brother got involved with that sport and that was my youngest brother. That is how he got out of the real dirty work at home; he was always at practice. It's not that we were deprived of sports growing up. We had a football field; it was a cow pasture. We turned sailor caps inside out and stuffed them with newspaper to use as helmets. You would catch a pass and be running like hell until your foot went into a hoof hole and you would fly into a fresh pile of cow cheers. Basketball was down the road from our house. There was one street light where we nailed some boards on the pole and used a barrel stave as a hoop. There you would be dribbling up for that famous back hand between the legs, when the ball would hit a rock and go flying into the creek; or your opponent's arms. Then there was ice hockey. The water at the dump used to freeze over;

and it was a fairly good size. We had metal 'buckled' on skates; the kind you attached to your shoes. We were lucky enough to have decent shoes, let alone lace-up ice skates. Again there you are skating up to the goal pushing the puck with your tree branch; when bang, your body went flying because you forgot about the truck tire sticking up through the ice. Yes sir, never say we didn't have sports. An ironic part of this is that my father had been in charge of all the sports on base while in the Coast Guard. To this day I have nothing to do with any game that has balls in it; except for one that I'll tell you about later.

The day after my youngest brother graduated from St. Vincent's; the school closed for good. Maybe it was the lack of monthly shipments from the new world, or an inability to secure adequate supplies of "The World's Finest Chocolate". It never failed to amaze me; we were all basically poor kids, except the few whose father was a politician, yet the priest had the biggest house, with a live-in housekeeper, and he also got to buy a new Cadillac every year. So, not only did our families have to dig up tuition for us, but the school was constantly asking us to sell something; supposedly for some other poor kids in some made-up country somewhere. It was absurd; we had to meet a quota for the dubious 'Bishops relief fund'. When you went into the church, everything seemed to be covered with gold. It made me wonder why they needed more money.

For some events, we were forced to attend services; usually a sales pitch. The padre would ascend up to his teak pulpit and tell us to sell, sell, and sell! The entire Roman Empire was on the brink of bouncing checks; God forbid; the priest may have to buy a Buick next year. All this blatant hypocrisy surrounded by all this opulence, pomp and ceremony; flashy robes, marble everywhere and Fort Knox up front. When they passed the basket, I put in an IOU and was promptly smacked in the head because the alms basket was attached to a long wooden handle with an angry old man at the other end.

35

At St. Vincent's, four years of Latin was a mandatory requirement; you could never tell when you might run into a bunch of drunken Centurions. They also required two years of French. Why French? I made it my duty to explain that Spanish was more of the Global language: French was only spoken in France, Quebec and Tahiti. I did not envision myself being invited to Marlon Brando's private estate, nor did I expect to run around Paris with the ghost of Hemmingway or Bridget Bardot.

After a lecture form Sister Bleu Cheese, during which she implied that even Christ spoke French; the truth was revealed, none of the sisters of mercy could speak Spanish; just the god given French.

One day at lunchtime, my future was revealed to me in the form of a book from the town's only thrift store. A book titled "How to Speak Yiddish". I brought it to my French class and began to teach myself Yiddish on the sly. It was a small book and fit right inside the larger one of French. So for all appearance's I was Jacque Strap; without the black beret and coffee sitting on the Rue de Mortis.

As with all good things, it happened. One day when the planet Venus was in Paris, and the class was reciting Parlez Vous and Michelle my Belle, I was reciting the Yiddish translation of something like "kiss my sewing machine, you stupid goyum". I hadn't noticed when the class had finished and I was the only one speaking out loud. Naturally Sister Cheese wiz noticed and the infamous oak ruler was drawn from its scabbard. My book on Yiddish (or exhibit A), was placed in a bag marked evidence. This was considered heresy because every catholic institution has "the Jews wacked Christ" carved somewhere in rare Italian marble that was donated by the Medici family, installed in all of their tax free properties.

I was expelled again, which was particularly embarrassing as I was the Sophomore Class President. Mary T made the trip upstairs again, but this time there was a slight twist to the plot. It seems that Sister Big Kahuna had just used the public address system and forgot to turn off the microphone. When my mother arrived, they went into this debate, and she noticed my "Yiddish" book sitting on top of a manila envelope addressed to the Pope, and marked exhibit A as I mentioned. Along with it was a sheepskin document which officially condemned my soul to eternal damnation on the 5th level of Dante's Hell, where the library was located. This lively debate between my mother and the Big Kahuna continued to be broadcast throughout the entire village, thanks to the massive exterior speakers, until another big cheese ran in and turned off the microphone. It was an interesting discourse because Mary T, who had become quite the antique collector, actually told this nun how she provided her 'boys' with books on every religion; hell, she even had a set of the "Black Books" in Greek for Satan worship. Another deal was cut and I was allowed to return but my Yiddish book is somewhere in the Vatican, buried with the lost books of the bible and everything else they don't want us to know about. The thing that kept me from being turned into a temple eunuch was my grade point average. But there were to be other trying engagements before my soul could be saved. What comes to mind is the dreaded 'book report' story. On one occasion, I failed to do a book report for English class. On Friday the nun asked me if did my report and I blatantly lied and said "yes". She then asked the title of the book, and I told her it was a new publication called "Blood on my Hands and a Knife in my Back". She then asked who the author was, and I said "me". The next sentence was bad; she told me to have a copy of the book on her desk on Monday morning; Or else, meaning my grade of course. All weekend I wrote a book, it filled one of those school pads with blue tape on the binding. I finished it early Monday morning, just in the nick of time. She read the book and kept it, the only copy in existence, but I received a B grade. Good because it was the final grade that period. I'm convinced the copy of that book is hidden deep inside the

Vatican archives, on the same shelf with my Faustian contract with the devil.

In terms of 'gene pools', my mother's family would be the summer Olympic size and my father's was that B-17 gas tank. My IQ test result was 168. I know the validity of the 'Intelligent Quotient' test has a considerable amount of controversy around it, and may be of no use to anyone, but I do know that I did not have to study very often. If I read something twice, or looked it over for 30 minutes or so, I could ace a test; except math, then I was doomed. I do feel that the real influence was my mothers' insistence on reading books and being saturated with information. After we became 'rich' during the 60's and 70's, she subscribed to a ton of magazines; Time, Newsweek, US News and World Report, the Atlantic Monthly and the best were Smithsonian and National Geographic.

Mary T started out as a collector; over 40 years later she died an authority on Chinese antiques. She even learned the Mandarin dialect, both in speaking and reading, no easy task.

She came from an educated family and studied at some of the finest schools in New York. She was in her own right a 'renaissance woman' versed in fine art and culture. For some reason, she picked me to follow in her footsteps. The negative side of this was, of course, my dear old dad and his image of me "taking after your mother'; which normally was the prelude to something physical. In school, it was the Sisters of Mercy using a form of mental torture to sway one's opinion away from the logical and into the dogmas breakfast. As a young boy I was called intelligent; then as a young man, a gallery owner referred to me as brilliant. While 37 years of age, while dying in a hospital bed, a nurse called me "pathetic'. I will explain all of this in the pages to come.

Graduation day came; I had turned seventeen several months earlier, and there were a few crowning achievements, I graduated with honors. Considering everything that was going on at the time, I marvel at that one. But, I had mastered the art of multi-tasking; before it became a buzz word in corporate board rooms. I graduated as the class president, and had also placed second in the State wide championship for 'debate' in the category of "extemporaneous speaking'. That was my answer to the basketball court.

On my back is a scar, more like an indentation, that is a perfect reminder of my dealings with catholic girls. I rarely dated them in fact. They all thought that 'fellatio was a Brazilian pop star, or a village in Italy. But one night, in my black souped up Ford, I took a nice catholic gal to the drive in. I parked the car and placed the speaker in the rear window, driver's side, and rolled the window up, standard procedure. One note about my hot rod Ford, it wasn't really necessary to have an emergency brake, in a car like that, unless you were racing on a dirt oval. So, anyway, I had the car in first gear, which was a mistake, and proceeded to make my first move. We were across the front seat and I was working my way up to her bar locks, while unbeknownst to me, she had quietly unscrewed my gear shift knob, so when I reached the point of stop in her mind, she pushed me onto the floor shift which set in motion a series of events. First, I had a hole in my back with blood running out of it. And second, it had kicked the car out of gear and it began to roll down the hill. As I scrambled to the driver's seat, I heard the speaker break out of the rear window and bust it all to hell. I managed to stop the car before it careened into the guy in front of me and then found a little towel to help with the blood. While doing all this, the little catholic actually giggled, which told me she had done all this before. I drove her home with a mind full of torture ideas, and then spent the next three weeks trying to locate a rear window for a Ford Crown Victoria.
Wyoming Valley had a severe problem with blue ball syndrome. The affliction was rampart due to the number of

drive-in movie theaters and the type of girls that left large holes in a man's back as a method of heavy petting control. If someone needs a definition of blue balls, I'll make it quick. When you were advancing successfully on the triple bra latch, you'd get a boner. Inside tight jeans in time it would lead to getting 'Blue Balls'. A drive in was a passion pit; hot cars and cool guys with too much grease in their hair. We spent a lot of time in our cars; and they meant a lot to us. Car radios only had AM; FM stations were just beginning to hit the air waves. We did our best to make the music sound great. If you added a little black box called a 'reverb', it added to the intensity of the sound. It vibrated your car, and made Chubby Checker sound like he was singing in a large metal drum. The top radio station was WARM radio with DJ's like Tommy Woods, Harry West, Joey Schafer and Ron Allen. They would come out to your school and do 'record hops'; and also the fire hall dances where boy met girl and the rest has been going on since the advent of time.

Some of us guys even put turntables in our car; just watch out for the pot holes. I knew a guy who had a draft beer handle on the dashboard that went to a half of iced beer in the trunk. And to finish off our 'look' we carried a pack of condoms in our wallet, mostly so you could see the round outline in the leather. 'Cool Daddy O'.

Well, beyond a shadow of a doubt I was cool. I had the spit curls, aka 'jelly roll', the DA, 'ducks ass' and a comb in the back pocket, always.

With the introduction of 'folk music' everything started to change. Black shoes with Cuban heels were replaced by penny loafers and no socks. Girls stopped 'teasing' their hair and let it hang down straight; which I liked. The Four Freshmen, and the song 'Greensleaves' started making me violently ill; the only cure was a highly reverberated rendition of "Wooly Bully". A friend and I used to buy cheap socks at the thrift store, roll them into tight balls, then cruise around town looking for a guy in Madras and penny loafers to use as a target.

During this period in 1967, I had laid claim to part of the property my father had purchased to house his "Goodman Excavating" business. There were two buildings; the newest section was a garage with four bays, to park, or work on the trucks. The old red brick part of the complex was the Boston Coal Company Building, circa 1869. There were lockers and showers for the miners, with a small bathroom in the rear of the building. The entrance on the street opened to the office and chart room, which was to be mine. I cleaned out everything except the pot belly stove, which worked great. I set up an art table near the side window where I did pen and ink drawings; I hadn't starting my painting career as of yet. I had gotten quite proficient in both welding and using an acetylene torch; which lead to metal sculptures. None of them were very large, that came later in the 70's while at Florida Atlantic University; but they were unique and I sold a few. I cut a piece of steel into the shape of an artist's pallet, painted it black and with white lettering and hung it over the front door, thus ALCHEMY STUDIO was born.

This was to be my gallery and studio for the next 30 years. My painting technique was developed there; and many of my best were done there in that small room.
With the sale of my souped up Ford and summer of '67' coming to an end, I was beginning to look towards college. I got rid of the hair cream and started wearing a black beret; it went well with my poetry and bongos. I had been writing poetry for years, but never told anyone; tough guys like me weren't supposed to write poetry; that was for sensitive guys. In the fall of 1967 I enrolled at Luzerne County Community college, LCCC, or the 'cube' for short. It was a junior college and the tuition was something I could afford. This was a brand new college, which did not yet have new buildings, so they leased a bunch of old mansions along the Susquehanna River in Wilkes-Barre. It was a top grade institution from day one. I received a great education; my degree was to be in Art and Advertising, also known as Applied Science.

41

My employer back home strongly suggested I arrange my classes from 8am until noon. Even though I was paying for them, he still held the opinion that I was being provided with 'three hots and a cot'.

Originally, my parents told me that they would pay for any of us that wanted to go to college. When it turned out that I was the only one of the four brothers to take up the offer, the money part fell silent. I ended up using a 'Pell Grant' and that leather thing in my pocket with the circle on it.

I scheduled my classes early and late in the day, allowing a window for me to change clothes and jump into a truck or onto a bulldozer. He knew I would oblige him because I needed money to pay for college. The original promise was taken off the table, and my paycheck was my education money. But by this time in my life I was accustomed to the money game; it was always a carrot on a stick. Eventually, things started to change even more. I became President of the college level of the Rotary Club; and simultaneously one of the biggest dealers of LSD in the area. My partner and friend of many years and I would drive to Hell's Kitchen or Boston's south Side and buy a cigar box full of the stuff; and it was good. We had a reputation for selling top quality merchandise; orange barrels, purple micro dots, strawberry fields and other aptly named products. My partner also dealt in hashish which came from Germany through the ROTC program, of which he was a member. Our philosophy on all of this was that we were cosmic love providers. We ran a clean operation, and made sure everything was as it was supposed to be. Our customers were very satisfied and about an hour later, very fucked up.

But the heat was about to come down. A student at Wilkes College began a crusade against drugs. Her sister in New Jersey, just a teenager, was given some pretty bad stuff by someone there, so she decided to protest here. My friend and I decided to dissolve our partnership. Harder stuff was on the streets in the late 60's; they were not the love years people may think, things were changing. Our last great finale was at the showing of the 'Beatles", "Yellow Submarine" at the local theater in downtown Wilkes-Barre. We supplied the bulk of the LSD and after the movie hundreds of long haired hippy types danced onto the square across the street, and just started grooving. The Police in town new something was amiss, but couldn't put their finger on it. It was the end of an epoch; new realities were in the wind.

Meanwhile, at the age of 18, I casually walked into a Pennsylvania State Liquor Store and asked for a case of Strawberry Galliano; which I knew they didn't carry, but they could order a case for me. The legal drinking age in this state is 21, but these guys recognized me from a photo in the newspaper. In their minds I personally cleaned out all the winos from under the bridge in town. So when I came in the store, it was all Mr. Goodman this and Mr. Goodman that. When the case did come in, they all wanted a bottle so I sold a few back to them.

The photo and write up were due to my bulldozer duty. The college in town did not have many places to park your car. But across the river there was potential. Under the four lanes Market Street Bridge was enough room for about 75 cars; if the place was cleared of the underbrush and weeds. So I borrowed a Goodman bulldozer and 'went to town'. Besides doing the parking space, I also cleared along the river bank and cut walking paths; which the biology department then used for field trips.

This was one of the biggest chameleon periods of my life. A few nights a week I hung around with a guy about 10 years my senior, who was into the whole 'Playboy' thing; his was the Hugh Hefner Philosophy. We wore double breasted blazers and ascots. Our haunts were the high end cocktail lounges in town. One in particular was a gay bar and women went there because they felt safe. Gay guys wouldn't hit on them, but we would. As my 'Hef' friend would say, "like shooting fish in a barrel'. For the most part I was being instructed in the 'new cool' ways; slow jazz, good clothes, a money clip with matching gold lighter and 'the' car.

I bought a 1956 Ford Thunderbird from a college student. What made it unique, was the fact it was a factory standard transmission with a floor shift; a rare find. I fixed it up, replaced the engine, (which I had to borrow money from my mother to do, this will come up again later), and she was a beauty.

At the time I did not smoke, but one of our stocking stuffers that Christmas was a gold plated butane lighter; the refillable type. It was called a "Swank"; which fit my personality perfectly. On one of our 'fishing' trips with 'Hef', I met this girl and asked for a dinner date. I was going to take her to Iorios Restaurant, one of the big leagues.

On the big night, I drove down to a weird place called Honey Pot. It was a suburb of Nanticoke, but not like any other suburb. It was surrounded by black 'colm' banks; a waste product from the coal industry; treeless, bleak, black mountains.

When I went into the house, her mother, speaking in a mixture of Polish and English, invited me to sit in the living room to show off her 'color' TV. I didn't tell her we had three at home. Finally, my dream date came out wearing a silver sequined dress with shocking pink shoes. Her hair was piled up like Marge Simpson's in a beehive. My inner self told me to vomit on the coffee table and excuse myself because of the outbreak of Malaria, but I went through with it. Knowing full well there wouldn't be any sex until after a church wedding.

We were sitting in Iorio's at a table for two. There was a man walking around from table to table playing a violin; the atmosphere was perfect; until she pulled a cigarette from her purse. I reached across the table with an international flow of hand movements and produced my "Swank" butane gas lighter; flipped the gold wheel and a flame about two feet long came out of it with the sound of a blow torch. The violin player scratched all of the strings, my dates' hair just exploded and collapsed inward, her eyebrows just disappeared and the entire universe stopped. The flame did not burn her flesh, and the waiter had the sense to throw his towel over her heavily sprayed hair and snuffed the blue flames. I did the only thing I knew how to do in a situation like this; I left.

I don't know how much money changed hands between the Duke and her father and needless to say we never went out again. When 'Hef' asked what had gone so terribly wrong, all I could say is that I didn't know there was a flame control button on the lighter. The most 'flack' I got was from my brothers; they came up with new material, at my expense, for months.

My chameleon life was getting even more involved. I was a beatnik who read poetry to bongos and sold LSD to the audience wearing bell bottom jeans; with peace, love and trees radiating from them. Then I changed into the smooth talking lady's man in a blue blazer with the ascot handkerchief that matched, puffed just right from the breast pocket. Then there was the guy scratching his scrotum, pointing into a hole in the ground with a bulldozer in the background. And there it was; the microphone; that you save for those gracious comments, "It is a pleasure to be at the Rotary Club annual awards dinner."

Now I was to add another piece to this growing puzzle. One day in October of 1968, I went and joined the US Navy. They offered a deal; finish college, go to boot camp, receive the best training, get orders for a ship in the fleet and see the world. Then, come home to four years of college money. Those were the golden words. Just sign right here, and here, and here, and with this one we will need a few drops of your blood.

Down the street I can hear the sound of manual concrete mixers, the back breaking type with a spinning hole you constantly feed all day with sand, stone and Portland cement, then add just the right amount of water. Here in Mexico they do everything by hand; the object is to install new curbs and sidewalks. Here in the U.S. there would be a line of cement mixer trucks lined up ready to feed a special machine that lays curbs all day, miles of them. This is followed by a sidewalk machine.

When I was a kid we had one of those godforsaken manual cement mixers. I fed that thing for more days than I care to remember in the early days of the house expansion. There was a formula for the number of shovels of all of the materials listed above, then you watched it glop around until it was ready, the wheel barrow came up to the other side and you pulled a lever that tipped the entire spinning tub into it, that was one quarter yard of very heavy slop. My youngest brother probably still has it, he had a knack for borrowing things that after a period of time became his somehow; cheap magic trick. It wasn't worth arguing over, it was a beat up piece of rust.

Getting back to the Navy, the irony of it was the fact that I was one of the leaders of the anti-war contingent on campus. My reputation was based on my ability of giving motivating speeches and I also wrote articles for the newspapers. This activity cost me my alliance with the Rotary Club which demanded an all American individual for campus president.

What made me snap into a separate reality as ' Carlos Castaneda' called it in his second book of the same name, was preparing for a large anti-war demonstration on the 'square' in Wilkes-Barre the next day. That night we all gathered at someone's house complete with undercover police, too discuss plans and strategies when I overheard people talking about what they were going to wear because all of the major television networks were going to be there with their 'action' news teams, now back to you Wolf! As I strolled around the more it seemed to be the focus of people's attention. They were not discussing the war, or the number of body bags being used in proportion to troop buildup, these supposed friends of mine were talking about what they were going to wear? I simply found this disgusting for some reason and quietly left the house and drove away. The very next day while this demonstration was taking place

I was being inducted into the United States Navy. I never asked to be sent to Vietnam, but no one in that room had been there and the only Vietnam vets we heard about were a few local guys that were shipped home in a box. Their parents were given a check for $250 dollars toward their burial expenses and a form letter from Mr. Nixon, Commander in Chief.

By this time the family business was fully entrenched (pun intended) in the excavating, we literally moved mountains and filled valley's. I became quite good operating both the backhoe and the bulldozers. One day I was sent to a job that entailed digging all of the dirt away from the foundation of the customer's house due to serious water problems in the basement. I could have saved the man a lot of time, work and money by telling him to sell the house. The sub-division his home was located in was reclaimed land; someone just kept dumping all sorts of things in the river at that point, covered it with some topsoil and sold building lots to smucks like this guy. He was never going to keep the river out, never. But in the scheme of things that was not my problem; his checkbook was, so I went to work. It was a tedious job and I was there all week.

It was getting late on Friday afternoon and I had this hit of LSD that would take well over an hour to kick in, so with the last of my thermos coffee I popped it into the black hole. My logic seemed perfectly sound, I would work until 5 pm then run up to the studio and take a shower and by then it would be party time because I had asked for Saturday off.
There was about 10 feet of dirt left with a chimney and a window. I parked the machine and shut it down, the owner came out and he was frantic, he begged me to stay overtime and dig the rest of the dirt out so that he could work on it all weekend. We went back and forth until he pulled a wad of cash out, money does not just talk; it lectures too. So I climbed back up on the machine and started to dig, only this time I was looking at my watch and it wasn't the kind of job

you could really power into. I was throwing dirt when I bumped the side of the foundation with the bucket which made a lot of noise and very little damage. What I did not know was that Granny was sitting in a rocking chair watching me from the window right above my bucket tap. I just kept on going and about 15 minutes later an ambulance backed up to the house and loaded someone on a gurney than roared back down the street, siren wailing. I dug out the last bite and by now I was really fucked up. I shut down the machine and locked everything then jumped into my car and got out of there having noticed that no one was around when I left.

Needless to say it was a great trip and a better weekend. On Monday I shown up at the garage, my brother Bill asked me if everything went well on Friday and I said yes and told him about having to stay until almost 6:30pm to finish it. He then told me that the owner's mother was sitting near a window watching me and had a heart attack, they had to call the ambulance but she was doing fine, bad mixture.
It was a great trip though that lasted until Sunday, naturally I felt bad about the lady in the window, but when you are digging like that it is just a matter of time until you bump the house.

My wife recently read this story and she found a stick pin button that reads: "Friends don't let other friends drive bulldozers while on LSD."
My education at the junior college was another good one. This was a brand new college and I would be part of the first class to graduate. In a bid to put the place on the map from the very start, the board went around with deep pockets and made top of the line people an offer they could not refuse to move there and teach. I was studying Commercial Art and Advertising, in my art classes were two really brilliant men in their respective fields. Andrew Palencar was from Pratt in New York and had designed the 'Ritz' cracker box and had a big hand in the 'Coca Cola' label, the list continues from there. Howard Purcell, also from Manhattan, worked for both

DC and Marvel comics. He was responsible for the 'Silver Surfer' and 'Thor's Hammer' these were his creations, plus he did the story boards for other comics.

Because of the 'Pell' grant and a few other small stipends I had to keep my GPA above 3.5, this will be the story of my academic life until I received my Master's Degree, it was their money and they called the shots.

One thing that I must admit is over a professional career of 40 years as an artist, I made more money with that 2 year degree than all of the others I have to my credit. It was called a degree in "Applied Science," where they concocted that title I will never know. Both Howard and Andrew told me that I had a natural ' eye ' for design and warned me not to take any courses in the subject because I didn't need them and secondly, I could run the risk of it being ruined by others input. As crazy as it sounds, I listened to them and never formally studied design, it actually does come to me naturally. Howard Purcell would invite me to his studio at his house in the country. It was quite an honor to sit there and watch him work, he drew pencil story boards then shipped them to New York where they were colored, and the dialogue was added.

Howard's wife told me that very few people entered his studio when he was working; it was quite an honor to watch a professional at work. Actually, I am the same way; I will not allow anyone in my studio during a composition. If by chance someone should drop by, I always hide my glass palette, which can speak volumes to the wrong ears. Picasso had a bad reputation for lifting other artists' work, he is credited with being the 'father' of "Cubism," but it was not his initially.

After watching Howard work for an hour or so, he would close up his studio and ask me if I wanted to 'quaff 'a few lagers at the local pub. I would drive him to the Checkerboard Inn, a few miles from his house, for Ballantine's India pale ale. It was an acquired taste. We would sit there drinking India Pale Ale and talk about anything, my favorite were his stories about his leaving Portland, Oregon at the age of 16 and arriving in New York with $3.00 dollars in his pocket. I'm a sucker for underdog stories. In Puerto Vallarta, I purchased a time share based on a painting of the CEO and President simply because he started as a bellhop in a Spanish hotel and now controls the Melia Group with over 350 hotels around the World.

As soon as Howards head would touch the bar, I would pay the tab, put on his hat and coat, and then drive him home. One night I met one of his daughters, we ended up in bed and to this day I think that was a mistake, it taught me a lesson about quick gains.

That year I did well except for an English Composition course. I needed a grade of 'C' to transfer and this guy gave me a 'D' with the reason being a clash of personalities. It was an insult, by this time I had read poetry at the New York Poetry Society; also I had just read poetry with Archibald MacLeish in attendance, who complimented me on my work. Then there was a list of poetry awards for that year, 1968. I think one of my 'performance' art pieces may have contributed to this entire clash and subsequent outcome.

In those days I used to carry a small cassette recorder in my bag. Prior to his lecture, I taped the sound of a toilet flushing, then during the middle of his verbal suicide chat, I replayed my recording in its entirety and then explained that it was one individual's commentary on his lectures, which were boring as hell, and he spoke in a monotone voice that made it even worse. Another important reason he may have held some deep distorted feelings was his alternative life style. Somehow I posed some kind of threat to him, or, he just didn't like real men I have not the foggiest idea.

Summer school to make up one 201 course meant no pomp and ceremony for me at graduation, I missed all of that. Even though we did not care for one and the other, I wrote a piece of English Composition which must have had an impact on him and I received my grade. This experience taught me something I would use later in life; never allow your personal emotion over ride professionalism in education.

Good old Uncle Sam, the last will and testament of I am not in, didn't waste any time, it was almost exactly to the day that I received the call. He held up the paper with my signature on it and said, "Get into uniform boy, your ass is mine." First stop was the Great Lakes Naval Boot Camp, it was a total nightmare, Eastern airlines had 'misplaced' my sea bag, or duffle bag and everything I owned I was wearing; and that was my dress white uniform. The Drill Instructor was very understanding. I thought that this had happened before so they would have some loaner clothes; this was far from the truth. He told me that I could wear that dress uniform every day, provided it was spotless in the morning, every morning. The airline had taken a week to locate my duffle bag, it went to Guam, for over an entire week I wore wet, cold clothes, they were pressed, but still wet.

After eight weeks of total degradation and insults, I was graduated from that hell as a bonafide US Navy man. But there is something I must relate because I came very close to becoming a chicken wing.

One of the worse things aboard a ship at sea is fire, so subsequently, the Navy spends a great deal of attention to this and has a fire fighting school with actual pieces of ships lying about a field with open fuel tanks full of number 2 fuel oil, some of these contain over 5000 gallons of this flammable liquid.
One morning we were going to put out a 'compartment' fire, one of the more dangerous exercises because of the cramped quarters and nowhere to run and hide. We sat on the benches while the instructor gave us the entire history with examples of what a fire like this can do and why they are both difficult and dangerous. I was chosen to be the guy on the business end of this 4 inch water hose. Just think about that for a while, I did, putting an oil fire out with water!

My end of the hose had this huge brass nozzle with a lever on it, the stream went from a single jet to a large fan of water, it was explained to us that this 'fan' of water was going to be the difference between life and death inside that compartment mock up. The instructor was keen to point out that once he put the torch to that open tank of fuel oil, all 5000 gallons of it, the temperature inside that compartment would reach death levels in a matter of seconds. I had 4 men behind me to hold the hose, that is the minimum number that is needed to keep a 4 inch water hose from becoming an angry anaconda, and if the brass control valve got lose it would fly around crushing anything it touched and finally, the 6th man on the team was on the water valve outside and he controlled the pressure by way of volume, when we needed a lot of spray, he had to open that red valve double time. We all realize that there are people in life that like to sluff off and get by without paying attention to instruction and detail thinking that they can make it up by asking someone later. This was the guy on the red valve. They fired up this tank of oil and we went into this black soot filled smoke with only a fan of water between us and a ceramic kiln. I requested more water pressure, which meant turning that big red wheel to the left, instead, Mr. "I slept with Liz Taylor' turned the water off. One of the guys managed to find his way out which was not an easy task because this was a very good mock up, it was a huge chunk of and old ship, he got out and ran to the water valve, where our 6th man was smoking a cigarette and telling more lies, knocked him out of the way and cranked the valve open, suddenly I had about 600 psi in my hands and only 3 other men to control it, by this time the heat had to be close to 400 degrees in this little compartment. Somehow, our previous training kicked in and we started to cool down our immediate area with the water then we proceeded to attack the inferno. The guy who dashed out to turn on the water grabbed a drink and ran back in with a wet towel over his head because he knew we would need him. I had to gently slide the lever from the fan position to the jet stream and blow the top of the flaming tank of oil; it was a way of smothering the fire. But at the same time, I had to pull back to fan just to cool the air around us so we could breathe and not turn into deep fried shrimp. It was a very controlled dance of the use of water for multiple purposes.

We emerged from our funeral pyre as Al Jolson & company and proceeded to beat the hell out of our valve man who almost got us killed, it was so close, I mean real close. The D.I. curiously was pre occupied for a while until he stepped in and called attention. Both ambulances' showed up, one was a van with body bags in it, they quickly placed our waterless classmate on a stretcher; spoke to the D.I. smiled, and then left the scene.

After boot camp, I was sent to Norfolk, Virginia and stationed aboard a c. 1942 destroyer called the "Henley". My lasting reminder of that bivouac is the constant ringing in my ears; a condition known as Tinnitus. I'll tell you how I got this little gift. My rating was that of a Boatswain Mate, which meant that I spent all of my time on the main deck; or 'topside'. We went out to sea and I knew there would be target practice, but no one seemed to know when. I was standing several feet from a big gun turret when both barrels went off; the concussion 'wall papered' me against the bulkhead. I couldn't hear a thing and there was blood running out of my ears. I went below to see the corpsman and he told me I'd be fine in a couple days; when the bleeding stopped.

My next port of call was the Philadelphia Naval base in South 'Delphia'; as they called it in those days.

I was placed on roving watch; which meant I walked around the deck for 4 hours looking for boogie men and KGB agents; but my back was killing me. I kept asking for something different, so I would not be on my feet for so many hours at a time. Their answer was a huge bottle of Darvon pain killers; this proved to be the answer for my entire duration in the Navy. I didn't know much about these pills so one night I just knocked back a hand full of them. I woke up in the hospital having my stomach pumped. They ruled out foul play after I explained what happened; but while I was there a Marine doctor started giving me a hard time about not "sucking up" this little bit of pain. We had a slight exchange of words and I think I suggested that he do something anatomically impossible with his head. He told me he had just the thing for me.

While I was stationed there, I met a bunch of guys from my area in Northeast, Pennsylvania. One guy named Tony had a big Caddy parked on base; so we all would chip in for gas and all six of us went home on the weekends. Sunday night we would meet at a Diner and drive back.

The Marine doctor fixed me up really well; I was issued orders to report to Vietnam. He had personally recommended it as I showed exceptional motivation.

On that last Sunday, I was leaving our house with my duffle bag, headed for Vietnam. The Goodman crew was sitting at the dining table having their big feed; I said, "Well, that's it, I have to go now". My father, who was sitting in his chair with the back to me, barely turned his head and said, "Take care of yourself". He then returned to eating, never getting up from the table; now we're talking about a cold 'Kraut". With that I left.

On this trip back, we had a couple cases of cold beer. So there we were flying down the Pa Turnpike, swilling cold ones. What goes in must come out, so we looked for a place to pull over to relieve ourselves. Tony wheeled his big Caddy onto the shoulder and all six of us lined up to have a pissing contest. Quite a sight; six Sailors, with their back flaps, and black neck covers standing side by side laughing like hell, having a pissing contest while cars drove by honking their horns. Then it happened; a car pulled up with a flashing light on top. We thought it wouldn't be too bad, until a woman State Trooper asked us why we were urinating on her highway. Angelo, a little Italian guy, tells her we were all being shipped out to Vietnam, and how only a few of us would probably come back. He said we had tried to find a less conspicuous place, honest we did. She then proceeded to walk up one side of us and down the other, all the while you have six guys trying to return their hardware to its proper location behind 13 button bell bottom pants. Angelo's big, wet, brown eyes must have softened her a bit because she let us go with a standard warning about not doing a foolish thing like this again. After she passed us, and our somber looks, we broke out the beer and laughed like crazy. I hadn't told them that I was going to Vietnam.

It's 7am in the morning, and I'm sitting here in Puerto Vallarta, on the balcony, sipping coffee from a huge porcelain mug. I have my 'Pirate' spy glass and my job is to look for whales. One cruise ship just slid into the harbor while another is on its way out.
I have been up all night, but one doesn't die from lack of sleep; a doctor told me that once. What really has been keeping me awake is thinking about what I'm about to begin writing. I am procrastinating because it has to do with Vietnam. It is a subject I have to quietly enter.

CAUTION: MAY POSE CHOKING HAZARD

"You're in the Navy now, and not behind a cow, you'll never go back..." That is how the song went. Allow me to relate a story of how I upheld the honor of the entire United States, single handed, against a group of German sailors.

It happened in Norfolk while I was stationed there. One night, I decided to walk to the NCO club for a hamburger and a few beers. I was sitting at a table by myself, when I was approached by a German guy who asked if I wanted to join his table of friends. His name was Peter Alphers, a lieutenant on his ship, a German destroyer. Seemed like a nice enough guy, so I accepted the invitation. After a while some of the guys started to bad mouth our 'American Beers'. My response was to foolishly challenge them to a beer drinking contest. A few hours later there were six cases of empty 'Black Label' cans stacked neatly in the center of the table. We could no longer see one another for conversation, not that any of it was of any consequence at that point. Finally, a cease guzzling order was given and we made our way out the door with more stagger than swagger and went our separate ways. I proceeded to walk the mile or so back to my row of ships; the destroyers' were tied up with four ships together to save dock space. When I left the tide was out and the gang plank was almost even with the dock, when I returned, it was like climbing the south side of Mount Everest.

When you leave a US Navy vessel, there is a small portable podium where the "Officer of the Deck" stands with his large green book. You would sign it on your way on and off the ship. When you reported back to the Officer, you asked for "Permission to come on board, Sir"! He in return would ask your name, rank and serial number and then compare it to the green book. He would then say, "Permission Granted", and you signed the book, noting the time, and you were on your way. When there are four ships you had to go through this at every vessel as well as your own.

I started up the gang plank and kept slipping, then falling down until I finally crawled up to a pair of highly polished shoes, saluted and asked for "per mis to, ah, come on, sir". He checked the book then put it on the deck for me to sign. I got to my feet and staggered to the next one. Now everything would be level, but the red hot steam lines, and cables became trip hazards. When I made it to the third ship, I slipped down a hatch and fell into a third level bunk and promptly fell asleep. The rude awakening came when I landed on the steel deck; the guys had undone the chains and allowed the three bunks to drop, with me in the very top. I was on the wrong ship; mine was the last one, number four. After my apologies and the tale of how I saved the Navy's honor, they threw me out. I made my way to my very own destroyer. Fortunately the Officer of the Deck knew me, doctored up the time, and notices that my shoes and socks were probably on the destroyer "A Big Mistake".

A few days later I received a formal invitation to join Lt. Peter Alphers and his friends for dinner and drinks aboard their vessel! This may have cut my skipper to the bone. Had he ever received a red wax sealed invitation to board a German Naval vessel for dinner AND drinks?

The spooks didn't have enough time to wire me with hidden microphones and other James Bond type equipment prior to this festive occasion.

When I saw Peter in uniform, I immediately snapped to attention with a crisp salute; and everyone burst out laughing. He told me that they dispersed with the rank and file when in port. He was also keen to let me know he was actually Bavarian, not German. After many introductions we sat down to a great meal served by the stewards.

Afterwards we retired to the ward room and proceeded to have drinks and civil conversation. German sailors were allowed to drink alcohol aboard their ship, and could bring their own beer on board. Peter pointed out that the beer I was drinking was from his hamlet of about 500 people in Bavaria. After the third one he offered to give me a tour of the vessel. Thank God we were at peace as this boat would have chewed us up and spit us out.

There was a movie being shown on deck and we stopped to watch it. After a few minutes he said he didn't know I could speak German; which I didn't, his beer did.

We said our farewells and I staggered back to my boat. The next day a guy brought me two cartons of H&B cigarettes; compliments of my host, I then watched their vessel leaving the base. Peter and I kept in touch for about 10 years with Xmas cards, and then it just sort of stopped.

Naturally for a few weeks I was the big man aboard our bucket of puke. It doesn't take much to get a crew talking or complaining; it is referred to as 'scuttlebutt'. On a small vessel for an extended period of time, men have to find something to talk about. "Don't ask, don't tell", doesn't mean anything, everybody knows.

Back in port, a dock was a pretty bleak and dangerous place. It smelled of fuel oil and fecal matter and was a good place to get killed during the day by a fork lift or semi-truck; they didn't look, or stop, for anyone. A pier is attached to the land and extended out into the water to accommodate ships. Whereas a dock was a long platform built atop pylons or posts and extended out into the harbor or bay. Ships could be moored on both sides. A Navy dock would be piled high with everything from engine parts to pallets of wilting 'iceberg' lettuce.

Because destroyers were relatively small and narrow, they would tie them together abreast, sometimes five at a time. Crossing them was a real treat, as I mentioned earlier. The hot steam pipes operated the steam generators and cookware in the galleys. Next to these were the cold water pipes, marked in blue, and in this octopus vulgaris of twisted rubber and steel were the high voltage cables. It wasn't an inspired sight and I rarely erected my easel with a canvas to capture a quick still life of a Navy deck parade. Now, consider navigating this maze of hot, hissing rubber snakes in the semi darkness, totally drunk from doing stupid things like taking on the "Bismarck" in a row boat. Please keep in mind, these were not small garden hose variety hoses, some were 6 inches in diameter and it was all referred to as "Ship to Shore" utilities. Finally I received orders to report to the Navy Shipyard at Philadelphia. At first I was convinced that the CIA had gotten word that I was drinking with Germans. Not only that, I was smoking their H & B cigarettes instead of real American brands like, 'Luckys' or 'Virginia Slims' but it wasn't anything so melodramatic, I was a planters wart at best in their organization and they could order me anywhere.

For the past few months Teresa and I have been living in this beautiful town of Puerto Vallarta, prior to leaving we had a long discussion about packing. This may sound mundane as hell though when you are traveling, especially for 2 to 4 months at a time, luggage becomes a real problem. I told her about my 'duffle' or in Navy speak, 'Sea' bag and how I was trained to pack 66 pounds of clothing into that one bag plus every other thing I owned. Everything was done by traditional methods which included folding boxer shorts (I hated those things) and the different levels within the bag. Each individual piece of clothing had a distinct way of folding. The purpose for this was to minimize the wrinkles. It was amazing how many articles were packed in that bag; it even included my shaving kit and other personal items. After everything was loaded the top of the bag folded over a long thin loop which was fitted through eyelets and a lock passed through the loop, securing all of the contents. They even showed us how to use our knee to help boost it up onto our shoulder. Pretty slick stuff!

As I walked through the Philadelphia bus terminal, a guy with two crooked eye's started to follow me and asking if "…Hey sailor, would you like to buy something' that's gonna keep you warm all night?" I told him to hit the bricks, take a hike and get out of town. But he persisted in following me asking the same question.

Now, what would you think he was selling? I thought so because I arrived at that conclusion also. But the guy was still very persistent until we came to a concrete arch and I saw a few cardboard boxes stacked up. As it turned out, he ran over and came back with a pink, cheap electric blanket. I burst out laughing so hard that I knew I hurt his feelings, but I did not buy anything either.

I was stationed in one of the old brick buildings on the base on the second floor. My job was in the sail locker while awaiting further orders. As for my job, I didn't foresee a run on topsails, or any other sail for that matter, in the harbor were nothing but giant battleships, actually most of them were cruisers, the only battleship there was the USS New Jersey. The scuttlebutt was that it was being prepared to make an appearance off the shore of Vietnam, now that is what you would call the 'big guns.'
Below us lived the cooks, and for some godforsaken reason they worked really late, then went out and got hammered. When they returned about 3:00 am, with our muster at 6:30am, they came in singing and shouting; went into the showers and played grab ass in there then proceeded to make additional noise for another hour or so. One evening when I was on the deadmans' watch e.g. 12 to 4am, I went down and approached these guys and explained our problem with their excessive noise every night and our mustering out time. The next day I was in the chow hall with my stainless steel platter, it had some meat loaf on it, mashed potatoes with gravy and a vegetable, there was one clean little corner where the dessert usually went. I made my way along the line until I came to the dessert guy who was holding a nice slice of blueberry pie on a spatula. Because of rank, I had to say yes sir and no sir to anything they asked, he asked me if I wanted a nice piece of blueberry pie, I stood at attention and shouted 'yes sir' he then proceeded to move the pie toward that open space on my tray and in the last

moment flipped it on top of my mashed potatoes and gravy, upside down.

I then had to shout; 'thank you, sir! As I moved on they all noticed that 'squid' from the second floor and laughed. While at work I explained the entire story to my boss and asked for his opinion, without saying a word, he went into the back and rummaged around and came out with a fistful of fiberglass insulation. He then proceeded to tell me how to make the sneak attack; and install the insulation. It consisted of pulling back their beds, then rubbing them with the fiberglass, especially down in the mid-section of the sheets, then remaking the beds exactly as they were.

A few nights later while I was on 'roving watch' the cooks came in and made additional noise out of spite, they did their routine with the showers and bad renditions of Dean Martin and then turned off the lights and went to bed. It was quiet for approximately 30 minutes; then it began; the yelling was that of wounded animals and the showers were full blast with curse words full of water. But I must say, from that evening, or morning forward, our cooking staff were complete gentlemen once they entered their quarters.

The day arrived; I was flown out to Travis Air Force base in California and spent a few days there. I guess they were gathering all of the lambs for slaughter. We then flew up to Anchorage Alaska, changed planes and boarded a plain white DC-9 with nothing but the tail numbers on it. One side was all Marines and the other was us, the Navy. I looked around for a drink cart but that wasn't about to happen. Our stewardess' had to be in their mid to late 50's, not that I am discriminating; it was not a regular airline, just sandwiches and sodas. All doubt was gone; we were not in Kansas, Toto.

Our flying hearse made a fuel stop at one of our bases in Okinawa where we were allowed to disembark and stretch our legs, though the area we were given was quite restricted and well-guarded by the M.P.s (military police). I learned a few valuable lessons about going off to war, except I can't stop thinking about what we are getting paid for, I'll soon find out.

Lesson one is that it's best not to have any women in your life. If you are not married then don't do it. There is one exception and I apologize for the over sight, your mother is the only woman you need. That sweetheart back in Lincoln Nebraska who promised to wait, no, she'll soon be checking out the hunks at the bowling alley on Saturday night. Another reason for this very important lesson is to save face later. You will not slobber all over yourself when 'mail call' is announced, then end up playing with a hand grenade when your weekly letters are down to monthly. When something does arrive it will be your mothers' cookies which will make you a big man for some time until they are gone.

As a soldier you become a little less professional in a fire fight, or when the order is given to mount bayonets, your mind is elsewhere; which is a small place between who is she boffing and a crushing reality.

Lesson two: considering all of the above, you may become angry inside; anger and killing people do not mix, the latter will get someone else killed instead because you aren't concentrating on your training and instincts.

Lesson three: do not, under any circumstances, with cum the operative word, take any flesh eating sexually transmitted disease back to your hometown. No one will call you a big hero after you leave and Nancy has to marry a guy with the same disorder. Another good idea is to promise to write every other day and then just forget about it, don't do it, the perfect excuse is always "National Security." Just remember they don't call these places warzones because of a cotton candy flavor! I will have some more lessons for you as time goes on, first I have to make the mistake and then they will be valuable lessons to you.

A personal example, I was living with my LSD partner's woman after he cracked up, lost it completely and became a

fixture on a ward somewhere with a nurse called 'Masher.'
She was a Lebanese woman and very mysterious, she
smoked Viceroy Cigarettes.

She allowed the ash to become almost 2 inches long before
flicking it in the ashtray; it drove me crazy, but she never
missed. I was 19 at the time and she was 27; it was only
logical that it had to be love. When I was shipped out she
said she would write to me and I promised the same.
Months went by as I diligently penned a letter every week,
beginning each one with a variation of 'you must be very
busy', or 'have you had the casts removed from both arms'?
Finally, several months later, sitting in a rusted scow in the
middle of a jungle 18,000 miles from home, I received a
"mail call". It consisted of every one of my letters, unopened
and tied together into a neat little bundle.
After hours of flying we finally landed at Tan Son Nhat airport
in Saigon. The engines were never shut down; as we
disembarked you could see a few hundred guys in different
uniforms, waiting to get onto the same plane. Our baggage
was hauled into a large hangar and dropped. The fork lifts
would then load the other guys stuff and head back to the
plane .As soon as we were all accounted for, the jet turned
around and roared down the runway, escorted by a jet
fighter shooting out anti-ground to air missile flares. The
thought that came to mind was the expression that Oliver
would say to Hardy; it's a fine mess you've gotten us into this
time".

The heat and humidity was beyond oppressive. I swear that
there was water dripping from my boxer shorts, then again,
maybe it wasn't just water. We were told "at ease" and
stayed that way for a few hours while our highly professional
and thoroughly trained military arranged transportation to our
final destinations.

About 60 of us sailors were crammed onto a bus with wire mesh on the windows. While we boarded the bus, I noticed that the driver walked around with a mirror on the end of a pole checking under the bus for any possible 'welcome gifts'. We were driven to an old hotel in downtown Saigon called the 'Annapolis'; which was to be our home for the next few weeks while we underwent 'in-country' indoctrination' classes.

We were told about the history of Vietnam; to the types of diseases du jour that the local ladies of the day & night were including with the price of admission. For example, I learned that it was not appreciated to touch small children on the top of their head as this was considered to be bad luck. Hell, having your child stand next to an American was bad luck; we stood out in a crowd. You could look down the street and pick out every American; we were about a foot taller than most of the population.

But there was prejudice in the courses. Every instructor would provide information and interject the word 'gooks'; then comment on killing them all. I would imagine that is what is happening in Iraq and everywhere else we are in a war. We never bother to learn as much as we can about the people whose land we just invaded. I wanted to know about the people, the customs; their beliefs. They bent over backwards to learn about us; that was evident when you went out at night.

Upon our arrival at the 'Annapolis' hotel, I couldn't help but notice that about 30% of the wall in the back of the building was blown off. It was covered with a blue tarp. We had to go down the street to an Army mess hall for our meals. Evidently, about a week prior to our arrival, the Viet Cong had blown the kitchen and a few floors above right out onto the street; killing a number of personnel, another little reminder that all of this was real were the huge 'tanks' tearing through town. When we walked to our surrogate mess hall a few blocks down the street, there were sand bagged 'pill boxes' on various corners with machinegun barrels sticking out of them and black shadows behind each barrel. Many nights we awoke to the sound of explosions that were not too far distant.

In small increments I was becoming painfully aware of the fact that they flew me over 18,000 miles to be part of a real war, and the truth is I was scared!

In the back of the hotel they had set up a small shooting range, hand guns only. Prior to receiving our personal hand held weapon, complete with a leather holster which had a pocket for an extra clip of ammunition, we were required to undergo a quick course in .Colt .45. After I signed about 86 pieces of paper in triplicate, the weapon was handed to me along with a web belt to carry it on.

In boot camp, I qualified for a 'Marksmanship' medal with a long gun, or rifle. Do you remember my childhood story about eating a lot of wild game (you could call it 'bush meat') mainly because we could not afford to go to a butcher shop? From that experience developed the one shot one kill philosophy; ammunition was expensive for one thing; the Duke's size 11 boot in your ass the other. If you wounded an animal in the forest, you had to chase it down and that could mean spending hours running around following a blood trail. Once it was found it had to be shot again and that meant another round, then you had to field dress it and I won't go into detail about that except there were 350 pound black bears in that same forest and they considered it to be theirs. The next step was to tie a short piece of rope on the beast and drag it out of the woods to our vehicle, with the constant thought of what I said above, we are not talking teddy bears here! Being a 'marksman' was a necessity; not an honor on that field of battle.

Having that big 'hog leg' strapped to my leg in a city full of the hostile forces was comforting in a sense. An 1918 issue Colt .45 would put a huge hole in you in close quarters; it was not the gun to disrespect.

One morning prior to completing my indoctrination into Vietnam, I walked to the Army mess hall and stood there staring at the green scrambled eggs. I decided to try something from my service, e.g. Navy, but I didn't notice this big silver back with the Master Sargent stripes on his arm. I asked the cook for something different this morning, how about two over easy?

The guy just cringed and stole a quick glance over his shoulder than told me that they only serve scrambled eggs. Meanwhile, Sergeant Silver back came over in a nonchalant way and leaned across the steam table, about an inch from my face and said in a loud enough voice so the entire place could hear him: "Did I just hear you ask my man here for two eggs over easy?" I said yes sir I did. He then shouted out for the benefit of everyone, "Gentlemen, this water logged excuse for a military person has just placed an order for two eggs over easy!" There was howling laughter at my expense of course. The man in charge then proceeded to call me every foul name that has ever crossed human lips, then he moved on to the personal stuff that included my mother, sisters, girlfriend and (because I was a Navy man) boyfriend. This is called being walked up one side and down the other, similar to the female State trooper during our contest.
He then grabbed the stainless steel tray from my hands and proceeded to pile a heap of the 'green' eggs in the center, this did not bode well because of the sign above that read; take as much as you can eat. After the eggs was a hand full of rubber toast which he squashed into a ball and shoved into the center of the eggs, he then said, "Because you Navy guys are so sweet, I will just drizzle some chocolate syrup over this gourmet delight." After that, he asked me where I was from and I said, Pennsylvania, Sir! "Well, why didn't you say that earlier, you coal crackers like Ketchup on your eggs too," with that he squirted ketchup on top of everything. It wasn't over, he then told me to go have a seat and take this tray, all of our waiters are busy and I will bring two mugs of hot coffee over and sit with you while you enjoy this

handsome breakfast, as long as you are not concealing a bar of soap! The Army guys were now pounding on the tables and rolling around laughing even louder. I went over to a table by an exit and sat down, soon he came over with two mugs of coffee and sat down, naturally I had to say 'Thank you Sir.'

As I started to eat this pile of resentment, also known as a 'dogs' breakfast' my benefactor was called to the back and I saw my opportunity to make a hasty departure with the tray et.al. My breakfast found its way into the dumpster and I found my way as far from that place as possible. For the few days I had remaining I would go native.
The same bus returned us to Tan Son Nhat airport where I was to catch a flight to Vung Tau, a few hundred klick's North of Saigon. Before I leave, let me relate one more interaction with fate. It turned out that they needed Sea Bees, a part of the Navy that builds things, roads, bridges, barracks and whatever else is needed. We were lined up in a room and before the selection process began, I had time to mention that I grew up in the business and could operate any machine they had, besides build walls, pour concrete etc. I was told to rejoin the group and some officer came in and with an outstretched arm, separated us into two groups, I was right on the line for the right side. He then said, the left will go become Sea Bees and the right side will join the 'Riverine' forces in the Delta and on the Mekong River. I tried to become my own attorney in this case and lost, there is the old saying about representing yourself in court and having a fool for a client. This was the way of the Navy, if you were a brain surgeon when you came in, they would make you an anchor instead. No rhyme or reason.

The Riverine force was also known as the 'Brown Water Navy', we'd be on the Mekong; MRF, Mobile Riverine Force.

We boarded this old C-130 twin engine cargo plane, when I say we I mean myself and about 5 other guys. The co-pilot came out of the cockpit and went into a routine, good morning ladies and gentlemen, my name is blah blah and I will be your copilot for this flight, we do not serve anything because we don't have anything to serve, but I would like to thank you for choosing Air Nam and we will be departing soon, we have two parachutes but they are for yours truly and his boss. Today our flight will take us at tree top level due North to the scenic city of Vung Tau known for its' women, booze and smoking materials. Please, just sit back and enjoy the flight."

The operative word here was 'smoking,' it occurred to me that these guys could be high on pot, everyone else was. Twice the left engine coughed and died, we finally managed to taxi out to the takeoff position on one engine, they then fired up the left engine again, it came alive and revved up until there was this huge bang, a cloud of black smoke came out of it and it died again. They started it again and we were flying down the runway just about to leave the ground when it coughed again and we bounced on the tarmac and back into the air after it revved up again. After takeoff and once we cleared the city we were at tree top level, I thought to myself that any bozo with an AK-47 could empty a clip into this thing and it would be called euthanasia. As I glanced around I noticed that the Marines were sitting on their helmets and I leaned over and asked, they yelled in my ear that the rounds come up through the floor; just like the Huey's, and no one needs two anal openings, it wasn't Gods plan. I looked around and found an old safety officer 'brain bucket' and sat my butt down on it. We made it without new ventilation.

There I am walking down this long dock past all of these nice new ships and boats, sleek warships, I pulled out my orders (there was a special little pocket inside the front of the jumper for this purpose,) and looked at the boat, it was Hull #

902 "The Luzerne County" this is where I am from in Pennsylvania, the coincidence did not bode well. I kept walking until I reached the end of the dock and there was the African Queen, an old filthy rust bucket, there was mold on the hull, a whore without five and dime make-up or any underwear. This will happen to me again in my life, just read on its not that far away.

An LST is an abbreviation, or in this case, an abomination for either 'Landing Ship Tank' or, 'Landing Ship Transport,' but on the Mekong River it stood for 'Long Slow Target.'

No one laughed at us, this was tough duty and proved to be very bad for ones' health, and could be lethal; death from lead poisoning. Our mission was to transport mainly ammunition in every shape and size throughout the Delta region and all the way into Laos and Cambodia; places that we were not supposed to be, they were called 'black operations.' Vietnam was a transparent war, not only because of the VC knowing everything in advance; it was our own newsmen that got us killed. Hell, they could sit in Hanoi and watch the news for most of their information. Our vessel was a target; why would the VC want all this ammunition to reach its destination so it could then rain down on their heads. If we had taken a mortar round, I'd be in 'Star Trek' being beamed up, one molecule at a time. We also carried beer that was loaded on pallets, 386 cases to a pallet, and was placed around the perimeter of the main cargo just to provide a little extra protection, like using cling wrap as a birth control device. The boat had a flat bottom and could steam, with a full complement, in about 8 feet of water. The boat was built for one assault on Okinawa in the mid 40's, they were called dispensable then, and I doubt if that definition changed much. The day I came aboard there were hardly any crew; they were on from R&R in Bangkok. I met an old chief petty officer and we hit it off. More importantly he had control over a secret space where he would hide his booze. This was my kind of guy. He did give me some advice before disappearing down the gang plank, he said, son, there are only two rules over here, don't sweat the chicken shit and rule number two is, it's all chicken shit! My apologies for the 'S' word, I do not care for that word because it is crass, but in this context it had to be used, this was a direct quote.

I had been issued a bunk in the stern division which had a ladder directly to the main deck. Above us were two sets of 20mm cannons, they were used as anti-aircraft weapons, and that seemed a little out of place here but they were used and killed people just fine.

I stowed my gear in my 'sea chest' and went topside to just have a look around. The air was refreshing up here in Vung Tau. Saigon smelled like an open sewer mixed with two cycle engine smoke, and it was oppressively hot, over 90 degrees with humidity that was almost the same. Saigon was a disgusting city when I was there.

We had .50 caliber machineguns everywhere, then in conversation I found out about our regular trips into Laos and Cambodia, as mentioned, two countries our fearless leader Mr. Nixon, promised the American people that we had nothing to do with. Some of the first serious causalities in Vietnam had taken place in those countries. The problem that it made for me was when I applied for veteran benefits, the official records made it sound like we were on the Love boat.

I began to realize that day, this was an ugly blind date and I was stuck for the duration and would end up with the tab. I went aft (sea talk, for the back) and below again to try out my bunk, it was O.K. and there were 3 big leather straps for holding you in during a sleeping experience at sea. In 1970 everything was still tradition with the Navy, my entire 'sea bag' fit into that locker perfectly. Space was a premium on a man o' war, every square foot had a purpose; this wasn't the Omni or Embassy Suites.

73

Something strange just happened; while I have been sitting here typing this in 2010 with the PBS radio in the background, an old Eric Burton song just came on which fit this period. I must be rehashing this stuff well, maybe too well; it actually does cost me in mental serenity. A week ago we had a major accident and erased 80 pages of text; all of it was about Vietnam. I am here re-typing those same pages and I have to go back there in my mind again to get into the details, I could just say fuck it and avoid the entire story, but it is critical to the next 40 years, without it, the story would not have the same impact.

I changed my clothes, taking off the sweat filled official uniform for travel in the tropics; dress whites. I donned my denim bell bottom pants, spit shined black boots and a denim short sleeved shirt with my seaman stripes on the arm. The finishing touch was the white cap with its bent sides and worn cocked on the head, just over the eyebrow. I then ran up the ladder to the main deck and thought that I was a rendition of Steve McQueen in the 'Sand Pebbles'. But reality has a way of slapping you in the face. I was in Vietnam and it was hot; in temperature and in danger.
My new home was an armed patrol/ transport craft bristling with automatic weapons and other means of destruction. Meanwhile there were guys with AK-47's all around us that didn't want the US armed forces in their country; unless they were tourists buying trinkets.
Several months ago, Teresa and I drove to Indiantown Gap; an Army base outside of Harrisburg, Pa. It was a 45 minute drive but we hoped it would be worth it as the commissary there is supposed to offer the military great discounts on goods; which we found not to be so. We walked around and I spotted a nice white shirt, perfect for traveling. I checked to see the washing instructions and found the label 'Made in Vietnam'. Hard to believe; as so many of us have found it impossible to forget.

The next day the crew started to wander back to the ship, in their dress whites. You could get a pretty good idea of what each man had been into. First, were the drunken guys with traces of vomit on their jumper's. Then came the barroom brawlers; with spots of blood on the white fabric. A few of the guys, especially the young farmer types from Iowa, had the telltale yellow spots on their trousers; a prelude to the screaming to come later when they hit the head. There were some really nasty STD's in Vietnam.

I had heard from a very reliable person that the United States government established a special island in the Pacific for the un-curable strains of some of these STD's; hence the number of MIA personnel. I have not been there myself but I have no reason to doubt the comments by this man and it isn't that farfetched.

After some time had passed, I made a few friends and settled into a routine on the boat. The Vietnamese dock workers loaded our cargo we rarely touched it except for the pallet of beer that would be accidently dropped. About 350 cases and only 30 would be left on deck, the rest disappeared. We would have the beer placed on the sides of the cargo bay, and then fill the center with the ammunition which consisted of anything from M-16 rounds to the ones used in howitzers. One thing was for certain, everyone knew what we had aboard before we left.

The Mekong River was strange. It could be over a mile wide, yet have only one channel deep enough for us to operate in. Many times we were so close to the jungle you could almost touch it. After a certain point, the Claxton would go to 'general quarters', which meant every gun, was locked and loaded. We had steel helmets and WWII flak jackets; that weighed a ton and made you sweat even more. Because of my 'marksmanship' medal, I was usually called on to make the long shots; otherwise I carried an M-16 like everyone else. But I was always trying to get my hands on a M-14 with ammunition; a rifle that I personally felt was superior to the M-16 of that period.

During my boot camp training, I spent a lot of time on the target range practicing with a number of different firearms. To be quite honest I could not hit the side of a barn with the Navy issue .45 Colt automatic pistol; Model 1918. The reason it was called Model 1918 was the date of its birth, and the weapon had never been changed.

I did not care for the original M-16 rifle because it jammed a spent cartridge in the injector quite often. Also, the M-16 on full automatic mode had a tendency to pull to the right. It had something to do with torque, something I was always trying to get in my racing days.
My favorite was the M-14, it was a solid go anywhere type of friend; the M-14 was the rifle that won me a 'Marksmanship" medal. The instructor realized my ability and gave me some extra training on the .30 and .50 caliber machine guns. This was out of the norm as I was not rated as a gunnery NCO.

The entire compliment aboard our vessel was approximately 96 men; the number included both officers and enlisted men. Normally, a ship like this would require 110 men; minimum. The ideal would be 115. In 1970, it was very difficult for all branches of the service to maintain their normal manpower. Vietnam was generating an abundant number of causalities on a daily basis. And I can assure you, people were not flocking to the recruiters office screaming, 'I want to kill, I want to kill, kill, kill', as in Arlo Guthrie's song "Alice's Restaurant'.

Being short- handed meant that we worked 12 hour shifts and stood 4 hour watches as well. The work was difficult; the heat, humidity and those mosquitos would drive you crazy. As the 'leading seaman' my job entailed having 12 men in the stern division under my command. I used that term lightly, because in Vietnam, there wasn't much to respect and not much reason to do so.
Our job during the day was to chip rust spots, prime and

paint. If a hole formed under the rust, we just welded a plate over it and kept going. We also used these beasts called 'deck grinders'. They looked like an irritating little creature with a mouthful of teeth in the form of slotted wheels; as the name suggests, they were used to grind the deck. And we did the sides of the ship, or bulkheads as they were called. As boatswain mate's our job was the entire topside. This extended from the main deck to the top of our highest radio antenna. Sometimes we would spend days doing this maintenance only to have some Viet Cong spray us with machine gun fire and put all these pock marks in our work.

A large portion of the stern division was covered with canvas; this was the location of the stern anchor and all of its related equipment and large electric wench. An LST can run itself onto a beach, or in our application, muddy openings in the mangrove swamps. The stern anchor was lowered a few hundred feet out and locked itself on the ocean floor or, base of the river. When it was time to leave, they reversed the engines and powered the boat in reverse with the stern anchor pulling at the same time. Most of the time it worked though there were those odd occasions when tug boats and bulldozers had to be used to push the thing back into the water. The canvas cover was to protect all of this very important equipment, not our precious skin from the Sun. On the bow, or front of our boat were two huge steel doors that were opened with hydraulic cylinders, then a large ramp would lower onto the sand, or mud, depending on its use. This is why these old rust buckets were brought over from our moth ball fleet, the combination of a 8 foot draft, and the ability to land supplies anywhere along the river.
The Mekong River was a strange piece of water, it did not move quickly, could be over a mile wide in some places and less than a few hundred yards in others. It had a 'deep' water channel which was difficult to navigate, under fire it was a nightmare and our adversaries knew it and used this too their advantage.
Our most vulnerable time was when we were beached with

our pants down around our knees. It would take one cheap hand grenade tossed into our belly and LST-902 would be vaporized. On one occasion this almost happened.

We were quite a distance up the river in some nondescript place delivering ordinance at a small Army firebase about a half mile down a small dirt road. One of the redeeming things about this base was its bar. It was a sandbag affair made with cinderblocks, 55 gallon drums and planks. I cannot leave out the centerfolds (all of Hef's girlfriends); I think they had all 12 months hanging in a row.

The best part was the cold beer and an adequate supply of liquor. That evening, about a few dozen of us drew a few hours of liberty and hiked down to the base for the sole purpose of getting a bit drunk. We were sitting there laughing, telling lies and drinking away when several mortar rounds hit the base taking out some supply buildings and punching a few good size holes in the landscaping. The base came under a full scale attack by NVR (North Vietnamese Regular Army) and these guys were well trained and knew their business. Our full contingent of Navy personnel was pressed into service. As we left the sandbag bar we were issued M-16 rifles with a belt of clips and one thing that made me stop, I had to because my stomach was falling out of my ass, the rifles had bayonets mounted on them.

Just stand there for a moment and look at a gun with a knife attached to the barrel, it does something to your psyche, the cold steel runs down into your arm and penetrates your very being, this is another one of those lessons about being in a war, the faster you can freeze your soul solid, the longer you may live. You have to be frozen inside, cold, bitter cold. All the things you learned in life about values and morals had to be covered with ice to the point of being unrecognizable. You had to be in a position to kill another human being, maybe several, men with families, a mom and dad, maybe a photo of a girlfriend stuck inside his helmet just like yours.

After you completely blew this guy away and the fighting ceased, you then sat down and ate some peanut butter from your C-rations, pensive, quiet and cold.

Because of my medals from boot camp and experience with a machinegun, or maybe they just needed somebody to sacrifice in the front row, they gave me this young kid and told me to take as many boxes of .30 caliber ammunition we could carry and head for the forward machinegun pit near the wire. We followed orders and made haste to our destination with bullets zinging through the air above our heads. Once there I set up the gun and went to work at the task that, "we were being paid for." After a few bursts I asked where the barrel kit was, the kid said he forgot it. This was serious. A .30 caliber machinegun is an air cooled weapon and has a barrel kit which consists of an extra gun barrel, a wrench and a pair of asbestos gloves, sometimes just one. If you kept firing without changing the barrel it would get so hot the thing would warp rendering the gun useless. I could only fire when they shot up star flares; these were burning lights with little parachutes on them so they slowly drifted in the air for a predetermined amount of time before the flare would burn out. It was a surrealistic scene; the flares cast a bluish light and bathe everything in this hue, as for soldiers, all I could see were dark objects making their way forward with small groups breaking off to silence the machinegun emplacements. Occasionally green tracers would come in tearing at the sandbags in front of us and as I glanced around, our red ones would be flying in their direction. This was some serious stuff, plus I was still thinking about the M-16 behind me somewhere with a bayonet on it; that had an impact. The mortar guys put 3 flares in the air at the same time; so I had to take advantage of this availability of light with short bursts from left to right, then I would swing back to the left again really fast and catch them off guard, expecting the fire to come from their right. Suddenly the gun just quit, I pulled the ejector and checked around to find that the belt had ended. As I glanced around this pit there were still boxes of ammunition then I smelled pot. I asked this kid what in the fuck are you doing, he was in the process of lighting a joint, he looked up at me and said; "Man that's your problem, you're all stressed out and need to get a buzz to calm down." At this point I pulled out my .45 Colt and placed it on his forehead and told him that if that gun stopped firing again I was going to blow his head off, and added that I would walk away from it as hostile fire. He butted the doobie, called me some choice names then re-belted the gun. The thing I remember most is being very serious, too serious in fact because I know I would have pulled the trigger.

It was only when those flares were in the air that I could do anything with the gun, without light or bullets it was a piece of pig iron. Hell I was scared, I knew what they were up to out there, they had to knock out all of the automatic weapons and when they got close enough the game would change, their weapons would change. At that point in time, we either died or got hurt pretty bad; this wasn't the movies with that "it's only a flesh wound" crap.

After what seemed like hours, another Army guy came in with a ton of ammunition and told me to get back to my boat as soon as I could. It seems like the brass wanted us out of there because these bastards could pull and end run and sink us where we stood which would mess up their 'dock' you might say. I grabbed the rifle and asked if they wanted it there and they both said no, so I ran up toward the headquarters in a maze of trenches, occasionally stopping to take a few shots when the flares went up and then returned it slightly used. My crew mates and I then made our way to the main gate where there were two Vietnamese soldiers in American uniforms with ARVN patches on them; that was the South Vietnamese Army. But, they turned and locked and loaded their weapons on us, we piled into each other trying to stop. One of the guys spoke a little Vietnamese and asked what the problem was, an exchange went back and forth until they stood aside and we ran to our boat. At first I thought that they were NVR's in our uniforms and I wasn't the only one with that thought. All in all, it was a hideous evening, when we got back, after getting underway, I was shaking. In one respect it was exciting and yet in the other more powerful after thought it was full, naked and unabashed war with its own set of horrors.

That was one of my ground actions in Vietnam and I was not eager to repeat them, but it will come up again, I assure you. It seemed that most of the crew that was on the boat, along with all of the officers, had no idea what was going on other than all of the gun fire and the frantic order to sail.

The full impact did not strike me until very early that morning. That's when I really started to lose it, it being my life, close, so very close. I jumped out of my bunk and mixed up a cocktail of Darvon balls and beer, waited for the balls to melt and slugged that thing back. After about 20 minutes, I started to calm down and placed the entire episode into a dream scape. Now that I think of it, I did this for many years with all of my experience in Vietnam, I tried to bury them in a remote section of my mind.

This past 4th of July, 2011 my wife and sister-in-law talked me into joining them at the fireworks display. I should have known better but I could tell it was important to Teresa so I went. They had 3 of those really comfortable stadium chairs with the solid metal frames and we set up in what turned out to be the forward position by the wire. It started out O.K. but about half way through they started to shoot off single explosion pieces that felt and sounded like mortar fire, then they shot these things in the air that emitted that same bluish tint. That is when I started to sweat and look around. I wanted to run, well, walk away, but that would have left one heavy chair for the two of them to carry. Then this thing went off and red and green tracers flew out of it in every direction, I almost threw up. Finally the ordeal ended and I was pale, sweaty and very quiet. It was the entire firebase evening reenacted in front of my eyes; sound, and even the smell. Just to make this recollection more intense, Jimi Hendrix just came on the radio playing his song, Machinegun!

The inquiring mind that Mary T instilled in me was at work in Vietnam. I actually did keep a journal there with sketches in it and a running dialogue of my tour of duty. I had taken an interest in our surrounding's, especially when we went to Vung Tau to pick up cargo and do some R&R. The French were responsible for that city and their fingerprints were all over it, outdoor cafes, royal palm lined wide boulevards and their trademark architecture. I had heard that there was an unwritten truce between both parties that there was to be no shooting and dying in Vung Tau, in fact, we were not allowed to wear our sidearm.

Outside of the city was a Buddhist temple and two of the biggest bronze Buddha's in Asia and possibly the World. My drinking buddy and I stopped at the PX on base and bought 4 bottles of Boones Farm apple wine, we then grabbed a cab into the city and sat at an outdoor café checking out the women. The women of Vietnamese and French descent were stunning, they were called "round eyes"; the French influence made them taller for one thing and made their eyes more like a westerner. Sitting at the table next to us were 4 AVRN troops drinking from this small brown bottle with these tiny little cups (I seem too use little a lot but you must keep in mind that in Vietnam things and people were smaller) I got up and filled their tiny cups with Boones Farm, I don't know if it was the carbonation or the taste but they all started laughing and pointing to their cups, so I filled them again; same result. One of their guys went into a store just up the street and came back with a little brown bottle and we traded 2 of our Boones Farm for it. We opened it and poured a few stiff ones, this stuff was rocket fuel, it turned out to be a rice brandy; distilled Sake, and it was powerful, 120 proof. Both of us were toasting one another, it was funny, every time they had taken that first sip, they burst out laughing; whereas our laughing was from another influence. We bid our farewells and jumped into the back seat of a big black French cab, I gave the driver an American 20 spot, which was illegal, and made the driving gestures with my arms and pointed in 4 directions at the same time. Meanwhile my buddy had just lighted a huge doobie, and the driver, after getting a whiff began to laugh and shake his head yes, he understood. He drove and we sipped our thorax, after burner liquid and smoked pot. We finally ended up on top of the mountain, or close to it, at the monastery. There it was, this huge sitting, or reclining Buddha, I can't remember which came first. We walked up to it and the silence was incredible, there were monks walking about without speaking.

As I backed up to get a better look at this statue I bumped into a wall, when I turned around and looked down my serenity left the building. About 30 feet below me were beer cans and thousands of those stupid pieces of grey paper you pulled off a Polaroid camera. I stared at this mess for some time and began to realize how ugly we Americans really are. It was so sad to see this mess in such a beautiful place. I figured the monks just gave up and decided to wait until we left before they cleaned the place up again.
Just a few years earlier they were pouring gasoline on themselves and setting themselves on fire, while the cops beat the crap out of the reporters that were taking their picture. Disillusion started to set in that day, even with the rice wine and pot, I had a heavy heart just thinking about these monks, they knew about the corruption back then and we were too stupid to get their message..
Whenever we arrived in Vung Tau we had a ritual of stopping at this small dive that sold a strange version of the hamburger, they called it a hamburger and the sign read; over 20 sold. After several visits we were walking away one day and my friend made the acute observation that "you never see any dogs in this country." We both looked down at

our half consumed pets and threw them in the waste bin; that was the end of one ritual. Our favorite bar was called the Beatle bar, we went in there the first time and saw a cassette player and the Beatles' White Album, I asked Mama Son and she led us out back where there was an old hit and miss, one cylinder engine connected to a small generator. The thing had a large crank on it and she demonstrated. We were both showered and in nice clean and pressed denims, after we finally got that son of a bitch started the both of us were soaked with sweat. The fruits of our labor, was sitting at the bar with wet underwear and socks, drinking beer, and listening to the Beatles among other recent albums. The time came when I had to take a urine break, while I did my business the family sat there on the floor having dinner from a wok, about four feet behind me.

After some liquid courage, we negotiated a fair exchange from the Mama Son, for two pretty young women; and headed out to the beach. For a few hours all we did was hang out. I think the girls were surprised that we didn't want sex; we wanted a party. An old woman with black teeth, from chewing beetle nut, came by selling pineapples. We bought a few, and this old lady brought out a huge knife, cut the shell off and filleted it until it looked like a flower; then stuck it on a stick to eat. It was amazing to see and well worth the 50 cents.

After a few hours we decided to go back to the bar and have some more liquor, then maybe a cheap hotel. I found out two things; the 16 year old girl I was with was 6 months pregnant. And the girl Boston was with had a husband in the V.C.; same guys we shot at. To make matters more interesting, the Mama Son wanted us to pay again if we wanted to go back out with the girls; so for humanitarian reasons we declined. To those two girls we were heroes; we had paid for them and just taken them to a beach party. It was a good day; we drank ourselves into a stupor then headed back to the base; we sailed at dawn and that meant the river and the war.

The old 'Chief' and I had become sort of friends by now. Mainly because he had a secret supply of booze hidden along with my supply; and I never said anything if my stash was gone, or greatly diminished.

We anchored out and pulled into some nondescript mud patch. The Chief told me there was a small town a few klick's up the road that had a great bar and restaurant. I requested 4 hours of liberty and set off in a modern day rickshaw that was pulled along by a guy on a small motor bike; thus guaranteeing a face full of blue exhaust smoke. As we approached the town, I could see bomb craters everywhere; some of which would make a good sized swimming pool. As the buildings came into view, you could see the pock marks from heavy machine gun fire. In the center of town there was a square with a nice fountain; with only a few corners of it shot off, this was my destination.

I walked into the building and the first thing to greet me was the bar, after that were the steps to the second floor 'house of ill repute', followed by the restaurant. It was quite a beautiful setting, right there on the Mekong River. A few swans glided by and there were fragrant flowers hanging from the roof; quite a different perspective of those muddy waters.

In the far corner sat 3 or 4 young girls laughing and talking; I figured they went to work later in the day. I lit up a cigarette, sipped some tea and just relaxed; a respite of peace in a war torn backdrop.

When my meal arrived, it came with chop sticks and they were the only utensils I was going to get. I was struggling to get just a bite in my mouth with at least some decency. I had the girls' attention now and they were have a grand time watching this poor 'swabby' trying to eat lunch. Finally one of the girls walked over to my table (still laughing) and placed the sticks in my fingers and showed me how to use them. To this day, I can pick up a grain of rice, provided my left arm isn't too numb.

After the meal, I paid my bill and stepped out onto the

square. There wasn't a soul anywhere, then they appeared, a group of street urchins, about 12 of them, and they were headed my way. The little bastards surrounded me and began pulling on my clothes and trying to reach into my pockets. I pulled out my .45 pistol and made them back off a little, while I walked backwards out of town. I could hear a truck coming down the road headed in the right direction, so I turned around and tried to get to the main road. The first rock hit me, then a second and third; these punks were stoning me with rocks the size of golf balls. The truck came into view and I could see two South Vietnamese army personnel in it. Even though they could see what was happening, they had no plans of stopping. I had to run after them and grab the back of the truck and was dragged along until I could throw myself into the back. I was pissed and hurt, there was blood running down my face but these guys didn't give a damn. Think of it, they were wearing American uniforms, driving an American truck with American gasoline and they wouldn't stop for an American sailor in a bad way; more disillusion.

The guys continued to point and laugh at me in the back for the entire trip. When we got close to where my boat was positioned, I chambered a round in my .45, which makes a very distinct noise, both of the goons turned around and I said "stop". Please understand, I am not a dislodged psychotic killer, truth is the Colt .45 is heavy and for the most part a pain in the ass to wear. There were only a few occasions that it came out of the holster; most of those appear in these pages.

The corpsman on board made me take a shower before he would treat me. As I stood before him completely naked he dabbed and poked and said; "if I didn't know any better, I'd swear that you'd been stoned recently". I was angry, I should have shot all of those bastards, maybe I was becoming a psychotic, or the freezing of my soul was near completion.

86

That is what war is, there is nothing noble about it. You have to allow Dante to explain the 7th level of hell where Satan lives, with all of the frozen heads sticking out of the lake, some of whom he knew. You had to give yourself over and forfeit all humanity just to become cold. With it came the look in your eyes, the reporters called the '1000 yard stare'. You see too much of the wrong things. Death was starting to win the game of Monopoly; he already owned Park Place and was buying up all the valuable stuff, no matter where I threw the dice, he owned my soul and I was to pay for all of this later, no one cheats death; even at Monopoly.

As I have mentioned in the beginning, the stern division was under a canvas canopy; any one standing on the bridge couldn't see what was going on back there. One of the guys had a large cassette player that he bought in Saigon. One day while we were working, sweating and doing our usual, I got an idea. I asked the guy if he had any blank tapes; and he did. We then proceeded to make a 60 minute tape of the sound of us working, banging, chipping, running the deck grinder; and all the other noise's, like cursing and music, like the 'House of the Rising Sun. After lunch, we brought up the speakers, plugged the whole thing in and proceeded to play the tape. Our most difficult job was deciding who was going to turn the tape over. This went on for about three hours, when this highly disliked lieutenant JG (junior grade) came around the corner. He stopped and turned a deep shade of red as he looked at the scene in front of him; twelve men, lying around, some reading books, others writing letters and a couple of guys asleep. In the middle of all this was the stereo kicking out our hit record.
Because I was the leading seaman, and that it was my idea, he wrote me up to go before a 'Captains Mast". This is court aboard ship and serious stuff. I could lose my rank, get fined and have a nasty cut in my records.
When the day arrived, I stood there at rock solid attention while this lieutenant JG described in glaring detail what he had observed on that fateful day. Meanwhile, the captain is

trying to stifle a laugh the longer the 'luey' went on. The skipper started to laugh out loud and told the accuser to stop.

The captain turned to me and asked if I had done this dastardly deed, and I answered 'Yes Sir, It was my idea and I take full responsibility for it". He then told me if it weren't so funny, he'd bust me down to a mop head, but, because it was so creative, he was going to let me go with the understanding that if I did it again things would turn out differently. He then told me to get out of his office. I gave him a crisp salute, did an about face and walked out. During this process I stole a glance at the 'luey' and he was red as a baboons' behind. I made an enemy for life, which was a contradiction because this guy was a bible thumper; one reason the other officers didn't care for the guy).

Twice I typed this story and sent it in to Readers Digest, for their 'Humor in Uniform' column and the $400.00 they paid for articles, not once did they consider it.

Every morning, except when we were motoring up the river, we had to mop the decks before breakfast. It was a suck job on a good day, what made it worse was when they flew over us and sprayed Agent Orange, not bothering to turn off their jets. The stuff was oily and difficult to wash off.

One night we were anchored out on the river because it was too difficult to navigate if you couldn't see the depth of the channel. I was sitting out on deck just trying to relax when this little ole' Southern boy came by and sat down. We both sat in silence for a bit, and then he asked. "We are in the jungle aren't we sir"? I said yes, we were surrounded by jungle. He went on to say that they assured us that Agent Orange was harmless to us humans, and I said yes, that is what they keep saying. He then said something that is now quite relevant in my life today. "Sir, if we is in a jungle, how come we don't hear ANY sounds'? He was absolutely correct, it was dead quiet.

My heart problems were first noticed by a doctor in 1976. Now I have major aneurysms that are being monitored every

3 to 6 months with CT scans and MRI's. The Veterans Administration has just added several conditions onto the effects of exposure to Agent Orange; my heart condition is one of them.

When we were taking on cargo in the Delta, or even Saigon, women would come up to our boat in these little sampans full of fruit. You could point to what you liked and she would fill a basket. You then dropped down a line, she would tie on the basket and send it back up to you; you put the money in it and lowered it to her. It was great having fresh fruit. But this treat was to turn against us. A little lady suicide bomber came along side one of our sister ships, and when enough guys gathered along the rail, she detonated a bomb, blowing off half the ship and killing about 40 guys, some of whom I knew. In less than a week we received orders to shoot everything in the river, it didn't matter what it was, dead bodies, coconuts anything. At night we were instructed to use 'percussion' Grenades, these things would kill anything in the water for a 100 yard radius, after you pulled the pin and tossed it as far from the hull of the boat as possible because it sounded like someone hitting the side with a giant hammer, all of the fish would rise to the surface, not stunned, dead. The order called for 6:00pm, or roughly sundown to go into effect.

We used both the grenades and our M-16's on single shot setting. One night it was 10 minutes after 6:00pm and I was on roving watch, I noticed a sampan with a woman and a kid or two in it a few hundred yards off our starboard side and simply ignored it, she was going west and we were heading north so I didn't see any threat in that. For 5000 years this river system and the delta regions were their interstate highway system. The people lived in houses build on stilts and made a living by fishing and picking medicinal herbs, if the conditions were proper they planted rice; though that was more apparent higher up the river.
Without any warning my favorite lieutenant came up behind

me, he pointed at the sampan and asked why I didn't shoot it and I tried to explain the bearings on a compass to him. He then gave me a chilling order, "I want you to shoot that craft because it is after six and they know the rules." I asked what rules, how do you think these people received word of our new executive order? Did they fly over and drop leaflets on them? I explained my reasons for not firing on that sampan and he simply called it ' failure to follow a direct order,' in a war zone this carried grievous consequences, again he told me to fire on that sampan and this time it was an order, so I shifted my selector switch on my rifle to full auto and aimed then squeezed the trigger, the burst of fire only lasted a very short time and the clip was empty, most of the spent brass cartridges flew in his direction and bounced off his person. I pointed to the sinking sampan and said, sir, they are yours for all time, he was staring at the position where the small craft had been and there wasn't any sign of life at all.

As he stared at the empty spot in the river, I hit the ejector and dropped the empty magazine onto the steel deck and slammed a fresh one in. When that empty hit the deck it made a lot of noise, yet he seemed to be transfixed on the river. As I stood there, I looked at that hypocritical bastard and could see the look of horror in his eyes, he did not have to kill anyone while on this boat, or for that matter, ever. Also he was a card carrying Bible thumper. During this time I had the M-16 pointed directly at him and it was still on full auto, my finger moved to the trigger and I started to put pressure on it. I was going to waste this excuse for humanity and kick him over the side, possibly the blast of an entire magazine of ammunition would have just blown him over the rail, I was locked and loaded and ready to make that call.
He was one of those people, the ones that start these insane degradations of human intelligence, or lack thereof. He was one of those that really instigated this corruption yet never actually shoved a bayonet into someone or shot and killed another human being, I gave him that sampan and told him it

was his, I hope he realized that his hands now had blood on them. As for my part in this bad melodrama, that single act has haunted me for over 40 years now, my feeble gesture of remorse was to have a vasectomy in exchange for those kids that I was ordered to terminate that evening. The question still begs to be answered, did anyone tell those people about this ridiculous curfew.

A few years ago my mother, Mary T was dying, she was in a lot of pain and had that look in her eyes. I sat on my porch for days and debated whether to give her a hand full of my morphine pills and do her a favor. But then I realized that I would have to carry this for the rest of my life, no one could ever know what I had done and I asked myself if I could live with that? This same line of reasoning came into play on the deck of that boat in Vietnam, if I wasted this arrogant bastard, could I live with it? Now my soul freezing was complete, I killed non hostiles at the bidding of someone who just wanted to see them die.

As I stood there, I flipped the safety on and he turned back to me and started to lecture me on following direct orders and our duty to carry them out, he never knew how close I came to issuing my own direct order. With that I simply turned around and walked away, it was my job anyway while on roving watch. The guy never said another word to me that evening.

It may be interesting to note that it had required 10 years of regular monthly visits to a psychologist at the Wilkes-Barre Veterans Medical Center before I could even think of relating this incident to anyone, up to that point in time I had not even told my wife even though she would ask what was it when I woke up in the middle of the night screaming and talking to myself from the same dream, over and over for 40 years.

While underway when we came under a major attack, they would call in the Cobras, helicopter gunships, and their reason for escort, 'Puff.' This was not a fuzzy thing you gave your two year old. Puff was a C-130 cargo plane which had been reconfigured to carry a pile of 'chain guns' that supposedly could place a round in every square foot of an area the size of a football field, and these were not tiny bullets by any stretch of the imagination, if you were down there, you were dead, plain and simple.

The Cobras (4) of them, would circle our boat and get the bearings of where this fire was coming from then go back up to 'Puff' who would find the location and you could see this puff under the aircraft, hence its' name and usually all hostile activity would cease completely. A couple of the Cobras would flip over upside down and descend to the jungle floor and make a few strafing passes with their chain guns as a mop up operation. I was completely dumbfounded when I saw a helicopter turn over like that and was told that only the Cobra gunship could perform that maneuver because of a combination of rotor design and sheer speed. During that particular attack is when I got busted up pretty bad. During our maneuvering we hit a sandbar.

At that very moment I was half way up a ladder when the boat just came to almost a complete stop, it threw me off the ladder and I fell over 8 feet onto the steel deck below, landing with all of my weight on my lower back. I heard the cracking sounds. There was some serious damage done but this was not the time for the corpsman to get all excited, if it wasn't a large hole with blood spilling out then a giant bottle of Darvon would do the trick and an order for light duty which never seemed to ever materialize.

We were understaffed in all departments; everyone on the boat was considered a 'critical rate' which means they could not go without. The vessel was a piece of junk, our fresh water system was always broken which meant a dirty river bath or a salt water shower which I hated, especially down in the more sensitive areas of the body. The laundry machine was always breaking, so we walked around in the same sweaty clothes for days and even weeks at a time. I think I mentioned that we worked 12 hours a day, and then stood 4 hour watches on top of that every day. If you were lucky you would have one day off without a watch either. Coming out of Saigon we struck a sunken tug boat and it ripped a hole in the side of our hull. The Navy divers came in and welded a piece of steel over it and we painted the thing grey, though it was still a patch job, and would make its presence known later on. It didn't matter though, we had this job to do and damn it we were going to accomplish the task.

I arrived at a definition of PTSD, I feel that being on pure adrenaline 24/7, day after day has an impact on your mind; mix this with some bodies and a lot of bloodshed and you have a serious mental disorder from which you never fully recover. My PTSD was not diagnosed until 1983. I walked around for 13 years without knowing why I was not a nice guy.

The Navy corpsmen used Darvon to fix everything. The original was a big fat red and grey capsule that came apart, you could pour the contents out on a sheet of paper and take the small black ball out and throw the rest away.

Taking 2 or 3 of these, dissolved in a beer produced the mobile home park utopia. This was how I managed to get through the worst, it kept me on my feet, but at what cost? My pain level was really bad and there was little respite because we worked long, hard hours in extreme conditions, Saigon's famous weather.

Today I live in "Acute chronic pain" and use very powerful medications to control most it. The days of Darvon are over for me plus somewhere the manufacturer caught on and made a product without the little black ball. As DuPont used to say in his advertisements; 'Better living through chemistry', I would imagine that he said that before the place blew up.

In Saigon you could buy a pack of Winston 100's in a sealed pack, with filters but filled with perfectly clean marijuana for around $1.50 American, that's 20 cigarettes! These people were really slick; they opened the bottom of the pack of cigarettes and removed them, then rolled the tobacco out of them with the paper still attached to the filter. After that, they refilled the 20 cigarettes with fine and clean marijuana. To them the tobacco was of a much greater value than some pot. After repacking the smokes they resealed the bottom of the pack so it looked like the seal had not been tampered with. For all intents and purposes these were just a pack of regular cigarettes; the only difference came from the satisfaction level. There was an Achilles heel, at night when guys were smoking these 'cigarettes' sparks would fly off in every direction. The 'scuttlebutt' was that there were a few officers that would take the pipe as they used to say about opium, and that isn't surprising, the oldest person onboard that tub was the Skipper at 26 or 27 years of age, hell I was only 20 and that was getting old over there.

LST 902 was a highly decorated vessel, it had 12 fleet commendations dating back to Okinawa and our boss wanted to get his own. The skipper was a real adrenaline junky, one night while I was on roving watch at 3:00am a small helicopter called a slick flew in and landed on deck.

Out jumps our Skipper wearing greens with his face all painted and he was carrying an Uzi sub machinegun. I saluted him and he just waved as he ran by for his cabin. I have no idea and didn't ask; it's just that he was always looking for a fight. I am surprised that he didn't show up at the Playboy Firebase affair.

To give you an example, on our last trip up the river we had dropped our cargo and were heading down to Saigon. We rounded a bend and there was a small village flying a North Vietnamese flag, the Captain wanted that flag so he ordered that both of our LSVP's be lowered, they were the type of boats you always see landing on D-Day with the front door that dropped open to let the machinegun bullets enter. He sent down orders that I was to suit up my division with M-16s and everything else they needed for an assault on that village. The men just said no, a lot of these guys had been 'in country' for over a year, a typical tour of duty, and they wanted to just get out in one piece. It was really a mutiny which is punishable by death in a war zone. I guess some of the other officers jumped in and had a long debate with the Old Man because a couple of them would have to go with us. I was there because of being a leading Seaman and these 12 guys were under my supervision. An order came to 'stand down' and to go into 'General Quarters' instead, he wanted every gun on this tub manned. I was greatly relieved, we were by no means Marines who trained and lived for this kind of madness, I could picture an ambush and half of the men cut down as soon as those landing crafts hit the beach. What we did instead was very American, if it moves shoot it; if it doesn't, cut it down.

We sat there in the river and blasted that village until nothing was standing and the tracer rounds had started fires in the piles of wreckage. It was a perfectly good village until we came along and they made a mistake by flying the wrong flag.

Now it was a heap of burning rubble and we won a commendation for it.

Before I go into the rest of the story about leaving Vietnam, there is something I have to tell you. If you've seen the movie "Good Morning Vietnam", with Robin Williams; I can tell you, it was true. All of our information was censored. We had a newspaper called the "Stars and Stripes" and in the May issue there was a write up about a riot in Ohio. But what really happened was revealed to me in a strange way. Towards the middle of March I wrote to my mother and told her to sell my 1956 Thunderbird to get the money I owed her. (there will be another story to follow about that request); also if she would please send me some boxes of Screaming Yellow Zonkers; a snack that went really well with marijuana. About two months later, I received a package wrapped in ragged brown paper tied with string. Inside were the Zonkers, but more importantly, there were a bunch of newspapers used as packing. Of course I had to read the news, and there it was; the entire story of what happened at Kent State, Ohio in May of 1970. No one in our personal swamp mentioned anything about the extent of killing unarmed American college kids for supposedly defying a stupid order not to assemble on their own campus. For this they were gunned down by our own troops. The seventh level just reached a new low in temperature and Satan put on his best Hawaiian swim suit. Needless to say, we were stunned and furious about these actions considering where we were upon reading this.

I felt my entire life's patriotism leave my body, I had the feeling that this war was a big mistake and felt ashamed about shooting up someone else's country with them in it, but I still held onto a single thread of the American way, democracy for everyone and kill those commie bastards who said anything different. Now it all dissolved in front of me, I was empty, a frozen wasteland of disillusioned ideals. Will someone please bring the Zamboni out here to shave this ice patch?

After our heroic demolition of that village of the damned, we returned to Saigon, right into the arms of an adoring public. There was a huge ceremony planned.

In attendance were front, rear and side Admirals, we all received a bunch of medals and the fleet commendation that our Captain had coveted. This was followed by a bar-be-cue and all of the beer you could drink. By this time though, I had graduated to hard liquor; beer became a pizza wash or something to dissolve the black balls in.

The United States Navy is the only naval force in the World that does not allow any alcohol on board their vessels. At least that was the way it happened in 1970. Whenever we had a party untied to a dock or pier somewhere, we would lower one of our LSVP's over the side and place all of the beer in it and that is where you went to drink. A 'Jacobs Ladder' was used to get both down there and back up. The only problem was the ladder; it proved to be a very tricky affair because the wood slats would wobble around which made it difficult to maintain ones pose and dignity. The rule of the beer boat was if you got too drunk to use the ladder, there was a 3 inch hawser, one of the ropes we used to secure the boat to a dock or pier which was the caveat. The loop on the end was placed under your arms and you were unceremoniously dragged up the side of the bulkhead, onto the deck, then down whatever ladders your quarters were located on. During this trip, many black and blue marks appeared all over your body, it wasn't a pretty sight.

At our heroes welcome they actually sprang for a band. These guys were great when doing the instrumentals; it was when they started to sing that the air became a bit dodgy. A lot had to do with the 'R' thing and its tongue roll.

A really unique thing happened, after the band had quit playing, they started breaking down their gear and I went over and gave them a hand loading the stuff in their small van. While working I struck up a conversation with the leader and lead singer/ guitar player, a logical choice of topics was music of course, I never mentioned the singing part because they were all on a good high from their 'big break' playing for the U.S. Government. I just hope they got paid in cash and not war bonds or gift cards for the Whitehouse gift shop. After everything was stowed away, they invited me to take a ride with them around Saigon while the boss man dropped guys off, it was a strange invitation and I was free for a few more hours so I said sure. Because this was Saigon, I had my sidearm strapped to my leg just in case we had to pay a toll or something. As soon as we cleared the main gates the big doobies came out, as soon as it was fired up I could tell it wasn't street smoke; this smelled like Thai stick. After a few hits and a couple bars from 'Lucy in the Sky with Diamonds'; I could say with certainty that it was. The leader of the group asked me to send him music when I got home, any of the latest stuff on the radio. I handed him my 'black book' which I still have right here and a pen and told him to write his name and mailing address for me and when I got back to the old homestead I kept my word and sent him a half dozen cassette tapes, one of which I made in my studio with some talk and a lot of music. I often wonder what happened when 'the peoples party' found these capitalistic pig noises, how many years did my guy spend in reeducation camp listening to Jane Fonda sing Ho Chi Minh's top 40.

The evening was a blur as most of mine were back then, I just punched in the word 'blur' on my Franklin Language 3000 and the first definition was smear. We drove all over the city, spent a little time at a club listening to another group play until it got down to just myself and the leader, he drove me back to the base and we bid farewell. It was a tad difficult explaining myself to the Jarhead guards at the gate as to my whereabouts, but I did.

The Marines were suspect of some swab, squid or anchor cranker being dropped off at a main gate by some 'gook' in a crapped out van with the words "Rock & Roll" painted on the side, then noticing that this sailor didn't have any pupils in his eyes.

We left Saigon after hawking our medals and made a trip up to Da Nang, it was the first and only time that I got really seasick. My nemesis officer placed me in the 'after steering' watch.

This was a metal room with two huge electric winches' that moved the rudder which in turn steered the ship. In the event that the bridge is blown away, you could still steer the tub by cranking two handles that were attached to the cables that in turn were hooked to the rudder. It was the South China Sea, and it was very rough, plus the place smelled of fuel oil.

I was fitted with WW II headphones that were voice activated; a tuna fish can was right in front of your mouth with a small button and piece of string that stretched up to the bridge. Every time the helmsman touched the wheel, one of those giant electric winches would click and grind, it was enough to drive you crazy. Finally I started to lose my dinner into the mouthpiece of my head set; I could hear this clown screaming at me but couldn't respond because a hunk of

Spam was stuck in the hole where my voice was supposed to be. They sent relief down and I was taken to sick bay for dehydration. Then it came to light that the maximum time spent in the 'after watch' space was 1 hour and I was down there for over 3. My nemesis was in a touch of trouble over his journey into sadism. I started to regret not shooting the prick when I had the opportunity and actually wanted to do it. Now I was just sick of the killing and wanted to get the hell out of there.

When we reached Da Nang it was hot as hell, and that is not the local weather report. There was NVR throughout the 'Monkey' mountains which surrounded the city and harbor. Another interesting thing was that the battleship USS New Jersey was off shore lobbing shells inland the size of compact cars. It is said that they could drop one of those shells into a swimming pool from 20 miles away. Also, I saw a documentary a few years ago that interviewed NVR troops that were there at the time, one guy said when a shell hit, his entire body would lift off of the ground about 4 feet! But that's not why I was there. It turned out that I was one of 5 men that were being sent to guard our laundry, our machines were busted again.

They loaded an entire truck load of jocks and socks, we then accompanied it to a Marine base at the bottom of the mountain. It was really reassuring to see all of that wire between the buildings and the dirt; I am trying to be a smart ass now.

This was bad, on the truck ride over to the base, the 5 of us were sitting on top of the laundry and this one red neck had a paper plate of baked beans he had been eating from our lunch onboard. On his side of the road there was this Vietnamese guy pedaling a bicycle on the shoulder, possibly on his way home from work at the docks. The guy with the beans starts laughing like hell and tells us to watch this; he leans out of the truck and smacks this poor guy in the back of the head with the last of his beans. In an instant I jumped across that pile of laundry and punched this stupid pig in the face while he was still laughing. Meanwhile the guy on the bicycle had stopped and was screaming obscenities at us and shaking his fists, he was pissed. The other guys pulled us apart and I ended up back on my side of the vehicle. We had been issued our own M-16's and mine was lying next to me facing forward, the thought crossed my mind and I had to really use some willpower to stop it, I was really starting to lose it in this place. In a very small way I apologized by way of saying: "Why in the hell did you do that you stupid piece of.....that poor bastard was just minding his own business going home from work and you have to go and do something like that, why?" His answer was what I expected, he was only a gook so what; what do you say to that mindset? Anything would be an exercise in futility.

We arrived at the Marine base and the Officer in charge told us that until we left we were to be 'baby grunts' and if they came under fire he said," I want to see your denim coated ass's on the firing line, (we just happen to use the same weapons and have beaucoup ammunition), and I want to see you killing gooks, do I make myself clear?" In unison we all said yes sir and I noticed my bean buddy laughing again because of the jarheads remark.

We were there for 3 days while our boat anchored out in the bay just in case there were a few errant cannonballs. One night at 3am the place went into full alert, the NVR were pouring down the mountain side though they didn't drop a lot of mortars first, or punch in rocket fired grenades. One of the Marines I was with told me they were just jerking our chain, he went on to say that at times they do this every night just to fuck up our sleep patterns and to see if we left any gates open. I remember being in this position before, it made me think of Steve McQueen in the 'Sand Pebbles,' only he ends up dead in the end of the movie. Maybe I should stick to the Three Stooges for fond memories.

100

The next day our laundry was done and we loaded up, said thank you and got out of there, actually they used a forklift because it was all on pallets, now that is a lot of dirty clothes. After we loaded up we proceeded to leave Da Nang in our wake. Later that evening my redneck friend told me that he was going to report my 'assault' on his person, when he worded it that way I knew someone else was behind it, I simply told him to go ahead, tell the XO what you did first, then report me as much as you wish. Americans are really great at making friends, just look around, there are signs that say 'we love you America, please don't leave,' at least that's' the way it was in the 40's and 50's I wonder where did we go wrong?

ALL LOCKING PIECES

After Da Nang, we sailed down the coast to another Marine base. There we loaded aboard a pile of shot up armored vehicles; jeeps, trucks and a list of other junk. On our main deck they chained down these large containers which filled the entire deck. To this day I have no idea why we carried this junk across the Pacific Ocean, and that's what it was; junk. We headed back to Saigon and loaded 'stores' for the trip, meaning groceries. Milk and Ice cream were really sought after items. Aboard ship the mess hall would lock up the milk machines right after meals were served; the ice cream was used for bribes and punishment.

We were to cross the ocean accompanied by three other LST's; this meant that the slowest one would set the pace for the others. These things were junk also. Why we were sailing these pieces of crap thousands of miles is beyond me. My boat had 4 men write to their congressman refusing to sail back on one because of how dangerous it was going to be; they actually got to fly home. They had good reasons to protest. Ours was patched in the bow and it had a cracked keel; the very backbone of the ship which hold it together on open seas.

We had other entrepreneurs stuffing every nook and crannies full of marijuana; and all of the junk on the tank deck made perfect places to go and smoke some of your stash. You could climb down inside, close the top hatch and blow the smoke out of the big gun barrel. I just made several trips ashore with my duffle bag and returned with it full of liquor, it was going to be a long, slow ride. I hadn't allowed for the dangerous part.

It was the end of May, 1970 when we set sail for the United States without any fanfare. As the hours passed Vietnam kept getting smaller and smaller until it was just a faint green line on the horizon. When that disappeared we were just surrounded by the blue Pacific; also the name of a Sushi joint a few miles from my house.

Our best speed was 10 knots; that is under15 miles per hour. And there was a lot of ocean to cross.

Part of my job as a Boatswain mate was to helm the ship. Above the helm was 'officer's country'; as it was called. Slightly above where you stood was a huge brass voice tube where the commands came from. In front of me was a large, lighted compass, identical to the one above. The officers would shout down the course coordinates; "Helmsman, steer 252 degrees north by northwest". I would have to repeat every order to the letter, back up the tube and then spin the huge helm and bring the ship around on course. This was all ideal in 'Leave it to Beaver', but an LST is a flat bottomed boat. It bobbed in four directions at the same time; like a big cork! They were fine for the rivers in Vietnam, but on rough seas, very difficult to maintain course at all times; which is what the officers expected. To show their displeasure they would pour coffee down the voice tube, or a set of keys, all of which would hit you in the forehead and face unless you were quick enough to realize what would happen. Then they would order your 'second' to return their keys or get them fresh coffee; double time. Nice guys, these college graduates; so kind and sensitive to those under their command.

Sea duties were vastly different that river work. The weather and ocean conditions dictated what could be done on deck. The LST of this vintage had two large rectangular, black, smelly holes on each side; port and starboard. They were the exhaust pipes for the engines and when the wind was blowing in the wrong direction, you wouldn't go near the stern of the ship. It even got into our quarters and filled the place with diesel fumes.

Because we lost 4 men to their congressmen's request, we had to stand more watches. A 'watch was four hours and they were 24/7. The worst was the 'deadmans' watch; midnight until 4 am. That was mainly because we had to muster at 7am, which meant three hours of sleep; you were the walking dead the next day; hence the name 'deadman'. After breakfast, we went to work; chipping rust and painting unless the ocean kicked up. Our skipper refused to stop at

Subic Bay Naval base in the Philippines; he said he lost too many men there. The reason was quite simple, too many crew members would take liberty and the SP had a notorious reputation for cracking heads and asking questions later. He could count on loosing half a dozen crew members. Allow me to explain that SP means Shore Patrol and are basically Navy cops with bad attitudes. This was going to have dire consequences later in our voyage. We steamed 350 miles out of our way to avoid a typhoon, but suffered its effects on the sea. For over three days we took on 35 to 40 degree rolls and our bow was being shredded by the relentless pounding of the waves which towered above us; some over 50 feet high.

My old chief buddy the guardian of the liquids, told me not to worry. He said that LSTs had a tendency to break in half and each half would float for a while; sometimes. I thanked him for the reassuring words of wisdom.

When you are in seas like this, you had to plan every move around a roll; eating, walking, sleeping, using the head; and just about everything else. Now is when the three big leather belts in your bunk came in handy. You had to strap yourself in, and there was a technique to doing that; so you could get in and out.

One night, I was nicely strapped into my bunk; sleeping, when a guy with a flashlight came around and woke me up. He said we need your help on the main deck, we have a serious problem up there that could tear us apart in these seas; and make sure you wear your foul weather gear; and duct tape all of your loose clothing. I jumped out of my rack and got dressed. In the mess hall, I slugged down some coffee while I taped my pant legs, and shirt cuffs; a juggling act. The boat rolled and I heard a loud noise, and that wasn't good.

On the main deck, the containers we had loaded in Vietnam, were banging into each other, the chains holding them were coming apart. On deck there were these things we called turtles, they were for strapping or chaining things down.

They had four corners with a special shaped piece of steel in each; this is where you could tighten the chains. They went up to each corner of a container; and some of them had already broken loose. Another huge problem was that there was only about 24 inches between each container; and they were smashing together. Our job was to get to those turtles, replace the chains and tighten the whole mess. We had to accomplish this without being squashed like a bugs. All of this at night, in high seas, in the rain and on a deck you could barely stand up on. There were six of us; four went down between the containers, and two went down along the rail. There was a special safety belt to slide along the rail, but the guys in the middle, well; timing was everything. First we had to wait for that few seconds when the deck was level. Then, watching the waves and containers for when the time was right, we all lined up, waited, and then ran whooping like Indians for the space where four of them met. To weigh us down we had our flashlights and a web belt full of metal objects. When the first turtle was reached, we went to work readjusting the chains and using a short piece of pipe, tightened the chain clamps. Each turtle required four of these adjustments. When one was done, we waited, prayed, signaled each other with our lights; and then did the next one. When you made it to a turtle, you had to watch where your ass was located; it had only 12 inches before it was against a metal box as big as a house, and it was smashing into the next one. This went on until we finished and ran to, or fell out onto the bow area; mission accomplished. Some of the guys had their fingers smashed pretty bad; I was lucky because at one point my leg got caught between a chain and a corner of one of these behemoths and I got away with a bruise, and my leg.

We finally made it back to the mess deck where there was a crowd of officers, including the skipper. He thanked each one of us and said he was going to make a recommendation that we all receive a medal for saving his ship; he must have forgotten to fill out the paperwork, I never did receive any medal for valor...

On another occasion we were called upon to perform super human tasks. Remember the story of not stopping in the Philippines? Well, right out there in the middle of the Pacific Ocean, surrounded with nothing but ocean, we started to run out of engine oil. Using our Morse Code dot & dash system, the engineers found one of our sister ships had a few extra 55 gallon drums of series 3 engine oil, the problem was getting them across an angry sea. The first order of business was to shoot a line across to the other boat; we then had to synchronize our speed and the distance between the boats. After this a 'boatswain's chair' was hauled across and secured, it had various devices on it for this purpose besides transporting a person from ship to ship. There is another story where that comes into play which I will save for later. Then, using 4 or 5 men on a rope, we pulled that 55 gallon drum of motor oil across to our boat. During the process the thing, which had some real weight to it, would be bouncing around and popping in and out of the surf, this in turn had an effect on our hands connected to the haul rope. Once it came on board they had to man-handle this fat chick down into the bowels of the boat where the engines were, logical my dear Watson! The reason I end sentences with the blah, blah, blah is to save us time and interest. I am not writing a technical manual here on ocean-going subjects. When I see that the conversation is beginning to get technical and complicated, I try and back out gracefully. But just in case you were wondering, we did manage to get all 6 drums onboard and without any major injuries.

Internal Naval records about you went ahead too your next duty station before you even arrived. They knew everything about you, good, bad and dubious. One evening 6 of us were down in the stores locker, 5 guys were playing poker and I was lying on a bunch of big bags of flour loaning money when it was needed. I never gambled and I think I related that story.

Being a money lender was a lucrative business and you could say I was protecting my investments. Suddenly the hatch flew open and a flashlight beam landed on every one of us. Naturally it was my do-gooder nemesis, the Bible toting JG.

He could see that I was several feet away from the actual game and lying on bags of flour, just watching. That is not what appeared in the report for the Captains Mast to follow. Gambling is illegal on a U.S. Naval vessel, you could gamble with your life dodging AK-47 rounds and mortars, or wayward cargo that would spell instant death, but 5 card stud came with 50 lashes of the catty nine tails.

By this time the Captain realized that I was an artist and we formed a bond of ideas, then application. He made me the official ships' artist and sat around dreaming up all of these things he wanted me to paint. The job allowed me freedom and I could come and go as I pleased as long as a paint brush was sticking out of my navel.

I painted his name on his cabin door using a fancy script style font and used some gold in it to make it 'rich.' The real 'tour de force' was the replication of the fleet commendation seal that we received in Vietnam. I located it in 'officer's country' below the officers' bridge. It was a beauty, red and gold with two blue crossed anchors surrounded by all of the Latin words for pillage, loot and rape, then blow the place up into chop stick size pieces. I used Latin because you never knew when you would run into a trireme of a Roman fleet. In Vietnam, while all of the officers were chowing down, a well-aimed rocket propelled grenade crashed through the bulkhead into the officer's wardroom and just bounced off a few walls, then it just laid there. The XO got up, and threw the thing overboard; someone was definitely watching over them that day. Afterwards most of the officers just went back to lunch. The bulkhead wall was patched and that was that. I went in there when no one was around and did this painting with cherubs holding a banner which read 'thank you' and a bunch of flowers in the background. The stewards went nuts

110

when they saw it; all of the Navy's stewards seemed to be from the Philippines and were very religious. The Skipper really liked it also but asked for the date to be placed on it.

When the day of the Captains Mast came, all 6 of us were lined up outside at attention, then called into the office one at a time. Every guy told them that I never played cards and did not gamble at all. I was just bored and watching them for a while for something to do. (Four of them owed me money so I cut a deal, no interest in exchange for the truth.) The 5th guy went along after we all looked at him in a certain way that said; expect some permanent damage if you don't go along.   There I was again, all spit shined and ironed with crease marks you could cut yourself on. When I went in, my favorite JG was licking his lips, I could see the word balloon above his head, it read, 'this time you will not get away with it Goodman!' The Captain was aware of the vendetta which started with the cassette recording; which was a flagrant abuse of his rank and privilege. He was also aware that this officer of his was a bit on the weird side and had singled me out on a number of occasions by sending me on missions that were dangerous, not to mention the after steering watch debacle. So after hearing this guy go on for a few minutes, he had half a legal pad of notes with 8 X 10 black and white glossy photographs with a paragraph on the back of each one. The Skipper just raised his hand and said, enough, Goodman I fine you $5.00 for being in the wrong place. Now there are some things I want to talk to you about, I had some really good ideas and; he then looked at a very red JG and said is there anything else? I am done with this man and you can go. God, it was great watching an ego deflate except for the spike in temperature in the cabin. He kept fucking with the wrong guy, and except for the cassette tape, I had done nothing to provoke this man.
 Maybe it was a case of him just not having the balls because he might miss the last bus during the 'rapture.' Fate has intervened on my behalf with the dealing's I had with this one particular officer, he affected my life with the asinine

order on the river that gave birth to an incident which haunts my conscience to this very day, war or no war I owe him a debt of gratitude, he forever defined the true meaning of the word Hypocrisy.

On payday I would hang around the paymaster's window with my muscle and the little black book and collect all of the money owed to me before they blew it on another card game. It just dawned on me that I had mentioned having a journal and doing some sketches along with a running dialogue of my experiences in Vietnam including place names and other information; well that journal was stolen from me somewhere during our crossing of the Pacific. It was a major setback and would have shortened my bid for benefits from the Veterans Administration from 30 years to maybe 1 or 2. My wife tracked down the Captain of our boat and he wrote me a glowing recommendation for full benefits based on my professionalism while serving under him and my unfortunate accident with subsequent long term injuries. Getting back to the pay window, my base pay as a seaman was $93.00 per month, then I received an extra $50 or 60 dollar hazardous duty pay while in Vietnam. That was taken away when we left and replaced with 'sea pay' a few extra bucks for being at sea in a chum bucket. My poker lending and the sale of the black balls to guys that wanted to escape for a few hours helped up the ante. I had to start conserving my cash now, my pal and I had some big plans coming up.

Remember the sailor who hit the Vietnamese guy in the head with the pork and beans? He was not only a bigot; but was also not the sharpest pencil in the box. He was an engine department grease monkey and spent almost all of his time down there; if you saw any of these guys on deck it was suspicious. One night he was on standing watch, (which is done there in the engine room), and he allowed sea water to come in through the sea cocks. This was done at times, but under controlled circumstances. Yahoo fell asleep; and the engine room flooded to within inches of the steam boilers. The ship went into general quarters at 4 in the morning. I got to ask the old chief what the ruckus was about and he said he could have blown a hole in the bottom of the boat big enough to drive a truck through; it was the difference between sleeping in a warm bunk, or in a cold ocean. A few nights later there was a blanket party; I attended because of an old score as well as this recent event, sleeping with the fishes.

The Navy used a super-heated steam system on their vessels; it was like taking regular steam and distilling it into brandy. It was so hot you couldn't see it. If you made the mistake of walking by a broken pipe; you were badly burned. This steam was used all over the ship. It heated vats in the kitchen, ran generators that produced electric power and warmed the compartments; this guy could have cost us our lives.

Our first stop was on the island of Guam for critical repairs. We didn't have a choice; the patch on the bottom was coming apart and needed to be welded. There would be a few more 'service' calls before we set sail for our next port of call.

The island of Guam wasn't very exciting, but I did meet a stripper from Anchorage, Alaska. She was trying to save enough money to get off Guam. Prior to going on active duty, I went out with a few strippers. I didn't meet them at the clubs where they worked; I met them 'off-duty' at other cocktail lounges. I never cared much for G-String joints; seedy looking characters, rough neighborhoods and watered down drinks. Contrary to most beliefs, in 1969 a stripper did not automatically mean you were a whore or escort. Some of these girls were working their way through college; where else could she make $500.00 a week. Sometimes I'd be asked to come to see the show, but for the most part they didn't want me anywhere near where they worked. I guess it is a bit strange that I went out with about 5 strippers in a row; Ms. Guam was to be the last.

One night, in a bar, I met a guy from Pittston, Pennsylvania; about 5 miles north from my hometown. He was our radioman and hated the Navy with a passion. He seemed to be on a quest to really tie one on and he asked me if I ever had a Mai Tai. I hadn't so he ordered one for me and then left enough money with the bartender for me to tie one on as well. He left the bar and stole some guy's motor bike. He tried to ride it up the gang plank to our ship; the tide was in and the ship was 30 feet in the air. He got half way up when the bike fell over and into the drink. All the time there was a bunch of angry natives standing on the dock shouting and cursing at this guy. They kept a vigil on that dock for the rest of our stay, just waiting for him to come out. The police came but the skipper would not allow them to arrest him; he was on US property and their jurisdiction did not apply. One reason for being protected was because of his rating; he was our only radioman. I think the Navy paid for the bike and then took it out of his pay. As for me I never drank another Mai Tai again. Finally we cast off and headed for Hawaii. The passage was uneventful except for the monotony; every day it was water, water and more water in all directions. One day, looking for something to do, I poked around one of the life boats we had on the side of the ship. Under the canvas it had a mast, a sail and provisions for 12 to 15 men; I felt like stealing it and sailing to some tropical island. We did cross the International Dateline and held all of the festivities; Neptune showed up, people got wet and we got the day off. It was on a Sunday and after we crossed it was Sunday again. The kitchen had to serve their Sunday meals twice, which are the Navy's most expensive; cold cuts and cheese.

I do have a framed 'Domain of the Golden Dragon' parchment hanging in the hallway of my house. 'Be it known that LST 902, and Jason P Goodman, crossed the 180 Meridian Latitude'; she's a beauty, and I'm proud of her.

One day I paid a visit to my Mai Tai friend in the radio 'shack' as it was called. I requested an old chart of the ocean area we were in at that time. After a few days he produced the chart I needed. I figured with that and a good compass, I'd do just fine bobbing along the Pacific Ocean until I found an Island that wasn't used for atom bomb testing and build a hut. I would be a modern day Robinson Caruso; without Friday.

On a number of occasions I would sneak under the life boat canvas and with my flashlight would check the stores to be sure no one had dipped into them for a snack and recheck the water supply. One evening I found a pound of pot that had been thrown in there. Was somebody else planning to steal my ride? I really got serious about this escape; guess I wanted to get away from the human race. But I lost track of the trade winds and the currents between Guam and the Hawaiian Islands; within days we would be in Hawaii. My plan was foiled, not meant to be; guess it saved my life.

After Vietnam, Hawaii would be like dying and going to heaven with 40 virgins. A friend and I both had 5 days leave coming to us, so we rented a small car and rented a couple rooms at the Coral Reef Hotel. We were determined to live it up in a grand way. Epicurus would be proud of us; wine women and song.

We did all the tourist stuff, drove around Diamond Head into a rain forest; very interesting. One side of the island was bright with the sun shining. We drove around behind Diamond Head where the clouds were backed up against the mountain and it was dark and raining. But the touristy stuff wore off quickly; we wanted pure debauchery, a bar & bush!

In the basement of the Hotel there was a bar called "Davy Jones Locker"; that is where I ended up one afternoon. As I sat there having rum on the rocks, I swore I saw a set of legs in my peripheral vision. I asked the bartender what he put in my drink. There were three large turquoise panels behind the bar, which actually were windows to the hotel swimming pool next to the Cabana Bar This basement bar was set up like a theater in the round, the tables were on multiple tiers fanning out from the bar and windows. That night there were two sets of legs, and you could see it was a man and a woman; but you could only see them from the waist down; no faces. The guys hand moved down into the woman's bikini bottom; and bar got quiet. Pretty soon the guy had a pretty good sized cod piece in his speedo, and the bar went nuts. About 70 drunken sailors were yelling and shouting like they were at the coliseum. Interesting to note that the bartender served quite a few drinks before he walked over to the phone and must have called someone topside; suddenly the couple shot out of the water like missiles. That bartender must have made a small fortune in tips that night. I must say that no one in that bar ever saw the faces of that couple, otherwise I may not have told this story. I still have some scruples left, dusty for lack of use, but still in working order.

After the Aquatic Sears catalogue Sir Robert Attenborough human nature show was over, I left to take a walk around Honolulu. I must say that the old saying is true, 'women love a guy in uniform'. They flirted with us all the time. Often you could see the tan line where their wedding ring should be. Maybe another attraction was that we would sail away soon, and never be seen again.
I had a technique of knocking on a girl's hotel door with a bottle of champagne and ask if she had a cork screw; it worked like a charm. Allow me to make something clear. I was 20 years old at the time; had just come from a war, and weeks at sea with a bunch of men who didn't read National geographic. Sex had its uses, but was never an overwhelming priority in my life. Numerous qualities in women held much more importance before that.

While in Honolulu, I found a club with a live band playing, it was 'Quick Silver Messenger Service'. They were a pretty big name at that time. They sounded great; especially the bass player; remember me wanting to be a rock and roll base player. I could hear him but couldn't see him. So I followed a cord from the amplifier and there he was sitting on the back corner of the stage, where he could look through the amps and see the drummer. I assume that is where a bass player gets his cue, from the drummer. Anyway it was great to just sit and watch this guy; imagining myself there, long hair and all. But that was never going to happen; I took the art road; that would be my calling for life.

Our leave was over and just in time as I was flat broke by then. My buddy and I made it back to the ship with just enough money for the cab ride; none for a tip. He called us some choice words as he wheeled away from the main gate; the guards just laughed, guess they had seen it all before.

Once we got aboard, I noticed they had painted out the entire rust bucket. I asked what was going on and was told the XO wanted us to look good when we passed under the Golden Gate Bridge. It was a bit absurd, as soon as we docked at Vallejo, this tub was going to be turned into Chevy's or toilet seat hinges. The ship was to be decommissioned and 'stricken' from the records; Navy 'speak' for nonexistent. The cost; my good friend John fell 30 feet and landed on his back on a painter's barge. That barge was a flat floating platform pulled along the side of the ship while the guys painted. The Jacobs ladder was dropped from the deck to get the hard to reach parts. Seems the slat in the Jacobs ladder broke in half from old age. He was a nice guy and the only one I could call a good friend on board that boat. He was going to be in the hospital for a while and I couldn't visit him because I had duty the next day.

Do you know how much paint it takes to cover a ship 300 feet long? And it wasn't just the grey paint, there had to be a primer of stuff they called 'red lead' put on first. It was a major undertaking and usually reserved for an overhaul; not someone's vanity.

In 1970, I envisioned people lined up on the bridge just to piss on us as we sailed under it. This was San Francisco, the hot bed of anti-wars protests. They didn't give a damn about a returning Navy ship.

During the last days in Hawaii, I was one of the few men still aboard; it was called a skeleton crew. It derived from wartime, in the event the ship had to get underway, there were just enough men on board to accomplish the task. When I reported for duty to the officer of the deck, he turned out to be my Junior Grade hate generator. Fortunately for me I had just dropped a hit of 'Strawberry Fields' that a Texan sold me. This would guarantee my sanity for the duration and make me susceptible to frequent outbursts of laughter. The first task at making my life as miserable as possible was the inspection of the contents of the 'sports locker'. It was filled with various sports equipment, a lot of sports equipment. Now this guy could have gone through a maze of hatches and ladders to inspect this while standing right in front of it, something he probably would have done if someone else was on duty. But for me, I was to bring everything up to his office for inspection. With a very peculiar smile, something that didn't escape his gaze, I said yes sir, thank you sir, you won't be disappointed sir.

I made my way down to the bowels of the ship to the sports locker, carefully removed the pounds of someone's pot and found at least a dozen balls; footballs, basketballs, soccer balls, softballs, Christmas balls, my balls and I had to devise a way of getting them up to his office. I found a large mess bag and loaded all of the balls into it, then proceeded to haul them, Santa style, to his office. As I got closer to my goal I noticed the bag was getting lighter and lighter. I turned around and there were balls everywhere. I was convinced we were still at sea and the ship was rolling. I found a hole in the bag, stuffed the largest ball into it and hoped it held. As I came down the passage in clear view of him at his desk, balls began to roll out of the bag as I bounced around to my imaginary 30 degree rolls.

I gathered up the balls and dumped them on the floor of his cabin, turned and staggered back to the locker for the bats;

Louisville sluggers, not the flying kind. This also proved to be awkward as the bats were longer than the hatch was wide. I almost made it until I tripped on the hatch going into his office and my armload of bats landed on his desk and I landed on the deck. "Sorry sir, it's an inner ear thing". Another bad combination of LST's and LSD; but I still had this comic book smile on my face.

This guy hated me, he couldn't figure out what was going on. I wasn't drunk, that would have been obvious, and this made him even more aggravated. He had ordered me to do a ridiculous job, because he had the rank to do so and now it sort of blew up in his face. It was 3:30 and I was scheduled for "watch' duty at 4. That was something he couldn't mess with, an order from someone with higher rank.

Consequently all of the smelly old WWII sports gear was left in his cabin for someone else to remove. That would make it back to the skipper, who'd wonder why he didn't go down to the locker for the inspection. It was another vindictive move on the 'lueys' part; and the skipper knew it.

San Diego was our next port of call; this entailed another 2 to 3 weeks of open water and sheer boredom. It was so bad, guys would take bets on flying fish off our bow and I financed most of the action. Meanwhile the Land of Don Ho singing "tiny boobies' to titillate all of the silver haired tourists; slowly disappeared into the distance.

I completely disbanded the idea of stealing a lifeboat; we had been in the 'doldrums' prior to reaching Hawaii. I would have ended up eating myself bit by bit and they would have rescued a talking head. During this down time I'll relate a story. Before leaving Saigon, I bought a Zippo lighter and had it engraved with information about my stay in wonderful and exciting Vietnam, it was like a modern day Iliad and the first time I ever owned a Zippo, so I was pretty proud of it. One evening a few of us were standing on the 'tantail' staring at the prop wash and our wake when one of the guys asked for a light, and me being the fool that I am, handed him my Zippo. He fired it up on a large joint, then, he dropped it over the side. We all stared as the Zippo tumbled down end over end until it hit the water. I asked a guy in our group to dash up to the radio shack and find out where we were; it turned out that we were steaming over the Marianas Trench. I tried to throw this dolt over the side but was restrained because the rest of our party didn't think it was a good idea. There it lay, to this very day, my pride and joy in the deepest water of the entire Earth, mocking me. Even if some toothy Denison of the darkness swallowed it, the Zippo would still be there. The moral of this, if it even deserves one, is to this day I use disposable lighters.

Another fantail story which happened in this same place, the round enclosed area of a set of 20mm aircraft guns, was the day that we had gunnery practice with our new, improved version of the M-16 fully automatic rifle. We were all crowded in the back facing our instructor as he flipped the gun around and showed us it's various exposed parts, but, one thing that I distinctly remember was him mentioning that this weapon had a torque to it, meaning on full auto, it would pull to the right. He mentioned this a few times. Naturally there was a wise guy in our group who was running his mouth and when you talk you can't very well be listening. Finally we all had our turns on the gun, a few single shots, and a few bursts then at the end a full auto demonstration with the rest of the clip of ammo. When it was time for dick wad to get up there he flipped the selector switch right to full auto, and holding the gun at the hip like Earl Flynn, he pulled the trigger. That thing spit out 30 angry parabellum rounds just an inch or two above the inside of the curved armor plating which encircled the gun enplacement; and where about 25 men were standing. The thought of what could have happened was horrible, a large casualty report at best.
Without saying, there was a blanket party that night, and the wise guy was more attentive.
A few days out of San Diego, they brought the narcotics officer out to meet us. This was a new policy of the Navy sending a man aboard with a complete set of blue prints for

the entire craft he was inspecting. We had to rig up the infamous 'Boatswains Chair' again, just like the oil drums I had mentioned before. As he was being pulled across to our boat a mysterious thing happened, our helmsman swerved suddenly to miss a rock or something and the chair went slack hitting the cold sea with its occupant strapped in the device. This unfortunate thing happened twice during the 'G' man's passage. Let us just say that he wasn't filled with joy to be onboard our boat, dripping wet, but it didn't deter him in the least when it came to his job. There were a lot of grown men sobbing tears that day when they watched hundreds of pounds of dope being tossed over the side. Just think of the money that was lost also, entire fortunes gone to the bottom.

We finally reached Coronado Island in the middle of the bay at San Diego. A pile of guys went to Tijuana to get: 'drunk, screwed, and tattooed!' On the advice of my Chief, I stayed on the island and did quite well again, there was the telltale sign of where a wedding ring once lived, but it didn't matter, I was only going to be there for a few days. At least I wasn't bringing home some nice presents from the girls in Tijuana. This was rather bleak for some of these corn huskers because their wives were meeting them in San Francisco.

We left San Diego only one man short, he was in a jail in Mexico, and we sailed up the coast to Camp Pendleton; a Marine camp near San Clemente, Nixon's West coast Whitehouse as the press called it. The containers from our main deck had been removed at Coronado Island.
Now we had to empty our tank deck of all of the junk we had brought back from Vietnam for these grunts. We rammed the boat up onto the beach and maybe we did it too well because it refused to leave. We were there for 3 extra days while they brought in bulldozers and then ocean going tug boats to try and pull this lump off of the sand, I knew it needed sunscreen rubbed on the bottom!

About a mile down the road was one of the gates and just outside the gate was a small drinking bar, our kind of place. Boston and I walked down there the first night, threw a pile of cash on the bar and told the woman behind the plank that we wanted 5 ounce beers and double shots of whiskey. We also told her that our glasses should never, under any circumstances, be empty until we walked out. As she set up the first round she said, you two are from that LST stuck on the beach, we said yes ma'am, then she asked where we had come from, we told her the Riverine Forces, Mekong River. She then asked if we were in the action over there, and I said yes ma'am every day and night of the week, without sounding rude, we came here to drink and with that I knocked back the double shot with a wash of beer, and continued to say, that is our only purpose for being at this bar. She was old and experienced enough to understand my drift without taking any offense; our glasses were never empty. I remember just sitting there at the end of the bar staring at this Olympia Beer sign that was a water fall with running water and knocking back one after another. The second night we showed up at the exact same time, wearing our dress whites, as the night before, assumed our duty stations; she said good evening gentlemen and set us up. A few hours later about 6 Marines came in and stayed up by the door at that end of the bar, I could tell that there was trouble coming our way, what are these two squids doing in OUR bar? Then, when she dropped everything and ran down to fill our glasses that really pushed them over the top.

We could hear all of the planning going on about how two sea frogs were going to be shown a good time until our bartender leaned across the bar and told these guys that those two sailors down there just came back from Vietnam and the Riverine forces, she went on to say, they must have been through a lot because they just sit there, never talking and just knocking back doubles, so you might want to think again about bothering them, they both have a strange look in their eye's that scares me, just leave it be and in another

122

hour they will get up and stagger out of here.

The Marines got really quiet after that, just whispering. A few came back to the men's room which was behind us and I noticed one of them just checking out our ribbons(same as medals only smaller and lighter) in the mirror. After his trip to the head, he would go back and the buzzing would start. We didn't give a flying fuck what these guys thought, if they wanted a war, we knew about those, though it would have been preferable to just leave us alone. That is what they did. When we did get up to leave, they parted to allow us to pass and one of them said something like 'goodnight sir!'

On the third night, just as we walked up to the road, a jeep came by and the driver told us to get in, he said I have been briefed as to you destination, and drove us to the bar. Boston and I just looked at one another and said nothing. We were dropped in front of the bar, after I got out I said thank you, the driver corrected me by saying, no, thank you. Inside our glasses were already set up and I waved to the barkeep, she told us that she heard it would be tomorrow before we shoved off and figured we would be in. So we assumed our battle stations and proceeded to drink ourselves into a coma, it would be days before we would have this opportunity again. We had to steam up to San Francisco next with our final destination being Mare Island near Vallejo where this lard bucket was to be 'stricken from the record' which is Navy talk for junked, or tuned into cheap toasters. Our Marine buddies showed up with a few extras, we ignored them.

Though we knew they had something to do with that jeep ride. We could tell that these guys had just finished boot camp and were undoubtedly going to end up in Vietnam. In a way I felt sorry for them. I think that is what the impact was that we had on them; this may have been their first time seeing two guys staring straight ahead, not talking or laughing, just drinking one after another. It may have been an insight into what that war will do to you if you make it back, and with that understanding came a form of respect for the unknown. When it was time for us to make our exit, Boston just fell off the bar stool, as we went through them I heard comments like, thank you and come back anytime, stuff like that. I greased the bartender really well; she waved and smiled when she saw the size of the bill under my shot glass. A Marine opened the front door and there was the same jeep waiting to take us back, this time he powered through the soft sand and drove us right up to the bow doors.

The reason Boston was broke all of the time was due to an accident in Vietnam. He was guarding the open bow doors and had climbed up into a piece of their super structure and fell asleep, in the process, he dropped his M-16 into the river never to be seen again. When it came time to explain himself he made up some story, sleeping on watch in an active warzone can get you shot as punishment. As for the gun, he offered to replace it on the black market for $50 bucks, but they would not have anything to do with that. They charged him $850.00 for a brand new one which came out of his pay every month, not leaving a lot left for drinking, I am sure.

On that glorious day of passing under the Golden Gate Bridge, the entire crew was assembled on the main deck in a long line, dressed in our summer white uniforms. The only problems were that we froze in place it was so cold, and the fog was so thick you could barely see the bottom of the Golden Gate. All of that frantic push in Hawaii with one man crippled for life, thousands of dollars for paint and here we are, under the bridge.

No flags waving, no brass bands or cheering crowds, just fog so thick you were lucky if you could see 100 feet in any direction. Also, if I knew then what I found out later about the love children of San Francisco, there would have been urine and other bodily discharges raining down on our clean, pure white uniforms; another Navy fiasco.

Later I found out that it was the XO who decided to paint the ship, not the Captain; and my friend John was still there in Hawaii with a broken back.

I checked with the personnel officer (who later, in 2006 wrote a letter on my behalf for VA benefits) and found out that my request for duty at a submarine base in Scotland had been approved, the orders just needed to be signed. I had it all planned, after a quick stop at home, I would fly over there and buy a brand new Triumph 650cc motorcycle and take 30 days leave just to go traveling around Europe before reporting for duty, then just putting in my time and collecting all of that college money after I was discharged from the Navy.

The only thing my plan did not take into consideration was a vindictive person with a mental problem. Instead of Scotland, I was ordered to the Naval Hospital at Oakland where I spent two weeks under the influence of very strong medications they injected me with every day, and some physical therapy for my back. It was during that period that I signed a bunch of papers and was tricked into requesting and early discharge from the Navy, which was the last thing I wanted to do, not now with all the dirty stuff behind me, I paid my dues in Vietnam.

One area that was difficult to take were meal times. We took our meals in a regular mess hall style arrangement. Three times a day I had to go there and sit across from some young kid with no arms, or half his face missing. The place was full of people with multiple amputations. It was depressing to watch, the look in their eyes, while nurses spoon fed them, or worse yet, sweethearts and mothers. This was the real Vietnam.

Today I have people thank me for my service in Vietnam, most of the time I haven't a clue how to respond to that. For all of those years, Vietnam Veterans were perceived as losers, I have been called that myself. I didn't ask to go to Vietnam but was ordered there and I went. I was over there risking my ass for the benefit of America, or so I was led to believe, some people made a lot of money on Vietnam so they didn't want that war to end, just like all of the other wars we have been in, behind the scenes are a hand full of fat cats cleaning up, just like our recent Vice president did in Iraq. No one wanted to hear about what we went through, not even my own family was interested. Presently, the highest numbers of homeless people in the United States are Vietnam vets. We were not perceived as heroes, we were the losers.

Allow me to explain the procedure as I remember it that had taken place at the Oakland hospital. First order of business was an injection of morphine, and then a doctor came in with a file and started to page through it. He asked me how many Darvon I was taking every day, I in turn asked him to qualify the question, first of all we worked 12 hour days, 6 days a week and then stood 4 hour watches. The second part of my bid to qualify his question was which part of the Darvon capsule was he referring too. He ordered a Darvon and I was to demonstrate. I turned the capsule apart and dumped the contents onto a sheet of paper; then I removed the black ball and handed it to him. The pile of powder I just blew into the air. He stood there staring at my balls for a few days until I explained what happened next. Well, you take about 3 of these and crush them up a tad then throw them into a can of beer and wait about 20 minutes for them to dissolve. While you were waiting, you prepared the second dose. After drinking 2 or 3 of these beers, the pain became bearable. I pointed out that in my file, which was under his arm unopened, he would find evidence dating back to 1968 which shows that I tried to change my rating so that I would not have to be on my feet for hours at a time, I had no desire to leave the Navy because I enlisted in this branch of the service in the first place. I also pointed out that I had a two year college degree and was promised money to return to college after my discharge.

He then opened the file to a part that was clearly earmarked and asked me about the sampan without any hostiles in it that I drilled and sank. I asked if he was a shrink and went into a complete tirade, why, of all the material in my file, was that of any particular interest, why that particular incident? Naturally he didn't answer my question, just called in another injection and before I became the Manchurian Candidate, I pointed out that I had a chest full of medals including a perfect conduct medal, so where was the problem? It gets a little fuzzy after that, the questions were like a game show. I made a comment about his methodology and asked if I was with the KGB or some other shadow organization? At that point he slammed the file closed and left the room. It was about the second week, I was getting regular shots of morphine than being sent to physical therapy. This proved to be a dichotomy, I am all whacked out on morphine and some girl is asking me in a baby talk voice if I can climb these steps to nowhere, or pedal a bicycle to the same destination. At this time, besides the internal injuries which they never looked at via X-ray etc. The entire time I was there, I was in the best physical condition of my life, as they say today, I was ripped.

In the mess hall, I would sit there looking around thinking that if I had my Colt .45 sidearm and a box of shells, locked and barred all of the doors, then went around and asked the same question of these poor bastards, do you want me to finish it? I would wager that 97% of the people in there would have said, or shook their head yes, the other 3% were just undecided. Most of these men were Marines, they were taught to die the good death, just take 10 of them with you, and this was the average and still is.

That was how I spent my days at Oakland Naval Hospital, getting loaded on morphine all day, falling asleep on a bicycle to nowhere and then dining with a roomful of men I really should have helped terminate. Then they could laugh again, just remember the coins!

OVER 2000 PIECES IN ALL

I will make this really brief because that is the way it actually happened. An orderly came in and told me to pack my sea bag and wear a dress blue uniform; I was being transported to 'Treasure Island.' This is a small naval base at the base of the first columns for the Oakland Bridge. I was discharged from the hospital and walked down to the street and put my bag down to smoke a cigarette while waiting for my transport. As I stood there a woman came walking down the street, I heard her clearing her throat and paid it no attention. When she arrived in front of me, she spit this huge wad onto my chest and proceeded to call me a baby burner, then just walked away. Here I am, standing there with this foul looking goo running down my chest and onto my ribbons. Welcome to the United States, its' great to be home, isn't it?

On Treasure Island I had very little to do except walk down to the water's edge and look at part of San Francisco from a different angle. I was there less than a week before I was called into the Commanders office. He handed me my DD-214, a.k.a. discharge paper, a plane ticket for Wilkes-Barre Pennsylvania and a check for $94.00 representing one month's pay; I had been given a raise of $1.00 a month. He then told me to sign papers for everything that I received and informed me that officially I was no longer a member of the US Navy, but I could wear the clothing in my sea bag until I reached my destination. I was then informed that there was a Navy bus which would arrive in a few hours and it would drop me at the station where I would receive free transportation to the airport; provided I was wearing my dress blue uniform. The whole thing was cold, cut and dried. Don't let the door hit you on the way out.

It was July 21st, 1970 and I just received an Honorable Discharge from the Navy 'Under Medical Conditions.' I stood and looked at this and thought, here is what I get for fighting in a war that I would not be able to talk about for close to 30 years.

It didn't take long for me to find out that they did this to a lot of men during and after the Vietnam War. The service branch did not matter either. This way a lot of benefits didn't have to be paid which had been promised when people like me signed up. It is just like the Agent Orange thing that I mentioned, 40 years after the fact they are assuming culpability, and that was helped along by a lawsuit a veteran filed, and won. Its' a shame, I had a friend who was 225 pounds and dropped to 93 pounds before he died from exposure to that stuff. His wife and two kids received a check for $2500.00 from the VA. That was it.

While waiting on Treasure Island I was allowed to go out at night. One of those nights I met a guy in a bar who told me that if I wanted, he could use me and offered a job, plus told me he had a good size house so it would not be any problem to put me up until I got on my feet. He wrote his name and phone number on a piece of paper and told me to look him up if I was interested. After my discharge I just could not see myself back in Wilkes-Barre just yet. I realize that I was being a bit naïve at this time of my life, there should have been red flags flying but I didn't know, so I did not care.

Mary T flew out to see me, though I think she actually came out to see antiques at the stores in Chinatown. I rented a car and drove her around to anyplace she asked me to. She bought a few vases and had them shipped back. Later on in life I drove her and those vases to Christies in New York were they sold for a tremendous amount of money, her cut after commissions etc. was over $8000. When I asked her how much she paid for them she just smiled. Mary T only stayed 4 or 5 days then flew back. I told her that I was going to stay on for a while and had been made an offer I wanted to look into. I drove her to the airport and saw her off. I then dropped off the rental car.

Prior to calling the guy who I had met, I placed my plane ticket and some money in a locker at the bus station.
My most important documents had gone back with Mary T.

The only uniform that I had to maintain and keep was my dress outfits; the rest of the stuff was dead weight.

Prior to my appointment mentioned above, I had walked out to the center of the Golden Gate Bridge and threw the rest of my sea bag into the bay, the tide was going out which meant that it would head West. I showed up in my dress blues and kept the dress whites in a small bag and made my appointment.

During my college years I became interested in psychology, one of my electives was Psychology 102 and when I landed on the subject of 'latent homosexuality' it stayed in my head for some reason. Here I am driving this huge dump truck wondering if I was gay. Something's should be left unopened. After a while I couldn't take it anymore and just decided to try this thing for myself and see what it was all about. From going to that one particular cocktail lounge in my hometown, I knew a few people to talk to.

The experiment didn't last long, maybe 15 minutes at best. The fondling of my penis felt good, though this guy didn't operate jack hammers either, but when we got to the kissing part I had to draw the line. The idea of kissing someone of the same sex with a three-day stubble just turned me right off and told me everything that I needed to know. I would not make a good gay partner to any man. I do not regret what I did, it was a question that I think everyman deals with sometime in their life, and I answered that question for my life, it was just another piece of the puzzle. I must admit that the experience proved to be invaluable over the years as it was about to be put to the test with my new 'benefactor.' I called the man and made the arrangements to meet him and I did, in my full dress uniform.

The man was well off for his age, he appeared to be in his mid-30's. We first meet at a bar of his choice and he both laughed and was impressed seeing me in a full dress Navy uniform, the old traditional ones did look good with the jumper, 13 button front and bell bottom pants not to mention the lines of colored ribbons on the chest. He owned a chain of men's wear stores, mid-range as he put it and needed someone he could trust to manage them all as an overseer you might say. I told him about my ability to sell a used car to a dead man and it may have sparked an interest. After a few rounds of drinks we hopped in a cab and went to his place. After I explained to him my situation, especially in the clothing department, he found me some nice lounge wear. It was a treat to get out of that wool uniform. He noticed the condition I was in and was impressed; I think that was the basis of the attraction from the start anyway. The first night we stayed up late snacking on some tapas that his maid had left and sipping some really fine wines. The next day I had awakened late and found a robe and towels laid out so I showered and shaved, then donned the robe to sit on the balcony in the back of the house with cups of coffee, just relaxing, I had decided that tonight I was going to explain to him how I felt and why this wasn't worth investing too much into. The guy came in with an arm load of boxes and bags; they were men's clothes that fit me to the 'T' as he said. These were not mid-range priced clothes either. They were top of the line and very conservative. Either he measured me while I slept, or the guy was a genius, even the loafers fit well and they were Italian leather. His presentation of the clothes was understated, he said that they had been lying on the racks at one of his shops for months and his wholesale price was nothing for them. I really appreciated his generosity. It was definitely better than picking up some hippy jeans and a tie dyed T shirt. Later that day I removed the ribbons from my uniforms and dropped them at a one hour cleaner. I rode a few Cable Cars, had lunch at the Wharf and headed to Haight-Ashbury to get some LSD. After a full day of touring the city; the evening came, and with it my confession.

That night after dinner we retired to the front room for brandy and cigars and I explained everything I just wrote down for you. He was impressed with my knowledge of self, and commended me on going the length that I had on the subject. He also understood there was not going to be any relationship between us; of which he may have expected and thanked me for my honesty. I asked if I could stay one more day, there were some things I still needed to clarify. He said it would be fine and handed me a couple hundred dollars. I told him I would repay him, and he said it wouldn't be necessary. He said he had enjoyed my company and honesty. He had found me attractive, but in my eyes was a look both inviting and dangerous at the same time. I didn't touch on the subject of the frozen soul; Vietnam was best left un-said. He encouraged me to become the artist I had talked about, and that I should return to the East Coast; and get out of San Francisco.

The following morning I woke up alone except for the house maid. I packed a small bag then laid out my two uniforms for my host to have. Everything was there including the ridiculous boxer shorts. Possibly he could use them for some fantasy. It just seemed like a fair thing to do; I would no longer need them.

Before I left the city I wanted to get to 'Ferlinghetti's' book store. It happened to be 'open mike' night and I was able to get up and read some of my poetry. Receiving a decent amount of applause kept me in the poetry market for a few more years.

My stay in San Francisco was at an end; I took a cab to the bus station to retrieve my plane ticket and headed for the airport. It would be 15 years before I returned with someone that was MY dream and fantasy, and someone that I truly loved.

Back in Wilkes-Barre, my old job was waiting for me. My mother had sold my '56' T-bird for $500.00, exactly what I owed her; that still hurts. I had also sent my Dad money and asked him to pick up a van for me, which he did, but later sold it and doubled the profit, which he then kept for himself.

It was now August of 1970. Part of the old 'Boston Mine' building my father purchased had not been used for years, and I decided to take over the front office and turn it into a gallery. It had two very large windows, as it had also been used as a chart room. Built in 1869, it was a solid triple brick structure that just needed some exterior repairs to keep out the weather and bats. I thoroughly cleaned the inside and installed a pot belly stove. I set up an art desk next to a window, added some spot lights; and Alchemy Studio was born.

It was a very productive studio and a lot of art was created there. Eventually I put a bed in the room and ended up living there. I also found a dentist chair, which became a permanent fixture. It must have weighed a few hundred pounds. It had a hydraulic lift and about 15 adjustments. I used that studio up until 2000, when Teresa and I finished building our "Tree house" and studio up on Larksville Mountain.

Upon my return to Wilkes-Barre, I went to the Veterans Administration in town. I was told I would not receive a dime in college benefits due to the papers I signed while at the Oakland Naval hospital in a morphine haze. I filed an appeal and went one step further; I filed for benefits due to the back injury I sustained while under hostile fire in Vietnam. I kept filing appeals right up until the year 2006, when I won the case.

After the news from the VA and the appeal paperwork was filed, I decided I had enough of this treatment from my government and was preparing to leave the states. It was bad enough to have the public spit on you and call you a baby burner, but then to have my government pull the underhanded action they did to me, well it was just too much. I bought a one way ticket to Australia. In Vietnam I drank with some of their troops and they were good guys; the kind that would cover your back in a fight.

Please understand that we never received any debriefing upon leaving Vietnam. One day you were in the jungle with a machine gun in your hand and the next you could be in your hometown standing at the bus station waiting for a ride.

That is how we were dealt with; thanks, but see you around. My ship was not to leave until mid-October so I had some time to just play. I borrowed a Goodman 'spare car', usually an old Lincoln or Buick that the Duke had around in case he did not want to drive his pickup truck.

One night I made my way to a new bar in town called the "Deep End". Little did I know that this would affect my life for years to come? I walked into the bar and immediately fell in love. There was this stunning woman sitting at the bar with hair down to her bottom. I wouldn't know her name for a period of 14 years as our paths would keep crossing without a word spoken between us. I'm sure there are other men out there that will understand what I'm about to discuss. You see a stunning woman, a real knock out, but there is a nagging doubt about yourself; not good enough. So rather than risk embarrassment or immediate rejection, you do nothing; you hide, and love this person from afar. She now became the benchmark of the rest of the women in my life. Deep down inside I knew this girl was my soul mate, but I couldn't or didn't take that chance.

Another friend from college recognized me and brought me to her table, sitting there in the corner was the woman to be my first wife; though I had no idea of that at the time. We were introduced and arraignments were made to meet again; all the while stealing glances at my dream girl, somehow knowing I was making a big mistake.

As it turned out, the girl I was introduced to loved my wit and dry sense of humor, her exact words. One date would lead to another and I ended up canceling my tramp steamer and got a refund on my one way passage. I bought a Triumph motorcycle, and became part of the 'business' again; plus developed Alchemy Studio. The bike was my main means of transportation and as the weather started to change I froze my ass off, it was time to go shopping for a 'bar car'; a bar car is a $250 to 350 automobile.

The technique was to hang around a gin mill known for its poker game and wait for someone who needed money fast. You would make an offer and then have the person turn over the keys; the paperwork had to wait until the next day. But you had the car just in case he lost again. In two days and a few hundred bucks you were riding around in a clunker. The bar car was ideal for the Winter months, if you plowed into a frozen snow bank and wrecked, so what, it was just a matter of repeating the process while the old one was being towed to the scrap yard where they paid $50 to 75 dollars for it. Since I would be back in the city of Wilkes-Barre for an undisclosed period of time, I enrolled in college at an all- girl school called College Misericordia which had a good looking art department. It was on the roof of a four story building and commanded a terrific 360 degree view; I wish I could say that for the instruction. I began by paying by the credit hour and at $60 bucks a pop it got expensive. One day I approached the business office and asked why I could not just pay the flat semester fee. This in turn opened a Pandora's' box, I did not know that there were two groups of nuns clashing, the younger ones knew that their college was doomed and something had to be done that was against tradition, allow men in. I was the first full time male student at that institution.

During this entire period I was painting with acrylics on canvas, doing metal sculpture and sending off poetry to various publishers. My old partner and I tried to start-up our business of dealing in LSD, but things had changed. There were guns everywhere and you had to be careful who you dealt with when making a 'score' because as soon as you walked outside you could be robbed of what you just bought, usually at gunpoint. It wasn't the type of crime you called the police in on and I did not want to start wasting people again. Another truth was that I was a drinker by now, hard stuff; it was the only thing that stopped the noise in my head from Vietnam. People kept telling me how much I changed, what was I going to do, tell them the truth?

Again, I was balancing a number of different lives on the end of sticks; the secret was keeping the plates spinning. Wilkes-Barre was not a very nice place, come to think of it, the place still sucks. The city makes it onto CNN news for the wrong reasons, toxic chemicals, corrupt judges and now tap water that you can light with a match. The place itself is toxic and a lot of men between 45 and 60 are dying left and right. Then there is that house of hypocrisy, the Salvation Army, which is paid by the state to take in these violent drug dealers and a few boozers, make them work like hell in their 'industries' and attend Sunday 'go to meetin' time, where they read the Bible. The program lasts for 6 months and then the inmates are placed in "… established neighborhoods where they can acclimate to a wholesome environment." In reality, within 2 weeks you have a crack house with kids as young as 12 toting 9mm Glocks; so much for the healthy environment. If you don't believe me spend some time in Williamsport, PA. Just make sure you lock your car and have extra clips.

I rode around on my motorcycle, operated heavy equipment and attended an all women catholic college. It sounds like a huge contradiction of terms; everything I didn't like became a way of life. It was again just a matter of spinning those plates and making those puzzle pieces fit.

While at Misericordia, I received permission to put on a play that I wrote called 'Mental Perspectives.' It was an hour and one half production which utilized a multi discipline approach. There were various mind tricks, guys with skulls, recitals and plenty of musical entertainment. My detractors said it wouldn't work because it was too 'far out man'. Combining a host of seemingly unrelated artistic entities is a challenge, but not a failure; I never embraced that word well. It worked, the production was sold out a week prior to its' opening, the house was full with people standing. We all made some nice money and paid the college for the use of their theater. The idea to travel with a show was discussed, but my interest span was short and I had more to do.

One of my electives was a 35mm photography course which gave me access to a complete darkroom. During the class our instructor wanted us to 'burn' a roll of Tri-X black and white film, develop the negatives and print 6 of the best in an 8" X 10" format.

It just so happened that an old nun was repainting an entire set of plaster statues used in the church for the 'stations of the cross.' I walked in the studio and there it was, painted in pure white (the gesso coat) Michelangelo's' Pieta. There is a remote possibility I may insult some people, but I say fuck it, this was a plaster of Paris statue, a graven image if I may add, Catholics really should study their Bibles, and on top of that it was art, not malice.

What I am referring to is the placement of a whiskey bottle in Christ's hand, it was an empty prop, and this was a shot made for film. I went on to shoot the entire roll and procrastinated the development process, with a deadline looming I went to use the dark room and there was some girl in their doing 4 loads of colors, I asked her if she would run this through for me, she was in my class, but I had honestly forgotten about the photo in the studio of the icons. What I did not know was she had made a print of the Pieta shot; this was to be submitted as a pure art photo, not the type of thing to pass around a catholic college. Of course I never found the catholic mind to be open to many opinions when it came to their belief.

Andy Warhol would have been proud of me then stole the shot and made a fortune on it.

Lo and behold the nuns caught wind of this and started amassing the kindling wood for the fire at the stake. They even washed the dried blood off of the inquisition machines. I approached this girl and asked her why she had done this, her reply was that it was blasphemy and I realized with a comment like that there wasn't any more room for logical conversation. It became a touch dramatic and I had to go before a panel of nun judges to plead my case, they simply wanted to throw me out. But I stayed, either my defense was convincing or they needed the cash.

As it would happen, after Joan of Arc developed the negatives another girl, who I think was gothic, actually in 1971 that simply meant suicidal, made a pile of duplicates of my photo and was selling them. I told you that I never much cared for catholic girls or for the entire church as a matter of fact. I still have an original here somewhere but I don't dwell on it. I found out that Jesus was a really straight guy who liked to laugh, he must have been set up and busted by the Romans for a controlled substance, I think it was love, and they gave him the maximum sentence, a one way ticket home. Could you imagine a bunch of crazy Jews blasted on LSD during Passover? Neither could the Romans!
After the sampan incident in Vietnam I went to every religious representative there was and asked the same question, how I justify what I've done to these people when every holy text has something in it about not killing folks. They would beat around the bush for a while then end up with a lame explanation that these people were heathens and it didn't matter. So in other words they are gooks and you aren't, is that what you're telling me? One thing that a lot of people failed to realize is that there were a ton of Christians in Vietnam.

It turned out that the girl I was introduced to at the 'Deep End' bar and I had been dating occasionally, was a millionaire's daughter, a few times removed. This was going to be a high wire act without a net.
Her mother lived out on Long Island in a very wealthy area by Stony brook called Setauket. She was the very first person in the United States to introduce the concept of the 'trade off' magazine, those rags that you place your ad in free until you sell the bar car. I was told she started out with $6000, all of the money she had after her divorce from the Doctor and the magazine doubled its income every year for 12 years and that was when they sold it for a lot of money.

Meanwhile, her father was a big shot psychiatrist who lived on Park Avenue in the low 70's, nice address in Manhattan.

What proved to be the fly in the ointment, you haven't heard that in a while, was he studied and practiced as a Freudian Doctor with psychoanalysis. This is an important point to take into account later in this text. His office was in his apartment but the apartment was the entire floor of the building with its' own elevator stop.

I ended up moving in with this woman, she and her roommate had an apartment in an old Flatiron building in Wilkes-Barre, one of the only ones left. The apartment was above a print shop and every outside wall was on an angle, a crazy apartment for 4 crazy people. We ran into a friend of mine and introduced him to the roommate, soon thereafter they were a unit, except he worked out of town as an engineer and only came home on weekends. We didn't have the heart to tell him of the steady procession of men that made the bed springs loud all week.

One of my more brilliant moments, was taking her to a secret swimming hole, it started to get dark and we ended up screwing in a poison ivy patch, don't laugh, it wasn't pretty. Then it took over an hour for Mr. Woodsman to find the way out to the car. It was awkward when the doctor asked me how we contracted this disease in such 'delicate' areas. After a few days of treatment we were discharged from the hospital and then the history of it set in, naturally it was my fault according to Freud.

It was bad, poison ivy of the scrotum and the girl had poison ivy of the ass, they even had to treat my Johnston, it was a mess now that I sit here writing about it. Because the treatment consisted of a series of injections, followed by a wash job with special chemicals than the application of copious amounts of cream to the affected areas, the stuff was gone in a week.

We made a lot of trips to New York; each weekend was a different household, one weekend in the city, the next out on

Long Island. When I first met her mother she said, I thought he was black? Go figure!

On the other hand her father had been stationed aboard an LST during WW2. There was a large picture of him standing next to his boat hanging in the dining room, when he was told what I did we were comrades in arms; that is until 'bizzaro hour' arrived.

At 6:45pm the maid would place a water glass full of ice on the corner of the counter with a bottle of Jack Daniels, cork out. After filling this l0 ounce glass with bourbon she would then return to fixing dinner. My little rich girl told me to never stand near that door at 7:00pm sharp, and sure enough, the door burst open and the Doctor made a beeline to the glass on the counter and drained it, he then refilled it and said: hello Jason, how nice to see you again. Every visit was the same, after his refill he would retire to the dining room and talk about the same thing every time I saw him. When the maid came with a tureen of soup, I learned to suck it down fast because by this time he was into the "…your fucking my daughter aren't you; fuckin' sailors are all alike, get out of my house you bastard before I throw you out." That was my cue to get lost for an hour or so until he passed out. If only he knew the truth about his daughter, this girl was no sex fiend that was for sure.

I usually went to a bar on Lexington Avenue called the Whiffenpoof because they had English Watneys ale on draught and I liked the taste of it. Sometimes she joined me and other times I was on my own. The same scenario took place every week, it was like an off Broadway play, same scene, same action at the exact same time. Welcome to bizzaro world. And just think, it gets worse, there was Long Island.

I learned a considerable amount about Manhattan, after a few years I even knew what subway lines went where. We were only a few blocks from the major art museums. The situation with the doctor the next morning was always the same; he would come into the kitchen for his coffee, ask me how I slept and be the perfect gentleman. I would tell him about the cardboard box I found along with a bunch of old rags, so yes, I slept well thank, you after a quart of Mad Dog 20/20.

The trips to long Island were even more demented because there were action figures. Her mother and step father would stop at their favorite lounge, Mario's, and get 'snockered'. On the way home, the step father would chase and smash into VW Beetles because he just hated them and it was obsessive, he drove a huge Lincoln town car and one night he started chasing this guy all over the county until the man pulled into his driveway which had stone walls on both sides, that is where the Lincoln got stuck when he rammed into the stone walls. The police came and he lost his ticket for two years, so now the mother has to drive, her problem was her Irish temper. One night they stopped her and the policeman must have insulted her somehow and she slugged him, you do not slug a cop when you can't run away, fast.
They ended up with a chauffeur.
Friday night was especially bad, as soon as they staggered in the house they were arguing, it of course escalated until they started throwing antiques at each other, smashing anything that was handy as a projectile. After they fell into bed, the maid would clean up all of the pieces and call the same contractor who showed up early Saturday morning and patched the drywall from the collateral damage. Later that day everything looked perfect. They would then go out and stop at antique shops and spend thousands on more cannon fodder for the following week.
During the Friday night antique massacre, we would hide in the family room, or in the swimming pool with the lights off. This was the use of money at its' best, I actually enjoyed it, here my mother is a respected antique dealer, so I grew up around them all of my life, she would always say that they should be used once in a while, well, these people knew how to use them with pin point accuracy!

None of this mattered, they were both very intelligent people and worth a pile of money. Now they turned their attention to buying real estate, the first place was a one bedroom condo in South Palm Beach. This purchase was part of a plan for their daughter.

South Palm Beach was a misnomer because it was actually Lakeworth, Florida. But everyone wanted desperately to be associated with Palm Beach so they had the boundaries extended south 2 or 3 miles.

My precious was quite a brilliant girl though she did have problems with depression; who wouldn't after going to college in Wilkes-Barre? She attended Wilkes College, it was an extension of Bucknell University at that time, and was considered a top college for 'wasps' on the East Coast. She'd stay in the apartment and not attend classes, while her siblings did extremely well in their respective colleges; which exacerbated her depression.
This was an invaluable educational period of my life. I was witness to the possible effects of having too much money. It seemed to me it made people a bit crazy.
Her biological father, the psychiatrist, was highly respected in his field. Some of his clients would fly in from Chicago every week to see him. He was also the head of a very prestigious hospital in New York City. Yet, he had his problems. One night, his fourth wife asked me if I would try to find him. She said he would probably be in a bar in the neighborhood. After about an hour of searching, many bars in the area; I found him in this Gay Bar. He was so drunk he couldn't walk. I threw him over my shoulder like a sea bag, and carried him back to his building. A surreal part was the doorman; he opened the door and said "good evening, Jason", the elevator operator did the same, like nothing was amiss. I got the doctor to his apartment and proceeded to take him to his bedroom and dump him on the bed.
I asked my girlfriend why the doorman and elevator operated didn't say anything to, or about her Father; she said a

thousand dollars in a Holiday card paid for their discretion. During this entire period I was still working in my studio, mostly doing metal sculpture. I made a piece I called 'Leontyne Price', a world acclaimed soprano. It consisted of a piece of exhaust pipe with copper tubing woven through it for arms and legs. I formed an abstract rendition of her head with a ball of steel wool (she was a woman of color). I then mounted it on a piece of polished plexiglas and presented it to the doctor as a gift. One night he had a formal reception in his apartment, complete with butler's in little red jackets. All night I had people coming up to me asking to touch my hands; the hands of an artist, they would say. I called them the hands of a bulldozer operator and mechanic. At one point I was cornered by a famous brain surgeon. After complimenting me on the sculpture, he bent my ear for 30 minutes talking about his exotic sports car. The entire party of individuals was more abstract than any art I could ever create.

The next morning the doctor mentioned something to me that had a great effect. He said I had something that no one else at the party had, even with all their money they could never have, and that was the talent of an artist. He added that I should never hold my head down because of the amount of money someone may have, but to hold my head high as you can have $2.00 in your pocket and be the wealthiest person in the room.

Meanwhile back in Wilkes-Barre one night I was driving my brothers' MGB sports car and had a bag of LSD with about 300 hits in it. I had it in my pocket, but decided to leave it in the car and headed up the steps to the apartment. I found myself staring into the barrel of a .38 police special. The place was being busted. Not because of us, but because of the nymph roommate bringing home a guy the cops were looking for. He stayed the night before and was gone, so they also left in time. The crazy girl laughed hysterically when they left, then put the Doors album on so she could listen to 'This is the End' over and over until someone had

146

the bright idea to give her a couple valium to shut her up. We got out of that apartment, found another one, right across the street.

Meanwhile my little rich girl received a brand new Toyota Corolla, lemon yellow and one of the first ones to be sold in the US, from her Daddy. Besides the new car, came a new college; Florida Atlantic University. By this time I had accumulated enough credits to receive a Bachelor's Degree in Fine Art from the girl's college, but didn't press for the degree. This new University was going to accept my A.A.S. degree in full and would start me as a third year student. They were also on the quarter system which meant I could really burn through some degree programs.
We both were admitted to F.A.U. so we planned to drive down to Florida and take up residence in the "Palm Beach" condo.

Prior to our departure, I decided to sell my 500cc Triumph motorcycle. I spit shined it and sold it to my friend Carl who was to pick it up the next day. There it sat, my 'Chrome buffalo' begging for a last ride. A friend came by and asked me for a ride across the river, about three miles, so I agreed. I dropped him off and turned around to head back to the studio. There was only one car on the bridge coming straight towards me, in the left turn lane; it was some punk kid in his Daddies Oldsmobile 88. I kept watching him to see what he was going to do, I did have the right of way so I shifter into 3rd gear; I was then going about 50 miles per hour. He turned in front of me and stopped. If he had kept going I would have missed him; but no. There is a law about a body in motion staying in motion unless acted upon by some brainless dope. I was lying on the Market Street Bridge, with blood running down my face, due to broken safety glasses; the helmet actually saved my life. You could say I hit the surface of the bridge as if I were still sitting on the bike. A crowd started to gather around me but it didn't seem that they were looking at the blood per se. An off duty nurse came over with a blanket to cover me until the meat wagon arrived. While in the hospital the doctor asked me if I could sit up. I then realized what the crowd had been staring at. I had quit wearing underwear as a protest of sorts from all of that time in those ridiculous Navy boxer shorts. Presently my hip hugger jeans had burst open in four directions from the impact, so I was lying there somewhat exposed to the elements you might say.

After that incident I went out and bought some jockey shorts. The relevance of this story is that I recently had a knee replacement done on the very knee damaged in that accident.

In our love nest in Palm Beach, my rich, no sex, partner, had a habit of locking me out of the master bedroom at night. So I spent a lot of time on the white vinyl couch, drinking cheap wine and watching old horror movies until all hours. I still have a liking for them.

At the University I was having a bit more luck. I was given the opportunity to have an 'out of state tuition waver'. It would save me a lot of money; the caveat was that I had to maintain a 3.5 grade average. Not an easy task when you are taking the maximum number of courses per quarter. During this entire period, I kept up my artwork and started to develop a signature style.

A year or two earlier I read about a new pigment that "Liquidtex' had introduced and they were looking for artist to try them, free of charge, so I signed on. They were iridescent acrylics and came in gold, silver, bronze, copper and the basics. Between the style I was working in and these new pigments I started to mature as an artist. At first my work resembled the grill of a 1948 Buick; you needed sunglasses to look at it. But with time, I learned to tame these things and make them speak to the viewer. Today my style is so pronounced that if you see one canvas, you could go half way around the world and see another and know it is the same artist.

148

My first love, that of sculpture needed a studio of its own, which was difficult to move around. It required welding material, heavy equipment and perhaps a junkyard nearby. But my paints and the necessities that went with them all fit into a foot locker; it could travel. All I had to do was find a lumber yard, build my art desk, find a few lamps and blank canvas'; I was ready for business.

To this day I am still doing this. In a few months we will be returning to Ireland and I will do the same as described above. I have my work in a Gallery there and like to give them fresh canvas's to sell. Without sounding too boastful, I can honestly say that I sell everything that I paint, it may take a few years sometimes, but in the scheme of things that doesn't mean much. I have painted my share of 'dogs' but it never fails to amaze me that someone will come along and love that bow wow.

For years I would listen to the 'Rolling Stones' to get a work in progress; it was a requirement. I have everything they have done on cassette tape. I used to have a full vinyl collection, but that story will come later.

Everything in Florida was moving right along. It was a good place to sell artwork and the university was tough, but I was doing well. One day at the beach, an old guy I knew asked if I was from a coal cracker town in northeast Pennsylvania. I said yes, so he threw a recent edition of the Miami Herald on my lap. There on the front cover is a full color photo of that same bridge I had the cycle accident on; except it was now almost completely under water. It was the 'Agnes' flood of 1972. Due to hurricane Agnes, the Susquehanna River rose to the point that it flooded the town buildings up to the third floor; it was really very bad.

I took a sabbatical from University for two months and flew back to my hometown. It was truly a disaster area, designated so by the President of the United States. The airport was on the East side and I needed to get to the West. There was only one bridge open at the time so I started walking in that direction. Thankfully an Army truck pulled up and a friend of mine was the driver. He told me to jump in the back and keep my head down. He got me across the river. The place was a mess; covered with mud and the smell was terrible. The river had cut through a cemetery and washed coffins up out of the earth. Coffins and bodies floated down stream, some got stuck in trees, and it was a terrible sight.

I reopened my red brick studio and moved in. Goodman Excavating had trucks, bulldozers and backhoes that were desperately needed. We worked 20 hours a day, sometimes sleeping in our truck. We would burst through a wall of a supermarket and go right down the aisle with a front loader, putting everything into waiting trucks to be taken to a dump site. People were told to throw everything of no value into the middle of the street and we would come by with the equipment to remove it; we worked our asses off. Sadly, people walked around like zombies from 'Dawn of the Dead'; it was such a shock. After two months of this work it was a relief to return to Florida

Upon my arrival back at the girl friends condo, I was offered a 'treat' by her mother. She had given us an all-expense paid two week 'Barefoot Cruise' on the four-masted ship, the 'Phantom'. We flew to Nassau and boarded our ship to the outer cays of the islands, some of which were uninhabited. It was a great vessel; four masts of canvas snapping in the wind; and you could sign up to take the helm after midnight. During one night of drunken debauchery, the captain married us along with a half dozen other drunken passengers. So my heiress, wasp, hates the male sex organ girlfriend became my first wife. The following day neither of us spoke a word about what transpired the night before. Maybe neither one of us wanted to comment on how we really felt. The incredible thing is that she hadn't remembered it happened. It would be years before the subject came up again.

She graduated before I did, decided she needed more

space, and went back to Long Island; with the keys to the Palm Beach condo. It would be another two quarters before I finished my Bachelor's degree in Art Education. Now my most immediate priority was a car and a place to live. I tried living with some of my friends, but there was too much pot smoking for me. I really didn't like the stuff or the mundane conversation that went with it, not to mention the eating everything in sight afterwards. So I moved into the dormitories on campus. They happened to need a 'resident assistant'; a job that paid $60.00 a month and came with a private room, a telephone and access to the rear door, excellent for late night trysts.

This period of my life consisted of many, different jobs. I made concrete septic system pipes for a family owned business in West Palm Beach. I did this on the weekends; I'd drive up there on Friday night and returned to campus on Monday morning.

I also wrote articles for the campus newspaper called the Atlantic Owl; because of all the real owls that were on campus, the Burrowing Owl. This was a nasty little beast. If you walked into one of their suburbs, they would swoop down at your head and draw blood.

For the art department, I posed nude; it was big money in those days. On one job, I was to sit on this big cube in the center of the room. Problem was I sat directly under the air conditioning vent and in the front of the room was a girl I had the hots for and was getting close to asking her out. It got to be so cold sitting there that I was very much aware of what was happening to my anatomy. I tried to keep the little fireman with the cap on it out of her sight, but it was futile. I modeled a bit for the photography class which entailed sitting out on the grass keeping a pose while ants bit my ass, but (butt) it paid $10 an hour. Nude modeling is not as easy as it may look; trust me.

I never heard from my new wife. Before she left I told her I would be at her house in several months with a sports car, and we would tour the West Coast, US #1; from San Diego to Seattle, that was the last time we spoke.

During this entire time I was still painting and exhibiting, I sold a few paintings to the University and had the gallery in the 'Pink' plaza in Boca Raton which did well. I used some of this money to make the first of several trips to Jamaica. I would fly over to Montego Bay and live like a king until the coffers went dry. Early on I found this neat little hotel called Mrs. G's, a short walk out of town. Mrs. G was a huge black woman who owned the place and didn't allow no problems mon! I went to drink rum, you could buy a quart of really good rum for $1.25, I preferred a brand called Mount Gay which I think was from Barbados. My room had a nice balcony with two large green louvered doors that opened onto a beautiful tropical scene, palm trees, banana and it was elevated above the road to town which you could barely see.

My waiter would arrive at the door with a tray containing two Coca Colas in bottles and a large bucket of ice cubes. He was wearing a small red jacket, white shirt and black bow tie. I on the other hand was bare foot with white pants rolled up to the ankle, no shirt, just tan, and a nice silver neck chain Mary T. had given me. It was a nice quiet time as I sat there and got pleasantly drunk while laughing at my situation; that was the key, work hard and live large.

Being a "Resident Assistant" had its' advantages and benefits. I controlled quite a few students living arrangements and ran a tight ship, word got out if you wanted quiet and a good study environment, my floor was the place to go. One day I was approached by a resident I quaffed a few beers with at the University bar and he asked me if I wanted to make a trip to Bimini to do some 'rock' fishing on his father's 28 foot cabin cruiser, I said sure, how much, he said for you a case of beer, little did I know what that case almost would have cost me.

His father moored his boat down in Miami right off the causeway where the famous 'Caulks' seaplanes landed. On the day of departure, I drove down to Miami and parked the car where they had advised and made my way down the pier with a small bag and a case of beer on my shoulder, we were going to spend a weekend in Bimini. As I walked I passed these multi-million dollar crafts and figured one of these had to be it, I walked further and spied the end of the pier looming in the distance and that's when it hit me, Vung Tau Vietnam; I had walked right back there looking for my boat. Finally I came upon the "African Queen" an old plywood cabin cruiser from the 1950's; it was blue and white and showed its' age. A quick overlook showed signs of bad repairs to the hull and open seams. Then my college friend popped out and bid me aboard and said, well this is it! He introduced me to his parents; his mom just made a large cooler of sandwich's and did not plan on going with us. There were 5 guys from the University already drinking beer and smiling.

His father climbed up onto the flying bridge and he joined him up there, it had its' advantages for seeing distance but was a wild ride if the seas kicked up and as soon as we turned right onto the causeway I could see in the distance a fairly angry sea. So I climbed up and joined them and looked at the clock on the dash, it was early afternoon and Bimini was less than 60 miles from here, but that horizon wasn't promising. We all looked out and I said it looks a little rough, what is the weather report for boaters, they said they never listened to that, it took all the fun out of it. I began to get the impression that these guys had more testosterone than grey matter; they just looked at each other and said, let's do it. With that the old man gunned the engine and we headed into the unknown. As soon as we cleared the outer marker, it started to get rough and the puking down below began, I went down the ladder with a bad feeling about this. I tried to tell the guys to keep eating and drinking no matter what, if you don't you will get worse as time goes on. They didn't listen, the sight of the big sandwich in my hand just made them heave some more. At first the ocean was somewhat manageable, but the deeper we got into it the larger the waves got, this old tub couldn't take too much of a beating from what I saw. I carried up two sandwiches and a couple of beers to the guy's topside on the bridge, I asked them if they had a radio beacon finder and they said yes but it was busted. On Bimini was a radio tower that emitted a steady signal, the beacon finder had a round hoop on top which, if working, pointed toward that signal and showed you were to steer, they were using 'dead reckoning' with a compass, but if you were off a few degrees you could miss your target by miles. I asked for the beacon and said let me see what I can do with it.

As we progressed the sea just became a raging torrent, I estimated the wave height by the distance of the flying bridge at over 30 feet, troublesome when you're in a 28 foot boat. I searched around and found a few flash lights with decent batteries in them, the beacon finder required a big 9 volt battery, and I had 8 D size to make it work.

By the way, this radio beacon was the same thing that got Amelia Earhart into trouble and she has never been found. There I was, sitting on the cabin deck with 8 batteries rolling around trying to use black electrical tape to tape them into a large pack. While I was puking, and so was everyone else, two guys were down below with buckets. Finally I managed to get the task done with wires on both ends for the connection, when I connected the two wires I have to admit there were a few silent words. It worked and immediately showed how far off course we were. I taped the entire thing together and ran it topside. By now the noise was getting so bad you had to shout to one another, so I told them the radio beacon was a one shot deal, use it wisely.

I then headed back down and heaved over the side, the salt spray was actually refreshing, after that I dove into the cooler and grabbed more food and a beer, this of course made my poor classmate sick again. Now the waves were hitting 35 to

38 feet, this was getting worse by the minute, we were in the Gulfstream by now. The most frightening thing a sailor can hear on a motor driven craft is silence from the engines. If you get sideways in seas like this they would roll you over into a watery grave as they say. It happened, the engine started to cough and sputter. I first pulled down 6 life vests and threw them at each guy with the instructions to put it on. One came apart in my hands; they were old canvas and cork things, left over from WW2, another bad omen. I then threw the engine cover off and exposed a 318 cubic inch Dodge V8, it was a gasoline engine with a carburetor. Remember the days of being a coal man in the beginning of this book; well we had two of these. My father had Dodge trucks before he went to Fords. This engine had a problem where the float would stick and flood the engine with too much fuel and the only way to fix it was to bang on the two barrel carburetor with a wrench or a small hammer, sometimes you had to keep doing this for quite some time before it corrected itself. I found a wrench in the toolbox and started to tap the carburetor, it fixed the problem.

In the dark I noticed that there was cold water splashing on my feet, I did save one little flashlight and shined it into the bilge and there it was, water, a lot of it. As I explored around I saw the problem, the bow was starting to open at the seams in the hull from the pounding. While the engine seemed to be running correctly, I ran out, heaved over the side and bounded up the ladder and asked where the bilge pump was and they told me, I asked if they could see anything yet and the answer was a negative. I went back down and found the bilge pump; it was one of those little things you use in an aquarium. This was bad, we were going down; there was no doubt in my mind. I told everyone to put on their life preservers and grabbed two for the guy's topside. As I scaled the ladder I saw the most beautiful sight, lights in the distance, it had to be Bimini because the radio beacon was pointing right at them. I told the father and son to push this thing for all it's worth, we were sinking.

He rammed the throttle forward and the engine coughed again, I said I will fix that just head for those lights; we didn't have that much time. I went below and tapped on the carburetor and the engine cleared up, I noticed that the wave action had become less violent, we were within the shoals, and then he ran the thing a-ground on a sand bar.

After a few attempts we were free and proceeded into the harbor at Bimini, as soon as we tied up, I put on the rest of my clothes and told them I would be in the nearest gin mill. As I walked into this bar the entire place turned to look at me, I went up to the bar and said give me a double white Mount Gay and leave the bottle (I always wanted to say that)) as I pounded back double shots a man in a captains hat and blue blazer approached me, the harbor was full of million dollar yachts, he asked me where I hailed from, I told him we just pulled in from Miami, he then said that's impossible, I told him that he asked, I told him, now go fuck off and let me drink. He then apologized when someone said a small boat had just arrived about 20 minutes ago.

I also apologized for being somewhat rude, and then went on to explain some of my ordeal, suddenly I was surrounded by Sunlight sailors, and I started to tell a tale of an old salt and how close we came to kissing death, the drinks started to line up in front of me, the more I told, the more they needed to hear. They could not believe we crossed in a 28 foot boat with 38 foot waves.

Midnight arrived and with it the closing of that bar, I was given a plastic cup, the famous Bimini Walking Cup as I was told. We made our way down the Queens Highway to a small hotel which had a bar and the party continued, my celebrity status was renewed when they got a look at the 'African Queen' and more drinks flowed my way, then someone handed me a key to a room and said that my story was worth every cent.

I finally made my way upstairs and collapsed on the bed then bought a ticket on ' Caulks' seaplane to Miami the next morning, when asked if I was staying around for the fishing I simply said no and offered a piece of advice, burn the boat down to the water line and get another one. One last thing, as we were making our approach to land on the Miami Causeway, a speed boat cut right across the pilots' path, I heard him say a four letter word and even with my seat belt on, my head hit the overhead, hard.

SIMPLE INSTRUCTIONS INSIDE

After the near death by drowning I decided not to go sky diving with the other student on my floor. In a way I regret that decision now because of the poor quality of my legs and back, in those days I could have handled it.

I never heard much from my trophy wife, the only thing that I told her was I was going to complete this degree and return with a sports car so the two of us could tour Highway #l in California as we had talked about, that was our last bit of correspondence.

It is interesting to note before I forget about it, but I read a newspaper article that the four mast schooner, the Phantom, had gone down with all hands while trying to reach safe harbor in Belize during a hurricane. There weren't any paying customers aboard, just l6 poor souls and the skipper who had married us; a terrible way of starting divorce proceedings.

When I enlisted in the Navy, I had a few more motives than mom, the flag and apple pie. They had promised educational benefits after my discharge. At the time I was signing the contract with them I found myself drooling on the page, but I signed and I made sure that the enlistment signed their part of it also. This was more important to me than any amount of money from looting, raping, or pillaging we came across during our travels.

To my dismay, it didn't work out that way, every time I filed for benefits they denied me, three times this happened, and it would take 2 to 3 years just to get a decision back from the VA. I felt like the character from B.C. in the newspaper who would throw the message on the water and sit on a rock while waiting for a reply.

After a while I was filing for benefits out of sheer frustration, my back injuries were really getting bad and the pain was of a chronic variety, it just never went away, it still doesn't to this very day. This went on for a period of 30 years but I never gave up, I am German and when you sign a contract with me and I hold up my end of the bargain beyond what was asked of me, I expect at least the original agreement to be honored.

To stay within the guidelines of chronology, I did graduate with a Bachelor's degree in art education on the 10th of June, 1973. It was the only graduation that Mary T. insisted on attending, so I rented the cap and gown for the occasion and photo ops. After the ceremony my father handed me a $100 bill and told me that my car needed two new tires, it was the only money that he gave to me without strings or hours of work attached to it. Keep in mind, this was the person who said he would never spend a dime on my education, and he didn't, but he was in every photograph that was taken, beaming with accomplishment.

They returned to Pennsylvania and I went to the tire store. I sold that car to a friend of mine who was pre-med and crossed the State of Florida every weekend, he sent me a card after a few years had passed just to tell me that it was the best car he ever owned. So I helped another doctor come into the World.

I flew back to Pennsylvania via Manhattan to drop in on an old friend of mine; it was a form of ritual. I would fly in, cab uptown, or subway from La Guardia to his apartment on 86th street on the West side, spend the night catching up, and then head down to Port Authority and grab a bus to Wilkes-Barre, usually the Martz express. Upon my arrival in Death Valley I ran into an associate who just so happened to own a carnival game and needed a "barker."

The name of the game was 'Shooting Waters' and consisted of 12 Colt .45 water pistols which sprayed into a clear plastic tube with a ping pong ball in it. The first person to get the ball out of the tube was the winner, and, on the back of each tube was a small basket (whose rim was almost the same diameter as the ball) if by chance the ball landed in it; you won a huge rat as we called them in the trade, the other rats were smaller.

He would pay me a decent wage and when we were on the road he paid for everything including the food, beer and liquor. Sometimes we used LSD just to stay awake while driving at night to get to our next gig. We had a route all through Pennsylvania and upstate New York. The schedule included State fairs, small church bazaars and a hand full of other functions. The game itself was self-contained and we pulled it with an old 'Grumman' bread truck that looked like it was on the same assembly line as the B-17 Flying Fortress.

It was all riveted aluminum without any paint; a large square example of bauxite at its best following a major World conflagration. In the back were two bunk beds and space for all of our outdoor needs, table &chairs, Coleman stove and everything else two people would need for food and drink. The two burner stove worked well and I must admit the food wasn't bad. The only thing that was difficult was getting a shower. We played a predetermined route through the States I mentioned above. It was a crazy life, one day we would be outside Pittsburgh, the next night somewhere in upstate New York. The game, when it wasn't set up on the mid way at the fair, had to be on the move. Time was money and more importantly we had to be at our next gig or lose our space, and our game was one of the highest earners on the Midway. It cost .25 cents to play and after our 'show' as it was called; we sat and counted quarters, this game made a lot of money, most nights were in the $1200 bracket though many times I helped count out over $1500 in one 6 to 7 hour show. The small rats cost him .30 cents each, and the big ones were about $7.00 dollars. He had a station wagon which was used for running to get supplies and the rats which were housed in a rented warehouse.

Sometimes I'd act as a 'shill' for our neighbor. They had a booth with .22 caliber rifles, (with slightly bent barrels), so most shots were doomed. But I knew how to angle it and lo and behold I'd be a big winner. Then proceed to walk around with a big ghetto blaster on my shoulder, to show the world. Then I'd sneak around back, give it to the guy's wife and it would end up back on the shelf.

When I did get a break, usually about 5 days at a time, I'd head home to work on my new auto. I bought a used 1963 MGB and had it set up on blocks. I bought it from a man up the street, so had no reason to think he was not telling me the truth about its condition. He assured me that the engine and transmission had been completely rebuilt. I ripped that car down to nothing and put it back together again; one piece at a time. The time came to start her up and the engine was pounding like crazy; the engine was junk.

He and I had a few heated words and some money changed hands. I found another engine; put the time in on replacing the old one, started it up, put it in first gear and clunk; the transmission was shot. And, in an MGB you have to take the motor out to get to the transmission.
It was around 10PM when I started up our biggest bulldozer; an H-16, the size of a D-7 Cat; in other words it would fill a living room. And I decided that's where I'd put it in this guys' house. I drove through the woods, knocking down trees, and revving the engine, so he could hear me coming. I stopped the machine right next to his 'above ground' pool. The police had arrived, but they knew the story and they knew me; and they weren't prepared to shoot. Needless to say he gave me another car, a MGA; worth 5 times as much as the first one. I also made him deliver it to our garage. It's handy to have a bulldozer lying around.

The 'Carney' is a strange business; it is the closest thing to a Gypsy lifestyle that you can find in the US. A 'rube', for example, is someone you cannot trust; and they were known to just disappear. If a stranger came around asking about a person, who might be traveling with us, no one said a thing, but the warning would go through the camp. I used to tell people that if they wanted to hide from the FBI or CIA, just join the carney. Once you established yourself with them, and you were trusted, you were considered family.
The only ones you avoided where the set up guys that put the rides together; most of them were drug addicts and really lived rough. Let's just say, I will not go on the Ferris wheel at a carnival, I know just a bit too much; they got pretty sloppy doing their jobs at times.

As it turned out, my associate paid for the entire game the first year. The second year was gravy and the third; he sold the game and moved to Costa Rica.

As far as taxes were concerned; he'd pay the taxman in cash. $50.00 if it was slow and $100.00 if it was a good day; no questions asked. The taxman did drive a very large automobile and wore very expensive boots.

Entering the world of sport cars opened new vistas for me to risk my life. I started to race and actually entered the "Giants Despair" hill climb which is located in Wilkes-Barre. This race was quite famous and consisted of a very steep hill with hairpin curves. The object was to start at the bottom and get to the top ASAP. It broke a lot of cars and a lot of egos. People from all over the US entered that race and I did pretty well for a newcomer; beating out some of the regulars who spent millions on their cars.

It was time for me to move on. I had been depositing my Carney salary of $1200.00 per month, in a bank account and decided to sell the MGA and keep the MGB. I had a tidy sum on which to travel. I loaded up the 'boot' as the English call it, with a case of Rolling Rock beer, for a friend in Utah. I borrowed my brothers' 'mummy bags', filled the MGB 'after-market' steering wheel that held contraband quite nicely and was capped with the MGB insignia; with some nice hashish. Filled the car with gas, grabbed a map and headed to Long Island.

I drove right up to her house, and said get your things together, we're driving to the West Coast, just as I had promised. It's then when the 'hems and haws' came into play. She wanted to talk so we drove to a cocktail lounge in Port Jefferson. I knocked back a few 'Manhattans' while she explained to me that living with an artist was no longer in her plans. She decided she wanted to marry a doctor, have 2.5 kids, a horse, a couple of dogs and a white picket fence. She didn't see that in my future; frankly neither did I. We headed back to the mansion of pain, I dropped her off and wheeled out of the driveway without looking back; another case of me keeping the contract and the other party doesn't.

I had forgotten a very important piece of equipment in Wilkes-Barre, a toolbox; so drove back to retrieve it. I spent one night with some friends, and was sent off the next day with a small pan of marijuana brownies.

West was my goal; I drove towards Utah. While driving through Indiana, I was into my second 'brownie' when I glanced out the driver's side window and there was the biggest, ugliest Indiana State Trooper they employed, and his gaze was fixed on me. He seemed to know something just wasn't right. Here is a guy in a light blue sports car, with a smile from ear to ear, driving along at the legal 65 miles per hour, chewing on a nice looking brownie. He stayed there next to me for a very long time, what seemed like an hour. I thought about waving, but didn't really want to meet the guy. He finally sped away at 120 MPH. Keep in mind what I was doing could have gotten me 20 years behind bars. I then saw the sign, 'you are now leaving Indiana, prison state for non-apple pie eaters and reefer madness types', ya'll come back now, ya hear!

I decided to stop in Boulder where my ex-wife's brother lived. He and I had a good relationship, so I was welcome to stay a few nights. There were also some other New York buddies there. My first impression of boulder was 'Yes, I could live here'. No pot holes in the street and good looking people everywhere. Money Bags' brother was a nice guy who just decided to get away from madness in New York. I don't think he was surprised by his sisters' actions. I was anxious to get on the road and in my haste I left one of my brothers' sleeping bags in Boulder.

I rolled into Logan, Utah and couldn't wait to unveil the Rolling Rock and when he saw it he said he was really a Stegmaier drinker. Nice. But he and his wife let me stay with them for 8 weeks. Enough time for me to decide where to go and what to do next. Logan was a bit strange. Mormons keep to themselves, and if you are not one of them, they look at you like you're something stuck to their shoe. I read the entire book of Mormon while I was there.

I preferred the ideology of the "Rasta" man in Jamaica. A man who claims to have talked to god directly makes me a bit nervous. It seems like all his actions can be justified in his mind; actions on the side of god or the other side. A lot of blood has dried in the dirt of Earth because of philosophies like theirs; I saw it happen and had no desire to see more.

The liquor stores were state run and had a strange method of selling. First you had to look up the product you wanted in these huge books, on high tables, with pencils provided. Then you filled out an index card with type, size and code number; then stood in line at a window. There were a couple old ladies that ran the place, so when your turn came they would go in the back, rummage around to get your order, (there was also a limit to the amount of bottles you could get at a time),then you paid the tab and left shaking your head.
 One of the things I liked to do for my hosts was provide wine for our dinners. So I ended up at the liquor store a few times a week. These two old bags decided I was never going to be a fine upstanding, albeit, non-Mormon gentleman. After standing in line, when I approached the window, they just happened to be out of the product I wanted. A trip back to the 'big book' and back in line and the same thing would happen; out of stock. Finally I grabbed a bunch of index cards, made my way to the window, and said what DO you have in stock; give me that and a quart of rum. This didn't happen too often due to the arrival of the police car when they saw the blue MGB in the parking lot. Fortunately it was toward the end of my stay and I'd soon be rid of this Mormon madness.

Some of my mountain crossings were death deifying. A MGB has a tonneau cover; with an opening for the driver, and a convertible top folded in the boot. I usually left the tonneau on. The higher I climbed the lower the temperature would drop. Then, usually the snow would start or worse yet it already had a head start. An MGB is not an all- terrain vehicle; it is about 10 inches off the ground. The heater doesn't work worth a damn, except maybe in the summer when it was 90 degrees.

One of the most memorable moments in crossing was the pass that leads into Steamboat Springs, Colorado; it is over 12,000 feet in elevation. It started out to be a nice sunny day in June and then I noticed that the air was getting a bit chilly. By the time it occurred to me that it was just plain cold, my hands were nearly frozen. You can't take a tonneau cover off and put up the top of an old MGB with frozen fingers. But with a lot of nasty words I got the job done. I wrapped myself in whatever blankets I had with me and the last of my Government Issued sleeping bag, oh yeah, and the wool watch cap pulled down around my ears, and headed up the pass. It was really bad, cars were stuck everywhere along with tractor trailers' jack-knifed into ditches. I put the car in 2nd gear and held the RPM's steady at 1800 and just drove; passing vehicles as I went. In blizzard conditions I barely could read a sign that named whatever pass it was. That's when it happened, the snow building up under the car pulled the exhaust pipe apart. I then proceeded to roar and backfire the other 8 miles down the other side. No one believed me; they said nobody could have crossed the pass in that storm. When they saw what I was driving, they were quiet with disbelief and awe. I found a garage that allowed me to use their lift; once they saw the snow packed under the car they believed me. I beat the tailpipe back into the muffler, snugged up the clamp and offered to pay. They wouldn't take the money just because I was the only one who made it across the pass that day. Another thing, I didn't have snow tires just 2nd gear, 1800 RPMs and a doobie the size of a cigar.

I swept the garage of all the snow that fell from my car, said thank you and continued on my journey. My name, Jason, means wanderer, and that is what I did, wander. But I decided to avoid the passes and took the lower routes.

I drove through the "Black Hills' one day, listening to Billie Holiday on the 8 track and drinking beer. Once in Wyoming, I stopped at a well-known pool hall and decided to unpack my two piece stick and see if there was any gold in 'dem thar hills'. I was shooting really well and the money was beginning to stack up. Once I started to feel the heat around me, I packed up my stuff and headed for the door. Some of these guys were pretty sore. I fired up the car and threw gravel on the way out of the parking lot. It would be a few years before I returned to Wyoming.

Regarding my friend in Logan, Utah; we met in Junior college in 1967. He was the first person I smoked pot with and he was another slightly twisted artist. His work bordered on ultra-realism which was 180 degrees from what I did, so we never clashed over art. I was there when his father died. I was at his wedding and saw his first born before anyone else. His wife was a friend of mine and I respected her. We kept in touch no matter where life had taken us. He illustrated my second book of poetry and was very instrumental in the production of "Mental Perspectives". Another important part of our relationship was that he also was in Vietnam. That may have been the reason I wanted to talk to him. The memories would not let go and my heart was heavy that day; I wanted to talk to another Vet. I stopped and bought a bottle of vodka on the trip down to Williamsport, Pa. where they were living. I remember most of the visit; seeing him and talking to his wife. After that, I have no idea of what happened. Whatever I did, it must have cut deep. To this day, he will not talk to me. He won't accept my letters or calls. I had to add this dialogue because it is painful and baffling in equal measures. It seals the memories of Utah as better times; I've moved on.

My arrival in Boulder was a bit 'charmed'. It so happened

that an apartment became available in the building where my New York friends lived. This was a large house on "the Hill". A very important address due to the fact the University of Colorado was there. The apartment was perfect. The living room was on ground level and the bedroom was behind it, in what was the basement portion of the house. The next thing that happened was being hired on the spot as a heavy equipment operator by a medium sized business, called Boulder Excavators. After several months on the job I became one of their top operators. The Union steward started giving me a hard time, so the next day I was in the AF of L-CIO Operating Engineers. This is one of the top unions in the world. People spend years trying to get into this union, mainly because it is the second highest paying position in any union. The first are the crane operators. Here I am 24 years old making $14.56 per hour (this is 1974) with full benefits and living on the 'Hill'. The Indians claim that Boulder is an enchanted place. Some people maintained the theory that it was because of the massive amounts of silver and gold in the mountains that wrapped around the city. All I know is that it was one of the best living experiences of my life.

I found a small weight lifting gym and joined; this was not a spandex haven, the owners were 7th day of Adventist and had the place strictly separated, both men and women went there and I can honestly say I never saw a woman anywhere near the place. I started lifting 3 days a week, real serious weight and within 6 weeks the results began to show, I was becoming pumped up like the days after the Navy. My back was still bothering me quite a bit, so as a precaution I wore a large leather belt that was specific to the activity.

My studio was shipped out to me at my request, the same old foot locker that contained an entire artist. I set up my desk and got to work painting with the standard goal of 6 canvas' framed and ready for hanging. Once I had this number of compositions I would start gallery shopping.

 I knew from experience what I was looking for, one of the

oldest in the city with a framing business also. The years tell you that it is well run and the framing business pays the salaries and bills. I've been burnt too many times by bright eyed idealists without any money and grand ideas, they usually only lasted 6 months to a year.

Part of the deal at the gym was a complete rub down by the owner, Howard Harvey. He was really into herbs and healthy living; the man hiked up into the mountains and picked his own various herbal ingredients for the rub down oils. Every 7th Day Adventist must preach to someone every day; for Howard, I was the one. I didn't have a problem with that it was the technique. He would start preaching on my back and shoulders and then as he worked his way down my leg's the intensity really picked up, by the time he was into my toes he was really wound up and would yank at my toe while yelling out 'Jesus' and it hurt like hell. I was polite for several weeks until one Wednesday at the leg I stopped him and said, Howard I do not have a problem with your preaching, in fact I rather enjoy it, but please, could you time it so that my toes are not children of Jesus? Howard also had a dry and wet sauna, in the winter when we got a decent snowfall; he would go out back and shovel the backyard snow into a large pile. He would then put up a small sign warning about weak hearts and this Swedish method of cleansing ones' body and mind. The object was to get the sauna up to about 160 degrees with plenty of steam and beating oneself with a Melaleuca branch then suddenly jumping up and running out to the back porch and diving into this giant snow bank, naked.

It was breathtaking to say the least, though I doubt if I would do that today, it does stress your heart and the rest of the body to the max. He was also a vegan, or vegetarian I am not sure which, but he would walk around the gym eating a jar of peanut butter with a spoon. The scene wasn't at issue; it was the vapor's escaping from his lower torso that really would scent the entire gym for hours, a strange form of incense I suppose.

All of that aside, after a complete session and a good hot shower I stepped out of the place feeling like a new man. One thing I failed to mention were the tanning booths, I think my mind was attempting to delete those thoughts completely. I used them every time I went, pop a quarter in and touch up with some color, especially in the winter when everyone was white. One night when I felt like a 'Rhodes Scholar' I decided to go in the stand-up booth completely nude, my idea was to tan my entire body and eliminate the tan line for good, I thought that George Hamilton would just have to weep once he saw me on the cover of 'Stupid' magazine. Stupid would have been a better choice of words over monumental unless you were combining the two into one large folly, mistake or complete misunderstanding of my own anatomical make up of skin in various areas of the body. My poor penis was pissed; it went through all of the phases of any bad sunburn, blisters that burst at inopportune moments, peeling skin, bright red coloration along with the pain. I am talking about unadulterated pain that lasted for the duration of any 2nd degree burn. Now that I reminisce about this lapse of judgment I think I should have taken some mustard and a hot dog roll and photographed the wayward appendage for use in medical journals.

Boulder Excavators had contracts with some pretty intense customers; Rocky Flats where they assemble warheads, and NOMA, the government agency that figures out all of the stuff that ruins a good afternoon, IBM a.k.a. Big Blue and Arapahoe Chemical, that had 30% of the Worlds raw chemical business from which everything is made from nose strips to serious heart medicine. That was in I975, they may be even bigger now.

During my tenure, I worked on the project which diagnosed the "Wind Sheer" problem that made planes drop from the sky. I also helped to put a dike around the entire facility of Arapahoe Chemical in case they had a spill. This earthen structure was designed to contain some very vicious chemicals. And then there was Rocky Flats, I dare you, go out there and stand on the mesa where Rocky is located and look South by South West, down in the valley is Golden Colorado, does it sound familiar? I was sent out there with a backhoe to dig two perfect circles for footers to place two one million gallon fuel tanks on. Here is a mesa with a guard shack, fence and a few small out buildings, that is a lot of fuel oil!

I was told that everything was underground, huge buildings buried in giant holes. I had a full security clearance and there was a two lane black top drive which was about one mile long running from the main road to the guard shack. I used to really put that old MGB through its paces, first running up through the gears to about 90 mph and then down shifting and grinding to a stop a few inches from their red and white boom. The guards hated it every morning, but they had to let me in; until one day. They had taken great pleasure in telling me that they had a small spill and my machine was impounded until further notice. I called the boss man and he just told me to come back into the yard to be sent somewhere else. That machine was there for two weeks.

The architect on the project was a big Indian guy with grey hair down to his waist and a Brooks Brothers' suit underneath it. We got along well because he didn't say much, but when he found out that I could read blueprints our mutual respect grew stronger and he would ask for me when he needed a machine. The guards that I harassed had loaded M-16's on their shoulders. Somehow they got word of my combat experience in Vietnam and I can assure you that I didn't tell them, that subject was still taboo to me. Afterward, I was called 'sir' and saluted after the gate was raised; I remember mixed emotions about that.

After the isotopes were removed from my machine, work got under way. This place was always in the papers there for spills, two headed calf's' and a host of other issues. Now I will answer the riddle if Golden, Colorado doesn't ring a bell, yes it is Coors beer. For the locals, Coors wasn't a popular beer back then for a few reasons, one was its 3.2 rating in the alcohol department and the other was Joe Coors who was inclined to speak his mind on camera. He was quoted as saying that he would not give a dime for all the Mexicans in Colorado, yo, that would cause nightmares in a politically correct individual.

There was a small supermarket called Eagle Market where I shopped, and many times ended up squeezing cantaloupes with Allen Ginsberg. After a number of visits of this nature we spoke beyond the condition of the fruit. He was teaching a course by invitation for a few semesters and that is what placed him in Boulder. We exchanged numbers after I told him about my years of poetry experience and one day I received a call from the head of the English department at the University of Colorado, on the 'hill' in Boulder. I met with this man and he asked if I could do a reading and have a discussion with his students to get them out of the moon, June, spoon mode of thinking. I accepted the challenge and proceeded to be a part of the department at the University.

My life in Boulder was living large, people had the right attitude; a pursuit of life and living to the fullest. After more than a year I became a believer in the old Indian saying, the only problem was the second part of that, it said once your soul found Boulder you would never forget it and long to return, it too is true, but then again I have not had much luck at returning to a place that I have already lived. Here I am, union scale, sports car, respect, rock & roll singer, poetry instructor, plenty of interesting women a good boss and a beautiful setting to wrap it all in. I drove around with just my tonneau cover for so long, when I lifted the top from the boot it was all dry rotted and useless, a commentary on the weather at over a mile up.

Everything was just rosy until one day when my 'little precious' showed up under the auspices to visit her brother who lived upstairs. In her baggage were a lot of negative and depressed things to wear. She tried to approach me one day and I had to explain to her that it was over, she decided to

174

meet Doctor Right and be happy until death does its' part, I went on to explain that I had built an entirely new life here for myself and was enjoying every minute of it. I refused to be a part in any way shape or form of her ridiculous jealousy. I refused to contract her sickness. I had my own soul to deal with and it was still a glacier, its' just that I couldn't go public with it. She wasn't very happy but that wasn't my problem "…Frankly, I don't give a dam."

One night there was a big party planned and I for one was looking forward to it, that afternoon the phone rang, it was my boss calling to ask me to go to work on an emergency job. It seems that a 24" waterline had broken and a lot of people were without water, plus it was a difficult job because of the location. What could I say, I changed and sped off to go to work, the job lasted until 11:00 pm, I came dragging back to my apartment and made a cameo appearance at the party, explained the long day and had to take a rain check. The work had been very stressful and dangerous, there was a steep grade next to the worksite and the material was loose, working under stress will wear you out. I went downstairs and walked into my bedroom and just fell across my bed, clothes, boots; everything except my jacket, and fell asleep.

The party upstairs continued and would so until the half's kicked. This story was related to me several years after the fact, my friend and her brother were concerned about what I would do if I knew what happened. She was popping valiums and drinking, then she disappeared, the two guys noticed that she was gone, so they ran downstairs and quietly entered my apartment, she was there, standing over me with a knife with both hands on it, both of the guys grabbed her and her brother put his hand over her mouth to muffle her while they dragged her out, disarmed. They had taken her upstairs and gave her something that put her to sleep. She probably thought that the water main story was a ruse so I could sneak out with some woman; I knew her way of thinking.

I remained ignorant for some years and when she woke up she didn't remember much, so that was how the story ended.

Winter was upon us and I planned on driving East. While making plans a friend of mine had a misfortune, her mother died at their home in St. Louis, I told her that I would be there for her, she appreciated that and said there was plenty of room. Without notice I was asked to take my 'little precious' with me. I protested and explained that I had to travel light because of a serious commitment I had made, it was to no avail, I was hit with the ' least you can do' stuff and 'all of the years we spent' and so on. I said all right but wasn't comfortable with this at all, it wasn't all right.

Against all caution I sped to St. Louis with the pedal to the metal as we used to say when you were running hot. I drove like a madman, blowing off States; all in all, I made good time. This girl was Jewish and they had a mansion with a view of the St. Louis Arch, I say Jewish because it has an effect on the way the final service is dealt with. Her mother was 'In State' in the front parlor and that evening there were Rabbis' all around the perimeter of the room in chairs reading the Torah.
Suddenly, my 'hideous hitch hiker' appeared at the top of the stairs on the second floor, she was in an altered state; valium and liquor. That in itself was not the problem, the problem was her outburst which could be heard throughout the house, the Rabbis in the other room stopped reading and all went dangerously quiet; this only made the 2nd floor tirade even more vicious. Again it was a case of a total mental breakdown in terms of imaginary and uncontrolled jealousy; she was screaming things about my fucking this poor girl with total disregard for her mother lying in the other room. I was completely embarrassed and kept apologizing to my

host and then ran up the steps and grabbed her and dragged her to the room we were in and shoved a pillow over her face to shut her up, now she was laughing, enjoying the pain inflicted and my humiliation was complete. I dug around in my bag and found a pill which would really quiet her; found it and shoved it in her mouth, I brought them in case my friend needed something to calm her; these were high dosage seconals and worked rather quickly. In less than 10 minutes the shouting and laughing had stopped, I packed our bags and made a trip down to the car. After stowing the bags, I asked my friend if I could address the group and would she join me. I began my conversation with a brief 'Yiddish" introduction, then proceeded in English to explain how appalled I was with this woman's behavior, I assumed complete responsibility for this crude and totally uncalled for action on the part of this person who allowed her true feelings to surface with liquor. I explained that my host and I were simply good friends in Boulder and shared similar interests. Upon hearing her unfortunate news I felt it my duty to be here, alone, to comfort her. It was not my intention to have this other person with me and will vacate these premises so that everyone can be left in peace during this painful time. I then made a comment again in Yiddish asking that God bless them all and especially the departed. I realized that it was a form of slang but it was the only thing I could think of which would help convey my sincerity. I then went upstairs and brought the source of my damaged integrity down the rear steps and dragged her to the car, threw her in and returned to the foyer. I again apologized to my friend and her father, told them that I was leaving because it seemed like the only thing to do. My friend followed me out and thanked me for coming and claimed that she understood the outbreak and didn't hold me responsible in anyway, my image was intact. I drifted the car out into the street before starting it and proceeded out of town. I had left a note for my friend in the room we occupied and explained again how bad I felt and how it would be impossible for me to stay after what transpired. It was one time that I actually thought of doing something quite rash, but instead just drove to rid my conscience.

My honor got in the way of any plans of retribution so I just drove North East for Pennsylvania, I had no intentions of taking this walking insult to New York or anywhere near it. Using coffee and sheer willpower I drove into Wilkes-Barre, stopped in front of the bus terminal, threw her bag out and then opened the door of the car and threw her out onto the pavement. It was over with a wounded sense of integrity.

When winter broke, I sold the MGB and bought a Ford Mustang, my father actually helped me paint it for some reason I will never understand. We had taken every shade of yellow we could find and mixed them together to make enough paint to finish the entire car. When it was done it was the most disgusting color yellow that I had ever seen, but it was too late now, it was stuck to the car.

Soon thereafter I returned to Boulder and resumed my old job but had to find another apartment; I fell into the same routine and slowly started to enjoy life again. My lady friend moved back to St. Louis because her father needed her, it made the scar itch when I read the note.

In Boulder there were a lot of corporate drop outs, very successful people that just burned out. Every month I went to a dude ranch and rented a horse, they had a small herd of buffalo and a few thousand acres. After a few escorted rides they allowed me to go out by myself, it was great, riding through these dry washes and chasing the buffalo around, afterward the price included breakfast. They had excellent pancakes and everyone raved about them, one of the ranch hands told me the secret, one morning they were drinking quarts of beer and one of them fell into the batter so they just left it there, and that was the big secret. This guy had been with IBM near Chicago and told me he was fighting his way home one day through traffic and decided he had enough.

He went home and told his wife she could stay or go it didn't matter, but he had it. She stayed. I asked what happened to his front teeth and he told me it was a cattle drive barroom brawl that claimed those, but it was worth it he said.

On Saturday I would stop at Tom's tavern and every week there was this guy that came in, he looked like one of the 'ZZ Top' guys. His beat up old truck was parked out front full of provisions with his dog guarding them. After several weeks; we struck up a conversation and he told me that he panned gold for a living, he wouldn't say where, but I didn't expect him to. He was another corporate drop-out; but his wife and kids agreed and followed him. He staked out a claim and every Saturday he headed for the assayers office and cashed in his loot. They took the taxes from what they gave him, so he would leave there with between $400 and $1200 dollars per week. He had a log cabin somewhere up in the Mountains, but only winked if you asked, where?

I worked hard that year doing all the overtime I could at my job. My goal was to save enough money so I could return to FAU and start my Master's Degree. But it wasn't all work; I hooked up with a band. Every Saturday night I made a guest appearance as 'Slick Dick'. I wore black clothes and a pair if wraparound sunglasses. I'd slick back my hair with Brylcream and put the jelly rolls in the front and the DA in the back. I jumped out on stage after a big introduction, grab a mike and say "…well baby, do you love me yet"? Then break into a wild version of "Mustang Sally". The crowd went crazy. I'd come back one more time during the next set, then disappear through the back door into my crap yellow Ford Mustang.

I sold that Mustang to a Mexican guy who loved the color. "Where did you find such a nice color, man?" Naturally I didn't tell him the truth, but went on about how it involved Detroit, security guards and a secret paint booth.

After I sold the car, I bought a ticket in the 'Silver Zephyr' and the 'Broadway Limited', which covered the Denver to

Chicago, run, then, the Chicago to New York route. The Crane operator gave me a ride to the train station because of his guilty conscience.

It was early summer and the boss asked me to drive the giant crane down to Denver for a job. This thing was big; one part extended out front almost 40 feet. Behind me was a truck carrying the other sections of the 'flying jib' as it is called. Inside the cab of the truck were the crane operator and two laborers. They were to direct me through town. They took me on a strange route; we went right downtown where the municipal building was.

Suddenly, they were screaming at me over the radio to look at '10 o'clock, quick, so I glanced over to the sidewalk. During this I was just starting to go into a turn, with of course, the large boom sticking out. Walking down the sidewalk was a beautiful girl with long legs and pink panties on and the wind blowing the dress up around her head. As I was watching all this, the boom was knocking all the lights off the fancy polls, all 8 of them. Some were still working, hanging upside down, others were just mowed down. The cops wanted to form a firing squad, but the supervisor, who knew everybody, stayed and cleaned up. After the formalities were taken care of we continued to Denver; but I was pissed. I had a perfect safety record up until then. That night went we finally pulled into the yard, everyone told me the Boss wanted to see me. That didn't help my situation. I went to his office and he started to act really angry, then he asked, "Was she really that good looking"? I said yes, and then some. He then said that's what insurance is for, now get out of here and don't let it happen again, or I won't have any insurance. I dodged a bullet on that one; after all is said and done, I was still responsible for that vehicle. The other guys just laughed and there were plenty of comments in the men's room for months afterwards. And the trains keep rolling.

During the train ride to Chicago, I was placed at a table with Mr. Chavez; the man who organized the migrant workers that picked all the fruit and vegetables. He had bodyguards with him and they gave me a quick pat down before I joined him at his table for lunch; there had been a number of attempts on his life. He was referred to as the 'Mexican Jimmy Hoffa'. He was on his way to Washington DC to speak before Congress. He told me he didn't like to fly and preferred riding the rails. We struck up a conversation that went from hard manual labor to 'Bacchus'; he was well read and could pick up on any topic with ease. We were kindred spirits of sorts because we both started doing a man's work when we were 8 or 9 years old. He said "he was embarrassed because these aren't the hands of a working man; I'm getting soft from doing all this speaking". I told him I felt he had paid his dues in the field and was now answering his true calling. One could not happen without the other; he liked that and told one of his guys to write that down, it would make a good speech.

We actually sat together and talked for a few hours; enjoying each other's company; I enjoyed the education. Eventually he said he had to go and read over some papers, even picked up the lunch tab. He was a great man.

It was getting towards evening so I headed for the Club Car. I parked my buttocks on a high stool with a small round table, and an attractive blond asked if anyone was sitting in the empty seat; and I said I hoped she was. We hit it off. She went on about how she was sick of wimpy guys, and could tell that wasn't my style. I agreed and we proceeded to drink the club car dry. After covering every subject you would normally find in the yellow pages, it was 1 AM and the bar was going to close. I remembered that I had a bottle of Moet champagne so told her I'd meet her in the Vista Car; which also would be closed but only had a velvet rope across the stairwell. I pocketed two wine glasses and headed to retrieve the bottle. We popped the cork, and toasted everything while the clothes were coming off. Serious breathing replaced the bubbles until an old man with a cap and a flashlight, bopped me on the head, he was offended and threatened to put us off at the next stop. The blond found all of this very funny, which didn't help my hardship explanation, in more ways than one, and we were duly escorted out of the 'Vista' car. That was the end of it, and I didn't see her again the rest of the trip, not that I didn't look for her. A girl in every port, the sailors would say; but Amtrak stations were taking the tale to extremes.

I decided to get off in Chicago and take the 'Empire Builder' to Milwaukee and visit a friend. He had been a roommate in Boulder, and left before I did, because his place was haunted, and I mean it. He was a true hippy; he lived simple and walked around in sandals in the winter. He spread a couple blankets on the floor and said there is your bedroom. We enjoyed ourselves as two Pabst beer drinkers and tried our best to empty Mr. Pabst's number one vat.

After a few days, I jumped the train back to Chicago and caught the East bound 'Broadway Limited'. During my stay in Milwaukee, sleep had deserted me, maybe the mattress had something to do with it; but I missed a stop, where they split the train, and I was headed to Baltimore instead of New York.

I had heard there was an Andy Warhol exhibit at the Museum there, so decided to make the best of it. I really didn't like the guys work, or more aptly put, the work his underlings did which he signed. As I walked around the museum, I noticed small flecks of dried paint under each of his canvases. At first I thought it was part of the exhibit. But I soon learned that he used a lot of cheap house paint; I heard he was tight with a buck. Any self-respecting artist went hungry rather than compromise their canvas. Obviously our Mr. Warhol, either lacked self-respect, or hunger. Years later I read where a London Art Gallery was suing him because they invested a bundle in his work only to have it flake off onto the floors. It's too bad they didn't call me; my work will withstand a Marine boot camp.

During those days I carried a 'little black book'. After the exhibit, I thought I was stuck in Baltimore until I remembered meeting some girls at the Elbow Room in Fort Lauderdale a few years earlier; and the one said 'if you're ever in …and I was. I called her and with great hesitation in her voice, she invited me to come over. She let me take a quick shower and then we proceeded to grill some burgers and drink a few beers. We were having a pretty good time, until I started to talk about Florida and the good times there. I felt the cold sea water on my legs and before you knew it I was on the Titanic. Guess somebody really hurt her there as it was the cold shoulder from then on. Here's a pillow there's the couch, be gone in the morning before my parents get home. I woke at 4Am and decided it was time to go. I headed out across a field in the back of the house and knew if I walked north I'd eventually find an interstate that would get me back to Wilkes-Barre.

Riding thumb is a fickle thing. Sometimes it is easy and you get a ride with someone from Earth. But sometimes you spend the entire time holding onto the exit handle. Then there are the station wagons full of bible bangers. There are two expressions used in those bobbing head Jesus vehicles, sweet Jesus and Ahura Mazda, wait, that's Zoroastrianism.

Hallelujah is the other correct expression used in large station wagons with chrome fish on the tailgate. Sometimes I'd make up a place for them to stop and let me out, just to do that; get out. The next guy could have a rainbow on the back. If they were women I was in good hands; if it was a guy, a single guy, it took great vigilance; you didn't really want to fall asleep in a rainbow car. And finally, if it had a blue light on the roof, it meant you were either going downtown, or getting dropped off on a side road by a big guy wearing a campaign hat; who'd tell you, to keep off his highway or next time he'd put some jewelry on ya. I always check to see if there were rainbows on the back of the cars just in case. If you think about it, you don't see many, if any, hitch hikers anymore.

My unemployment checks started to roll in and they were for the maximum amount because of my union status. I bought a 1968 "ram air" Buick; a simple muscle car with a bench seat and four on the floor. It also had a healthy appetite for gas.   I had to remind it at every gas station that this wasn't an 'all you can eat' place. It ran well and did all I expected from a muscle car, but it was a stupid purchase. Maybe being 25 had something to do with it. "That's right baby, I'm a man, spelled m-a-n, MAN. I spend half my income on gasoline; but I'm the guy you've been waiting for…enough, it making me sick also.

After a few months of work with my brothers, I kissed Mary T on the forehead and set off for Boca Raton. I had put aside money for university and wanted to get going on my Master's degree.

Back in 1975, I-95 wasn't finished in every state, so you could go like hell for an hour or two, and then roll along behind a truck full of watermelons or hogs; I preferred the watermelons. Then, zoom again, another new part of the road, until you came to a river and the bridge hadn't been built yet. So, look for another detour.   Eventually I made it to the university, got set up in a dorm and signed up for my classes.

 That first quarter, I really packed on the credits and was doing well; I had to maintain the 3.5 point average to maintain the 'out of state tuition waver'. It was almost like receiving a scholarship as the difference in money was substantial.
One day as I was walking down the corridor towards my room and a poster caught my eye. It simply stated; would you like to live in Australia? And a phone number, my response; where do I sign. I called the number and was told they were setting up interviews for teaching positions. So in

answer to where do I sign; well, I had to travel to Madison, Wisconsin for the interview, so we set a date. I called my hippy buddy in Milwaukee and he said he'd pick me up at the airport, and we'd go out for a few Pabst.

On a previous visit, I had met a girl who said she had friends who lived in Madison, and that we both could stay there. We were going to travel together by bus. On the way to the station, she stopped at her 'pharmacy'. Little did I know she was a crazy Jewish valium addict; she was screaming so loudly, demanding her 'script', I decided I'd wait outside. It was 20 degrees out there, and I had just come from the 89 degree Florida winter. The minute she stepped outside she opened the bottle and dumped a pile of valium in her mouth. She chewed a few times then gulp, they were gone; hadn't ever seen that happen in my whole career.

The only reason I had agreed to this fiasco was to save a few dollars on a hotel room in Madison, but it was too late, I was locked in and stayed focused on my reason for being here.

We had taken the bus to Madison, the interview was the next morning and I just made it through the night. That morning I dressed in my best, though it was a warm weather suit and the temperature outside was 8 degrees, with snow. I met the woman conducting the interview and she fired numerous questions at me, and then asked the one I was ready for, why do you want to live in Australia? My diatribe began with Vietnam and meeting Australian troops there and how we had fought together (mainly in barroom brawls) and, then went on about the tramp steamer tickets in 1970, but now I was completely unattached, no wife, no kids or pets just my ambition, knowledge and a leather bag. She told me that I would receive her decision in the mail within two weeks. On my way out of the door she asked me where I came from and I explained that I flew up from Miami for this interview. The woman then said could you be ready to leave in 6 weeks after receiving a notification, the answer was yes ma'am!

Somehow I knew that I would get the contract, hell, there was 2 feet of snow outside and I came from Miami? Another thing was the contract; it was very lucrative and heavy on money. But when you think about it, the Australians were very smart. They send a person to the US to hire some of the best teachers in their fields, and overnight, your country has a world class educational system and the tax payer didn't spend a dime to train them.

It was back to the crash pad, gather up the crazy lady and grab a bus back to Milwaukee. After we made it back we cabbed to her flat and she immediately undressed. I did not. As I descended the steps from her apartment there was a steady barrage of plates and other glass objects directed at my head. I managed to escape undamaged and went to my friends place on the East side of town.

That little episode in Milwaukee gave basis to an award winning poem which had been printed in a number of poetry anthologies. The ugly scenes were rewarded. A word of advice, if you are going to Milwaukee in the dead of Winter, you should do two things: 1.Get involved in a get help group and sit on a cold metal chair drinking bad coffee with powdered creamer in it, and tell the group why you are going to Milwaukee, then allow them to talk you out of it. 2. Find a haberdasher who specializes in outfitting polar expeditions with stylish garments and outerwear to withstand temperatures of 40 below, minimum.

I flew back to Florida and returned to my classes to finish the quarter and get my credit hours tucked away. Then prior to my return to Pennsylvania (The contract was mine) I booked a flight to Jamaica for another stay at Mrs. G's. I started out with my room and the Mount Gay rum, and as I sat there looking out there was a new addition to my view, so I approached Mrs. G. and asked her why there was an 8 foot chain link fence with barbed wire on top of it. She sighed, and explained that a new government had gotten in and things had changed, there was more crime especially toward tourists and that is why the fence had to be installed, it was

186

for safety at night. That had an impact on me, time waits for no one.

While walking around town one day, I ran into a "Rasta" man selling tourist crap, he asked me if I wanted to buy anything then looked at me again and said, you don't want to buy this stuff, I said no I am not interested. So I sat down with him and we talked for a while, he told me of his home in the 'Blue' mountains and how he had an extra cabin for guests, it started to sound appealing. My only expense was to give him $12.00 dollars for a pound of Ganga and I did. He told me to check out of the hotel and meet him in this same spot the next morning, I was there and he wasn't. I waited for over an hour then decided to head back up to the hotel with a bottle of rum when he came around the corner apologizing for being late, he had to wait for his 'main mon' for the ganja. We then hopped on a bus and went into the mountains on one of the most frightening rides of my life; our driver was going like crazy and I looked out and noticed that there weren't any guard rails with a several hundred foot drop two feet away from the road surface. When a corner came up there was usually a truck or something and we passed each other with a coat of paint missing. Finally we reached this spot under a light on a pole and that was his stop. Then we proceeded to hike through the jungle for a few miles before coming upon his compound. His name was Masuha, pronounced 'Ma-sue' and he was the real thing, a Rastafarian, complete with dread locks before they existed anywhere else. My cabin was simple and clean, there was not a bed per se, just a matte and a light blanket, the floor was highly varnished and each morning he spent time cleaning both of our floors. The morning began with a simple breakfast followed by the rolling of a 'spiff' don't quote my spelling. It was a very large joint shaped like a cone; we smoked that while he prepared his pipe, which was a large bull's horn with a bowl that held at least a quarter of an ounce of pot. To a true Rasta man, smoking the herb was a religious experience and not to be taken lightly. At one point

I started to talk and he stopped me with a finger over his lips, than he wagged it at me, the message was clear, silence. After he lighted that pipe, it was like hyperventilating the smoke until he had taken a drag that seemed to last for 5 minutes. Then he handed me the pipe. At one point I coughed, and he was quick to correct me by saying that was the problem with Americans, they didn't take ganja seriously enough. I did not cough after that.

We would hike through the bush to a waterfall and that was his shower, then he owned another plot of land where his vegetable garden was, and that was his bathroom, nothing was wasted, perfect fertilizer if you don't eat meat. Dinners consisted of fresh vegetables and rice, again, simple fare. On a few occasions we went out to this little bar where they only served Guinness Stout in pony bottles, there was a huge juke box there from the 50's with two records in it, I gave his friend 'The Spider' a buck and the same reggae songs played over and over, it was all part of the experience. After a few weeks he was stuffing pot into an empty corn meal box and I asked why, he said that another couple was due to arrive and he was giving me my share of the ganja. I told him that there was no way I could carry that into the U.S. and it would land me in jail for a long time. At this he was dismayed, a country without ganja? His philosophy was we would not be in wars if everyone smoked ganja and became a Rastafarian. I had to agree with a heavy heart. It was time to go anyway, so I did not mind, he walked me to the bus stop and saw me off.

Can I say that this experience changed my life? I must say yes. I've never forgotten the peaceful atmosphere and spiritual presence of my friend.

After a few days I flew back to Florida, and then onto Pennsylvania. I bought a 'bar car' for $75.00, a Mustang convertible that was so rusted it was ready to break in half. I am quite serious, I looked. If this car had a V8 in it, the thing would have just shredded itself with me sliding down the interstate holding a steering wheel in half a car. While waiting for the particulars on the flight, I made the most of the time by painting in my studio and reading books on Australia. Did you know that the largest solid gold nugget was found in a wagon rut in Australia? It now sits in a museum. It was enormous and required several men just to lift it. Could you imagine, just lying there on top of the ground covered with mud. A hapless rancher ran over it and busted his wagon wheel, so when he kicked it, besides the pain, he knew something wasn't right, it did not move and that was the story.

Allow me to tell a tale of loss. The girl that I was dating in Florida who had achieved so much by her own hand, the one I was supposed to take out for dinner but got drunk with my Cuban friends instead. Well, she disappeared, her apartment was empty the next day and she was gone. The night before my flight to Australia the phone rings, it is her and she was living in Hartford which was a 4 hour drive from my studio. She wanted to get together to have the dinner I promised her. I had to explain that within 12 hours or so, I would be flying to Australia for 2 years. The silence was wrenching and I felt like a heel. I have never heard from her again. For the sake of continuity, I dated this girl after the rich one left me and that was in 1973, it was now the spring of 1976.

I sold the 'bar car' with a proviso that it was unfit for human usage and a danger to body and mind. I made the person who bought it sign a paper to that effect just in case it broke in half on a railroad track with a speeding freight train flying through the gap. It was actually worse when I sold it because I actually sped over railroad tracks trying to break it in half just because I never did that before. Lead balloons, Mustang convertibles that come in two pieces, broken hearts; no wonder I had to fly half way around the globe.

At JFK the chartered plane was waiting, we flew to Los Angeles to pick up some more teachers and then headed off

189

for Hawaii, our first fuel stop. After we landed in Hawaii I tried to talk this girl into getting off with me for a week or so, and that we could arrange another flight later. She was too afraid to be that adventurous, of course, she was from the mid-west.

It was March 1976 when we landed at Melbourne International. As we disembarked I saw about a dozen protestors holding signs that said: Yankee Go Home. They were being kept in check by uniformed police officers. It was pretty stupid for all the reasons I mentioned after my interview in Madison. Couldn't someone explain these basic facts to these people? I simply ignored them; this wasn't the first time I got off a plane in a place I wasn't wanted. So I grabbed my two small bags and went looking for my surrogate family. It was almost like Vietnam, the feeling that is, I'm completely alone with a bag on my shoulder; I just flew 18,000 miles to be in a place that was hostile. After a few months, that attitude would change somewhat.

As I walked through the terminal there was this smiling guy holding a sign that said 'Goodman' on it. He was my contact and the person I would spend some time with. I walked up to this man and introduced myself as the person he has been waiting for. He checked his note and said: welcome to Australia mate, I am Trevor, your guide. At least it wasn't Vergil and there was a creepy river to cross.

When we got into his car, he reminded me to put my seatbelt on and then said something that proved to be pure truth, he said: "…we Aussies are nice people until we get behind the wheel of a car." With that he wheeled out into traffic and it was a matter of minutes that I understood his comment. I told him that some of the antics of these drivers would get them shot in the U.S.

We arrived at his house and everyone was excited, his wife had made a large chicken for dinner. It is a good thing I kept my mouth shut, because chicken was the most expensive meat you could buy there, the reason was simple, they didn't have the soil or water to grow corn, a staple feed. My faux pas came after dinner when I leaned back and said that I was stuffed, the kids started to giggle and the wife had to run into the kitchen. Shortly afterward, Trevor and I were in the study having cigars and brandy, one of the first things he said was that you never say 'stuffed' in Australia; it was an insult that made 'get fucked' look like the motto of a cub scout troop. He strongly suggested that I avoid the word at all times. As I went to explain he stopped me and said he knew, there were a lot of American television programs on the 'telly' here.

The next morning we were off to my home for a long time to come, during the drive, he used the word stuffed numerous times directed at other drivers; a bit of a dichotomy here. When we arrived, because of his timing to the minute, there was no time for any introductions or period of adjustment. The bell rang and I was told that my first class was in an out building, one of those temporary classrooms. I walked in to see 25 kids seated and staring at me. I felt like they were thinking, so here is an ugly American! I did not have a clue what to do other than Trevor's parting words, teach them art. After my initial shock, I sent a few boys to bring back 25 scissors, 12 glue pots and a pile of construction paper along with pencils and rulers. While they were gone, I sat on the edge of the desk and said, right, any questions?

It was a fucked up way of doing business and I felt that way for about two weeks until the paychecks were issued. I used Trevor to translate the codes on the check face, when he saw it he just whistled and told me that I was being paid a lot of money to be here. I explained that part of my contract was a tax relief for the first two years; this added about 40% to my base pay. As time went on, he looked at my checks again and told me that I was making more than the principal of the school, I assured him that he was the only person that ever saw those documents, he and the bank teller.

The terms of my contract stated that I was being paid to

write and implement curriculum for teaching sculpture; then instruct the existing teachers how to teach the subject.

My work was to involve the latest approach to the subject and how to establish a modern sculpture classroom. I arranged for maximum usage and storage of tools and equipment behind locked doors. Here I was, standing in a mobile home with 25 13 year olds, tough little brutes because this turned out to be a 'technical' school, which meant that the academic side of education was not of great importance; that was a different high school completely in their system. Did I mention the fact that I spent 20 hours on a plane and had what is commonly referred to as jet lag? My first assignment was to have every kid build a cube out of paper with glue tabs, crisp lineage and as close to square as possible. Every class had to do this, put their name on it and place it on a shelf. The next day it was a triangle, a rectangle etc. All day other teachers would just pop in to see what I was up too. One told me to just let them draw and I told her that it was my job to teach sculpture, and this was the beginning of the process, three dimensional shapes. She left in a huff, too many American telly programs I believe!

Eventually I received my own space in the main building, bought a car and rented an apartment with rental furniture in it. I stayed late and started to 'borrow' things from the wood shop and build my storage of tools and equipment. I set up a number of sculptural disciplines, bins for plaster of Paris, clay, wood blocks and another for a volcanic stone they had that carved really well without the need for power tools. During this entire time I was writing everything down and doing schematic drawings of everything I built; the furniture, the benches and storage bins etc. This I would compile into one complete volume on the subject they were paying me to introduce and teach, as per the wording of the contract. I found out through the grapevine that the sweet thing I tried to introduce into sin in Hawaii flipped out and went home. She had requested "Alice Springs" the very dead center of

Australia. They had a river and every year there was a boat race, the problem was this river had not seen water in close to 30 years. They built these boats and wore them like clothes then ran down the dry river bed. I had to laugh, years later I saw a piece in the paper where this famous boat race had to be cancelled because there was water in the river. No one in their right mind goes to Alice Springs except to see Aires Rock; they then get drunk and leave on the first flight out the next day. I'm being too harsh; Alice Springs is home to a lot of good people and supports a lot of cattle and sheep 'stations' that is why it is where it is. The truth, I didn't go there to look at a big rock, it wasn't my style back then.

After getting settled in well and earning the respect of both teacher and student alike, I was approached to teach night courses for adults, there wasn't any pay, but two night courses equaled Friday off; long weekends to paint and write. I taught figure drawing (hence the modeling experience) and ceramics from slabs, it was a different technique than using a wheel. The boss of the art department had all of the other slots to himself, its' good to be king!

In the meantime I rented a house in the mountains at a little town called Upwey. This town used to be the place to be in the 30's now it was an old whore with bad lipstick. I liked it, there was everything there I needed including a real weight lifting gym, plus this house had a terrific studio, all glass overlooking a tree lined valley. The place was 262 years old and it did have a ghost, I kid you not. The resident Cockatoos would fly around and I would feed them hamburger meat. The meat was cheap and I was told that if they stayed I would never have a problem with critters around my house. The studio saw some of the best work of my career up until that time. I found a small gallery in another mountain town called 'Emerald' and they sold almost my entire output of 32 paintings over the period of time I was there.

The Emerald Gallery owner's husband was a well-known

wood craftsman; he specialized in carving maiden heads for large sailing vessels. He worked with the Australian wood called 'Black Melaleuca', supposedly the hardest wood in the world, once it had completely dried. The grain of this wood was breathtaking; it was so deep and mysterious. He didn't care much for people disturbing him, so I only met him once, I think the story of him totally disliking people was just to keep them away because when I met him he was a perfect gentleman and happened to really like my work. I had taken that as a great compliment. The feeling was mutual, his work was stunning, though his medium was a very difficult one to work in and he was not a young man. He may have carved the maiden head for the schooner Phantom, I'll never know.

My house in the mountains had a strange bathroom arrangement. The sink and shower were inside and quite modern, but the W/C was outside like an outhouse, but it wasn't an outhouse per se. It was called a 'dunny' house and everyone had one. It looked like an outhouse. There was a small door on the side down by the ground, behind it was a large 'dunnycan' or, a big galvanized bucket with handles on it. Every week at 5 am the 'Dunnyman' would come along in a truck, insert a new can with disinfectant in it and take away the used one. Naturally, my little donut could not stand using this place, but she had too.

The reason was logical once you understood the logic, as it turned out the soil in Upwey was terrible and they didn't have sewers in the street. The dunny house was the only way of safe guarding the water table from contamination with un-desirable ingredients. Water was/is a serious issue in Australia, wasting water would get you noticed. Another serious matter in this country is the bush fire. If you look in my car there will be a blanket in the back seat; that habit comes from Australia. Sometimes bush fires moved at over 60 mph. If you are in a car, you get on the floor in the back seat and cover yourself with the blanket. The fire would not touch the gasoline tank but would blow out all of the windows and for a few seconds the heat would kill you. It was the law, if you were driving down a road and there was a bush fire you had to stop and help fight it. These things were nothing to trifle with.

Down under, a term that most Australians do not care for, the seasons are reversed. In the winter it could be 90 degrees at night. In this house I leased, I set up a guest room, because if friends came by and you were drinking it was expected that your friends would stay the night. It had to do with the drinking and driving laws. So I set up this bedroom and two sets of friends woke me up at 3 or 4 in the morning asking for blankets. I thought they were crazy, but it was true, there was a cold spot in this room, when you stood in the corner you could feel a 10 degree temperature change. I had to walk through this room to get to my studio and stood in the corner, it was freezing; I didn't spend a lot of time there.

There are a lot of poisonous things down there, besides the snakes and weird ducks, there were the spiders. One day I was sitting in my 'dunnyhouse' with the door open reading the paper, I turned the page and there was an article about the number of deaths in men from using a dunnyhouse and being bitten on the Johnston by the 'brown back' spider. Its poison had to be sucked out like a snake bite, or you died. With my little catholic 'Hoosier', a bite like that was a death sentence.

Remember the joke, Tonto say, Ke-mo-sah-bee, you goin' to die! There I just gave away my age. Anyway, I jumped up and ran down to the little hardware store in town and bought every can of 'Black Flag' he had, then ordered an entire case. I went back and sprayed every square inch of that dunnyhouse, there wasn't anything under gods Sun that could live through the carpet bombing I provided.

Up to this point I have not spent anytime describing my wife #2, its' easy to understand, when I go there my blood will crystallize in my veins, I will get to it, but not now.

Let's get back to spiders. In my bedroom was a giant spider called a Huntsman, This 'animal' had big hairy legs and was as big as a dinner plate. I asked my colleagues about it and was told not to scare it away; they were harmless to humans. As long as they were there nothing would bother you, meaning everything from an insect to a snake. So we lived together under an uneasy truce; until one night. After a period of time I ignored it because it was always in the same place. Then one night I went to bed and had been reading the hardcover copy of the 'Omen' I was on the part about the dogs in the cemetery with yellow eyes. Well, I picked up the book and brought it up to my face, you guessed it; my Huntsman was sitting on the book. We scared each other to death. I threw the book up in the air and bolted for the door naked as the day I was born. Huntsman must have went and packed its little bandana on the end of a stick and found a new home.

I also had possums living inside the walls, they would chase each other around and then there was heavy breathing. My neighbor brought a man who successfully trapped them all. It didn't fix the haunting.

One day I was approached by an English teacher from New Zealand, she asked me to tape books for the slow readers. They had a program where the kid could check out a cassette recorder with headphones and pick out a book and cassette tape, they would then read and listen to the tape at the same time. She was having trouble getting the right books, so I said yes. I built a boom in my studio with a microphone on it. Then set aside a morning when I would read the book, we aren't talking 'War and Peace' here. I popped in a cassette and read aloud. I decided to give it a bit more life so I used some voice changes or maybe some sound effects. There is a tab on the back of a cassette tape that can be broken off which won't allow anything to be taped over it. On Monday I'd turn in two or three tapes. I must admit, it was the most gratifying experience I can remember. Kids would come up to me in the halls and say all kinds of good things about the book they were reading. My teacher friend said there was now a waiting list; and the new books were like major 'show openings'. It feels good to know I may have influenced some young person; at least to continue reading; they needed professionals in that country. At that time in Australia, they 'main streamed' classes, which meant putting all of the deadheads in one class. I had an all-girl class like that every Thursday; my last day of work before a long weekend. Some of these girls were real bad. A few of them would sit in the front row of desks and show me they didn't have any underwear on under their skirts. Fortunately I had a 'Masters' class of 'proper ethics' which dealt with this exact type of behavior; it helped, to a point. There was another girl who would chew on a leek while in class, smelling up the entire room, really distracting. One day she showed up with a black eye. I asked the school social worker about her and she said the girls' father had been sexually abusing her for years. We had a parent teacher night and I had the pleasure of meeting this piece of crap, it took everything in my power to not beat the fat bastard to within an inch of his life. But I couldn't do a thing. After that I treated this girl differently. I let up on her, and was pleased to teach her a little bit about sculpture. One day I asked Trevor to look at my paycheck because there was a good size sum added to this one. He told me it was a bonus for showing up every day. I said you can't be serious, they reward you for being here every day; isn't that just part of the job? He said so many teachers called off sick, they just didn't want to come into work and would rather stay home and put some meat on the 'barbie'; that was the attitude concerning work. Now this is in 1976 & 77, I do hope that has changed. Trevor himself would be standing by the door promptly at 3pm; in fact all the cars in the lot would be vying for position at the gate. That was why there were so many kids wandering the halls; and many begged to get into my classroom. That holiday break I received 10 weeks with pay.

My holiday was prior to my inviting future wife #2 to join me. Up until that time I was a happy bachelor. I did a bit of traveling before I was approached by a friend who asked if I wanted to make some money during my time off. He offered me a job with a funeral parlor business in Melbourne called Tobin's. I decide to give it a go. I was fitted for a few suits with some light blue oxford shirts and burgundy ties. We worked 12 hour days, 6 days a week, and remember this is the Australian winter; hot. I made a lot of money just being paid as a casual laborer; but there was nothing casual about the job. We did up to four funerals a day; usually two cremations and two 'dirt burials' (as they called them). I met my friend, Ian, at a small gym in Upwey where we were both pumping iron. He could actually jump, do a back flip, and then land in the same spot; so he was in really good shape for a small guy. So we both were capable of handling some heavy weight.

On one job, when we showed up at the church, he said 'mate, we're screwed'. It was an extra wide casket, built to hold at least 350 pounds. The Tobin's also provided a man in top hat and tails that monitored everything so it all went smoothly. He'd stand at the door to the church; Ian would ask' what's he doin'? He look in and say "he's getting ready to feed 'em" a bit later, "he's washin' up." We would then put on our jacket and ties; show time. There were little signals that the pall bearers would use. One tap on the casket meant get ready, and the second tap was to lift, the third tap was to place it on our shoulders. On this particular job, we had trouble lifting it; on the third try we got it and then had to walk steadily out of the church down the steps to the hearse, without dropping it. The real horror was when we got to the cemetery; the grave site was about 100 yards from the road, thankfully a couple of the workers gave us a hand.

On another occasion; I opened the hearse, grabbed the coffin and the end came off in my hands. There were two bare feet sticking out; Ian quickly hammered the wooden end back on. The families supplied the wardrobe, so I guess they didn't think he'd need shoes.

On another occasion, Ian and I had plans with two hot dates at 8pm; it was now 6pm. The dispatcher tells us that we have to drop off two caskets for the next days' services. When Ian saw the manifest he started cursing like a sailor; which wasn't like him. He said the churches were on two different ends of the city. Melbourne was a huge city; it could take 4 hours to drive across it. And so we set out, he let me drive, and that I did; almost 100mph most of the way. The cops never stopped a hearse. We rolled one casket into the church, wiped it clean then sped to the next. We made it back at 5 minutes to 8. The only problem was we had put the catholic in the protestant church and the, well you guessed it. Tobin had to eat both funerals, about $12,000. Ian got his butt chewed, but they needed us, so we still had our jobs. On occasion we had to pick up a corpse and transport them to one of the 13 Tobin locations; we would go to a hospital morgue for the "candidate" as they were called.

One memorable time was when Ian pulled off the sheet at the morgue and there was a beautiful 23 year old woman who had OD'd on something. They hadn't done an autopsy, so there she lay, naked, and beyond a '10'. We stood there staring, until we realized we were transfixed. The trouble was we weren't repulsed. Then Ian said "There is hot water in that hose, mate". Then I said the Greeks had a word for this, necrophilia. We lingered a bit longer and said no, we can't, this is for life. With great care we transported her to the location on the manifest.

The next one must have been our punishment; another female corpse. We transported this young woman to the hospital. After she was in the hearse, a man in a white coat came out and handed me a cup to take with us, he said it was the afterbirth; the woman had died in childbirth.

I did my share of killing in Vietnam, but never stopped to look upon them as anything but dead people. I created dead people; they were hostiles. And now I'm working for a company that ritualizes their burial. Is this more than one person has to know?

Now it is time to tell you about wife #2. While living in Boulder, I was drinking in a club called 'Potters', a 'meat market', and I met these two women. One was a brunette and quiet, the other was a blond, and, well, let's just say she liked to party. The blond was from Texas and having a great time while staying with the quiet brunette. The blond and I hooked up and partied for the entire week. She left town, but left me with a dose of STD without any symptoms. Clap in its original form comes with symptoms a man never forgets. This petri dish was carrying something new, but I'll spare you the details. So the doctor tells me I must tell this to any partners I had sex with, and pay for their treatment. The brunette, wife number two, didn't know any of this, and I don't know how she found me, but she shows up one day at my apartment with a loaf of fresh bread. After she left, I found that she had left behind a small purse. (This is an important event, as it will show up again in a future chapter). The next day I got a call and she was back over to my place again; and again and again. We then continued an on again off again relationship; which eventually landed her in Australia.

Before she was allowed to leave the United States, she had to settle her credit problems. She had maxed out her credit cards, so me, the dope, paid the $6000 for her closet contents, so she could join me. She was given a Visa limit of three months; after that she either departed or got married. I could stay because Australian citizenship was part of my contract, of which I still have.
I'll tell you a little story about her. I decided to take her on a nice weekend getaway. We went to the beach and that night we were to have dinner at 'Maxims;' yes a real Maxims. She loved the sun and a tan, but the sun in Australia is strong, and I tried to warn her of that. She ignored me and spent the whole day in worship services. At the restaurant, I had

to order the entire meal and wines as soon as we had a chance to look at the menu. As we were sitting there waiting for the first appetizer, sipping wine. I happened to glance up, and miss tanning lotion had turned white and unresponsive. I knew exactly what it was and it was serious. About that time, the stuffed mushrooms arrived. I asked for a cab ASAP, and gathered her up; she was barely lucid. With my free hand I grabbed a stuffed mushroom and popped it in my mouth on the way out the door. She ended up in the ER where she was treated for heat stroke; the doctor said if left untreated it could have been fatal. Meanwhile $181 dollars went on my credit card, Maxims does not do 'take out'. That was one expensive stuffed mushroom.

I completed my work on the curriculum that I was hired to write and presented it very professionally in bound volumes with clear illustrations and instructions. It was a big hit with the big shots of the Victoria Educational Department, so while I had them, I asked to have my contract reduced to 18 months, rather than the two years I had signed up for. After taking everything I had done into consideration; the night classes and the taped books, they agreed. I really didn't want to do this, but I didn't want to marry this woman either.

I apologize for being slightly out of sequence with my Australia experience, but there are a few more stories that I'd like to fit in. I traveled around this huge continent as much as I could on my holiday breaks. I toured all of the state of Victoria, then made a trip to Adelaide and drank my way down their grape producing valley until someone called ahead to warn them of the American on the way; and I had only three more winery's to go. I took a train to Sydney and back. Interesting to note; you had to change trains at the border as the rails were a different gauge. There was a rivalry between the states, each had its own game, beer, vineyards, everything. If you weren't from their state you were dog poop. The capital, Canberra, was in the middle of nowhere; which is exactly half way between Melbourne and Sydney. They actually dug a lake to look like a river, so you could drive over a bridge to get into town.

I made a few trips to Tasmania, and my only regret is not taking a plane that flew from there to South Antarctica. The plane didn't land; it just flew around so you could see the sights. They had taken a few rows of seats out so you could get some good photos. It cost $250 which included food and booze, Years afterward I read about the plane that crashed into the mountain in the middle of the continent.

And finally there is this little piece that could be called "Snooker to Shark." I would have deleted it but there is a large presence later on after I return to the U.S.

One of my other mates was a guy named David, he worked for 'Foster's Brewing Co'; come to think of it all my mates had decent jobs. But David had another passion; he was a 'star' snooker player. The game of Snooker is played on large pool tables, 9 X 12 feet to be exact. It is a form of billiards which in America would be simply called 'dirty pool.' I have no desire to write a complete description of the game because it would be boring and a long time has passed so I would question some of my own facts. Let me just say, you could be losing a game by l50 points, and through the use of 'english' on the cue ball, come out winning. All of the games were based on points earned and you kept score by taking the long cue stick and moving the wooden markers above your head that were suspended on a tight wire. If your opponents could not make a critical shot, they forfeited the points to you.

David had me join the RSL club, or, Returned Servicemen's League, similar to our VFW or American Legion. Every Sunday (that was another reason to join; beer on Sunday) they would have a solemn ceremony dedicated to the fallen Australians at 'Gallipoli' during WWI, and they had really great snooker rooms. It is interesting to note that back then, women were not allowed anywhere near the snooker tables, it was strictly a man's' sport.

David made me his 'apprentice', he would draw in the other guys and run up the value of the game by using me as his decoy, missing shots, scratching and other stupid things. Then when it was time he would step in and clean their clocks, we would then split the money 60/40 because I still needed a lot of work. After playing snooker for well over a year with him, I learned a form of reserved finesse. David spent hours with me, showing me the finer points to proper 'english' on the cue ball, being able to knowingly place that ball anywhere you wanted. He needed me as his stooge or 'shill' if I can borrow a carney term, in order to draw in the bigger money. We travelled all over the City of Melbourne, mainly playing RSL clubs because they were safer, as my game improved so did my earnings.

One weekend we drove to 'Angels Cove' a small beach resort off of the Queens Highway, a two lane blacktop road without any guard rails. The road ran right along the coast and at one turn you could see the 12 sisters; large rock formations sticking out of the ocean.

We started at the first RSL near the turn off onto the Queens road, and played our way until they ended. In the process we made enough money to pay for our entire holiday. It was night when I drove the last miles into Angels Cove. We had a case of beer in the back seat of my 1967 VW, a car that I grew to really dislike even though it didn't let me down. There's David and Jason wheeling around these corners with headlights that were like church candles, but we made it and so did our reputation, no one wanted to play us on the snooker tables, it seems that someone had ratted us out in advance.

One thing that I can tell you is this, after playing on those huge tables, a typical 8 ball table in a U.S. gin mill was sheer massacre.

When I returned from Australia, I bought a really good two piece cue stick that came with an aluminum case; the old man who sold it to me told me that it would come in handy and that was all. I then set out to make some money, but the only problem is that shooting for large money in America is not always the civilized game I was accustomed to. More than once that cue stick case stunned my irate loser long enough for me to make my exit, the old man was right. It didn't take long for the word to get around when there was serious money on the rail. One game of 8-ball could go for $500, and if I won the coin toss for the break, the game was over. I had become a pool shark, that was my title, usually when they saw the case come out from under my jacket, they knew at that very moment that they had been played like a one holed piccolo. I preferred the term' out-played. In the game of straight pool, you would set a number of balls to be played 100, 200, then arrive at a value for each ball. If it was a 100 ball run at a dollar a ball, you get the picture. Again, if I won the toss it was over, I rarely missed, but if my opponent won I would just sit and listen for that unmistakable sound of the cue stick mistake; and then it was Showtime! I ran the table, picked up my cash and left. The night finally came when I was playing a large money table in New Jersey; I didn't like it, but had no choice. I hustled this guy and did really well, as I was getting ready to leave, I felt the cold steel on the back of my neck, he not only took his money; he grabbed mine as well. That was when I put away my stick and never played pool again. End of story.

We disembarked at Hawaii. I had a gay steward who decided how much I was going to drink during that long flight from Sydney. Wife Halo and I stayed at the Coral Reef Hotel, my old Navy haunt and I was happy to hear that Davy Jones Locker was doing just fine. We walked around Honolulu and heard that distinct song, Don Ho was still belting out his only hit 'Tiny Bubbles', well it was his nightclub. When wife 2 heard this she told me that she loved this song! I looked at her in disbelief. Then she told me again, another red flag. I could not believe how anyone our age could embrace a stupid piece of music like that. In the distance I heard Bikini atoll blow up again and turned and walked away looking for another once in a lifetime experience.

After a few days and the coffers almost empty, I thought a thousand dollars would go further than this; though I didn't look in her suitcase, I am sure there would have been some designer bathing attire stuffed in there somewhere. She was going to San Francisco to visit friends so she needed more money, whereas I was flying right through Chicago to Wilkes-Barre so I wouldn't need a lot. What her plan did not take into account were the many drink carts they pushed around on the plane. My pockets where almost dry, after all of the money I made in Australia, I was broke. On the flight I met a few sailors who just happened to have Thai stick. It had such an exotic scent that it didn't offend anyone near us, so we passed a few joints the size of a blue tipped match and I was bonkers, this stuff was crazy. The stewardess came back and told us it was 3 am and that our laughing was keeping passengers awake. We apologized, bid our farewells and returned to our seats and went into a dream sleep; probably the American Indians have. We were the last flight allowed to land at O'Hara airport, as usual there was a blizzard and the place was socked in. After a few hours, I finally got a hotel and meal voucher from those cheap bastards and went below to catch a shuttle, when the two glass doors opened I nearly fainted from the blast of cold air. It was 95 degrees when I left Australia. Finally the right shuttle came by and I asked if I could sit on his dashboard where the heat was, he said no, then drove me to my hotel. I then went into the dining room and approached the bar manager and asked how many Manhattans this dinner voucher was worth, I explained that I was on a strict liquid diet and it had to be alcohol to kill the parasites. She gave me a number, I drank them and tipped the waitress with a handful of Australian coins I found in my leather bag, she wasn't impressed. It was on to the room and a shower, a little sleep then back on the shuttle the next morning; to grab anything going east.

Allow me to explain something. Because I had no intention of marrying this catholic nun candidate, I had to work twice as hard. I finished my rather lengthy curriculum package, complete with pen & ink illustrations ,so that I could approach the Victoria school board and make my presentation; with the caveat that I could shorten my contract. What they didn't know was that there were the two guys in black suits at my front door asking me if I was married, the 6 months were up that day. I begged them and explained my work and they gave me a 3 month extension but that was it, no marriage certificate and she was gone.

Before leaving Australia I gathered up a collection of items and packed them for transport by ship, back to the U.S. My father and I went to the World Trade center where the shipping company's office was located and found out the crate was there on a dock in New Jersey. What they didn't tell me was to take a fistful of $50 dollar bills with me to grease the forklift wheels and a few other Marlon Brando's. It was our third attempt when I received this information, suddenly the crate appeared and the grease allowed it to slide right into my father's truck with great ease. Everyone was smiling except me; three times we drove down here. That crate had some valuable stuff in it; cases of aged tawny port, some musical instruments from the native people, about a thousand slides some of which I sold the rights too for $120 bucks apiece. I made a tidy sum off that crate and finally had some money. I bought another MGB from my younger brother, it was an l970 'split bumper' version with electric overdrive that actually worked; don't laugh it was a Lucas arrangement which usually was broken.
I applied for a position as a Drug and Alcohol counselor; I had the undergraduate work in psychology for the certificate from the State but the boss lady knew I was over qualified for the job, she hired me anyway. This in turn allowed me to rent an apartment in Wilkes-Barre on the 'river commons' as it was called. I worked a 6 week swing shift and it was difficult to adjust to. The place was a 7 day in-house rehab that supplied food and a bed. Most of the customers were snowbirds as they are called, they checked in to a place like

this to build up their strength, see doctors, and then head south for the winter to continue drinking in Florida. The guys I worked with were real dopes and I grew to hate this job until the boss approached me about putting a slide show together to raise funds for another year, this was during Mrs. Reagans' just "say no" days. What she meant was just 'say no' to any funding for alcohol and drug addiction; that is how it turned out. With the help of a retired disc jockey, who did the voice over, I put together a really convincing piece of propaganda. Unfortunately it fell on deaf ears and the budget was not renewed. At that very time the employment office called me about a job opening working in a maximum security prison. Because I was a veteran, I had a 10 point lead for all of the good jobs in town. After several meetings with guys in suits, I was offered the job under one condition, in front of three witnesses' I had to sign 2 serious documents, #1. Was that they would not, under any circumstances, negotiate for my life if I was being held by inmates; and #2. I agreed to submit to complete strip search and body cavity inspections at any time they deemed it to be, meaning of course, without warning.

My first job was to take an extensive 10 week course, 8 hours a day, 5 days a week including gunnery practice to receive a diploma from the Department of Corrections Institute in Boulder, Colorado. I passed everything with flying colors except the hand gun exercises, which were really close. I had to really do some target shooting over a weekend and take the test again, just squeaking by. Upon completion of this course and a full security check, I was now a Civil Service employee of the State Correctional Institution at Dallas, PA. The first call came from the big cheese; he wanted me in his office ASAP. Once I got there, he threw a set of keys to me and a State Visa card and told me to take my time and go to every other prison in the State and visit their Arts & Crafts shops and to steal all of their best ideas and bring them back here then implement them in our shop. This man had big plans and I was to answer to him

207

only, he told me that I was the prefect man for the job, my education, the Vietnam experience, everything. He was looking forward to a long and fruitful relationship, but I was to tell no one of our plans. I picked up the credit card, gave him a sharp salute and said: Sir you can count on me and thank you, sir! I then turned on one heel and headed for the door out to the parking lot and into a waiting brand new Ford with State tag's on it, this meant that 100 mph was the norm without worries of State Police interdiction, just remember to wave. I stopped at our garage and made arrangements to have my car brought back from the prison, packed a bag and was on my way. The Superintendent had called ahead of me so they were expecting me everywhere I went. Except King of Prussia where they have some great men's outlet stores, top labels and low prices, it all went on the card, I had to look the part didn't I? This also went for the hotels I stayed in and the cocktail lounges I would hang around in both before and after dinners of King Crab, lobster and steak. I knew a thing or two about padding the daily account.

It was the spring of 1977, my position entailed taking and old, well equipped arts & crafts shop and turn it into a production facility. We were to create products to sell in our visitor's center and I had made some arrangements while on the road to sell certain items in other visitor centers where they didn't have an excellent leather person, or wood worker. I used the two guys that were left over to spit shine the place while I went into the records office and found my 16 man crew based on a number of criteria. I didn't want any nut case's, and I found out that 'lifers' made the best workers because they never bitched. I would not hire anyone with less than 6 years in the joint. After this, I sent the two guys away that cleaned because I smelled a rat somewhere and brought in the first 15 guys one by one with orders to show me their wares. It basically worked; I had a good crew of 12 men to start with and would add the rest via recommendations. We had a leather department, with an Indian guy who hated everyone, a wood working shop run by

208

a guy doing double life, he was older and wiser than most, a ceramics department run by a huge man who had, well it wouldn't be proper nor beneficial for me to mention only he had 4 life sentences for murders but was deathly afraid of bats.

The most interesting part that very few knew was that all the profits went into the prisoner relief fund. This fund was designed to help wives and their kids during their husbands' incarceration. A worthy and noble cause made even more important by the fact that the man behind it wanted this to be kept under wraps. I got anything I asked for, if my leather man said buy $4000 worth of hides, in different thickness and quality, I ordered the hides. The guy I replaced became paranoid of the inmates and only allowed one or two down there at a time, in the tool shed, there was at least $25K of hardwoods, 25 years old, perfectly dried and ready for something. I wanted cutting boards and special handmade chess sets for starters, everything was standing on grain, because I had all of the power equipment needed, my old lifer was in heaven being put in charge of all of these machines. I wouldn't go near them; I liked my fingers too much.

One thing I did on our first day when everyone was gathering around my desk was to put my finger on a spot. I then dropped this large ring of keys on that spot and told them they would be there every day if anyone needed them for any reason. I then told them that I was here to kick ass and I wasn't a lawyer or a judge, I had nothing to say about anyone's past, it was the present that mattered. I didn't care what anyone did to get in here but I was going to work their balls off and pay them the highest wage there was from the start; .16 cents per hour. These guys at first were dumb founded, they were not accustomed to being treated as men; they were a number. I put a stop to that, I told them that we used our real names or, nicknames and there was never to be any numbers mentioned in here, ever.

I had a man from the education department upstairs who

tried to tell me he was my boss. He was a sneaky person and had a couple of little inmates that he used to get information about what went on in my shop. He tried real hard to have me busted for something, but failed. When my leather goods started to disappear; expensive purses and wallets; I laid a trap. It always happened on weekends when no one was supposed to be in there. Fortunately, the Captain of the guards used to work for my father, so I approached him when there was a large inventory, waiting to be shipped. He quietly posted a guard in my shop and waited, it wasn't long when the axe fell.

As for his little spies, the one wise guy was making Nunchucks, a martial arts weapon of two sticks with a chain between them. I waited until he had them almost done, the fool actually put his name on something which could increase his sentence up to 10 years; these were considered deadly weapons. You do not make yourself a deadly weapon in prison. Just at the right time, 4 guards came in and cuffed the guy; he was in a world of hurt. More importantly my secret boss had him banned from ever setting foot in this space again, he figured right; there was another big dog on the porch.

Coming up on 9 months I had the place running like a Rolex watch. Then winter set in and I hate winter, always have since I was a child, this would prove to change everything.

Late in the winter the year before I had broken down and went out to Indiana and picked up Ms. Fashion plate. It was a crazy thing to do, my car acted up so I borrowed my brother Marks 350 Porsche. It was an I963 'bath tub' model that ran like great guns. The only problem was they are not known for heat. So I drove almost straight through, stopping once to sleep for a few hours at a truck stop. This car had less room then my MGB and she brought out a ton of luggage, capped off with a guitar. I asked, since when did you play a guitar, she told me she didn't. Anyway enough of that dribble.

She lived with me until I turned in my resignation. During that time she landed a job at the City prison. This was really great, if you want to go through life without talking, become a Buddhist monk or have you and your significant other both work in prisons. There won't be a sound at night.

While all of this was going on I was still painting at my studio, I used an electric heater to supplement the pot belly coal stove. My paintings were being handled by a gallery in the Poconos, anywhere the money was and in the winter the Poconos were the place to be due to the ski resorts and the people from New York and Philadelphia. I was working on my poetry at that time; I won a few more awards and published a number of them in a few college anthologies. This was in preparation of putting together my first book to be published. I also was pool sharking at that time so early 1978 wasn't bad in terms of finances.

Undoubtedly my glowing success for that year had to be my work at the prison. I met and exceeded my secret boss's expectations. The shop was really getting a reputation for its quality wears. I had a full complement of employees, I6 in all. But the most amazing thing was the fact that during that entire period only one small screwdriver disappeared. It was taken by a Sunni Muslim because he feared for his life from the Shiites. The guy wasn't even connected with the place, but the guards came down, lined up my guys and stripped searched them right there in the shop, it was terrible and so demeaning a thing to do. They found the thing and it was with a guy who lifted it on a 'visit' to the Arts and Crafts area. We had hundreds and hundreds of tools in the tool room; anyone of them was a weapon. I gave that job to a guy who was perfect; his inventory and methods proved to be excellent for the control of so many potential weapons.

On Friday I had to go in at 1:00pm and stay until 8:30pm then open again on Saturday morning at 8:00am. Somebody had threatened to sue the prison because they were denied access to this area, it was a nuisance suit but it had to be addressed. That was a difficult few days for me. One Friday evening I came out and there was my MGB completely buried in a snow drift, 6 inches of the radio antenna was the only thing exposed. I called my father to come out and get me, then on the next day he gave me a ride out to work and afterward my oldest brother came out and the two of us dug out the car. That was it, my mind was made up; I was going back to Florida to finish my Master's Degree. On Tuesday I turned in my resignation allowing one month.

There was a lot to do, I bought a car and my other older brother and I fixed and re-painted it. The car was an old Ford 'Maverick' with a small 6 cylinder and a stick shift. I really hated to drive the thing but it wasn't for me, it was for her. I then got rid of the apartment and moved in with my older brother Bill for about 10 days, both my little dumpling and I kept working until the end, I had to because of my civil service contract and wording of the resignation, basically the dates.

Many things did transpire during my stay in my "Dirty Old Town" and I can assure you it was just that. During the final days at the prison, a few guys came up to me and asked a favor which amounted to turning my back to something that wasn't well received there. It dealt with a little guy named 'Cheeseburger, who gave head for a living; that was his job in jail; as it was explained to me. The price would be one carton of cigarettes. I told them to go ahead but to be very discreet about it or my ass would be in a jam. Cheeseburger showed up and went into the bathroom that didn't have a door, this was standard policy. They posted a lookout and one by one the guys would make their way to the bathroom to be serviced you might say. I stayed at my desk with my back to it all; my desk faced the other way to begin with. He made this trip on a few occasions and one day my guys asked me if I wanted to indulge, their treat, I graciously declined.

By treating these men as human beings and with respect, they in turn treated me the same. To have a tool room like that and only have one small screwdriver go missing, and it wasn't even one of my crew, was a milestone in the prison. Just before I left, while the Superintendent was away, I saw my opportunity to bring in my 35mm camera and shot the inside of the prison. This was so illegal and banned I could have been burned at the stake. Actually I used my network you might say, to compose a letter with a forged signature on it saying that I was allowed to do this for a very professional reason. I shot 136 shots using available light so as not to draw too much attention to myself. It was the perfect coup; these photos were like gold and would help me later that year. On one of my last night's there, an old friend of my fathers from the coal mines sat down with me in the dining room to have dinner. He started by telling me that he heard about my decision to put in my resignation. He then went on to say: "…Goodman, I've been here 27 years and I wish I had the guts to do what you are doing now; getting out. Listen the money is good, the benefits and all of that other crap, but after a period of time this job and this place rots your soul and leaves an empty hole. Don't listen to anybody about that good job shit, keep doing what you're doing, and get out of here before you rot. It can't be much of a job when you can't even talk to your own wife when you get home. Have you noticed that when you stop for a beer nobody wants to hear a word about this place? (I had noticed that at my local watering hole.) You go and don't look back and tell your old man that Stash the Hunky said hello." He then got up and walked away without looking back.

I prepared my MGB for the trip, tires, brake's everything it needed. I helped load her stuff, including the guitar which sat in the corner for almost a year and never was played, into the Maverick and sent her off to Indiana, hoping that this was it, or at least that's what I told myself. The entire horizon was covered with little red flags and I still could not see, I was color blind due to a touch of esteem issues, I didn't know at the time, it was crazy.

213

I bid my family ado and jumped into the little green sports car and took off South, it was cold but I thought I would drive out of it as I headed over the Mason Dixon Line; but that wasn't to be, I froze my lily ass off all the way to Boca Raton and then some.

I failed to mention that during my stay in Pennsylvania I attended classes at college Misericordia and racked enough credits for another Bachelor's Degree in Art History but no one handed me one because I did it with electives rather than the prescribed catalog course. I went out of the lines with my educational crayons, but I know. One thing about knowledge, it turns into wisdom if it's fermented correctly.

Mary T. once told me that if you hit your late 50's or, early 60's and have one really good friend, you are fortunate, if you have two then you are truly blessed. I had a couple more but they died young. One of my best friends lives in Florida, when I could get away from my classes I would run up to Lakeworth and visit him. On one visit, his older sister was there. I didn't even know he had an older sister. She was quite nice and very pleasant to the eye in every respect. As it turns out, she had just finished going through a very ugly divorce from a real prick and she was visiting my buddy. I think that I was supposed to be there at that time. We hit it off from the start.   I was in good shape and still had my looks and a full head of hair. She had several years on me but it didn't matter; the conversation was vibrant and full, I made her laugh a lot and Rick was happy to see that. He told me she had been crying since she got there and that this divorce was an affront to her personally. I asked her if she was busy for a few days and free to go 'walk about' with me. She hesitated then thought why not; what did she have to lose. If I was Rick's best friend I had to be a decent guy or he wouldn't condone it. To begin with, I told her we had to cleanse her soul and mind, with that I had brought her to my old German lady's place. I had called ahead and told her to fire up the boilers. Fraulein ran an old fashioned sauna which included her own steam and each sauna had a wooden bucket and Melaleuca branches for slapping the skin to bring out the toxins. I explained this to my date, it seemed to me that she needed to have some toxic entity removed from her soul and this was the way to do it. She was game, at first the nudity was somewhat awkward but she got used to it quickly because it was just that, being nude, nothing else. These places were really funky, old and reeked of personality. After our cleaning, we headed south. It was a nice night so I threw back the top and we drove along with the breeze in our faces. After a few hours we were in the upper Keys and I found a nice hotel with a great view of the ocean. Prior to leaving I told her to pack a little bag just in case; Rick said, with Jason you never know where you will end up, but where ever it is it will be nice. I stopped at the university and threw some stuff into my trusty leather bag and threw it into the boot. After checking in we went for a walk on the beach and found a great little seafood place for dinner; and it was great simple fare. Afterward we headed back to the hotel and sat around on the balcony sipping wine and talking about everything, I didn't press any issues and kept the conversation innocent and happy you might say, when it was time to go to bed we did just that, I said goodnight and put my back to her and fell asleep. A man can feel the atmosphere if he is in tune with the person he's with. I didn't even ask for a kiss, nothing but a nice sleep with the doors open and the sound of waves lapping. The next morning after a light breakfast, we slowly made our way down the Keys. That first stop was Key Largo. I was in no hurry and the slower speed made conversation humane. I thought this is Ricks' sister, that is blood, and Rick was my friend; plus I got the impression she had a broken wing. Our next stop was a small hotel again on the water. I ducked out and grabbed some provisions, wine, cheese, bread and a few sweets. We used the pool and then ended the day with our beatnik dinner and nice jazz in the background from a Miami station. That was when she took my hand and led me into bed, slowly stripping off my clothes, while I did the same to her. The love making was passionate and almost needy; she had to have this tender touch of a sensitive man. I just let her go and make up the schedule. It went on all night like this and I did nothing to disrupt it, this woman had a deep sorrow and an even deeper need. It was not my place to ask where it was coming from, I just knew that she needed all of this and was happy to have supplied the blank canvas. She now had a smile on her face.

We both knew what this was, it wasn't a relationship, it was what it was; two people, a man and a woman, and one of those individuals needed an emotional release from a very painful experience.

I told her I would only stay until her darker thoughts had passed and she felt like herself again. After a few more days and nights a transformation had taken place. She got her strength back and seemed to once again enjoy her life. We returned to Rick's place and he was pleased to see her happy. We both knew this was not to be a permanent thing, but just to make it easier to part, I showed up drunk the following night. She went on to meet Mr. Right and they made a fortune building spec houses in Las Vegas.

While looking for a part for my MGB, I met a man who was in need of an English car mechanic; and happened to have a room to rent in his large house in Boyton Beach. I said yes twice, and moved into my "en suite' room. I worked and was making a good wage. Then I did a stupid thing, I invited the soon to be #2 down to Florida; a bigger mistake than I realized.

The guy who hired me was in his 40's and he had a 19 year old girl friend that was living with him. The girls didn't get along from the get go. The 'chick' had a dirt bag 'friend' who needed a place to stay, so he moved into the garage. She called him 'Grandpa'; a real mooch who would eat and drink anything he could find, that wasn't purchased by him; which was everything. One day I made a beer run and took a path through the bushes in the yard. On the way back I fell and cut my leg pretty bad on a piece of rebar. It quickly became infected with a flesh eating disease from human fecal matter; grandpa had been using that area as his latrine. I went nuts on him and then the girl wanted me out. Now she hated both of us.

He had an Audi sitting in the Shop garage and the motor was scattered everywhere. He asked if I could put that thing back together; nuts and bolts everywhere. It wasn't an easy job, but I did it and with that won the respect of the other guys in the shop; as it had been sitting in the garage for over 6 months. Boss called the owner and he shows up with his typical spoiled rotten Florida teenage son to drive the car away. The next day it was out there in front of the shop. The guy was screaming and threatening attorneys etc. So I got the job of ripping the engine apart. Every push rod was bent; the result of his kid driving the thing like a hot rod; which neither one of them were. Boss charged him double to fix the damage.

I made money and I went to university. Future wife #2 got a position as a paralegal and started working for a big law firm. We then began looking for another place to live. Finally, I quit the job and just concentrated on my degree. She was willing and able, to support me for a while.

I found a nice two bedroom end unit at a small self-contained little community just a few hundred yards from the beach. I finished my Masters and told them to mail me the diploma; it was sent to my old boss's house. He immediately gave me a call as he was afraid his girlfriend would tear it up; and told me to come by the shop on Saturday afternoon to pick it up. When I arrived the guys were all there and it turned out to be a party in my honor. I was really touched; nice guys, we grease monkey's. There was a big cooler full of freshly caught oysters, limes, hot sauce and Miller High Life to wash 'em down. Boss presented me with my parchment and a large wad of cash from a few jobs I hadn't been paid for. It was like winning the Nobel Prize.

They say that oysters put lead in your pencil. I went home full of them, but my catholic girl had no desire to put a point on mine. I will figure out why I stayed in this relationship; I'll tell you about it later.

There were a few small houses in the community where our apartment was located; and one of them became available. It was a one bedroom with an ocean view, we moved in around the end of 1979.

An old associate/ friend of mine from Wilkes-Barre arrived in Florida from Iran. He had $50,000 duck taped to his chest. He had been working there as an engineer and got out when the politics got dangerous. I found him an apartment right on the beach; same place my parents would stay when the big day arrived. Meanwhile my little 'Hoosier' decided to fly back to Indiana for Xmas. Not long after her departure a rental convertible pulled up in front and there were the Wilkes-Barre guys; the one with the cash and the attorney on vacation. They told me to pack a bag and hop in; we're going on a tear.

First I had to feed my dearest ones sour dough. She had this big glass jar for about twenty years (remember the loaf of bread in Boulder?) and you constantly had to feed it as it was a living organism. I figured it was possible I could be gone with these guys for two weeks so I dumped sugar and flour in the jar, closed the fridge and made a dash for the rag top. The Cash man bought a half kilo of top grade cocaine from someone he knew and packed a bottle of Percodan for any hangovers. I supplied the booze for the trip, and loaded it in the trunk; this was looking like a deadly combination. We started out on A1A, the ocean road near my house, and headed to the Keys. At every stop we were an attraction for girls; those who liked to screw for copious amounts of cocaine in exchange. It was a madcap adventure and should have been videotaped; especially since I can only remember parts of it.

Remember the sour dough? Well when I got home and opened the refrigerator, a huge blob fell out onto my bare feet, the thing was a monster, and worse yet, it was a bitch to clean up and there seemed to be a half ton there. When little bumpkins came home, she asked me where her sour dough was, I told her it either died of old age or commented suicide. Another 7 day period with no talking except the initial, how could you? Well, it was simple, you should have written the instructions down about how to feed this thing, plus if you go to 'Piggly Wiggly' up the road, they sell it there. But you don't understand, that was given to me by divine intervention I suppose, look, there is an old saying, don't cry over obese sour dough, now, can we put this behind us?

IMAGES MAY VARY

Prior to leaving for Maine, I had acquired an 'agent' to handle my artwork in Florida. It started out really well; paintings were being sold and he was getting commissions on every one. I told him about going to Maine and said in about three months new work would be arriving. He was also in the framing business so receiving my rolled canvases without stretcher bars was no problem, he re-stretched and framed and exhibited.

This house had an outhouse also; it was round and made of stone. The shingle roof was firm and it really had a nice look about it. Naturally I sprayed the place entirely and placed a bucket of 'sweet lime' in the corner…hummm does a circle have a corner? Anyway the lime controlled the smell and the finishing touches were toilet paper and a Cosmopolitan magazine. It was 'store bought' toilet tissue, but she hated it just the same.

The house was looking good. I had a 1943 'Gibson' gas operated refrigerator; it ran on propane. That thing was a real mystery; there was a flame at the bottom that shot into a black box and then less than four feet away were ice cubes. I am still intrigued! The kitchen had two stoves; one a cast iron wood burner and the other fueled by propane gas. I bought a chainsaw and on certain days I worked as a lumberjack cutting wood for the four fireplaces and the kitchen stove.

I bought two brass platters at a yard sale and polished them. Then I nailed them behind a tableside kerosene lamp; you would be surprised at the amount of light that system could project.

She took a job at an ocean front resort as a hostess, which meant that I would not have a car; but I had my boat. I bought a sweet 1957 Mercury outboard motor for it; the thing was only a couple horsepower; but it never let me down.

The only problem I had to face was the tide; it would go out 12 to 14 feet. I had to use a tide chart and keep a close eye on the time. If I spent too much time screwing around in town, when I returned, I could be 50 feet from the dock. I'd have to walk through the smelly mud; sometimes up to your knees. I had a window of about three hours. I could get up to the store, get groceries, and a case of 16 ounce beers; and then wander down the river, drinking beer and steering the boat with my bare feet, with hardly any house in view. That is when I got this nasty idea. I talked my loving wife into going with me, and then when we were in the middle of the river, with nothing around, I let out the one eyed snake and wanted her to take care of it; not too much for a husband to request. She did but she hated it more than the outhouse, or swimming back.

I started to have trouble with this stupid neighbor about the right of way. I went to the court house in Warren, the small town we lived in and produced papers 262 years old showing the road, but he didn't want to listen.
We were coming home from dinner in town one night, and there were trees across the road he had cut. I went ice cold and told her to hush. I grabbed my 410 over and under; it had a shotgun on the bottom and a high brass 22 caliber shell on top. There were two triggers and a selector switch; I went to put the feud to bed once and for all. I called that piece of dung out and told him to bring a gun; I wasn't going to fuck around anymore. He came out on his porch with a long gun and I shot the light out right next to his head; about 6 inches away. A nice shot if I say so myself. Then I let loose with the 410 shotgun and blew the window out of a dark room to his side. His wife started screaming about me being one of those twisted Vietnam vets and how dangerous this could be. He couldn't see me because I had the dark woods behind me and I could move undetected. The next shot came at him from an entirely different direction; about now his dinner was in his overalls. The State Police showed up; went to his house to speak to him, then came looking for me. The police told me that this guy had been a pain in the ass since he moved there and gave lots of people a hard time. He'd have to take my weapon for a period of 30 days; and took the extra rounds that were in my pocket. He then

224

told me to jump in the back of the cruiser. He drove me downtown, had me sign the papers for the gun and shells, and then drove me back home. Thirty days later I went to town, picked up my over and under, (which I still have) and suddenly I became a hero in town.

The policeman said he was glad I didn't have any 'claymore' anti-personnel mines with me, which made me think that was what he hoped I had used. This neighbor of mine needed someone to scare him; "The Man Who Shot Liberty Valance", etc. Suddenly people were waving to me, smiling; I was the guy who took matters into my own hands, and I never had a problem with him again.

My father wanted to come up and visit, probably to see what kind of job I'd done on the house. So I told him to bring another chainsaw. We spent a whole day cutting cords of wood for an old lady who lived up a dirt road from us. We not only cut it; but I split it and piled it. We cut enough wood for the entire winter. She came out with her little pocketbook and we told her to put it away; it was a gift.
All of that work was worth the look on her face.

Since I was mister popular du jour, we received an invitation to have dinner with the Mayor and his wife. During our conversations; the story about cutting the wood for the old lady was brought up and he thanked me for my generosity. But he also added that one of her neighbors, (a convicted felon) who lived down the road had called and reported that I stole the wood from her; but he knew the truth. Perhaps he should not have told me that part of the story. It was a shot at my personal integrity, again.
On the drive home I pulled up to the front of his house and did a donut on the crushed stone driveway, and stomped up onto his porch. I could see him inside and told him to come out. I could hear his wife begging him not to, as it was that crazed Vet guy from down the road.   After telling him I'd make hamburger out of him if I heard anything like that

again, I left. He was another guy that quit stirring up trouble. It was getting on into winter and the cold showers were even trying my strength. And at that point I had to cut wood for two days to provide enough for one. So we decided to pack it in. The owner came by and took a look at the place and said it was money well spent. I had just finished making shutters for all the windows and it was pretty secure. Now only he had a key for the place. He had a trunk full of whiskey and we had a fine send-off party; just what my woman wanted to see and hear!

My checks had run out, the sublet apartment in Florida would again be ours so we headed south. It had been quite a long time since I heard from my 'agent' so I decided to make a stop in Washington DC; at the Watergate Hotel, where my artwork was on display. They were pleased to meet me and asked if there was anything they could get for us to make us feel welcome. Not thinking they were really serious, I said some liquor and cocaine would be nice; but it all showed up in our hotel room.
The next day they gave me a check for the paintings that had sold. Those that did not, they would roll up and sent to me. I did some serious damage to my career that time; in other words, I was out. The rising star just faded, and fell from the sky.
It had to do with something I was unaware of at the time, a disorder called PTSD, as I got drunk on the balcony, something had triggered a memory and the rest was this uncontrollable urge to leap off the deck into the night, it was a terrible way to live I grant you, primarily due to the fact that I could not prepare for any given trigger. A certain song would come on and bang, I was there, color, smell everything and so was my frozen soul, which made me less than gracious.
Please don't misunderstand me; I cannot blame #2 or any person for what happened in Washington D.C., though I often wonder what she talked about after I passed out on the bed.

226

My little sweet thing had a lack of diplomacy in matters concerning her soon to be ex-husband.

As I sit here at 3am on my second floor porch with all of my writing equipment set before me, a nice discreet lamp, a fairly new black & white composition book and fine black pens that are not ball points, I hate ball points.
I know I haven't talked too much about my second wife; but it seems there are mostly bad memories. All the cars and plane tickets I paid for; Florida, Indiana, Australia and even Pennsylvania. Going without money so that she could line her wallet, and those maxed out credit cards which paid for a closet full of fashions. Then comes the blatant pile of hypocrisy, did she tell her priest about the well positioned purse during the pre-nuptial classes? How she 'set up' her husband to be. It's still hard for a man to live with the knowledge of being duped and taken advantage of. I am sure there are plenty of female readers saying join the club pal, we know all about it, how does it feel, is the shoe a little tight maybe?
The Chinese had taught me to 'save face', it didn't matter how much time passed, time in itself was not relevant, if pay back required a few generations it did not matter a bit, it was all about being patient, and striking when the moment arrived. I was making those plans because the moment was at hand.

It was early 1983 when we arrived back in Florida. I had decided that none of this was working and that we should reconsider our options. I was a victim of entrapment and as such there were certain rules. With this type of ruse you can never, under any circumstances, expose the real truth to the person who was deceived. As soon as the truth is revealed to the person involved, you will have lost the prize; one that a lie and other means helped you get.
Allow me to apologize for the harassment of my sweet, loving companion, she was a trophy wife and I had to say yes when the question was presented to me.

Also, allow me to comment on some of the violence in the past few pages. Some, if not all of it was warranted, there are those people that simply do not respond to civil gestures. But more importantly, Vietnam was really starting to manifest itself in the form of PTSD. As I mentioned prior, I had no real knowledge of this and if I had perhaps I would have sought some sort of treatment. Vietnam vets do not talk about what they endured, we kept it all inside; all of the danger, death and denial. I was a dangerous person to be around under the right circumstances, usually liquor, my only medication for the affliction, was involved in a sick ill- conceived soap opera.

There was only one woman of my dreams that meant anything to me and I didn't know her name, where she lived, nothing. I did not have a full definition of the word love in my itinerary of emotions. This word is still difficult for me to say and I do not take it lightly, I do not love New York, nor do I love breakfast cereals. It was an inward vision that I did not possess in 1983, it was another visit to the 7th level with Virgil again; there would be no peace or relief this year!

The answer is yes, I did end up marrying the one from Indiana who had lied to me and tricked me. It wasn't my desire to get married. I didn't think there wasn't any need for it. I gave this union 2 years and was right on the money. When I was told that I had to attend pre-nuptial classes and pay for the privilege, I went crazy. I went to exactly one, during the session the most violent electrical storm I have ever seen in Florida took place above the church; a catholic church. I stood up and told the priest that this was balderdash and to save his church from total destruction I would remove myself.

The day of the big event my good friend Rick and I went looking for my father, he was M.I.A. in Delray Beach. We stopped at the light by the tracks and there was 'Morley's', the most famous Irish drinking bar in South Florida, it was where St. Patty's parade started and ended every year, Rick turned to me and said, just one for old time's sake. I looked at that bar and knew exactly what would have occurred, both the groom and his best man would not be seen for days. One of the last times I was out drinking with Rick I ended up in Boise, Idaho; please do not ask because I don't know. Finally I said Rick, you know what will happen if we go in there; he reluctantly agreed. So we returned to my big mistake. There isn't much else to say except, doubt.

I became one of the walking dead until close to the end when I bought a motorcycle and started to hang around " Harry's" bar in Palm Beach with Ted Kennedy and the boys; this lead to a regression into debauchery and unabashed sexual encounters.
Prior to the stopover in Washington and the Watergate affair I spent some time in Pennsylvania, my brother Mark helped me again with a paint job on my Mercury Capri, and he was paid for all of these paint jobs I may add. In Maine I had to have the top of the engine rebuilt, so with new paint, sexy racing stripes and a rebuilt engine it was good for another few years of service. We then headed to Washington D.C. and on to Boynton Beach.

One day the UPS guy stopped and handed me a cardboard tube, there were 3 or 4 rolled paintings in there and a note explaining to me that they loved my work and realized a great future for it, I was the problem, as an artist I was too difficult to deal with, so here are your compositions and a check for one that was out when you were here. That was that, I just got fired from a prime location. I then found out that my 'agent' did not do a thing for me, his wife called the shots in that household, I gathered up my artwork and filled the MGB with it. I went to a gallery I had already had some work with, The Holly Daly Hermann gallery on Worth Avenue in Palm Beach, it was next door to Gucci's and Chanel. I suggested a one man show with this number of paintings available and she agreed as she picked out the best compositions and set the date. After a few weeks, I saw the advertisement in the newspaper and pointed it out to my Nun. The day of the show opening I was at my friend 'Bad Bob's house. We were sitting around sipping Ron Rico and lime on the rocks, telling lies until he said "...Jason, you have a one man show going on in Palm Beach right now!" I told him to grab the rum and some ice and get in the car; totally oblivious to what I was wearing. I had on a 'Ginny T-shirt, cut- off jeans and my 9 inch leather lace up work boots; quite an outfit for Palm Beach. When we got to Worth Avenue it was packed, I drove around a few times looking for a parking space, got angry, and pulled my car up on the sidewalk. Ladies in gowns had to part for us to make our way in. Bad Bob, who was a bartender by profession, chased the bartender that was there, fixed me a drink and proceeded to really serve some drinks. Actually it was a good move, the police didn't bother me once they found out that I was the main attraction, plus everyone who was anyone was there, sponging free chow and booze without spending a dime and using words like, esoteric and moving, same old stuff from people that don't know a thing about art. The one thing that caught my eye was a young blonde that lived behind my ex- boss, who was now a coke dealer. She was there and throwing eye's at me while I noticed that Scarlet O'Hara was nowhere to be seen. I made the Palm Beach paper that day, front page and a typical attempt at trying to describe what this brute was doing to their little village, Bad and I were the barbarian hordes. There was a lot of interest in my work but no sales yet, just promises, which in Palm Beach get flushed with the scented toilet tissue.

Finally Bob and I decided to make a break for it, we were in rough shape when we arrived, now I was having difficulty remembering my artists' dialogue of mysterious words. Plus I didn't want another Watergate on my hands. It did bother me that my lovely Miss Vatican could not find it in her busy schedule to attend her husband's one man show on Worth Avenue; just the address alone should have brought her out to this one, except maybe St. Therese Hovel.

I really must stop with these comments about the Catholic Church and the papal state; I am probably insulting a lot of people out there. Our constitution, which I fought and almost died for, allows for the freedom of religion. It is just that I spent 12 years beating back that propaganda, so I know a little more than most about how the organization works and I was never impressed. I apologize to anyone I may have offended and yet I must be true to myself at the same time. Let me just say this, soon it will be over, almost. There was one attempt to stay together but you will be upon that soon enough.

I sold the MGB for a large chunk of change because of it being an l970 'split bumper'. The car was rare, need I say anymore. I then signed up with Shaw Trucking again and decided, with Master's Degree in hand, I would climb up onto a bulldozer and put it between my legs. My new ex-wife worked for a lawyer, so the divorce deck was stacked against me, what I didn't sell she laid claim to.

I must tell you a quick story about one of the best painting sales I ever made. My old neighbor, H.H. who lived next to me when we first moved up to this little neighborhood; had moved away. It turned out he became one of the bigger pot dealers in South Florida and had two wives, figure that one out, I never could. Out of a clear blue sky he drops by my studio one day and besides hello and remembering the days we used to dive for lobsters together, he said he needed some artwork for his new house. I just happened to have a load of it, he started picking out canvas' and I think he had taken 5, most of which were pretty good size. Then, without talking, he started to peel $50 dollar bills off a big round wad, he would peel a bunch off and look at me, I would simply tap my desk with my index finger and he would peel more off, then repeat the process. this went on about 5 times before I shook my finger. He smiled, grabbed the paintings and a guy with him picked up the rest then turned to me and said, thank you; then drove away in his expensive automobile. Back to the rape of the Sabine man, her excuse for grabbing everything was pain and suffering, I told her she should try blue balls someday. I sold my antique brass bed and carpet which Mary T. had given me and bought my friend Ricks old crapped out Courier pick-up truck; it looked like an experiment but it ran well and never let me down. The motorcycle had gone awhile back after I fell in a cactus patch with it on top of me, nothing like several hundred pounds to drive those barbs through. We were evicted from the house because I found a wire that had been running their sons' massive a/c unit, all this time at my expense. When I approached the canoe head owners they simply threw us out rather than discuss it.

I found a travel trailer to live in, but then Bad Bobs crazy Jewish girl friend got me evicted from it, screaming dirty words at 4 in the morning and my landlord being born again was awakened again too. She didn't care one bit, never apologized to me once for that, I often wonder about that. My job with the bulldozer went by the wayside and I got a job moving furniture with a crazy guy and his pot head brother; cash money every time we went out, simple math $10 bucks an hour. I had found a small cabin to live in closer to the beach. This was my life though I still had an art desk set up and was painting, between baby grand pianos and sectional units.

Then there was the blonde I mentioned, the one that came to the art show. Well she saw a hungry man and knew very well how to play the game. The song 'Tainted Love' was a big hit back in early 1983, hummm…a flag? One problem with the blonde was that she really liked to put on a show when we were doing the nasty. She was so loud, my neighbor in the next shack went to the landlord, the last thing I needed.

I had to promise on the fate of the universe that this action would not happen again, and it didn't; another good use for duct tape.

But all enchanted places must have an evil witch. One night she brought over this guy who said he was a hit man for the Mafia; or so he claimed, but he looked like one. He just got out of prison somewhere and was 'chillin' in Florida. We started drinking and smoking pot, and then Blondie brought out the coke; she never went anywhere without the stuff. It was all quite friendly until he started putting unwanted advances on the blonde; but then they may not have been completely unwanted; just unwanted in my place. So I, for no other reason except it was right there next to me, shot a staple in this guy's leg. I guess it must have hurt because a fist fight broke out. The blonde was beating this guy on the head with my boom box (the only source of music that I had); it did get damaged but still worked. So, back to the fight, we pretty much wrecked the place; elbows went through windows, my art desk was flattened. I won the fist fight, but lost the cabin; my landlady was livid. She gave me one day to get out.

I decided to get out of Florida; it was getting crazier than even I could take. I sold everything and bought a plane ticket to Pennsylvania. I was going back to live in my studio. I had been warned about this Florida blonde. My old car repair/ coke dealer boss told me she was crazy; like her mother. She was just another Florida air head with perfect teeth and an empty space behind them. Once she said hello she told you just about everything she knew. But did I listen? No, I was too busy making sperm deposits and using that part of my anatomy to make all the important decisions.

I moved back into my 'turnkey' studio. Swept and dusted, put clean sheets on the bed and went out and bought some canvas to start painting. The family business got me right to work, so I had money in my pockets. I'd soon be back into the old routine.

Mary T got a call from my ex. She felt badly because she was just finding out about the actions of Vietnam Vets and how they 'not always knew what they were doing' and why. It wasn't just me. She told Mary T that she would like to talk to me and to try to reconcile. She said if Jason will come down to Florida, I'll also have a special gift for him.
Well, I didn't like to fail. And I also didn't like to be alone. I don't know why I did some of the things I did either. Even Mary T was hesitant about the arrangement, but she never did tell any of us what to do. But her silence usually was a sort of answer. I decided to give it a shot. And the gift; well she did have my entire Rolling Stones collection on vinyl. I even had 'Black and Blue' and the cover with the little zipper on it. Why she ever took it I never understood, but at the time of the split; she wanted it all.

I flew down to West Palm Beach and took a cab to the restaurant she had suggested. I had an hour to kill before she would arrive, so I started on the Manhattan's. I verified the reservation; it was in my name (I had made her take her old name, the one with the 'ski' in it); but strangely it was a table for three. I went back to the bar and continued the conversation with my mind.

The Mercury Capri pulled into the parking lot. One mirror was missing and the side was a bit stove in. I tipped the barkeep and told him to transfer the tab to the table under the name 'Patience'.
I stepped out and she gave me one of those fake 'European' kisses that don't actually make contact. She then introduced her retired female marine DI who proceeded to pulverize my knuckles with the handshake. We went through the pleasantries script about the flight, the weather, etc. and then I asked about Sargent Major. My little sour dough explained that she was her 'guardian angel'. I said I thought

they were cherubs; although she looked to be working on the part. She said to me that she had accompanied us in the event that "you made unwanted gestures towards me". I thought; these people are crazy. We made small talk while the Ninja didn't say a thing, but then again it is difficult to speak when you are shoveling copious amounts of food in your gob. She ordered everything; a bowl of Bisque, Oyster Rockefeller, and for the entrée, a surf and turf; Bacon Wrapped Stuffed Shrimp and a petite filet mignon. My 'until death do us partner' was oblivious to this dumpster sitting next to her. Finally I asked the burning question…"Where are my Rolling Stone albums"? There was an awkward pause, and then she said they were burned in a fire. I asked "at your apartment or house"? Then she went on to explain that it was at a church fire in the parking lot, where they were burning Satan's music.

Now I was really getting heated. "You mean to tell me you took MY Stones collection, some of which were worth more than you earn, just the jackets alone; records that didn't even belong to you, and threw them on Satan's bon fire"? In a very small voice she said "Yes". "Did it ever occur to you to call me and ask if I wanted my or Satan's albums back"? Her gestapo sidekick tried to interject and I just held up one finger and said "No, don't say a word".
This piece of play dough knows my Mother is an antique dealer, and well respected at that, she didn't have to wait to find out their value from a fortune cookie.
I turned back to Fahrenheit 451, who had head down, a few watery eyes; everything I've seen before. She began eating again, she was going to dodge another reality in life; substitute sour dough for Satan and you'd be closer to the truth. She knew my feelings about her religious institution, and didn't want to risk a confrontation in front of the walking stomach; whose lunch I ended up paying for.
So, my albums were gone, along with some of those ideas of reconciliation. So, the albums weren't the surprise.

After lunch, we drove the Capri to the West Palm Beach Auditorium. The car was a mess, the doors wouldn't close correctly and there was rust showing; she hadn't spent a dime on it. I was heated up enough at that point and didn't want to ask about the smashed side. As we drove along, to my great surprise, she complained about the car.

I kept my silence and we walked up to our 'nosebleed' seats; this was going to be an Italian Opera. I sat there for about 10 minutes, and then walked out. While standing there at the rail smoking a cigarette, she came out and asked what was wrong. I told her, after all the years we spent together; you don't even know that I despise Italian Opera. You bring a cow to dinner, burn my prize record collection and then take me to an Opera. It was never about me was it? It was always about you; what you could get out of the relationship. How much can I cost this guy and give nothing in return. You never supported my art, but liked that it supported you. I'm afraid that this is definitely not ever going to work. You can live with your twisted religion, but not with me.

 I took a cab to the airport to look for the next flight to Wilkes-Barre. Back then a ticket was like cash. You could take it to a different airline and use it for one of their flights.

My studio in Larksville was built in 1869. It had plenty of ghosts and things that went bump in the night, but they weren't as scary as the ones in my head, so I ignored them. I did buy another 'bar-car', some people call them heaps or clunkers; it didn't matter, I held the title.

I made up my mind that this booze love affair was not doing me any justice. Using my experience as a D&A counselor, I would lock myself in my studio with about four gallons of apple juice, a few valiums on board just in case, and then go into a hell that lasted about 4 or 5 days. It was bad; sweats, chills, and shaking like a cement mixer. Sleep was fretful at best, maybe an hour if I was lucky. The worst part was 'Michele my Belle' by the Boston Pops and multiple violins

236

playing over and over again in my head. I wasn't crazy about that Beatles song, I was a Stones man as you recall. What part of hell did that dredge itself from? Guess it was one of those gestalt phenomena's from a deep recess or scar. There was vomiting involved, but that's enough to say about that. After I felt human again I would emerge from this self-induced exile. I'd take a long cold shower, which was out back in the grapevines. Then I'd show up for lunch at the 'big house'. That is what we called our homestead. Mary T made a huge meal every day for all her men. My brother Bill gave her money every week to do so. She liked to cook and the door was always open to us and a guest if we wanted. My mother liked these periods of me not drinking. She could actually have a conversation with me. We'd talk about art, hers and mine. She liked to work in oils and our techniques were different. But we were kindred spirits.

One of the jobs with the brothers entailed standing in a sewer manhole, about ten feet deep, with a jackhammer hanging down from a chain. Every bit of debris had to be put into a bucket and pulled to the surface; nothing could go down that sewer line. It was an 8 hour day and took 7 days. We had to bore a hole through a pile of "high early" concrete, which simply means exceptionally hard. Up the street was an ice cream factory. At exactly 9am, the chamber would fill with the smell of chocolate; at 3pm it was vanilla. It was between those times that I'd rather not tell you about.

Finally we broke through and a new sewer line could be put in to the Plymouth High school. The old line had been blocked and when we got to that part of the pipe, lo and behold; a triple D cup bra was pulled to the surface. The supervisor of the school hung it in his office. It was the $8000 dollar bra.

For some god-forsaken reason, the blonde thing from Florida darkened my door. I had not called her and don't even know how she found out where I was. She decided she couldn't live without me, quit her job at IBM bought a crapped out Chevy station wagon and drove to Pennsylvania; naturally she had a huge pile of Florida snow with her. I should have listened to my inner voice, and that of Mary T's, who said "that woman is no good and going to cause you grief". She was 100% correct.

I got a long distance call from my former Florida 'Agent'. He and his controlling wife, who wore the pants in the family, were now living in Las Cruces, New Mexico, next to a missile testing range. He had this idea of putting on a 'one man show' of my work. I shipped a number of the canvas' I had to him and then the blonde and I flew out to El Paso. He picked us up at the airport and drove us to a rental car dealership, where I was handed the keys to a nice car for my unlimited use. My agent's house was out on a table mesa; flat, red desert. On the main road a mile or so away was a liquor store. I tend to notice these places; it is called preoccupation. At this time it was over thirty days since I had any alcohol.

There was a week before the show, so blondie and I went on a motor trip. Southern Arizona is quite beautiful and I wanted to see the Petrified Forest. We drove and drove until I saw a sign that said we were 'IN' the Petrified Forest. There were a bunch of round stones on the ground, reminded me of a collapsed Greek temple, with the fallen columns stretched out in a straight line. Yeah, I was kinda stupid; I was looking for a forest made of stone, with tall trees. We kept driving so we could find the Painted Desert. Well that's another thing. You have to be up at dawn, or watch for dusk to see what that was all about; otherwise nothing jumped off the canvas at me.

The big night came, the one man show that would kill all of New Mexico. The wine was chilled, and the cheese, crackers, fruit and vegetables were laid out. Nice mellow music was playing in the background, the lights were dimmed, except the ones over the large pieces, and we were all smiling. The smiling stopped after a few hours when not a soul came through the door. We stuck around until 11pm, put everything away and went back to their house.

The next morning, I woke up and everyone was gone. My hosts were at their jobs and blondie took the rental car to go somewhere. While I was having coffee, I went to the sink and there it was off in the distance, the 'we don't serve Indians' liquor store. So I did what anyone in my state of mind would do, I walked over to the place. I bought two quarts of cheap vodka and stepped outside; it was hot as hell. I could see a shorter route back to the house through some brush and headed that way. I kept falling down into these 'washes' as they were called, and stumbling through cactus; when I smelled something dead. It was a big steer with intact skull and horns. I ripped the head off, emptied what was left of the brains, and scraped off most of the skin. It was a perfect trophy for my hosts with the perfect white teeth! When I got to the house I searched for the biggest pot they had; filled it with water and the skull and set it to boil. I then mixed myself a drink and went to the hammock. Whenever I got up to mix another drink, I'd stir the skull around and watch the skin fall off. Due to the excitement of finding this perfect specimen, I didn't realize the house was filling up with a rotten stench.

As the sun went down the first to show up was the blonde, she came back out of the house, vomited, got back in the car and drove off. Then my agent and his wife came home. As I lay in the hammock, I could hear a lot of screaming; I guessed they were really surprised. He came out of the house to the big tree I was swinging in and said his wife wanted me to be at the El Paso airport as quickly as possible. I asked what was wrong and he just shook his head and told me to go pack my bags. When he asked me about the blonde, I told him he could keep her. I flew out of El Paso that night; alone.

I returned to Wilkes-Barre, the home of aluminum siding and dirty front porches. Gone were the days that people sat on them and waved to you. It was a 'depressed' place; every other house was a 'section 8'. Some eggheads gave it that name and the people just seemed to roll over and become part of it.

It was going to be a depressing summer for me. Blondie eventually returned, I asked where she had been, but I really didn't give a damn. Whenever she wanted to take off for some tryst or whatever, she would start an argument, storm out of my studio and disappear for a few days. Don't ask me why I let her come back; she was really getting on my nerves.

I had this pristine place to go skinny dipping. It was out in the country; a clear mountain stream with great trees as a canopy. I'd take a bar of soap and a towel. She'd take a bag full of various extra special shampoos for her blonde hair; numerous, odoriferous conditioners for it, and soaps and creams for the body. I'd look at the mass of bubbles and gunk floating down the stream and would want to pick up a bolder and throw it at her. I was getting disgusted with the company I was keeping. These treks to Beaumont Creek had been one of my favorite things to do.

She made sure I was always in vodka; it was a form of control I suppose. People stopped coming around because I was usually drunk and made unkind remarks. A good friend suggested I go and talk to C.C., I made an appointment and this time showed up. He was a nice older Italian guy with a great sense of humor and was quick to laugh. He suggested I go into this special hospital which also had a very good psychiatrist on staff. I was immediately defensive; what was he implying? He talked a bit to me about my experience in Vietnam and suggested I had unresolved issues from that time. In the back of my mind I knew he was right, but I told him I wanted a little time to think about it.

One day a package arrived at the studio with most of my artwork and some apologies from Las Cruces. In the letter was a check for a few thousand dollars. My agent said he made a few sales after the opening. He also told me that the blonde (he didn't know she was back on my turf) had hooked up with some cowboy type and rode around in his pickup truck; going to rodeos and giving him blow jobs. I guess a good blow job could keep you in the saddle; reducing friction on the leather or something. Maybe that's how I got some of those 'private' rashes she said were most likely from the creek.

I didn't tell her about the letter, or the money, she'd claim half of it. I felt her share was all those free rodeo tickets. Besides she was in and out of my studio, mostly out and I didn't know where she was most of the time. She'd just show up with vodka and some 'snow' when she had nowhere else to go.

Finally one day I asked her to give me a ride over to town. I had been drinking rye whiskey all day. She had no idea where she was taking me and I didn't tell her. We pulled up in front of the hospital. I opened the door, took another slug of whiskey and told her I'd be here for an unknown amount of time; and that I didn't want any visitors. She threw the bottle at me as I was slamming the door.

What inspired me to make this decision to enter the chamber of horrors was an ill-fated suicide attempt. I went to one of my art clients who was a doctor and got a quantity of Valium. I was glad the blonde 'petri' dish wasn't around, I stopped having any relations with her anyway, I was afraid of getting 'Hong Kong Dong'. Seems a bit ridiculous now; I was about to take myself out and there I was worrying about getting a STD.

Upon my return to the studio, I landed on a course of action; I would take the entire bottle of pills and wash it down with some vodka. Naturally I decided to have a cocktail to celebrate this momentous occasion and a few days later

I was still there, in the studio. What I did not know was that I forgot to take the pills and this never occurred to me until several months later, it is a good thing I didn't work for the good Doctor Kevorkian. This was all flashing through my mind as I scaled the steps into the' institute.'

It was the first time I heard the term 'PTSD' and had the doctor repeat it and its' definition. All of these years, since 1970 to be precise, I had been walking around with a dangerous and unpredictable mental disorder caused by being exposed to a traumatic event, which in my case, just happened to be the war in Vietnam. I spent 46 days in this place and I can assure you, it wasn't the type of joint you just got up and walked out of. The doors were always locked and they kept tabs on your every movement.

This experience, as dreadful as it sounds, was actually good, it opened my eyes to the questions of why I did the things that I did, it explained the failure of two marriages, or, maybe why I had gotten involved in them in the first place. Why could the U.S.Navy not have explained this to me years earlier, it would have saved a lot of misery.
During my entire stay at this clinic, the blond was using my studio for whatever, I did not know nor care. During one of my sessions I reached an epiphany, this was another one of those relationships, though bad, I stayed in rather than face the fear of living alone. What difference did it make; I was alone even in a bad relationship. I made up my mind to put an end to it as soon as I was discharged. I asked the doctor to write a report for me and submitted it to the VA as another claim. A few days later I was pronounced cured and sent on my merry way. My new associate, C.C. had set this all up and I didn't know who was paying for it and did not ask; it improved my outlook and gave me clarity of vision.

After I returned to my studio, it was like Jason and the Argonauts sneaking in and throwing all of the bums out.

I would have preferred the slaying and slewing parts, but our society frowned on such actions.

Blondie didn't take the new and improved Jason too well and went off on one of her get a ways. While she was gone her unemployment checks arrived from Florida, a pile of them and I knew as soon as she saw them she would have to return to Florida sans me of course. So I went out to my farmer friends place and told him that I needed 2 buckets of really fresh cow droppings. He had dairy cattle so I went in and just held the buckets right up to their ass as they relieved themselves, now that is some pretty fresh material. I then went to my father's house where she had stored a pile of her 'stuff' in his open air garage, threw the plastic off, and then carefully spread the cows present to her all over the boxes of 'stuff.' It seemed like the least I could do. Later that night I ran into my attorney's tenet who was one of the guys she latched on to after one of her disappearing acts. I knew him, and when I entered the bar I told him to step outside into the parking lot. He told me to listen to his side of the story, and afterward if I still felt the same way I could beat him into ground beef. After the story, we shook hands, and I went my way. Her stay with him was a short one, and I knew in advance it would be. I gave her the checks and told her to pack up and leave, I didn't care where she went but she was no longer welcome here.

My father said he heard all of this cursing outside and went to investigate, she was loading her 'stuff' which was slightly altered, I provided a nice country fragrance for an 1200 mile trip without A/C and a taped up front window. She asked my father why I would do something like this. His response was simple; you must have really pissed him off.

After a few weeks had passed, I sent her a $20 dollar FTD with a card that read: This relationship is terminated! They always advertise to say it with flowers, so I did.

It was almost winter of 1983 by the time all the dust settled; I was quite myself and made a deal with an auto dealer who was also an art collector, for a car. It was a big land yacht called a 'Grand Marquis' and was commonly called a 'lead sled'. The thing was like driving down the interstate a furniture showroom, but it was mine and paid for.

Clothing was next, I went to the better thrift shops and bought a new wardrobe, when all was done I was styling and doors would open for me.

One item that I failed to mention was the night I went to beat up the guy in the bar, 'she' was bartending, and I averted my glance. I knew that the drinking was over now, how could I sit there getting stupid with the woman of my dreams serving me? Up until this time I didn't even know she lived in the area. The timing was perfect. I had completely cleaned my slate of all previous women in my life just to allow a place for real love to come in. Also, there was no 'ex' I cared to talk about; a major mistake most men make.

I had been smitten by this woman for over 13 years and didn't want anything to tarnish my character; that is what character I had left! Somehow, deep in my being, I knew that we were going to be together, this was my soul mate.

Things started to change quickly, I was introduced to a man I knew that was loaded, but had a reputation for not paying his bills. He was having an addition put on his house and needed someone to manage the work. He also needed a design for the new room so it transitioned well from the oldest part of the house to having a new addition tacked on. I lied through my teeth, but assured him that I was more than qualified for the task.

The guy had married a woman at least 25 years younger after his wife of 30 years had passed away. This Babe was a real piece of work; she wore entirely too much perfume and the wrong color lipstick. He told me to listen to her for my cues as to the design of the place; I secretly decided that this would never happen We rode up to the next city she was from and she showed me her apartment, it was despicable and as a designer I wanted to run out and vomit on her Mercedes.

The place was done in green and red with a lot of gold thrown in, gold grapes in a vase; someone shoot me.

Back on the job, at first the general contractor didn't like me at all, but I gained some respect when I solved a span issue. As time went on and they knew that I was on top of things, their respect grew. I also came up with some additional structure work which added to their contract. I went to the studio and cut up a few Ikea catalogs and pasted up a few designs for the bathroom. You never show an entire catalog to a client or they will never make up their mind, and I never submitted more than 3 designs for any given space for the same reason. After the young wife saw this she left me alone. This guy was cheap with expensive tastes, a quality I became an expert at perceiving later on in life. I gave myself a trophy on the subject when I became a fulltime 'Building Designer.'

Incorporating artwork into the design was important. I gave Mary T a plum commission to build a leaded glass window which was going to hang from a beam and make the initial transition from old to new; plus it put a wad of money into her hand, his money. I designed a large canvas using a lot of green and gold as a concession to the Italian princess, when it was completed and hanging, she could not speak at the first viewing, she loved it, and he had to bring out the checkbook.

I then went to a few electronic firms to find out what was on the horizon in the future for sound and television, and proceeded to have the contractor install a complete control panel with wiring for a number of speakers. The place was being set up for surround sound which was a few years away.

Speakers and televisions have never struck me as furniture, so the television was placed behind two doors, and all of the speakers were hidden in the walls; or 'surface mount'. After they were painted, you could hardly notice them. My boss fought me all the way, he couldn't understand a hole under a window seat with power and wires going to it, or wires in the walls that went to nowhere as he called it, I just said you hired me to do a job, now either send me home or get out of my way, in time all will be revealed. In fact, years later he and his brother called me to redesign the façade of their office buildings, cheap of course. During the meeting, my boss from 1984 asked me how I knew about surround sound and flat screen picture tubes on televisions; I simply told him that was why he hired me! The only problem with this guy was getting paid. I would pull up in front of the house and go to the front door, his maid would stall me until I saw his Mercedes 450 SL back out of the garage and take off. After that I parked in the driveway. Plus he was always trying to cut my fees; I grew to get very impatient with all of this and ended up telling him. I was hired to do a job and I did one beyond what was expected, what was the problem with paying for it? It didn't make that much of a difference, he was still a cheapskate.

It was in the early summer that my ex-attorney asked me to do something for the cover of his invitations to his 40th birthday party; his house was turning 100 the same day.

One thing that I rarely ever do as an artist is work on-site. I did it once early in my career and became so sick I couldn't work for weeks afterward. But, for this invitation I did. It was a pen and ink drawing of his house, which was a large coal robber barons mansion so it had all of the gingerbread and porches etc. The artwork came out fine especially when it was shot down to size (commonly called reduction, an old artist trick, draw big then shoot down, it looks like a million.) My payment was an invitation to the party, though I can't complain considering what transpired.

The party was held on July 22nd. All of the food had been catered by a fine Italian restaurant. Another friend brought his ice cream truck, with over 30 favors, and parked it in the driveway. My father showed up in his Model T Ford and gave people rides around the neighborhood for a few hours and then went his way. Inside they had different rooms for different vices, a booze room, and a snow room and so on; there was even a place up in the attic, the ballroom.

In the side yard was a metal sculpture I had done a few years back and had given him and his wife as a present, I was standing there when it happened, 'she' showed up. I quickly turned around and bumped into a guy we both knew who owned a few men's clothing stores. He said "what is the problem, the look on your face was like seeing a ghost". I said close to it, do you see that beautiful brunette with the great looking blue eyes, well I first saw her in 1970, when I was fresh out of Vietnam. I don't know her name or anything about her except that I have been crazy about her since that first encounter almost 15 years ago. He said I know that person, is it that one and I glanced over my shoulder and said yes, that's her. He said that's Teresa Fee and I know her well, so I'll go and make quick work of this. I began to protest but he was gone, a few minutes later he came back with her and said Jason I would like you to meet Teresa, your mystery girl. He then saw someone and said good luck, I am out of here.

She asked me what he meant by the term 'mystery' girl. Hell, I was embarrassed as if I wet my trousers. But then we found an empty bench and started to talk. Finally I broke down and told her about seeing her in a bar in 1970 when I just got back from the war. To my surprise, she told me she noticed me that night also. As our conversation went on it was as if I had known her for years. She was so easy to talk to and very funny, she had a fast sense of wit. As I sat there listening it struck me that this must be what love feels like, I must be in love, so I decided to be very careful and not prick

247

the balloon over my head. After a while I told her that I was going to leave and she asked why. I then went into an entire description as to what was going to happen starting about 10 pm. The ties would come undone, someone would slap their wife and then a fist fight would break out. I would rather not be here when all of that occurs because meeting you has made my evening complete. With that I gave her my card and a brief description of where the studio was located, told her to stop by any time, and I left. It would take dynamite to blow the smile off of my face, I was so happy and relieved, 14 and a half years I waited for this moment not knowing if it would ever really happen. So many things could have stood in the way over a period of time like that, she was so good looking I was surprised that some rich guy didn't scoop her up to go live in Europe or something. She definitely did not strike me as the type of person who would settle for a mobile home existence with 4 brats running around, this lady had class, and it showed.

Later that night, it was after midnight, I was lying on my single bed watching a television I had rigged up under my art desk and a tap, tap, came on my door. I thought, who could that be, no one knows I am here, who would stop by at this hour?

As the door opened, there was Teresa standing in the doorway, parked behind her was a nice Datsun 240Z car, she even had good taste in cars; I wasn't surprised. She came in and I offered her a drink of seltzer water, I explained that I didn't drink, so I didn't have anything stronger. Her first question was how I knew what was going to happen after 10 o'clock at that party, I simply explained that I had been there so many times before and it's always best to leave on a good note. Sort of like James Brown, push off on your good foot. We talked about a number of things well into the night, after what seemed like several hours, she told me she had to go home. I asked if she wanted to get together again and she said yes, we left the planning go until schedules were checked etc. After she drove away with a smile and a wave, I went into the studio and started to jump around like a kid and almost knocked over my easel with my latest composition on it. I sold that painting but years later Teresa asked me to get it back, I had to trade the guy two paintings for the one; it now hangs above our dining table.

With Teresa I made up my mind that this was going to be the old fashioned way of 'courting' as opposed to dating. So I had taken my time, aside from an innocent kiss here and there I did not place a hand on her. We went for hot dogs, then ice cream cones. I had my fill of sex for the sake of sex. I could see a much more fulfilling relationship with this woman. An acute case of 'blue balls' set in for quite a period of time and it was OK, occasionally embarrassing, but OK. I believe I've explained what this old teenage phrase meant in a previous chapter. One used often when getting shut down at the drive in. And in fact Teresa and I did go on drive-in dates; although sex in the car was something I didn't expect from our relationship. A simpler story would be to tell you not far from where I presently live are towns named Blue Ball and Intercourse, I kid you not.

At this point in time I was finishing the house project, all of the pieces came together well, much to their satisfaction and my anticipation. Mary T's leaded glass piece was back lighted and really made the transition flow from this old low ceiling house into a vaulted 1800 square foot space with a loft. My support trick was to build a fireplace which supported the ceiling, the roof, and a loft. The loft/master bedroom was surrounded by folding doors for privacy. The finished product was ahead of its time for 1984 and looked like it. Without wearing out my drum, let me just say I gave this conniving old fart more than his monies worth and his red lipped bimbo bragging rights for a few years to come. But still, at this point he only saw dollar signs; not art and pure design. It really bothers me when some guy wearing $2000 worth of casual wear, sitting in a leased 450 Mercedes SL at $500 a month, has the babalone's to tell me that he had a bad week and can't afford to pay me the $16.46 he owes me. Don't they realize how that sounds? It's just not believable.

I know the art business too well and have very mixed emotions when someone gets really excited because they just touched the hands of a 'real' artist. This has actually happened to me at one of the fancy cocktail parties the doctor and his wife would throw at their Park Avenue apartment.

I do not begrudge anyone their money, if they worked hard, or had their name on the will; all the best to them. All I want is my fair share that was originally agreed upon, no more or less. I do not covet the money of others, it is an evil thing. Some people get too much of it, they then lust after power. If I am not mistaken, Maslow addressed this in his "Hierarchy of Needs." There is one thing that I am very much aware of, as an artist growing older; people just keep pushing more money at my work. Being an artist, of any strength, has its' own built in retirement program, that is provided that my hands and arms retain their nerve endings and I can still feel things. My duty in Vietnam has had an impact on the neurology of my body, especially on the left side, and I am left handed.

As it turned out, Teresa was a well-travelled individual with much of it done solo. This I respected because it takes a certain quality of character to step off a plane, boat, train or even a donkey cart, in a strange land. And then proceed to learn customs and enough of the language to get by. It takes a lot of Moxey to stand there with a bag in hand and say, what now and where to next. And she had done this; traveling through Europe and then on to the Middle East, where she lived for a year.

We spent every day together. As mentioned I courted her by introducing her to my secret place's, 12 inch dog's wit/or wit out. It was a great way to start this relationship. I had every intention of being with this beautiful Irish girl for a long time.

A night did arrive when we returned to my studio and I turned the radio on to my favorite PBS DJ named George Graham, who had the best taste in music. He played one of Marvin Gaye's hits called 'Let's get it on.' That was all that it required, we danced then fell into a sweet embrace. I must admit that I undoubtedly climaxed before my pants were off I was so much in love. We made love and it was the sweetest evening that I have ever had with any person to that point in my life. Just holding and touching this woman completed something esoteric in my life that had been missing, she completed the circle; we fit together like pieces of a long awaited puzzle. Needless to say, 'Lets' get it on' is our song to this day and we usually drop everything and dance to it, real slow. Since that chance encounter of July 22nd, we have been together ever since. The only times we've been apart would be for a few weeks when I have been away, or, when she would go ahead and scout out a new apartment for us.

Before winter set in, and we had to cross the Rockies, we decided to get out of Wilkes-Barre and head for the West Coast. Teresa found out that there was a room available for a few months in the old apartment she had shared with a few other girls in San Francisco. I went completely over her stock Datsun Z-car; gave it a tune up, oil change, new brakes; anything it needed to be dependable for the trip and afterward. She had picked a nice one, stock sun roof and mag wheels, automatic transmission; it was a beauty. I tuned up and set the carburetors, there were 3 of them, but they were the same English models that they used on the MGB cars. The Japanese had bought the rights to them and used the parts on their new 'Z' series of cars. They had not been done in a long time, so it was a good thing.

I sold my 'Grand Marquis' to my oldest brother who happened to like big lead sleds; it was much to the chagrin

of his wife who hated me anyway, so what difference did it make. I gave it to him cheap to make up for that stain on the seat of his brand new car in 1967, I still felt bad about that. Again, my brother Mark and I had just repainted the car in a stock two tone green, so it was good for a while. Bill never, if ever, washed his cars, but he took good care of them otherwise.

As I type this I realized that I never fully told the story of the infamous front seat spot. It was in 1967 as mentioned. I borrowed his new car, with only 500 miles on it, to impress this girl. We went to the drive in and one thing led to another, bingo a spot right dead center of his front seat. I tried every cleaner known to man, and that spot never came out. I wonder why I never thought of just having the seat cover replaced by Ford, it just didn't occur to me. Though you can assume correctly that it was a bone of contention for a long time, he gave the car to Mary T and every time I got in it, there was that spot mocking me, as it turned out, this girl had gone out with her ex-boyfriend who just came back from Vietnam, so, afterward I was in the Doctor's office again suffering from 'Hong Kong Dong.'

One of the last things I had to do was get my final payment from that cheapskate client, he dragged it out as long as he could until I told him that I was coming out there and was going to start removing artwork. I had a key for the place and knew he was too cheap to pay to have the locks changed. That is one of the first things you do after having god only knows, how many workers in your house; have all the locks changed. There is no telling how many copies of that key are out there and some guys wait a few months then come in and clean you out, believe me, I did a lot of residences' and it was the laborers you had to watch.

When I pulled up to his house real fast, I locked the brakes up so all of the tires would make a horrendous noise of anger, it didn't matter because he was in the front door with a check in hand, I checked the amount and noticed it was

drawn on her account, but the bank was a few blocks away and I turned that into cash before the ink was dry on the signature. My fear was her finding out that she was paying the final bills on their little love nest, when he was supposed to be the sugar daddy.

Teresa and I had a pile of cash, pointed the car west and did not look back. I always tilted the mirrors when I left that hell hole, that way you wouldn't be turned into a canister of salt, or pepperoni on a pizza if you did turn around. We drove west for days; it was 3300 miles coast to coast. This trip was more enjoyable than my solo MGB voyages across country, as we drove along, my past just melted away. I had enough sense to not discuss my ex-wives or any other woman for that matter; this was the only woman I needed now.
On one of our fuel stops in Echo, Wyoming, I bought wine, bread, cheese and sausage, a typical bongo and beret luncheon for two old beatnik's.
I had not touched alcohol since late into 1983 and we were into 1985 on our way to San Francisco. Without any trepidation I opened the wine and poured two glasses, yes I bought plastic wine glasses, and we toasted, Teresa noticed the wine and I told her it would be fine, I was never much of a wine drinker anyway and she believed me. That was it, she believed me when I knew that I was playing with fire here, it was like that Bob Dylan song: "Well I started out on burgundy but soon hit the harder stuff…"

After we reached California, we were somewhat north of the city so we decided to check out the Northern coastal regions. Our idea was to possibly stumble on one of those great artist towns somewhere in the redwood trees. We went to Mendocino and then inland to a town called Eureka on the

Red River, finally we jumped on the interstate and made a trip to Sacramento before driving into San Francisco. This was the artist town, I always enjoyed gay clients, they had good taste and a lot of money, plus they rarely argued about price, if it was liked, it was sold.

Her friends had kept the same apartment for 25 years and were locked in on some rent agreement. We kept looking at the papers and checking out apartments but it wasn't the cheap place that I recall from 1970, all of the love, peace, and tree stuff was over, the city was into money now you could tell by the financial district and the Embarcadero.

We finally found a place in the 'Mission' district on the corner of Guerrero and 15th street. It was a 4th floor walk-up but had very large windows facing the US Mint and the business district, it was a decent view. I found a wood worker to build me an art desk to my specs at a reasonable cost, and proceeded to set up my art studio. My foot locker followed me when I called it in. When I looked around this huge city I saw walls; and walls needed artwork and I was an artist. Sausalito was an artist haven. There were some exceptional galleries and my goal was to be in one; that was going to be my 'grail'. I began to learn quickly about the West coast, there was an emptiness behind the invitation, my favorite was the expression; 'we should DO lunch!' This was simply a polite way of saying don't wait by a phone booth. But that wasn't enough to dampen my spirits I was going to sell art in this town, period. After the employment office, I ended up in a welfare office. I refused to be a dishwasher with a Master's Degree. California welfare turned out to be quite generous; they supplied rent, money, food stamps and medical assistance. The perfect set up for a starving artist. Even though I was successful it was still feast or famine, any artist will tell you that and if they don't they are lying.

Every artist is looking for a guaranteed annual income so they can concentrate strictly on art work. I happen to be a disciplined artist; I'd go into my studio between 9 and 10 am and not emerge until about 6pm. This is every day until the composition is finished. I then take a break for research. Even though my work is semi-abstract, I still base each composition on researched subject matter. In Ireland a few years ago, I did a series of paintings that were based on early Celtic art from 850 BC. My job is to bump the image and knock it slightly out of focus at times, or add something to the established imagery. The system allowed me the freedom to paint and I used every moment of that time for this purpose.

After the third ticket and tow expense we had decided that the Datsun Z car was not long for the streets of San Francisco. What had happened was the strain of backing out of parking places on steep hills had its effect on the reverse gear in the transmission, it broke. Now we had to park somewhere level and that was when the tickets arrived. I placed an ad in the paper and the phone rang off the hook all day. I finally sold the car and the guy just threw the cash on the table and asked for the keys, he told us to mail the paperwork to him, and he had already removed our plate. We followed him out and cleaned out the rest of the stuff in the car. He started it up and drove away. I returned to the apartment and got another call where the person offered me more money. Teresa was upset, she really liked that car, but I had heard the engine bearings rattling in it and knew they were next to go. The car was at that age where it needed a complete overhaul and this was not the place or the time to do it. She has never let me forget that car.

Another re-animation was my poetry; San Francisco was the home of the famous Ferlinghetti book store called 'City Lights'. Allen Ginsburg had told me about this place because he was also one of the 'beat' poets as they were called. I believe I talked about the Boulder, Colorado poetry readings at the University, I read with Allen Ginsburg and we became fast friends, he said my work was rare, the way he liked steaks. It turned out that the 'City Lights' book store had an open mike night. I stopped by to get the information and told them I was a friend of Allen from our Boulder days, so when I was about to go on stage they would introduce me as such. I teamed up with a girl who played interpretive cello and she would accompany me during the reading, they allowed me about 15 minutes which was more than anyone else got. I read from my old book, 'Simple Reflections on a Frozen Surface', and the new manuscript I had entitled 'Nervous Reader'. It was quite successful I may add and went on for a few months until the cellist had to leave and I showed up one night with one too many drinks under my belt and was yanked from the stage. Again that crap had gotten in the way of my career.

San Francisco was a big 'trigger' town for me. I spent time here in Oakland, was discharged here, and had been spit on here. The place reeked of Vietnam and it was slowly creeping back into my life with the introduction of its road map, alcohol.

Poets are like rock bands that haven't made it yet. They travel around playing almost any gig that they can get, and then sell copies of their CD's during the breaks. I read everywhere, New York, Melbourne, ah yes Melbourne. I was reading every week at this small beatnik style club downtown and started to attract a following of sorts. Things were 'fair dinkum' until I saw guys coming in with black shoes and short hair, it doesn't take much to see cops under cover. They always wear their cop shoes and never buy a wig. Anyway after a few weeks they stopped me one night, though I never used 4 letter words in my work, I did imply quite a bit of personal things and body parts, this is what they objected to and threw me out with the promise of being locked up if I returned. That was the end of reading in Melbourne. Eventually though, especially after I had two books published, I had to make a decision between poetry and art. When I was young I could multi-task the two art forms rather well. But as I got older, it became more difficult for me to concentrate. That is when I set the two book

256

maximum, I told myself after I publish two books I would stop writing poetry and I did just that. My publisher was a small outfit in South Carolina, they did two editions of each book and they sold well, hell they sold out, then the publisher had some problems and that was it, I never pursued another one because there were a few thousand copies of each book out there and felt that was plenty, I had paintings to concentrate on and one man shows.

In San Francisco I did 'in home' showings of my work. I sewed together a canvas sling that held about 5 paintings and was on call with some advertisements in a few publications; gay and straight. I would show up at your address and give an on the wall demonstration of the work, then negotiate price. It worked fairly well, I sold a number of paintings this way, but my eye was on the prize, Sausalito.

In San Francisco people wanted large canvas'. In order to manage this and avoid the hassles associated with 8 X 8' paintings, I used the diptych and triptych device, 2 and 3 panels tied together as a single composition. I did this for the Sausalito gallery; they were 48 inch canvases and a bitch to carry on the ferry over. I made my appearance and got into the gallery, he had taken everything I lugged over there. This gallery was the perfect location, it was right where the ferry stopped, you could even see in the windows of the gallery from the ferry as it pulled in. This was the coup de gras, as an artist I was again at the top of my game. The owner and I became partners in crime, if a customer wanted a composition but had a price ceiling in mind; he would call 'dial a prayer' or the weather forecast and act like he was talking to me. The deal usually went down this way, I would always reluctantly agree, or insist on just a few hundred dollars more and the sale was made. He liked this approach and another thing, I used a Time and Material pricing structure, the galleries loved that, there wasn't any emotion attached to the painting. Have you ever noticed that? In a gallery is a huge canvas for $1000 dollars and a small piece by the same artist for $3000! That is called emotional pricing.

Teresa always worked; she was an experienced restaurant person. She could work any job at any place, she was good. Her tip money paid the bills. She actually was hired back at a restaurant she had worked in four years prior, when she lived out there with a bunch of her girlfriends. It was in the Business District, downtown, places where the young lions liked to brag about the money they made, and also liked to throw it around; so they'd leave the big tips. They knew their pig bellies, yes sir.

After all these years, I honestly know what my affair with alcohol was about; it was a catalyst to Vietnam. It helped to take me there, yet the alcohol promised relief from the sounds and nightmares. It was in San Francisco that I had another relapse into that insanity. It was affecting my art work, my poetry reading and my relationship with Teresa.

I had met this young guy at the welfare office. He ended up helping me with a lot of the paperwork that needed to be filled out. It was obvious that he was the kind of guy that liked men, but that was ok, I didn't care. He called one day and asked if he could come and visit Teresa and I. He said if I allowed him to come over he would clean and make dinner for us. Why not; so we all became friends.

Teresa's brother-in-law was in San Francisco on business and we were to meet him at the St. Francis Hotel; this would be my first introduction to this man. But Teresa and I got into an argument and I stormed out and went home to sulk. David came over to talk and made me realize it was a ridiculous argument. I had wanted to celebrate with her as that day I had received a check for painting sales in Sausalito. David and I grabbed a cab to go looking for her. I went to all the places I knew she liked or where her friends worked, but couldn't find her.
David offered to take me on a tour of the city that only 'his

kind of people' gets to see. He laid down the rules first; you are to say you are with me, period.

Don't talk to anyone at the bar except me, and don't let anyone buy you a drink. He said some of these places could be pretty rough, but I was game. We then proceeded to explore the world of the bizarre. We instructed the cab driver to wait for us outside everyplace we stopped and I tipped him in advance. One place was full of guys in leather outfits, most of them were really pumped up, muscle wise; David said, "Steroids'. These guys could have been ex-cons, right out of prison, bunkmates from hell. Then we'd head over to a place where everyone was dressed in drag. The guys were dressed to the 'nines'; expensive outfits and lots of makeup. The bar had silk couches and loveseats, and an aquarium behind the bar about 15 feet long. Next was the cowboy bar; complete with six guns and ten gallon hats and guys in 'character'. When 'little Joe' from the Ponderosa asked if he could buy me a drink, we left. What a night; an artist could do a modern version of Toulouse Lautrec type compositions.
The night was over, I saw San Francisco from the inside out. The cab dropped me off at our apartment and David left. Teresa was asleep on the bed. I gently undressed her and put her under the cover. Then went and showered off my adventure.

One afternoon we went to the theater to see the movie "Rambo'. Before the film started a couple of guys seated behind us were talking and one of them said, quite loudly, that all Vietnam vets were losers and suckers. Teresa could tell right away that I stiffened; which was a prelude to action. I got up, walked up to where they were siting, grabbed the guy by the collar and punched him square in the face. I then asked the guy next to him if he had anything to offer about the men that fought in Vietnam. There was a weak "no". Before anything more could happen Teresa got us both out the door. She was really upset and made me promise to do something, go somewhere and get help.

A few days later I checked into French Hospital; another locked door facility like the first one. They assigned me a psychiatrist who was under 30 years of age. This was a mistake, how could this guy know anything about Vietnam and PTSD, after a few days I wanted to leave because this wasn't going to work. At that point, they held up the 'AMA' banner in front of me which meant that my insurance would not pay for this.

Without an out, I stayed, but it went from bad to worse, one day he asked me not to smoke during our sessions because it was getting into his 'Herringbone Tweed.' I was furious, I had been talking for 20 minutes and this basically told me that he wasn't listening to a word I said, so I screamed at him to meet out there, on that bench, what in the World are you thinking about? The caveat was I had to see this guy every day. On another occasion it was late in the afternoon, suddenly what sounded like a machinegun went off, I dove under the table and told him to take cover, and he leaned over laughing at me and said they were fireworks. The poignant thing was I had been reflecting on the land battle at the small Army firebase, reliving the entire experience. My first impulse was to beat him into a pile of Herringbones then I thought better of that idea. The entire experiment was doomed from the very start, after that I simply put my time in; 21 days. Every day I had to sit with this arrogant person, who actually didn't care what I was going through; after all, I was just another crazy, whining Vietnam veteran, a loser who was stupid for going there in the first place.

After 21 days I was discharged with a month's supply of 'lithium' one of the medieval anti-depressants still left on the market since the days of Eric the Red. This compound had to be closely monitored with blood work ups, he didn't order them and it required up to 6 weeks before it even worked, I tried it and in a week, my ankles were burning so bad I could barely walk, when I called he told me it was in my head. So I returned to my usual medication, it was a clear liquid.

One day I received a call from the director of events at Penn State University, Hayfield campus. This was and old and very wealthy farm property that a family donated to the University. Penn State needed a satellite campus near this major population area. The main house was a mansion with a large formal parlor that probably saw gala dance's in its day. They wanted me to put up a one man show of my work, I told them yes even though it was a logistical headache, the site was in Pennsylvania and I was in San Francisco.

Prior to diverting my energy to this undertaking, I wrote formal letters requesting information on how this show was going to be handled. I pointed out that there would be months of work involved on my part plus a considerable investment in getting all of the compositions back there. They assured me that this was to be a premier event and they would advertise it and send out invitations to very wealthy patrons (I thought of my good old buddy the cheap skate) and there would be plenty of finger foods and wines etc. and etc. I had to be reassured of this because I had some bad memories of artwork sales and my hometown. We established a date and it was tight, I had to work hard every day. I was preparing to ship the work to my studio in tubes and then re-stretch it once I got there. That day a check for $1000 came from my insurance company, the method was to sign it and send it on to the 'provider.' As I sat there staring at this, it occurred to me that nothing was provided to me by this guy except pain and aggravation, so I signed the check and cashed it and bought one plane ticket back to Wilkes-Barre. Teresa stayed behind, unknown to me, she was thinking about leaving me at this time because of my violent behavior and excessive use of "medication."

Upon my arrival, before I even stretched a canvas, I drove out to the campus which was in the country. I had bought all of the local newspapers and did not see one add for this show, even though it was a week away. With her letter in hand I drove out there and approached her, there weren't any ads or invitations, finger foods or wines, nothing. This was the kiss of death to an artist, just like Las Cruces coming over the horizon. I refused to hang the show, 20 paintings I had amassed for it, her excuse was that she got busy with other matters and just placed it on the back burner! I could not believe this excuse and showed her the letter, with her signature on it, promising all of this activity. She was totally non-committed as if it did not matter, I explained that I worked my ass off and flew in from San Francisco for this based on her request and then you tell me you forgot? It was bad, I imagine I could have taken some kind of legal action but that wasn't going to fix my current problems, plus it would be difficult suing Penn State University, they would simply say that she wasn't in any position to make this decision on her own. She was a painted up nothing trying to be a big shot at my expense. I made up my mind that I would not show my work in this place again.

I went to some regular customers and explained the raw deal and my desperate situation, one of my regular clients traded me a really nice VW Rabbit car, and I sold a few paintings for some cash. That was all I needed. For some reason Key West started to call out to me again, it was autumn of 1985.

The herringbone kid in California quit sending me letters after he received my 'bullet' letter concerning his ability or lack thereof; I suggested that he return to school or better yet, join the Marines and go kill some people, he would know what PTSD was after that!

My return to Key West was going to have to take a rain check. My friend and patron of the arts had gotten himself into a World of hurt by being a 'silent' partner in a construction company with $3.8 million dollars in HUD contracts. This was the Federal Governments' money. He called me to his office and almost begged me to take over this company as the General Manager. At first I was reluctant and had a pile of excuses, but this man was always good to me when I was in a jam. So I looked over the paperwork to see where the problem came from. It didn't take long to find it; the guy he got involved with was a thief, cheat, cocaine abuser and a boozer. He now was acting the big time, a big fish in a small pond.

He was turning up on job sites blasted and would tell a US Government inspector to go fuck himself. You don't tell a G-Man that; especially when he is holding the checkbook. I did some more research and in just over a week, I told my friend I'd take the job. That night we used his 'roll back' from the dealership to 'steal' back his own car from this jerks driveway; he then handed me the keys. I went into the office and interviewed every employee. There were fifteen guys on the payroll; getting government rate I may add. I knew some of these guys and they were bar flies, thieves and whatever adjectives that would apply to a basic scumbag. For three weeks I sat in the company office looking over all the files. The jobs were bid well, they stood to make a 22% profit, but there had been so much theft and so many outstanding accounts; one alone over 22K; that any profits would have to go towards making this thing right. The guy I replaced was bad mouthing me all over town, but I ignored that for the time being. I fired 10 of his employees. I found out who was running up the debts. It was obvious when you drove by his house; it had that same HUD siding on it. I was going to have him arrested, but instead brought a civil action suit against him; the money was more important at this time and the evidence was everywhere. Calling in the IRS was sheer vendetta. My position was supposed to last 8 weeks; I could see that was grossly underestimated. Along with a company car, I now had a 'beeper'; what a big shot. I ended up hiring more men; ones that I already knew and could trust. Patching up the relationship with the HUD inspector allowed for a payment to go through every week to cover payroll.

Although there were times I went to cash my own check and the funds were not available, so much for the Mr. 'big shot' part.

The jobs were being completed; I knocked off those close to town and moved out from there. There were two firehouses to re-fit with new additions and upgraded equipment. One was in the Poconos, Bushkill Falls; and they were ready to lynch me for how the place was left by the thief. I stood in front of this packed room of angry, blood thirsty people and told them I'd have a crew there on Monday. I put my guys up in a motel down the road and they stayed until the job was completed; I wanted a smile on every fireman's face. I told my guys there would be a bonus for them if they finished in two weeks; they did and it was a week before Xmas.

On one of the jobs, in the middle of the thief's turf; things had disappeared, and I don't mean screws and nails. It was big stuff like generators, and compactors that had been rented for the jobs. Unfortunately, there were some hands that were out, mostly behind someone's back, that I had to 'grease'; even some of the government guys. My boss didn't know about half this stuff, but he saw there was a light at the end of the tunnel. There wasn't any profit as of yet, but I had managed to save him $250,000. It was a bad investment for him alright, but a quarter mill was something, it made me feel like I did what I was hired to do.

I found another big problem at the office; there was a leak somewhere. Too much information was getting passed along to another thief on the payroll. If I said that Home Depot was going to deliver something that afternoon, it would be gone before it hit the ground. Turns out this piece of crap was dating my office secretary even though he was married and had three kids. She even left her husband for this liar. In her divorce she got $50K from the sale of the house and she gave it to this prick so he could build her "dream house". Every Sunday, probably after church, he would drive her out to a house being built and told her it would soon be hers. Then he torched the place and told her "sorry, your money is gone; there wasn't any insurance on it". It was all a big lie, it wasn't even one of his spec houses, but he burned it anyway so he could keep her money.

I contacted the State and local police and planned to set a trap. I ordered a shipment of 16 air conditioners and had the police there when they were delivered.

It was this event that exposed the secretary; after which she spilled the beans to me. The scumbag loaded all 16 units on his pickup and then was busted. He was the final black hole that money was being sucked into.

It was some time later that I was told this, but to make this story even more dreadful, was the fact that this guy was HIV positive. So this poor woman, and I've been told at least 8 more had been having sex with him, while he was conning them out of something, telling them how much he 'needed them'.

A problem with this whole arrangement was the huge amount of stress I was under. I'd take a couple of strong belts at night when I got home. What I called home at that time was a trailer on a piece of property I was to inherit. It was on a lot just down the hill from my parent's home, where one of my father's sisters' had lived until she passed away. It had electric heat and I tried to heat just the rooms I used, but it was cold, very cold, in the single digits, and I hate the cold, always have.

The winter kept getting worse and I was ready to get out of the mountains. I called a good friend of mine who was out of work and brought him on as my replacement. My boss knew this person and was alright with the transition. I stayed until he was comfortable with the set up.

I wanted to get my life back; and Teresa.

FUN FOR THE ENTIRE FAMILY

Teresa had elected to stay in San Francisco for a while. I could feel the scales tipping from one side to the other. She was deciding if a future with me had any future in it. After the collapse of the 'one man show' I had a decision to make. I could feel sorry for myself and drink myself stupid. Or I could quit the alcohol again and possibly regain the respect I lost for both my own being and that of Teresa's. It was a no brainer there; I loved this woman.

While involved with this construction company I asked on several occasions if she would return to me. This time I called and told her of my plan. I would give her the car I got in a trade for some of my art work, and a pile of money. She was a great scout and could find an apartment and even a job in no time at all. So I asked if she would consider going ahead of me to Key West and as soon as I finished with my work I would join her.

After what seemed to be an eternity she agreed to return to Wilkes-Barre. I got her a plane ticket and waited. She had already given up the apartment and was staying with her friends. She gave notice where she worked and it two weeks she was back. Even after this period of us being apart, we still held the same feelings for each other. Though our relationship had some dents and serious paint scratches, we were still intact.

She stayed with her own family for a few days then joined me on the mountain. We made our plans for heading south. Teresa also decided she was going to finish her two Associate Degrees at the community college in Key West. She had begun her studies at the same Luzerne County College that I had gone to prior to going to Vietnam. She was able to transfer all of her credits and would only need a few more semesters.
I filled her pockets with as much cash as I could and she set off in the VW.

The day did come when I ended up in a real fist fight with the thief I replaced. I'm sure my boss would have preferred if I had finished him off completely, but Pennsylvania frowned on that. As it turned out, his MO was to find some wealthy doctor or dentist that wanted to invest money, then he'd promise a very handsome return; all of the time they would remain silent partners, as most of these investors wanted. He lost his license a few times, but he would just get another contractor license in his wife's or his dog's name.

I knew which local gin mill this scumbag hung out in and avoided it, but heard something he was spreading around about me that was a flat out lie. So I went to his lair and questioned him about these rumors. He denied it of course, but I was ready, the spring was wound tight. As bar room fights go this was a good one. He was a bit rotund and out of shape and didn't expect the roundhouse that knocked him to the floor. Even though I may have had a few years on him, I had taken some 'hand to hand combat' lessons when I was younger; as well as having earned a brown belt prior to going to Vietnam. I got in a few hits and then his brothers jumped in; then I was fighting four guys. But I ran my antagonist into the cast iron radiator and he didn't get up. Some other guys at the bar thought it unfair for the brothers to jump in, but I was already done. I fixed my wardrobe and walked out. There is 'honor amongst thieves' as that encounter ended the feud and the whole affair was over. Not another ill word was spoken about me, and I appreciated that very much; I had enough to worry about.

The State Police got involved again when I found that he used my friend/boss's money to purchase materials for the house he was building for himself. I found the receipts and they were verified by the serial numbers; it was the same merchandise. There were also payroll checks made out to someone who'd been dead for quite a few years.

But justice does make its way around one way or another. Several years later, this guy was traveling with a new partner in crime, they pulled out in front of a tractor trailer; and died. .

Teresa had been successful, after a few days stay at a Bed and Breakfast; she found an apartment at mile marker 12; or twelve miles north of Key West. The rent was reasonable, but it was unfurnished. She would take care of that quickly at the 'rent to own' store. She actually stayed the first night there and slept on a beach chair, now that's my girl.

At the same time I was fighting a hard winter. It was eight degrees for over a week; eight! I was also suffering with lower back pain, seems the cold weather made it worse. It was just as severe as after the injury in Vietnam. I started medicating the pain the only way I knew how, liquor. It was a good thing I had my new man on board. If the beeper went off, it usually meant a problem. And he was willing and able to go and check it out.

By this time I had completed two of the four projects which injected much needed cash into the account. The third one was almost done, and the last one was a 'dog's breakfast'. It consisted of 16 houses that had been completely gutted inside and out. They were then reassembled using all new materials. It would have been cheaper to tear those down and replace them with manufactured housing, but HUD had this crazy idea of 'matriculating' welfare families into established neighborhoods. What that did was lower property values for the poor bastards that lived there all of their lives; laying in an automatic weapon with plenty of extra clips, and placing a half dozen locks on doors which used to be left open as long as anyone can remember.

The charge accounts had to be reined in so I tied them up with litigation, eventually, my friend would settle for pennies on a dollar, this also froze the interest rate charges and any penalty's, naturally it was all based on an 'ongoing' police investigation. My good friend who I used to double date with was the lieutenant at the police station involved.

After careful examination, I found a few loop holes in the original contracts that paid off really well, but it still wasn't enough. One day as I drove through the 'Lemon Grove' (a place where they kept the real clunkers) on my way to see the main man, I noticed an l972 'Dodge Demon.' I stopped and checked it out, the seats were covered with clear plastic covers; this was some old bugger's ride. Under the plastic they were like new, under the hood was a 'slant 6' engine, it actually was on a slant. They were known for long mileage and decent gas consumption and it had an automatic transmission which made a nice tight package. I went into my meeting and discussed some of the things mentioned that raised his spirits quite well, anytime I mentioned money savings he was smiling. Finally I asked about the car and he told me I could have it as a bonus, after the meeting I went downstairs and had the girl transfer the title and plate the car, paid her and received the keys to my next car. The HUD loopholes I found were worth $33,000, not a bad trade.

The 'Demon' received the whole treatment, tires, brakes, tune-up and oil change; then into our paint shop. It had a black landau roof that made the paint work easier; we only had to do the bottom of the car in gold, its original color. It ran like a top and was great on fuel; I parked it in the paint booth garage for safe keeping.

One reason my man lost more money was he refused to grease the proper hands. I went to him with a proposition. For $500 cash, the HUD inspector on our welfare apartment job told me he would go 'away.' When I mentioned this to my boss he went absolutely nuts, he started screaming that he would not pay anyone a bribe. I explained that we could save almost $28,000 if we did but it didn't matter. So, I put up my hands and said you are the boss, consider it to be a null and void discussion. As I left I both respected his position and at the same time thought it was stupid, a bag with some dead presidents in it would have gone a long way. My protégé was groomed and briefed and eager to take over the mop up operation. Most of it was punch list items; which is not an act of violence, it is an inspector walking through a finished project and noting little things that had to be corrected before he signed off on it, a sign off meant a long awaited payment, a final payment.

The placement of the crew in the Pocono's was one of my shining stars of reverse psychology. It had the desired effect on the town council and the firemen, I showed them the punch list based on their complaints, which we had repaired and they 'signed off' on them. I then explained that anything else was going to be viewed as add-ons and they would be charged for the work, not HUD. It worked like a charm; they didn't want to spend their money so they accepted everything as complete; another final payment check; another completed project. This one was great to get rid of because it was an hour drive one way to the job site. A few weeks later my boss received a check for $90K and he was no longer pissed about the hotel and bar tab, it had worked and cost us a pittance.

Now it was my turn, I gave my guy that fucking beeper and the keys to the company offices and car and wished him luck. It was February 1986 and I wanted to get the 'Demon' on the road. I made one last stop at my friend's dealership and walked into his glass and leather office. I then said,"…Mr. Dictator for Life I am here to officially announce my retirement from your construction debacle, I intend to get in that car out there and drive to Key West where it is currently 86 degrees and I miss Teresa a great deal. He stood up and came around his desk and shook my hand and thanked me for all that I did with his personal nightmare. He said his only regret was that my predecessor didn't expire in the bar brawl; little did we know how the scales would be balanced. I sincerely apologized for not getting to the point that he could say he broke even; but the damage done by this coked out hood was too much to surmount. I tried every trick that I knew but it was too far gone when I came on board; costly mistakes that I could never fully recover from. He reached into his crumpled tweed jacket, the same one from yesterday which said 'I slept under a bridge last night.' He pulled out a white envelope and stuck it in my lapel pocket with instructions not to open it until I was gone. The phone rang and I let myself out, closing the door very gently.

The envelope contained a month of my regular salary in cash, there was a small note that said this was a tin can parachute and the least he could do, he wished it was more and thanked me for a job well done. I sat there looking at this and thought it was too much, then had another idea. I drove down to the studio and fired up the pot belly stove and electric heater, then returned to the mobile home for some cocktails and a change of clothes. Afterward, it was back to the studio where I did a 16 X 20 painting of him, I used a mixed medium of felt tip pens, pencils and an acrylic wash. This was a rare piece because I never did portraits of people, ever. I achieved a very good likeness of him by having a picture of him from the newspaper blown up to life size then placing it on the canvas. I swiped a frame from one of the ill-fated Hayfield 'one man show' disaster, framed it, wrapped it and dropped it at the dealership prior to 10am, before he got in, with instructions to take it up to his office for him to un-wrap.

I loaded my art trunk in the boot of the 'Demon' along with my leather bag and headed to Key West. My back seat was full of artwork; I would sell it, not to worry. I heard through the grape vine that my ex-boss was quite taken by his portrait and placed it at his house in a place of great prominence, there weren't any notes or cards, just mutual respect. Artwork, framed and ready for hanging was currency in my World and I had a very enviable reputation for selling everything I painted. Part of that was simple, it was the T & M pricing method I used, it leveled the playing field and both client and gallery owner appreciated it.

A good friend of mine said you will not become a famous artist as long as you stay in Wilkes-Barre! He was correct in every sense. It never fails, whenever I have a number of paintings all boxed and framed, I can usually turn a tidy profit. My first stop in Florida was the 'Pink Plaza' art gallery in Boca Raton who still handled my work, though they were down to a few dogs as inventory. I never said that everything I painted was a masterpiece; even Picasso had his dogs.

They were glad to see me and even happier to see an entire show of artwork, over 20 canvas' in all. I kept bringing them in from the car and de-boxing them for the owners to look at, after about 12, the flow stopped, that was enough. While we were gathered around looking at all of this artwork; it was really an impromptu art exhibit. A woman entered the gallery, she was a regular customer of theirs and they made a big fuss over introducing me to her while pointing to the recent work standing all around. She held my hand, another one of those 'I actually felt the hand of a real artist 'ordeals, but I played the part well. She fell in love with one of the compositions, first sale of the day, it was boxed, money changed hands and she left happy. I then told the owners to pick out six paintings they would like to manage which they did. I put the remaining five into the car, when I came back in they had a check ready for me, my 65% of the mornings' sale. It was great, their bank was right there on the way out of the plaza; another $650 to put on the pile.

Over the years I had gotten bits and pieces of information on my old boss who had the foreign car repair shop, well it turns out, he sold that and bought a small locksmith business, talk about the fox in the henhouse. He was somewhere on US #1 so I drove north slowly until I finally spotted it almost into Lakeworth. I found a van out front of a two story building, with the locksmith shop on the first floor and I assumed correctly an apartment on the second. I parked and went in and asked for him by name, they said he was upstairs so I went up and sure enough he was there, cutting a pile of snow. He almost knocked over the table when he saw me, getting up to give me a hug, and a long handshake. This guy was one of those born genius types; he could master anything if he could study it long enough. When he bought the auto repair shop, he knew nothing about cars and ended up doing all of the high end jobs, Turbo Porsches, huge Mercedes etc. I had to laugh thinking what would happen if he was called to fix the lock on the case of the Hope diamond; they'd probably find an IOU in there instead.

During this entire book and for the years from 1970, I have been living in chronic pain from being slammed to the deck while under heavy fire, my lower back, the L4-L5 and S1-S2 region was a mess and is getting worse. This may explain why I was attracted to anything that would relieve some of the pain and stop the crazy nightmares that resulted in awakening covered with sweat.

It was great to sit with an old friend and catch up on all of the dirt; his former neighbor, blondie, did return and became a real pain in the ass, he then leaned over and said "Did you really cover all of her stuff with cow shit?" I said yes I did and it was less than 20 minutes old. I told him how I stood there and held plastic drywall buckets up to the cow's ass and waited. The laughing went on for many minutes; talk about tears flowing and falling off chairs, it was that type of reaction. Then he leaned over again and said "Did you really send her FTD flowers telling her it was over?" Before I said anything I corrected the quote, I told him that I said:' this relationship is terminated.' There was a howl at that and the word terminated kept going around the room between fits of laughter. Finally I gave my car keys to a young guy and told him to run down to Big Daddy's and pick-up a couple of fifths of bourbon and a couple cases of Miller High Life and a few bags of ice, I peeled off a few $50's and sent him on his way. I then resumed my conversation with my friend, he told me that he had some real special stuff if I was interested, I told him yes and that I was going to put together a little party in the back, he told me he'd join me when everything was ready.

I went downstairs and out into the backyard, a guy was setting up some tables and chairs and had the coolers ready, he also set out a half dozen glasses, one of which was a jelly glass that had Fred Flintstone and Dino chasing each other around the outside. Someone poured me a glass of Jack Daniels and handed me a cold beer, the party had started.

It wasn't long before a voice came out of the back of the building that said "your room is ready"! That was my cue to go upstairs and take care of business. He had a few lines laid out and warned me to be careful, he told me the stuff would make your nose bleed, I did the lines and became a new person, we settled our business, money changed hands and I said lets go down and join the party in progress. It was late in the evening when, like a fool, I decided to drive to Key West. I didn't tell anyone else that, I just said that I had to go. In the parking lot of a Burger King in Florida City, I mixed some vodka with an orange drink and washed down a Percodan, and decided to be on my way, it was a huge mistake, the next thing that I remember is waking up in the ICU of the Homestead, Florida hospital, from what I gathered, I hit the bridge going into Key Largo.

The police were very low keyed about the entire thing, I don't know why; the only thing I could think of was they somehow knew about my service record, it usually had that effect. I didn't damage their bridge because I wasn't going that fast when I hit it, they assumed that I fell asleep at the wheel and didn't bother with a blood test. I was there about 4 days when Teresa drove up from Big Coppitt.

We went to the yard where they towed the car after I was discharged, I paid the man for storage and then realized that the car wasn't as bad as I thought, oh, the front end was smashed pretty good on the passenger side, but with a few pulls on a piece of pipe I bent the fender out from the tire. After that I tried the ignition, the engine fired right up, so Teresa followed me for the 100 mile trip to Big Coppitt Key where she had found the apartment. I had to fix the car and made plans to get the parts; after I had time to recuperate a bit.

What was really strange after I started to look at the car more closely was the fact that a bottle of vodka rolled out from under the seat, between the seats there was a bag full of Percodan's and finally, in the glove box was a white envelope with a plastic bag inside containing premium cocaine; they could have locked me up and literally melted the key down for its' metal.

If there was a memoir of the party and that which followed, it was the 'Bama' jelly glass that I mentioned with Fred Flintstone. I must have taken a 'Bimini' walking cup.
After a few calls I found a junk yard with basically the same car and bought the 'nose' from it, but it had to be taken off and I hardly had a mechanics tool set. The people who owned the yard had towed the car up to their office trailer for the sole purpose of entertainment, watching me, in a neck brace and a relentless Sun, dismantling this car. I could see them in there laughing their butts off at me. Finally they came out and loaned me some basic tools which made the job go faster and I drove it home. I was fortunate that a neighbor of mine, who was also a Navy lifer as they are called, in for the 20 years, then retire at age 42, came and helped me re-assemble the car and offered to paint it after it was done. He told me that somehow he knew that he would end up with this car anyway!
When I reflected on my buddy the locksmith, I remembered that he had followed me out to the car and thanked me for the stop by and the money I spent; he said he needed it in a bad way. I told him, he didn't owe me a thing because years ago he had taught me the correct way to make real French 'Bouillabaisse'.

A few short weeks after all of the work on the 'Demon,' Teresa and I went for a drive up the Keys to a State park called Boca Chica. This place was infamous for its really advanced raccoons, it was said that they could figure out extremely complicated latches and enclosures, so when you returned from fishing or something, all of your food was gone and the rest of your stuff was thrown about the place as if done on purpose, even the old hanging your food in a tree trick didn't work. I was surprised they didn't leave a note,

278

"Get a haircut or get out of town…' On the way back, without warning the engine started to pound like crazy, it was called a bearing rap and not something wearing baggy pants with underwear exposed. As I drove very carefully down our street, my Navy friend was laughing his head off. He walked down and said I told you I would end up with this car. On the Naval base we use all slant 6 engines in our tractors for towing those jet fighters around. The base was NAS, or, Naval Air Station located on Stock Island, and it got the name from the old days when they kept their meat cuts on the hoof until needed.

First he traded me a French turd called a Le Car, the starter was bad and after I looked into it I knew why he never fixed it, the part was over $400 dollars and had to come from Paris! This was not going to work so I returned it and he gave me a huge aircraft carrier called a Catalina. It started, ran well; that was all I needed. With my neck brace off I looked for a job, but first set up my studio, then found a gallery on Duval Street, the main drag downtown Key West. After setting up these items I started to look for a heavy equipment position.

The first place I stopped hired me, though the wage was disappointing. I started at $6.25 an hour but was promised a big increase in 30 days of $1.00 dollar per hour; this was fairly standard for South Florida. I had taken the job not knowing how it was going to impact my life for years to come. It is interesting how fate operates, we are thrown into situations without any idea of what piece of the puzzle is in its' future; how that particular future would affect our entire lives' later and to the degree of impact, in my case it was going to be a very large impact, similar to the one that wiped out the dinosaurs.
From day one it was a difficult company to work for, the father who ran the business was an arrogant little prick with a Napoleonic complex, he was also a liar. At first I was thrown into a labor gang and came to find out title or

experience didn't matter, whatever they needed that day, you were it. I did everything from dig ditches to water palm trees, most of my heavy equipment experience came in the form of driving a truck, a job I did, but didn't care for. After digging with a pick and shovel, or walking miles beside a road grader spray painting spots on the shoulder I couldn't take it anymore. So I went into the office and told them that I was hurt bad in Vietnam, this type of work, especially spending a load of time on my feet was killing me. It just so happened that the boss's son was there, well, one of them. The other one was a prick in the making and had taken after his father. This son was somewhat more sensitive and better read. He told his dad that he needed a laborer, with experience in shooting grades with a transit, that I had, and I could read prints; the father with a touch of disgust said, "Take him".

Number '2 son' and I rode around in a small station wagon laying out the various jobs. If you travel to Key West you can thank yours truly for the four lane highway from mile marker 12 to the new, smooth flowing intersection at the entrance to Key West; he and I did all of that work. #2 son was a little on the tubby side so I will just call him Fats from here on in. Fats and I got along well; we hardly talked on the site because I knew most of the time what his next move was going to be.

The college offered a course I wanted to take and you could actually earn grade points from it; a scuba diving course. I talked Teresa into taking it also; it was the YMCA course, the most respected in the World.

The company got this big job, making a huge pad for a home improvement box store that had to be done in one foot lifts. The site had to be filled over 10 feet. A lift has to do with compaction of the fill that was brought in. They had their own pit for making a fill material called 'marl.' They didn't actually make it; they blasted it out of the Earth.

280

The stuff was pure white once exposed to the Sun and was actually just the ocean floor from a long time ago. But when it came to compaction, it was like concrete. The first 8 lifts were one foot, then it dropped to six inches, this was done so that the whole store didn't sink into the mangrove swamp later on.

In my scuba class we reached the point of using tanks in the canals in back of the college. Our degree was "Open Water One", which was diving to the depth of 40 feet. "Open Water Two" went to 90 feet but then you had to figure out math to surface due to the bends; Open Water One was plenty. On Saturday, I would dive and my lips would split open in the salt water from the mouthpiece of the regulator. All week we would make at least 2 visits to this building site and it didn't matter if you had a hat, the Sun would reflect up from the Marl. I looked like Clint Eastwood from that scene in 'The Good, The Bad and the Ugly' when Eli Wallach had him crawling across the desert. This went on for weeks, my lips never healed until we finished that job and I stopped diving for a while. It was sheer brutality, I was screaming into my regulator 40 feet under water and I could only blame myself and Jacque Cousteau for making it appealing as a kid.

Though Fat Son and I got along well, I couldn't say this for his crazy big hipped girlfriend. If you don't believe me when I say she was crazy, munch on this, she drove an AMC 'Pacer'.
This was the car George Jetson drove in the cartoon series on television. She was another Florida blond gold digger with a fear that I was filling Fat Son with ideas that didn't include her. I know when she first met Teresa, she was jealous; maybe she thought he'd realize he could be with a better looking, less pain in the butt, sane, woman. Once the four of us got together for dinner and within 10 minutes Fat Son, who thought of himself as something of an intellectual, using a large combat knife, tried to open an oyster with it and ran it

through his hand. End of the evening, no dinner at his house that night; they went to the hospital and we went home.

As you would have surmised, she talked him into having me thrown off his little crew, and he did it without any real manly gonads, he brought up something stupid I did weeks before and used that as his excuse. I never knew what it was with these girlfriends or wives of friends; there was just bad mojo.

With that job kaput, I ended up on the water truck, which they had hobbled together. They put a big square tank on the back of a Ford truck and a gasoline operated pump, but they never welded any baffles in the tank, which allowed 3000 gallons of water to slouch around and make the truck pitch and lean. The other son had just rolled it over a few weeks prior. He smashed the windshield and dented the roof, so they just cut the roof right off, and there was nothing; no windshield, no roof, just that Sun in the sky.

After a few minutes I knew why the son rolled the truck, besides the lack of baffles, the power steering unit needed a small 'O' ring which came in a kit from Ford that cost $3.00; yes, that is three dollars. I reported it to the mechanics at the office; the old man came out and said he could get a Haitian to drive that for $4.00 an hour, what will it be? On the way out I turned and told him that the truck was going to hurt or kill somebody and it could cost him a hell of a lot more than 3 bucks.

My father had all Ford trucks; I knew exactly what the problem was and even offered to fix it myself. In the power steering unit was a directional valve, when the 'O' ring went bad it would only allow fluid on one side, so you had power steering in one direction, and sheer force in the other; because the pressure made it harder to turn in the opposite direction. I was sent out to water the shoulders from the widening of US 1; a distance of 12 miles. There were culverts for drain pipes that I'd have to back up to in order to get close. I backed up to one, turned on the water and started to pull away, suddenly the steering wheel spun out of my hands and I was going over the embankment instead of up onto the road. The truck just flipped on its' side and shot me out like a catapult, I landed on my back on a pile of marl rocks left there in the 20's by Henry Flagler's track men. I couldn't move but was awake, I looked up to see this truck rocking back and forth on its side deciding whether to squash me like a bug. I was hurt and I knew it was bad, I could feel it.

They sent me home and I signed up for Workman's Compensation, they sent me to a doctor that was a friend of the family, an orthopedic surgeon. He kept telling me I had a muscle strain and I told him he was nuts. I needed an MRI and fast, but he would not order it. This accident occurred on May 26th, 1986 at 10:00am and here I am, arguing with a stupid doctor about something I needed bad. Finally I retained the services of an attorney and stumbled on the best firm in Miami; all they did were workman's compensation cases.
Things changed overnight, I was given more respect, I found out that by law I was entitled to a 2nd opinion and I was to be paid mileage for everything I did relating to the accident. I tried to sue Ford but it was too old a truck; plus, in Florida they do not pay for pain and suffering and I could not sue the company I was working for because they paid into workman's comp; as its' called . Finally, after a few months, I drove up to Miami and had an MRI. That same day, before I even got back from Miami, the 'company' doctor called Teresa and told her to have me at the hospital the next day for surgery. She told him, "You aren't touching that man; you misdiagnosed this from the start. You are an incompetent idiot and a puppet of the family who caused this".
You don't mess with an Irish girl who is pissed.

During this time lapse of a number of months I was working another job; the company was night and day compared to who I had worked for. Now I was operating heavy equipment and even had my own laborer. The only caveat to it all was that this boss had all of the contracts with the Navy and Coast Guard bases.

I really didn't have a choice but to keep working, the workmen's comp. payment was $600 a month; it just wasn't enough to live on in that town. With the new company we worked 7 days a week 6:00am to 6:00pm, it was so difficult and the pain was almost unbearable but I muscled my way through; Mr. Tough Guy. I basically just lived to work, by 9pm I was falling asleep and 4:30am came early.

It was 5:45am when I got to my machine, it was already 94 degrees and the humidity was about the same, then there were the blood sucking mosquitos which travelled in hordes. They would eat me alive until I could get the machine running, the diesel fumes would drive them away. I had to check out all of the fluids and put a few squirts of grease in the major fittings, and then the day began. We built roads and parking lots in these obscure places on the NAS, one time I was lost out there and ran close to a large cargo plane with armed guards hiding in the bushes, they turned me around.

One night I ran into Fat Son and he asked how I was doing, I told him not really well, I then went on to explain that his fathers' stupid attitude was going to cost him a lot of money. I said I wouldn't be surprised if that $3 dollar 'O' ring wasn't going to cost his company $500K before it was over and done. My calculations were fairly accurate after a few years.

This new company was something, one night Teresa came home from the restaurant with just over $400 dollars in tips; cash. This was for a 6 hour shift; I had my paycheck and after all of the taxes, my take home pay was $483.60, for 84 hours of work! What was wrong with this picture? I worked all summer like that. One day our boss told us we could have one Sunday a month off; the first one of the month, wasn't that special.

Some days I worked right next to the runway when the F-14's would do touch and go's. This is when they just touch the tires to the runway then kick in the after burners and scream back into the sky. The problem was my entire insides would turn to jelly when those after burners would kick in; these planes were only about a 100 yards from me, maybe even closer.

As for artwork, there wasn't much time for that right now, though the gallery in Key West was selling a painting once in a while. The problem with Key West is everyone you talk to is an artist, and they don't buy another artists' work usually, and the tourist rarely spent heavy money at this port of call, they went for the key lime pie, cheap knick knacks and photos of Earnest Hemmingway. Just that the gallery sold a couple of my paintings was a milestone in itself for that town; I made out later.

My Cuban Laborer was sitting on the fender of the backhoe as we rubbered down a deserted road. As we rounded the corner, there were two squids trying to hold a huge jet engine on a special trailer from falling in the swamp. I said, should we help these poor bastards, and he said, yeah man maybe we should! So we grabbed our chain and pulled the trailer back onto the road, then hitched it back up to their tractor. I asked them how it happened. They got lost and tried to turn the engine around on this two lane road, barely wide enough for the trailer, and we saw the rest. I then asked them how long they were there holding that thing and they told me if they didn't hear my machine coming, it was almost over. Oops, there goes another 4 million dollar jet engine into the swamp, little did I know that act of kindness would prevent my lynching in a few weeks.

We finished all of our small contracts for this area and we were going to move all of our equipment across the runway and get out of there. For a few days I was operating a large road grader, cleaning up the dirt roads and laying down gravel in the wet spots, naturally we had to make sure that the machines were spotless before driving them over the runway. The F-14's were still active; the control tower was going to give my boss instructions when to 'go'. I cleaned and sprayed every square inch of that road grader with a high pressure water hose, then inspected everything I could possibly see, even using a mirror on a stick(like in Vietnam). When it was my turn, I gunned the engine and had it in 3rd gear, I came flying down the little dirt road and the wheels hit the 4 inch layer of tarmac, when they did all of these round rocks blew out onto the runway, its" called "FOSS" Foreign Objects Surface Survey I believe; don't quote me I was never on an aircraft carrier, maybe it's search? Whatever, the gist of the matter is the place went crazy, jeeps showed up with dozens of swabbies with brooms and shovels. Everyone was frantic because there were angry expensive bee's flying around above us with rockets under their wings. This caused a real snafu, even the big brass showed up, with a rope. I was going to be in a real large pile of trouble for this. When I reached the other side, I told John my supervisor that I checked everything more than once, he knew where the rocks came from. He told me there was a place behind the blade that you would never find until you hit a hard bump; and that I did. He then told me to get back on the machine and get the hell out of here before all hell breaks loose. I reminded him of the jet engine we saved and took off. It was bad, but it got worse. A few days later, I was sent up to pick up a backhoe with a tractor trailer. It was some radar station and it was Super Bowl Sunday. I loaded the machine and this guy came to direct me out because it was a tight place. The next thing I hear is a giant electrical zap, the last 3 inches of the backhoe boom had ripped out their 400 amp electrical service right in the middle of a big play. These guys were mad. I jumped out and said what the hell, he was guiding me out; but the guy shot back, you are the driver.

I was starting to lose it, drinking more, taking pain medication, but I tried to keep working. My next bonehead mistake was taking the guys dump trailer up to his own private key which he was slowly developing. The dump hole was for landfill and was way out almost to the end of the island. So I drive up there and dump the load, then as I am ready to leave the 'maxi-brakes' jammed up. These are special brakes that will kick on if you lose air pressure in the event of an emergency. But I had air pressure and remember being told that they were acting up. I tried every trick I knew to make them kick off and nothing worked. Finally, with 8 brand new tires on the trailer that had just been installed, I tried dragging them; that usually broke them loose. I dragged them all right, after a while I heard what sounded like gun shots, 8 of them, I stopped the truck and got out to look, all 8 tires had been sheered flat on the bottom until the tubes blew up. I disconnected the trailer, which I should have done in the first place, and drove in, parked the truck and went home after a quick stop at the liquor store.

The next day all hell broke loose again and he was going to fire me. My supervisor came to my defense and saved my job, but I had to change all eight tires by myself, I mean take them off the rims and mount different tires; this was a monumental task, which damaged me permanently.

The end came when we were laying 24" diameter steel pipe on the naval base, I was setting the pipes with the backhoe something I've done hundreds of times, when I jerked the pipe and three laborers looked up at me from the bottom of the trench, their look said it all; this pipe will take our heads clean off. John came up and said: 'Jason, you better lay in for a while.' This meant go home and don't come back.

The people that owned the house at Big Coppitt Key rented us the smaller apartment which was on the street. In the back was the main part of the house, and was situated on the canal with a boat slip, it was actually at the end of the canal and very nice. They decided to move to Miami and just keep renting the place. They rented the main house to a 'biker'; which we didn't really understand, but it didn't affect us so we ignored the entire arrangement. That is until the biker and his biker chick did so much damage from parties and fights they were asked to leave, and so were we. The owners wanted to come back to the Keys and also wanted the whole house.

Teresa and I flew up to Pennsylvania to seek a second opinion from a neurosurgeon who had come highly recommended, it was late Fall of 1986 just prior to the holiday season, she asked for time off from her job downtown and planned on spending a few weeks with her parents and sister's for this holiday season.

I met with this doctor and he called up a CT scan and a MRI to get a better idea of what was going on in my back. After reviewing everything I was called to his office. He had concluded that I needed extensive surgery in the L-4 & L-5 regions as soon as possible, there was a blown disc and what appeared to be bone fragments pushed into the spinal cord cavity. This doctor wanted to know why it had taken so long for me to address this problem and assumed quite rightly that I was in very heavy acute pain. I told him that he was correct. After the holidays I went into a hospital in Scranton called CMC and had the first of many surgical interventions. This was November 1986. At the time I had no idea that these would continue until 2003, which proved to be the last and final surgery.

This began an entire new chapter in my life; it was a steady stream of doctors, surgeries, physical therapy, medications, MRI'S, and more doctors; and then repeats all of the above.

I will not attempt to paraphrase the several years and just deal with them as they occurred. One truth that I did learn was an expression: 'one back surgery is one too many'. The doctor had noticed that there were damages that were older then the accident of 1986. I explained my injury in Vietnam and he said that it made sense because what should have been a 2 hour surgery turned into a massive 5 plus hours, a long time to be inside someone's back.

Teresa left for Key West and stayed with a few girlfriends while she looked for a new flat. I attended some physical therapy sessions and did a lot of walking, even though it was difficult. After I was stabilized and found fit to travel, I too returned to Key West and moved into our new apartment which was in a part of town called 'Hilton Haven.' This was right across from the yacht club and a liquor store. With the new found knowledge and my steady growing files, I submitted another claim with the Veterans Administration. At the same time, I re-animated my workman's compensation claim and sent in all of my expenses, they were required to pay for anything relating to my medical reports. It was a frustrating game, I'm sure my ex-employer had something to do with challenging all of the medical invoices submitted. I would receive regular checks, then they would stop and it required a call to my attorney in Miami to bust up the log jam. I did manage to continue to write poetry and edit the manuscript which was to be the first book. I also wrote articles and did some artwork, usually pen and ink, for the 'Solares Hill' newspaper. This brought in a few extra dollars which I spent on liquor which helped quell the pain. My artwork never stopped, this has been a continuous thread throughout my entire life, especially since 1970 when Alchemy Studio was established. I had given up on cars completely and picked up a 'conch cruiser' that is a bicycle with an extra-large seat, one gear and huge handle bars holding a basket and a bell. Teresa used the VW Rabbit and I sold the Catalina back to my Navy friend. Life was changing in a very fast way.

Prior to my surgery in Scranton, the doctor said something to me which I found very disconcerting. He had asked me how much I was drinking, I told him the typical social menu of a cocktail before dinner and some wine with the food. He looked at me and said, Jason try another answer, something more convincing. His next comment was even more interesting, he wanted me not to drink for 10 days prior to the surgery, and said he would verify this with blood work. Then came the bomb shell, his comment was, I don't want you to go into D.T's on my operating table. I acted highly offended and he just smiled and said you know what I am saying. He said he had another friend named Jason, who he asked to stop by and talk to me during my recuperation. It turned out to be Jason Miller, the playwright and actor. Mr. Miller did come by to see me, he sat down and told me his story of struggling with alcohol in his life; his comment was that it's an occupational hazard for people like us, meaning people in the arts; nothing to be ashamed of, just something that needed to be really looked at with a clear view. At the time of his visit he had not taken an alcoholic drink for over 10 years and told me he was doing his best work ever. He told me it was instrumental in his part in the 'Exorcist' but was quick to say that would have never happened if he was still drinking. Before I returned to Key West he called me and arranged a meeting at a coffee shop in Scranton. He told me that he saw I was having the same problems he had and I should look at it long and hard; I was told not to wait until I was within an inch of death in an ICU before doing something. I listened with one ear you might say; I had been the drug and alcohol counselor at this table, not him. But I was kind and considerate and looked forward to seeing him again, maybe in one of his plays, he gave me his number and said just call first and it will be arranged.

After I returned from the operating room and was up and about, I met a 'goomba' from Dunmore; the place where all of my rental equipment disappeared on a regular basis, back in the construction business days. It was one of the HUD contracts, another fire hall extension.

This man owned a night club in town with dancing girls, they would visit him every night at the hospital and bring in a bottle of Crown Royal, so after dinner was served, it was happy hour in the hospital lounge; pure undiluted insanity. The fact that I was the guy who built their brand new fire hall made me a hero to these guys. And there were a lot of them, all in leather jackets, black of course, they came in to see my Demerol compadre, and in true Italian fashion, he would introduce me to everyone and pile accolades on me for being the guy who fixed their fire hall 'problem' meaning the guy I replaced. Not only that, when things disappeared I didn't call the cops in, and that gained me more respect than anything else. There were Paulys and Tonys, Guido and Joeys; all of which I had to shake hands with. All of these guys would lean over and tell me quietly, if you need anything done, I mean anything capeche? Just call and we will take care of it. It made me feel real tough, hell, I could have somebody whacked, and these were the guys who really made people disappear, permanently. Plus every night one of his girls came in, these women were not nuns, they would make a brass pole speak dirty words. Under their very short habits was the bottle of Crown Royal. It was just crazy, I'm in there for a major back surgery and he was there for his heart and we are getting pleasantly drunk every night.

The Don of Dunmore was being checked out before me, he stopped by my room and slipped a bottle under my pillow, then gave me his card and said; "…Listen, Jocko, youse come by my joint and remember your money ain't no good there, capeche?" I did.

Now it is time to get back on track, I started to talk about Key West and got side tracked into a few stories that were told because of the perverse humor in them, because in Key West there wasn't anything to laugh about. It started with drinking Bourbon one night (have you ever noticed where different liquors would always get you in trouble?) and suddenly got this craving for pot, this was unusual because I really didn't care for the stuff. I made my way down to 'little Havana' the section of town for matters of this nature, and bought a dime bag, which is $10 and only had a $20, the guy told me to wait right there for my change, what an idiot I am at times. I then got a claw hammer from the car and went looking for the guy. As I walked around, I shoved the hammer into my shorts and then came upon a lot of laughing, this was it. Sure enough, there he was telling the story of the stupid white boy. As I was ready to beat this dude into oblivion a cop car came by, saw the hammer and that was it, chrome bracelets. Teresa let me cool my heels in a 9 by 12 until the next morning when I was brought before the judge. His honor must have had a good cup of coffee because he fined me a few hundred with a warning of course. How could I tell him my side of the story, it would have leaked out to CNN!

As the months passed, I never noticed that Teresa, the love of my life, had enough and moved out, she rented a room off of a Navy guy in town who was never there. I was forging new roads into unknown dimensions of time and space.

I had started to have problems with my pancreas that landed me in the ICU of one of two hospitals in Key West, the other one I was not welcome in, Persona Non Grata. The first attack of a pancreatic nature had come in 1986 right after my accident. I think it was early summer when I was rushed to Depoo Hospital. I was confined to a corner bed where the nurse's couldn't see me unless they came out from the desk. Having nothing to do, no drinking or eating for 7 days while a tube in my nose pumped out my stomach 24/7 I figured out how to dis-arm the pump machine. Allow me to define the word insanity for you.

Teresa came in to visit me one evening, after some small talk I finally worked up the nerve to ask her to bring me a pint of vodka, she just stared at me, burst out laughing then said why do you think you're here? Now I was becoming angry, so I told her to forget about the vodka, make it a 6 pack of Colt 45 malt liquor. She then said no and that was final, then turned and started out of the ICU, I began cursing and shouting things I am not proud of until the nurse's came in with a needle and shot it into my IV. That 'was all she wrote' as they say; I was out cold for about three days and when I came to, my wrists and ankles were tied to the bed, I shouted for the nurse and asked her what the meaning of this was? She told me they had no choice because of my two IV's and NG tube, she then added, you went into full blown DT's, screaming things about Vietnam and disrupting our other patients. We had no other option but to keep you sedated.

The day I was released from the hospital I walked across the street and bought a 16 ounce can of Colt 45 to sip on while I walked to Tom's 'Caribbean' liquor store where I actually had a charge account. It wasn't until I got back to Hilton Haven that I realized I was still sporting all of my plastic wrist bands from the hospital, all four of them. I hacked them off with an old steak knife and proceeded to start all over again, trying to reach liquid 'Nirvana.'

The insurance company and my attorney decided that I was suffering from depression and needed the services of a psychiatrist, so once a week I went over to this guy's office and sat there. He decided, in all of his medical diploma wisdom I was suffering from an acute case of Librium deficiency and prescribed a heavy dose with unlimited refills at my drugstore where I also had a charge account. I was also being prescribed a serious dose of narcotic pain medications with an open ended, use as needed, label. Of course now my mixing all of these Smith & Kline wonder drugs with a copious amount of liquor had me sliding sideways in this distorted reality. The amazing thing is I kept painting!

This efficiency apartment was furnished with the best Goodwill had to offer. I had a circa 1940 stuffed chair and hassock; the chair had a broken spring in the cushion which stuck into my ass in the correct position. Why I never fixed it

I shall never know. Maybe it was my idea of a hair shirt or self-flagellation, but then again, when you have 100mg of Librium in you washed down with a quart of vodka, a spring in your ass doesn't really amount to much. The kitchen was one of those really old 'all in one' porcelain units containing a stove, refrigerator, sink and a storage cabinet. Another thing I still had was the 'Bama' jelly glass with Flintstone and Dino chasing each other. I had this idea that as long as I used a glass, I still could maintain a modicum of civility. I bought a floor lamp with a round table built into it as the perfect addition to my easy chair. On a few cinderblocks was a 13" black & white television with balls of aluminum foil stuck on the 'rabbit ears' for better reception. Now I could sit there with a cocktail in my hand and lust after re-runs of the 'Donna Reed Show' on the 'telly' what more could a man want?

It would take approximately 30 to 45 days before the pain in my chest would start, I knew what that was; so I charged a few large bottles of store brand 'Maalox' to have on hand. I would need this every morning. The following few tales are pretty disgusting, it is your call, but I promised an unabashed, truthful autobiography, so here it is.

When I came to, I would reach for my jelly glass and knock back whatever was in it just to get up and walk to the sink. Most mornings there would be dead ants in the glass and I would try to pick them out with a teaspoon, but my hands would be shaking so bad I was afraid of breaking the glass. Then one morning there it was, a palmetto bug suicide. The remains were floating upside down in a half glass of cheap red vermouth I purchased from Tom for $1.00 a bottle, I bought the whole case. This should have told me something, you can drop a shipping container on a Palmetto bug and it will just get up, give you the finger and walk away. At first I responded like the incident in Australia with the expired young lady, but then I just brought this to my lips and sipped the vermouth while this dead bug bounced off my nose. After that, I staggered to my feet and walked the walls to the kitchen, all 10 feet of it. It was then that the ritual started.

In this hand was a bottle of store bought Maalox, and in this hand was a glass of liquor, usually vodka and on the counter was the bottle of Librium. I would drink some pink goo and follow it with some vodka, then vomit a pinkish froth into the sink. I did not mention the internal bleeding did I? This ritual would go on until the vodka stayed where it was supposed to be, then I would throw a handful of pills in my mouth and wash them down with Count Vomitski vodka. I was now ready for my date with Calvin Kline's' girlfriend, or a trip to 'Uncle Sam's' pawn shop, I had one gold ring left that carried me over while waiting for my checks, which came every two weeks. When the money did come in I would go and retrieve my ring and pay the $5.00 interest. Checks could be a problem, when I went to the bank my hand was shaking and they would not accept my signature even though they knew who I was, just another of life's' degradations when you look like hell and smell worse. I would then have to tell the girl, I shall return, it all had to be melodramatic. I would duck out and get a half pint of something cheap and slug it down by the dumpster behind the bank, then make a grand entrance and with plenty of flourish, sign the check and the countertop with it.

After approximately 2 and one half months, my ritual would not work, the pain was unbearable and nothing would stay down. It was the fourth visit to the ICU, my Internal Medicine doctor was an old Cuban family name in Key West, plus he was the only one in town at that time, it was the end of l987. He came into my room one day and was checking my chart. I started the conversation by saying; I am dying doctor aren't I? He spun around, came up to the side of my bed and pointed a finger at me and said: " You sir are not dying(his face was red) it takes great nobility to die, what you are doing is killing yourself and I refuse to have your blood on my hands, this is the last time I will treat you !" He knew as well as I what that meant, I had to leave Key West. After my discharge, I packed up my studio and shipped it back to Pennsylvania, then moved all of the paintings down to my gallery on Duval Street. I then booked a flight for Wilkes-Barre, arriving on December 20th. At the time I didn't know that Teresa had spoken to my friend C.C. in Wilkes-Barre, so certain things were already in the making up there and I would be walking into them, if I survived.

Virgil had shown me some new levels of hell; it was like the Guggenheim in New York, a spiral in continuous descent. Frank Lloyd Wright must have seen his own future in that design, what neither of us counted on were the gnashing teeth, constant moaning and that feeling of being so far removed from anything even remotely spiritual that all was darkness except the glass as you raised it to your lips and heard a voice telling you that all was fine, it is everyone else that doesn't understand how complex this thinking has to be in order for it to be correct. You know, you are the only one that understands the levels, you're not going down, you are going up; the universe is upside down, no one knows this except you. I must go now, but I'll be back, have another!

There I was spread eagle on the bed with a cheap, metal blade ceiling fan above me, running on high. Everyone's greatest fear of having an overhead fan above your bed came to pass, this thing dropped and landed between my legs.

It left two handsome cuts on my inner thighs. With great fanfare and marching bands, I will have you know that 'Happy Johnston' was undamaged in any way after very careful examination, not that I used this instrument that often during these troubled times, unless of course Donna Reed came by begging me to put her in that way with my child. I also saw myself as the temple eunuch in the Forbidden City, if nothing else, a soprano that guarded concubines while singing high C's.

Many years earlier while living in Australia, my little croquette went to see this 'white witch' who lived in one of the small mountain towns. The woman was very well known in both Australia and Europe and she supposedly had a secret list of clients who conferred with her. After she returned from the witches' house she bugged the hell out of me to go, finally I did. As soon as I walked in, she said; "Do you have problems with your neck and back?" I said yes I do. She then told me that I was hanged as a heretic in a past life. She then did the tarot cards and told me that I would face a life and death struggle in my mid-30's (I was 27 at the time) but I would survive and my life would change completely. She then went on about living to be 86 years and realizing my true fame and ambitions during my 60's. I never forgot that and here I was in hand to hand combat with death for my very soul and I was 37 years old.

ONLY THE FINEST MATERIALS

The curtain didn't just fall, it shredded as it hit the stage. To this day I haven't any recall on the period of November 1987 until well into December of the same year. On December 20th I sat in the 'Propeller' lounge at Key West airport awaiting my flight to Miami and onto the far cold North. I had Bloody Marys' and Librium lined up on the bar, there would be no fear on this plane ride.

While I sat there I had plenty of time to think; that story I related about the palmetto bug in the glass, it would be simplistic to say why not just get up and wash it out! The answers are not that simple after you go off the path completely. It becomes complicated once you allow your brain to go on vacation and a relative is operating your mind. This relative is not someone you particularly like but he is always there on the night stand and he is not reading Tolstoy's "War and Peace." I knew I was in bad shape, in fact I knew that I was dying from the pursuit of immediate relief and serenity. My pancreas was cooked, I had internal bleeding from a hole in my stomach wall and my liver wasn't functioning properly. My skin had turned a shade of yellow and the whites of my eyes ceased to be white, they had turned a light orange but my brain, controlled by that relative I mentioned, kept telling me I was a stud, god's gift to the World, it was absurd.

Here I am; I'll present the Jason of December 20th, 1987. His clothes are from the finest of Salvation Army collection, a pair of linen pants that were 4 inches too short, the shirt used to be white but was showing the ghosts' of many stains. I was 262 pounds and it was all puff. My normal weight has always been below 220, size 36 or, 38" waist, depending on my habits and exercise regime. I was wearing $4.00 canvas shoes from the drug store, the inner sole would wear away and you had to fold a piece of cardboard and stick it in there. But! I didn't see any of this. In reality I was Jack London's' character from John Barleycorn. Suddenly the memories of the past few months came flooding back, I could not stop them even by switching to

Black Russians. The hospital stay when I was tied to the bed, the nurse told me that if Teresa had not found me I would have perished from hypothermia because I was lying on the terrazzo floor which was sucking all of the heat from my body, then there was the trashing around, the vivid dreams of Vietnam, no, they were not dreams, you have to sleep to have dreams. The images I had been experiencing came from somewhere else in my brain. Then the doctor's statement about nobility in death, he was 100% correct, I understood now. All of those years I tried so hard to drink these thoughts away; along with the constant pain, and it stopped working. Oh! Sure, it was going to stop the thoughts and the pain but at the ultimate price a person can pay, your life.

In Miami, I had a layover and was falling asleep at the bar, the barkeep came over and told me to go sleep somewhere else, I told him I would fix that problem straight away, I had some cocaine on my person, a going away present, nice friends are they not? I went into the men's room and started to chop out a few lines on the stainless steel T.P. holder, I swear you could hear it all over the airport. Soon I returned to the bar talking my head off, sure, hit me again Ambrose.

Then the flight to Wilkes-Barre, they still had those roll up steps back then, I came off the plane waving like some .50 cent politician. The Duke was picking me up and I could see him, then it hit me, 8 degrees above zero. He dropped me off at the bighouse and I borrowed my mother's car to go to the liquor store to get Kahlua and vodka for black Russians. Then I drove back and sat with Mary T. We talked and she actually had a small drink with me. I told her that I was finished; I had squandered a perfectly good life in search of something that lied to me. She listened and told me to do what had to be done, the problem had been oblivious for a long time, how much time have you spent on the solution? It made sense, I didn't spend any time on that, but first I had to survive.

As I got dressed in more appropriate winter attire, I told her how sorry I was for calling collect to tell her how well I was doing. Isn't that statement in itself ridiculous? After packing a few warmer clothes in my leather bag, I grabbed the vodka and told her that I would be at the studio tonight and a friend was driving me to the hospital the next morning.

As I walked down the mountain road; that same dirt road which was all paved now and had lines painted on it, will wonders never cease? For some reason I started to howl like a dog, this in turn started a few more dogs, the more I howled the more dogs joined in until I had a complete cold nosed classical orchestra playing the same tune. Years later my brother Mark told me about it because his dog, Zack, was one of my bass voices.

At the studio I fired up the electric heater and pot belly stove, it had taken a bit of time but the place became warm enough to be comfortable. I finished my vodka that evening at around 11:30pm and have not had one since; it was 24 years ago. But, it wasn't over by a long shot, I had a long way to go, it was like crawling naked, over broken glass up hill to hear myself say I love you over a pay phone.
I spent a few days in the hospital and on the morning of the 23rd I was transported to another hospital. After being checked in and assigned a bed, they told me that the next day my work would really start. In the morning my breakfast consisted of mush, my condition warranted it. Then I was placed in a red folding chair in the middle of a room. All of a sudden, a ton of people filed in and sat down in a big circle around me. Soon they were all asking me these crazy questions, how did I get there? Simple, it was a Ford I think. This went on until I felt myself growing distant like everyone was getting smaller and farther away; I then just remember falling over, chair and all. Later they told me when I fell over a puddle of blood spilled off of the chair and unto their antique carpet. I had gone into pancreatic shock and they rushed me back to the other hospital by ambulance.

This is where it really gets bad. All of that day and night I was given a battery of tests, blood work-ups, X-rays, CT scans and on and on. Finally, on Christmas morning at 6:30am three doctors walked into my room with clipboards, one was the spokesperson. He was short and to the point. Mr. Goodman, we have the results of the tests and what they show is that your insides are toxic, after careful consideration we have arrived at the conclusion that you have roughly 10 days to live. He apologized for being the bearer of this news but it was clear cut and medical.

Death at 37, an interesting present for the man who has everything! One of the nicer nurse's had placed a small green Christmas ball on the stainless steel tree they used for the bags of medicine. I laid there and stared at that little green ball just thinking of all the things that I had not done in my life. I never walked through the cave of the winds at Niagara Falls; I did not drink espresso under the Eiffel Tower in Paris, and other thoughts of this nature. I thought of Teresa and felt really bad, I almost cried, though I had not cried since Vietnam for anything. Then I became frightened, I began to think that nothing good can come of my death, I had screwed and hurt so many people, I would need another 37 years just to make that right. In fact, the fitful dreams started, they were all the same, it was moist, humid you might say, the walls were stone and wet, it was dark and there was water dripping somewhere in the distance, I felt the walls and they were covered with a slime, a wet slime. This was a reoccurring dream every time I managed to doze off. It was always the same, day and night.

As I was lying there two nurses walked down the hall and one must have whispered something, the other one said, loud enough for me to hear I am sure, " I have people on the other wing that are REALLY dying!" I felt like I needed a bed pan after that remark, god what a stupid thing to say for my benefit. Welcome to wonderful Wilkes-Barre, the valley with a heart, that was an actual sales pitch for the place.

My first chore of the day was to fill a torpedo with orange liquid. Next came the thumb wheel that controlled the drip rate of the Demerol, I adjusted the bed to the most comfortable position and dimmed the lights. Now I had a steady stream of painless, semi-comatose existence, the pieces of the puzzle were now complete. The one thing I had not counted on was the strength of the human mind to jack-hammer its way through very thick walls of chemically fortified concrete.

Small phrases from the doctors dialogue started to buzz around in my head, you are dying and there is nothing we can do, 37 years old, life in the fast lane, race cars, motorcycles, irate husbands with spear guns (that actually happened in Boulder, he was a professional diver that came home early) war, steady showers of Agent Orange, atomic bomb factories, and a score of other ways of dying. At least they carried a stipend of dignity, but cheap booze trying to shut out the noise? This was absurd.

In case you may have wondered, my family allowed me a company health insurance card, plus I had the medical from my accident. If it weren't for those, I would be in a cardboard box under a bridge somewhere.

Another good one was, 'your internal organs are toxic and ruined,' hell I couldn't even part myself out like a junked car and save some other poor bastards life, or eyesight. After I go what will be left behind, a putrid mess that someone will have to clean up. This was only the physical aspect of my demise. There was the emotional impact, many people had never seen the levels that I had stooped to, the ones reserved for dictators and court jesters. Then it struck me, the girl I loved from a far for almost 15 years, what did I do to her? She was a package that only God himself could assemble and deliver, I blew it, a waste, shame, nurse I need a sleeping pill!

Sleep wasn't a respite, that same dream was there, it was still as humid and dark as ever. There must have been

Banshees flying about just waiting to grasp that black mass of past failure.

If I crossed the River Styx, the Greek warriors would throw me back into the river with a warning. I was in the process of dying a death of despair; a black death you might say, a black death without boils. All excuse's seemed so pitiful now, being an artist, combat veteran, depressed, none of it mattered.

Every time I dozed off I ended up in that same place, dark, humid stone walls, this became my personal reality. The stones had been cut like a Mayan ruin, perfect fit inside an atmosphere of quiet stagnation, no movement, just blackness. When my lungs would heat up I would awaken, completely covered with sweat, the nurse would have to change the sheets most of the time. Whenever I closed my eyes I could taste that old stagnant air, it had gotten to the point where I did not want to sleep because everything would repeat itself in precisely the same detail.

My PTSD from the war in Vietnam, interesting enough, would never appear in my dreams anymore as long as the dark, rank stonewalls were present. This only confirmed that fact that what I was seeing was undoubtedly my new home in the afterlife. The result of living in a negative way, abusing those around me, who loved me, and damaging those that didn't. I made a mockery of the entire idea of emotion; my understanding of emotion was reduced to just lust and anger. If a higher intelligence created us to see with love in our hearts, then guys like me fell into the company of people like Hitler and Edi Amin with their self- inflicted genocide.

They needed my bed one day and moved me to a different floor and into a regular room. Many of the tubes and wires had been removed from my person and they just used needles to inject me with whatever it was they wanted inside me. I was placed in a room with a view of denuded trees and cold snow covered mountains. One day, I decided enough was enough, I would become more proactive.

I called the nurse and asked to be taken to the chapel in the hospital, I remembered Jim Morrison screaming out in one of his rants: you cannot petition the Lord with prayer! Well, I could try. Nurse hatchet came and loaded me into a wheelchair and drove me downstairs to the small chapel. On the way down I don't know whether it was an accident or she wanted it to happen, but as she blabbed with another nurse the elevator doors closed on my toes. We eventually got there and she prudently stood outside while I tried to make a deal with whoever was in control of these requests.

After about 15 minutes, I thought that this is ridiculous, I had my chance in 1983 and blew it; so what was the sense of crying the blues now. I called my nurse and asked her to return me to my room.

When we returned my bed had been all made up and there, in the middle of the covers was a small card addressed to me. As I sat in the wheelchair, I opened the card and it was signed by 74 people, the entire staff and population of the high end hospital I was in before I hit the floor. Allow me to explain this, I am of German heritage, I am also an Aquarius, I am not inclined to fanatical behavior in any way, I do not attribute paranormal events to anything in particular without a thorough investigation. But what happened in that room, holding a get well card in my hand is something that I could never explain. It seemed as if the room became very bright, I could not hear anything other than a voice that was embedded in my head and did not belong to me or my thoughts, in essence I was told that I would survive this ordeal, my life had been spared, and, most importantly, this was how I would maintain that existence, meaning the people on the card. I'm sure it wasn't just those individuals, but all of mankind. Then it all changed back, the nurse was saying, "I need this chair, are you getting out or what"?
One of the first things I noticed after this event was my

reoccurring dream had stopped, I actually fell asleep for a few hours and awoke refreshed.

I knew beyond a shadow of a doubt that I was going to live, and to maintain my life I would help others who were on the spiral of self-destruction. I felt free and for the first time that I can recall I felt good inside. Please understand, this wasn't Fatima, I was still a very sick person internally and that would require over a year to repair with medications and diet, or lack of a diet I should say.

Most of my life I was an agnostic, my thoughts on organized religion agreed with Karl Marx; it was the opiate of the masses. I was not raised in any religion, nor was my house a temple to any deity. Mary T. having been an antique dealer for 40 years acquired all of the books of religions from around the world, she even had a set of the 'Black Books' for Satan worship if that was your pleasure. Her comment to me and all of my brothers was the same, there they are, religions, pick one that interests you, or try them all. That was our religious training at 7 or 8 years of age. I honestly can say that I leaned toward Zen Buddhism; it made you personally responsible for your own life and that appealed to me. One of my early critiques of the Catholic doctrine was the confessional. It allowed someone to commit the same crime over and over yet still opened the door to heaven. And of course there was always the devil, like the fate of my Rolling Stones records, Satan may or may not exist, who cares; Zen makes us totally responsible to ourselves without any outside influence.

After I received my orders for Vietnam I had to go and get my 'dog tags' made up. A rather obese lady sat behind a small window with a typewriter that typed metal, she was chewing gum, had a Jersey accent and was wearing those glasses with the fins on them like a Plymouth Fury they used in the movie 'Christine.' Anyway, she inserted two blanks in this machine and asked the standard questions, name, rank and serial number then the question of religion. I told her that I was a Pantheist, she turned and looked at me over her eyeglass's and said; "youse can be katholick, protasent, or jewish, or just 'no preference", and that is on my tags to this day, no preference.

On my dresser in the bedroom is my "manbox," every male of age has one. Mine happens to be a cigar box, a nice wooden one with brass hinges and a clasp; it held "Churchill" size cigars. Inside, under my wrist watches and rings etc. I have treasures of a lifetime. A guitar pick used by the lead guitarist of the "Quick Silver Messenger Service" in a small lounge in Hawaii when I was on my way back from Vietnam. There is a real wooden nickel good for one drink at a bar that no longer exists, a tooth in a small plastic box which I may have to explain. I went to a dentist in Charleston with a tooth that was killing me. He looked and said it would have to come out, I asked why couldn't you just save it? His comment was that "Not even Jesus can save that tooth." He left the room and my inner voice told me to run away, but I stayed and he pulled the tooth, when it landed on the tray in front of me, I could see that there was nothing wrong with it, the thing was healthy and pink etc. here he had pulled the wrong tooth. So I grabbed that one and have saved it all of these years as a reminder of the money I spent, and the pain, of having implants installed. One day I'm reading the paper and there is a story about an alcoholic dentist who gassed someone while he was drinking in another room. Also, there is a P-38 can opener, boardwalk pennies which are squashed into ovals and at the bottom, what this detour is all about, are the dog tags with the words 'no preference' on them.
I went off on another tangent there and do apologize, but getting back to whatever place we were, I have no idea of what happened in that hospital room that day.
They decided to move me back into the other facility, their reasoning was I was dying anyway and had health insurance, so why not, it was as if I was dying until the

money ran out then it was time to go. They loaded me down with all of this stuff, a waffle bed cover, a case of absorbent pads in case my butt started to bleed again and I wasn't near a blood bank or even a drive through. Its' been real, there is the front door, bye now, take care of yourself, we hope to not see you again, here are some peanut butter crackers for the ride.

A car came and drove me back to the psychiatric hospital in the small town outside of Scranton, PA. Besides the grounds and architecture, it was an old mansion that some rich family donated to this trust from which the hospital emerged. The people I shared this place with were very interesting. There was a 'Doctors without Borders' guy who one night was talking a lot and sort of slipped up when he mentioned who he really worked for, they were spooks from the CIA, and trained doctors of course. There was a rich son of an Iranian or one of those sand piles. I ended up sharing a room with one of T Boone Pickens corporate raiders if you remember the days of the hostile company takeovers. One day he told me that his plane ticket was only one way.

The entire World, or a good part thereof, was represented in this facility. Then I arrive, the Red Badge of courage returns and check back in December 30th l987. I would celebrate the New Year in this environment. Most of us were stress and self-medicated cases, they did have an understanding of Vietnam and PTSD, which helped me out, and they dealt with chronic pain, another issue on my shopping list. I spent over a month there and the only thing that sucked was my diet. I was on a special no fat, no taste diet. For the first few weeks it didn't matter because everything I ate came right back up in a few minutes. I really should have taken my meals in the men's room, chewing on a few paper towels and washing it down with some hand soap, I didn't care for the toilet tissue (it had a floral after taste). I may have been informed of my survival, but I can tell you, the first year was difficult, I lost a lot of weight from not eating at all, and the problem of keeping it down was always an issue.

While I was there for two weeks, they finally allowed me a phone call, and of course I tried to call Teresa but couldn't get her, so I left a message with her friends as to where I was and the number, a few days later she called me back. I could feel the physical distance between us over the phone.

Our conversation was basically 'fluff'. We had been accustomed to practically reading each other's minds prior to this. I knew she was hurt, and probably even scared; for me that is. And why should someone watch the person they love, die. She didn't volunteer a phone number where I could reach her; I had a feeling I wouldn't talk to her often while I was here.
I did tell her that when I was discharged, I was going to approach her father with hat in hand and promise to be the best man that I could be if she and I were reunited, with that, the conversation was over.

It was about 11pm when I placed the receiver down in its cradle. Joe, the night councilor had a very interesting past. He was short and tight; perfect for the Navy Seals. He told me of a few old diesel submarines in Vietnam that he had been on. They would sneak up the river as far as they could go then fire him and his demolition pack out of a torpedo tube. He would then sneak into a V.C. camp; then hide in the swamp. He did this on a number of occasions until he had enough C-4 in place to blow a pretty good hole in the jungle and the V.C. encampment.

I liked talking to this guy, guess I was telling him I was unsure of what Teresa would do if I didn't get back to Florida soon; this time he felt like I was just complaining. He said "Listen Jason, make up your mind, you can stay here and get better, or if you want, there is a bar about a mile down the road. If you're not staying let me know, we need your bed". With that he walked away. At first I was highly offended, but he was right; I was here for me, no one else.

311

If Teresa and I were meant to be, then it would happen. If not, I was in store for a new adventure, a sad one I must admit, but a new one.

Here I was taking offense to the truth. A few weeks ago I was afraid to fall asleep; now 10 days had passed and I was still alive. If I wanted to end my life all I had to do was to walk down to that bar I was told about. People that are serious about committing suicide, for the most part, do not walk around with a big sign on their back; it is illegal you know. I never understood that, how can it be considered illegal? I'm talking about an individual's right to end his/her life, whatever the reason may be; disease, pain, love lost, it should still be their right.

But I was still in that bed the next day. They did a lot of testing. One was the MMPI (I believe that is the proper term), it consisted of 538 questions and was administered at a computer. You had a choice of two responses; true or false. No maybe, or sort of, or it depends. They had another one the CMPI; that was used for people who had been in combat. All of these required about three hours to complete. They then placed a profile of your personality on a graph; and it was pretty accurate.

My roommate Jack introduced the 'broken brain' theory to me one evening. He drew an analogy of our brains being expensive, exotic sports cars parked in the driveway. We could jump in and start it, rev up the engine, turn on the radio, play with the seats and windshield wipers but we couldn't drive it anywhere. There was a part broken in the transmission and it was impossible to repair or find a replacement. In other words, our brains were in perfect condition except for a small part that dealt with drinking any alcoholic beverages, that was the part that could not be fixed. A normal application of Jacks theory would be to bring out a bottle of fine red wine, we could admire it, discuss the label and talk about its' vintage but once it was uncorked, the waiter would only bring three glasses, none for me thank you. For myself, I found that the removal of drinking from my life was both good and meaningless. At an event that took place in Greenville, SC with Teresa; a very posh affair, there were waiters everywhere in little red jackets and bow ties with trays full of champagne. My business representative whose corporation, Fox TV, was responsible for this gala event asked me several times if he could get me a drink, he was being polite, this was Southern hospitality, plus my accounts represented a large portion of his commissions. About the sixth time he asked, I said:" Bill. I tried that stuff on a number of occasions several years ago and it just did not make any sense." As I walked away, I glanced over my shoulder and there was this man standing there just looking into his drink.

Naturally cliques would form and there were a few romantic encounters, occasionally you would stumble on one of these under the cloak of darkness. A marriage made in heaven. The psychiatrist would perform the vows, everyone in the wedding party would be given Prozac prior to the big kiss at the end, and the table centerpiece would have a Glock 9mm pistol in it, sprayed pink and all nicely decorated with ribbons and flowers.

My clique was the egghead group, the intellectuals who, in reality, were very dangerous. My intellect had failed me in Key West; what normal person would endure the pain of several pancreatic attacks.

During my entire stay, the only person who made an attempt to visit me was the Duke, no one else of my entire family even called. We Germans have a habit of cutting lose a family member and letting them drift. I wasn't especially well received in my hometown or at my family's house. Over the years I had pulled some real blunders like driving a bulldozer down the main street on my way to crush a bar because they had insulted my honor. When I saw all of the gun barrels in my path of travel, I decided to save my honor for another day. One day at the institute I was going about my business when the P.A. announced "Mr. Goodman, you have a visitor in the main lobby." I made my way out to the lobby and there was my father, sitting in a French provincial chair, wearing his flannel shirt and ear muff hat. After a few weeks had passed, here he was; my first and only visitor.

It was just about lunch time, so I asked him to join me, my buy! After we were seated, I asked what brought him up here.

He said he just so happened to be in the area and decided to drop in. That is a typical German answer. 'Oh, I was an hour and a half drive away, with snow up to my ass and the roads all covered with ice because it was 10 degrees outside; so I decided to take a ride and see how you were doing. It was strange that he came by; he was either boffing a woman who lived nearby or Mary T. put him up to it. Maybe he just wanted to see me; that was the last thing I would think of.

Anyway, we had a nice lunch; he thought the food was actually very good. Except for my dish with no salt, no fat and no taste; a slice of fluff bread with the crust removed, celery sticks which had not been deveined, a piece of some kind of square fish, and 23 lima beans that were probably used the night before at church bingo, artificial mashed potatoes (two tablespoon full) and finally, behind door number three, a cup of gelatin jewels, or Jell-O. After lunch he had to leave, so I walked him out to his truck; frostbite set in.

On February 1st, 1988 I left that institution and booked a one way flight to Key West for the following day. The Duke picked me up and drove me to the 'bighouse' for the night and he brought me to the airport the next day.

Teresa was there to meet me. I had one bag and $380 dollars in my pocket. An appointment with a local doctor was set up by the hospital in Pennsylvania, so she drove me there. It was then she said she gave up the apartment, and was renting a room on the other side of town. She had put all of my art supplies in storage and threw away most of the other stuff as it just held too many bad memories. She also said she wanted to keep the car. I was taken aback by these statements, but how could I argue.

According to some scholars, they say that the concept of 'hell' came from a dump outside of Jerusalem. People would throw their trash there and burn it. Occasionally a body would end up on the burning pile. In the bible there is no reference to 'hell' at all; not even the word is mentioned.

You could say I felt like a heap of burning trash somewhere. The Doctor was a real charmer. He told me that I wasn't going to last the year, but he would still treat me, and then proceeded to write about seven prescriptions. I asked him what part of his ass I should kiss for this courtesy.

That night I stayed at the Days Inn; but I knew this could not go on. Teresa and I parted ways at the Hotel. I didn't know where she was now living and in fact didn't even know where I was going to live. I made a few phone calls and found a room available in a trailer out on Big Coppitt for $300 dollars per month. Food was not included, but that didn't matter; I still couldn't eat anything or keep it in my digestive tract.

As it turned out my new landlord and his girlfriend liked to smoke joints before she went to work as a nurse. He stayed around the house, as he had injured his back and was taking a lot of Percodan and washing them down with Beck's beer. Then when she returned they'd roll more doobies and she would bitch about her job.

In Key West, at the end of Duval Street, is an 'all addictions you can think of' club. It was a place to hang out, shoot pool, or just sit in the air conditioning. There was always a meeting going on for something; overeating, gambling, sex, just think of something and there was a meeting for it. I went there just to get away from the place I lived; and it was a 12 mile thumb ride. Once in a while my landlord would give me a ride, but mostly I hitch hiked. Out back there was another canal that looked great for swimming, but in the water were these little red things that would bite you everywhere; yes even the vault and the tunnel of love. So, I just looked at the water when the mosquitos weren't too bad.

It was a boring existence; I couldn't paint, that wasn't practical, plus I made a deal if I was NEVER to paint again to maintain my existence, then so be it. I still had a considerable number of paintings downtown in the Gallery. One day I borrowed a 35mm camera from a friend and an easel from the gallery owner. I set the camera on a tripod, set the canvas on the easel, focused the shot, looked at my signature on the bottom and realized I had no recollection of painting this canvas. There were several of these; and they were actually quite good pieces of work. But these paintings, most of which take 35 to 40 hours to execute, I could not remember painting. Interesting though they were some of the first paintings I sold in the next few weeks. My old boss's daughter bought four of them and I made about $5000 dollars on that one transaction. They had finished their private island and needed artwork for the reception center where the maps and models were. Years later the entire island was covered with homes. And they had picked out the best ones for themselves; nice to own an island. Their family must have made a fortune in that business deal and I don't begrudge them at all, he was a good 'working boss', I respected that about him. Plus I think he secretly enjoyed my lawsuit against my previous employer, they weren't exactly friends.

My trailer mates were quite loud when it came to, well how shall I say this with finesse; consummating their evening of Becks Beer, Pot, Percodan and Vicodin in the presence of the matador painted on black velvet hanging over their king size bed. During these evenings of sexual bliss I would fill my ears with cigarette filters, like I did in the Navy.

While lying there one night just waiting for the manly man to do his thing, I started thinking about the last evening at the institute. They brought in a man who was a multi-millionaire as a guest speaker. One comment he made, which I still remember was..."The only difference between you and me is that I had 15 more bathrooms to be sick in". At first it sounds gross, but when you think out of the box; it tells you money doesn't mean a thing on a path of self-destruction. After he finished speaking they turned the mike over to the big kahuna, the resident MD of the place. His comment of merit was..."this is the only terminal disease that is treated with a philosophy for living". I found that thought to be of provocative value and use it on myself to this very day. Then the microphone went into the hands of the guy who ran the place; Big Nick. Actually we are friends to this day. Anyway Nick asked for 6 volunteers and then picked us out; I was one of them. He lined us up on stage and said, in six months to a year; only one of these people will be straight; look at them and decide. This also applies to everyone here today; one out of six will make it.

I was 57 years of age when my father died, in all of that time I never saw him drink any alcohol. What I came to realize was that I never heard him explain to anyone why he didn't; why should he? That thought has added new strength to my own personal resolve. Especially during these dark days of serious medical problems I am engrossed in. I'll address more of that issue later, but for now back to the double wide in Paradise.

One morning, I walked up to the main road to hitch a ride into town. While I was standing on the side of the south bound lanes; two things happened. First my landlord drove out and turned south; and then waved to me. But the real show stopper was seeing in the distance on the other side of the highway heading north was the green VW Rabbit. I knew it was Teresa. When she passed, she had the 'moon' roof open and a young blond surfer type guy in the seat next to her. He had real long hair and it was blowing up through the open moon roof; and they were laughing like crazy.

I knew the laughter wasn't directed at me, Teresa wasn't the type to be cruel or vindictive. Perhaps they hadn't even seen me, and that made me feel even worse, they were both looking straight ahead as if I didn't exist. I couldn't help but think about what had just passed me by; my car; and my girl with some young punk, enjoying the ride. Years later Teresa told me she did see me, but had such mixed feelings she pretended not to. Life is for the living.

We will keep an eye on that last statement because the issue will come up again later, but for now I must finish a final chapter prior to leaving Wilkes-Barre.
After the Duke and I returned home from my discharge I called Teresa's father and asked if I could drop by for a few minutes to talk to him; he said yes. I borrowed Mary T's car and drove up to the small city where he lived. I was nervous and didn't know what to expect because I didn't know what information had made its way up to her father. If he knew a lot, I was screwed, plain and simple.

I sat down with John in the front 'parlor' and explained my entire ordeal and promised him, on what was left of my personal integrity, that I loved his daughter completely and had since 1970 right after I returned from the war. If she would have me back I would treat her accordingly, and as we spoke, I had no desire to use alcohol in my life. It was true, I looked at it like a job, I had put in a shift and now it was time to put it to bed. I also told John that after an adequate amount of time, whatever it required, I would marry Teresa, if she would accept me.

John was a man of few words, unless it came to Ronald Reagan, then he cursed like a sailor. But he thanked me for being so honest with him. He had been deeply involved in combat in the Second World War and had been wounded on several occasions; so we had something in common, and

318

mutual respect. He was quick to point out that ultimately it would be Teresa's decision, though he felt I was sincere and would tell her that. I thanked him and stood up to leave, we had a man's handshake which paraphrased his observation of my sincerity. The next day I flew to Key West.

After my huge painting sale, I started looking for a decent car. Key West, because of being a small community, word could travel quickly. I was told about an American Motors 'Gremlin' that was owned by a retired sea captain. This was more than a car to him; it was part of the family and they were crazy about the car. He brought out a large envelope full of invoices dealing with an engine overhaul. As I leafed through it, I realized they had done a complete overhaul; this engine was as good as new. They also had the automatic transmission completely gone over. They would sell me the car with the promise that I would complete its overhaul and treat it with respect; I agreed.

I stopped in this auto parts store and the owners were art collectors. I showed them my work and they loved it, we made a deal on the spot. They could pick out a canvas they liked, and we would agree on the price and I could use that as credit in their shop. I handed over a painting and a list of brake parts. I went to Uncle Sam's pawn shop and bought a set of mechanics tools.
One day I was out there covered with grease working on the brakes, a complete overhaul which I photographed for the 'family', to show I was keeping my word. A car pulled up and stopped, I climbed out from under the car to see Teresa standing there. This was the first time she actually stopped to visit me.

Naturally I knew where she worked and could have gone in there any time, but I didn't. I knew she needed her space; so I avoided the place. It was an awkward hello; I still loved this woman to the depth of my soul; but under the circumstances, I wasn't in any position to talk about that, not now. She knew I could put cars together and tear them apart, but she asked what I was doing anyway. I told her I was getting this ready for some heavy interstate driving; high speed and many miles. She then asked me where I was going. I didn't have an answer. I told her I hadn't decided, that I thought about San Diego, nice weather; and I had been there while in the Navy. She asked if anyone was going with me and I said no, I was travelling alone; just me and the Gremlin; nice combination. We talked for a bit, and then she said she had to go to work and wondered why I hadn't stopped by the Half Shell. I didn't want to tell her, I still wasn't able to have any kind of food I wanted, and they had a great fish sandwich; my system was still healing. I watched her drive away until she turned right onto the southbound lane, the one I helped to build.

After Teresa disappeared, I went back to work. I had to just keep my mind occupied on something stupid. While I was re-assembling the front brakes, I noticed that the tie rod ends where loose, another replacement set of parts. If a tie rod broke, the two front tires would go in different directions at best, this is something you would not want happening at 70mph. Another painting produced a few tie rods and some other parts, an exhaust system, 4 new tires and they threw in a piece of heater hose and a box of clamps.
When we started this art for car part transaction, we settled on no more than four compositions, I was on my third and wanted to save the fourth for a new radiator and hose's, the State of Florida had a habit of eating exhaust systems and radiators on cars, it was the salt air, salt and copper, or tin did not mix well. This concludes the chapter on geographical places and the universal element chart.
My double wide dream was furnished with a double bed, a set of drawers and a small desk and chair, plus there was a built in closet. I had to hide my wad of loot in the car which I kept locked, this guy was of dubious character and I could see him jacking up my rent if he knew.

As to where the car repair money was coming from, I made up a few stories that were plausible and no one knew the difference, I did not expect my land lord and his girlfriend running in the same circles as my ex boss's daughter who owned their own Island.

I went out and bought a set of 8lb dumbbells from Uncle Sam so that they looked used and started to work out on the living room floor. Surprisingly, they rarely if ever used the living room so it became my gym at night, in front of the television. They would just lay on the king size bed and smoke pot with their painting on velvet. Many times when they were both pretty high and drunk they would ask the same question, can you paint on velvet like that? My answer was always the same, why? I broke down and bought a new mattress cover and sheets for the bed along with a nice blanket and cheap bedspread. On just one occasion they had friends over and told me to sleep on the couch, so I put all of their old crap back on the bed for that festive event. On the rear deck he had about 8 large pot plants in even larger clay containers. Well, the police drove by a few times nice and slow, this of course made the guy lose it. Here we are, both with messed up backs, moving these big heavy things down to the next level where they would be harder to see. This is the same person who would just pass me by when I was hitchhiking into town, or ask for $5.00 for fuel money! I was keeping really nice company and started to work harder on the car, I was putting a plan together. His girlfriend was a 'critical care' nurse at one of the hospitals. This is the same babe who smoked pot in the morning then again on her break. That bothered me quite a lot, more then I cared to admit, it reminded me of the 'boomer' sailors in Hawaii getting high surrounded by nuclear missiles. Here was a person with more than one life in her care, blasted on pot. She also was a slob at home, they both were, leaving dirty dishes in the sink and food stuffs out on the counter, you did not do this in the Keys, every ant and bug in the vicinity would be at your house. I can't remember if I dropped a dime on her or not, I do recall thinking about sending in a quiet letter. I may have suggested a urine test unannounced. It would have cost her the job and take a chunk out of the RN hat I am sure!

I know that I wasn't near the place when it happened; those fan blades must have sure been a mess after that.

One night I just lost it, I kept all of this emotion concerning Teresa under tight control, but that night, I started to think about the incident on Highway #1 with the surfer 'dude. It was around midnight and I decided to drive downtown, go into all the bars until I found this guy and beat the crap out of him; this was a really smart idea. Going in and out of Dirty Harry's, Captain Tony's, Turtle Crawls and any other gin mill where I knew the bartenders. I'd ask if they saw a surfer type guy with long blond hair, then came the question "what's his name?" I had no idea; I had about three seconds of visuals that day in the car and needed to beat him. It was going on 3am when I stopped myself. The stupidity of it all; there were plenty of guys in Key West that fit that description. Teresa was with this guy whether I liked it or not and I had no idea how she felt about him.

I had to think about what she had gone through with me those last few months. When she came home from work at night, she would look in the window, if I was in bed asleep she'd come in. If not she would get back in the car and go to a girlfriend's house to stay. She told me all of this later; she had no idea what state of mind I would be in, and mostly it was one of rage. She did this for a month, till she finally moved out; without me noticing.

When I was drunk the only thing I was somewhat capable of was a sloppy form of lust. I'd take what I wanted, then fall asleep; no fore or after play. When I was in 'my cups' as they say, I could not love anyone, even Teresa, I didn't love myself. I held myself in distain. I was a putrid bag of flesh filled with pus and unpredictable anger. I was dead but

322

didn't have the sense to just lie down; although I was very close to it at that point.

To this day I am at peace with Teresa's decision. It was probably a great relief to be away from my death wish. She would have to learn to trust me again. Trust that I would want to stay alive.

Before I sold all of those paintings, things were pretty rough; $300 dollar a month doesn't go very far, and I smoked cigarettes. I got a call from the Gallery and was told I had just sold another painting and could come in for the check. It turned out to be bought by Teresa. It was one of my 'Nude studies'. She had it hanging in the room she rented when a friend of hers from California came to Key West to visit. This friend had been doing 'standup' comedy in San Francisco and had now gone on to be part of New York's "Saturday Night Live" show. She and her husband were checking out Key West to see if they wanted to buy property there for a house in the 'sun'. Her husband was a screen writer who spent time on both coasts.
Teresa's friend really liked the canvas and offered to purchase it from her; but Teresa refused to sell. This canvas was later to be given to one of my doctors as a gift. And to this day, I have been reminded of that. Teresa gets 'first dibs' on my work when it is finished. I still owe her for giving that one away; and Teresa now has quite a nice collection. Her most recent acquisition is one I did in Ireland.

During the period I'll call the 'doublewide madness', I was still seeing a doctor on a regular basis. He had me taking 42 pills per day, the lions share were artificial enzymes for my damaged pancreas. It took about 6 to 7 weeks for me to hold down certain food.

Teresa was stopping by now on a more regular basis. The old Zen story was coming true; how to catch a butterfly. The first way is to run through the forest with a net; always looking up and not noticing the briars, thorny vines and poison ivy. As opposed to the Zen method of finding a nice flower, full of nectar, and sitting comfortably, and quietly next to a big tree. Eventually a butterfly would come to the flower. You could study the beauty of this creature without damaging it in any way, and when it felt it wasn't in any danger, would just stay.

There I was the grease and oil covered Zen Monk, with hair, leaning against a palm tree, holding a 1972 American Motors Gremlin, waiting for a beautiful butterfly to come by. Then I could sit and admire the beauty and ask for another chance with one caveat; if I broke my promise and made a mockery of my solemn word, she was free to fly away forever.

I wanted to thank some people that really helped me get through some of these rough times. I drove out to see my favorite old boss who owned Shark Key. I had a few paintings left and asked if he needed one for his office. He picked the one I thought he would and said "how much".
I told him it was a gift, he had already paid me.

We started to make some plans about returning to my favorite suburb from hell, Wilkes-Barre. I had a valid reason, my digestive tract was improving, but something was wrong with my back; I was in a lot of pain.
Teresa gave her two week notice at the Half Shell, and had finished her degree at the community college. She was to follow in the VW, as I was leaving early; I'd had enough of the people I was living with. I drove the Gremlin up to my friend Ricks' in Lakeworth. Seems I was just in the nick of time; he needed a vehicle right away. The van he bought from me many years earlier was literally duct taped together, because of the rust. I purchased this Van from my Mother in 1981 when I started a delivery business in south Florida; called "Vanguard". My premise was to guarantee overnight delivery to anywhere across the state. I had cards made up and my motto was "anything, anywhere without questions normally asked". There was nothing written on the Van. If my

driver was stopped by the Police and asked what he had back there, he was instructed to say…"no disrespect sir, but I haven't a clue what is in there, I am simply supposed to deliver to this address". Our clients were only required to supply an address, no PO Boxes, airports or international purveyors. I hadn't expected to put Fed Ex or UPS out of business, but I believe it really could have taken off if it weren't for my drinking and crappy marriage. Bad Bob and I made about three deliveries, and that was it. That's when I sold the van to Rick.

I don't know what it is with the wives or girlfriends of my buddies. I was always courteous; I never leered at them or made unwanted advances. I didn't walk around in a speedo or jocks. They just didn't appreciate me being around. I mention this because it's happened many times over. Rick's wife was one of them, so I hadn't planned to stay long. Teresa's opinion is that they are possibly afraid of my wild ways; past or present, maybe they think their men will take off for an adventure; like joining the foreign legion.

When Rick got behind the wheel of the Gremlin, he said "yes". We drove the van to the junkyard and the car was his. This vehicle was his for another 8 years! No wonder the Captains family loved it. I know I make many references to automobiles in these pages, but they are a way of marking periods in my life. Cars act as a clock that reads years rather than minutes or hours. This may explain why the automobile is many times rampart across my page's, for some it will be a trip back down memory lane, for the younger reader's it may just illicit an image of a generic metal box with a complex engine in it, not knowing they had really fast cars back then, and finally, there is the possibly of someone saying I wrote an automobile recognition manual. For whatever its' worth; look upon them as years on a clock face, simply markers in time. As I discussed in the early chapters, I came from a family of motor heads and grease monkeys as we were affectionately called. My brothers and I used to eat and breathe horsepower. Now, you can go to a dealership and buy as much of it as you can afford and still get decent gas mileage. Our 1932 H-gas drag racer with the four carburetors would use a gallon of high octane fuel for one quarter mile race! Enough about that subject; thank you for your patience in allowing me to explain one of my tools for maintaining accuracy in the chronological order of this book.

My back was getting really bad again, the worse part and dead give-away was the sciatica pain radiating down the back of both legs to the heels, this was bad. Teresa and I drove back to Pennsylvania with intentions of staying for the summer months. The long ride back gave us plenty of time to talk candidly about the events of the past few years, even though my diet was restricted, I could eat as much crow as I could stomach. I knew that all of the talk in the World would not make much of a difference, hell I could have the UN put our relationship on their schedule and it would not have mattered. There was a lot of hurt and deep emotional pain in those early raving's and me not quite remembering them didn't count; Teresa did. So much depended on the new person I was inside, I could not explain the new Jason with words; it had to done with actions over a period of time. The length of time was not in my control, it depended upon her satisfaction and the final dispersion of any fears that she had; like walking in and finding me blotto on the floor. I hate that word TIME, a few months ago, when I was dying, I wanted it to stop. Now I wanted time to speed ahead into the future so we could be the way we were; eating 12" hot dogs and ice cream cones. Time can be a wearing and grating on the nerves, I can't stand all of those sage expressions, only time will tell, it's going to take time, time is of the essence, a stitch in time, fuck time, I feel like giving all of my watches to homeless people and mess their lives up with it, time that is. After I retired from my design business, I stopped in the middle of a bridge and threw my last cellphone (with the time on it) into a river and haven't owned one since. I started with those things in 1990 and before that was the pager, enough!

My back was only good for about 6 months after that first surgery; pretty bad turnover when you think of it. Six months divided by $85,000 dollars; let's just say it's more than a heat pad from K-Mart. At first it was the left leg, then as time (there it is again) went on it migrated to the right leg. This pain is really insidious; you cannot stand, sit down, or lay down to escape it. The pain is always there, and pain medications simply take the sharp edge off of it, like tumbling broken glass, it was still glass without the dagger tipped points.

We called the doctor and made arrangements for a visit, I told his receptionist to have the orders for a CT scan w/ enhancement and an MRI ready for that same day; I was going somewhat mad from this. The next day she called back with all the scan's arranged for the same day prior to seeing the doctor, which made sense. The tests were done and I was with him when he pushed his finger into my back and hit one of the pain spots dead on, there were a few others but that one was the worse.

By this time it was late Fall of 1988 and I wanted to return to Florida to re-new my teaching credentials, this required two 4 credit hour courses in art at the main campus in Florida at Boca Raton. He arranged the surgery and the night before, as they normally do, the surgeon comes in and gives you your percentages for walking, pissing, screwing, pooping and so on, with each surgery the percentages were in favor of the house, there were a ton of nerves in there that affected all of the above; my signature was required. So if you woke up with a Johnston that just lay around and would not stand at attention when ordered to, it was a shame, but, here is your signature!

That particular evening, the doctor who came in to give me my percentages and have me sign the consent forms was not my regular doctor. He had been flown out to Ohio to perform a delicate brain surgery on an accident victim. So I was stuck with this guy, he had the bed side manner of cold dish water and the back of my brain was screaming, just like the dentist in Charleston; though a few vertebras would require a bigger cigar box. But, practically took preference over common sense, I was in a hospital bed, the 'OR' was ready and scheduled for the next morning, and I wanted to get it over with so I could recuperate and head back down South. It was a mistake. This fill in surgeon, though highly recommended, did not think out of the box at all and I will explain that.

A few months later, I'm on campus at Florida Atlantic University; which was built on an old WWII air field as most of Florida Universities were. Hey, cheap land with paved parking.

This meant that the parking lots were a hike from the main campus, but I made it to the new sidewalk and was on my way to the 'College of Education' when I suddenly just fell over, that was it, my legs were both numb and did not move. An ambulance had taken me to Boca Raton Hospital. Allow me to tell you something about this institution. First of all, there is more money in Boca Raton than Palm Beach had ever seen. The fat cats here decided they needed their own hospital, so they chipped in a few billion a piece and built this one and staffed it with the cream of the crop in doctors and support staff. On the two top floors, the penthouse floors, the rooms were suites furnished in real period antiques. You could actually order a bottle of Rothschild wine with your dinner, to the tune of about 6 G's. You had to have a certain tax return to get into these 'rooms.' Lucky for me I was given to one of the best neurosurgeons in the World. This guy, a millionaire in his own right before he even went to Harvard, was a genius with advanced brain techniques. At first he looked at me like I was something stuck to his shoe, hell a lowly back surgery, give me a break! Until that is, he found out I knew a lot about cars. The good doctor was a high end car lover and had a garage full of them, mostly top of the line Italian names. I had gleaned from the nurse's all of this information prior to actually meeting the guy, so I waited and slipped in something about fuel injection systems, I forget, it was attached to his medical terminology somehow.

In Pennsylvania, the doctor there was supposed to do a standard intervention for a disc at the L-4 & L-5 level, and, I repeat, look for any bone spurs on the vertebra, this is what came back to hurt me in a big way in Boca Raton. My car loving neurosurgeon, as reluctant as he was, told the nurse to check his schedule then prepare me for surgery as soon as it allowed. About a day and a half passed when I was being wheeled into the operating room, you really get used to staring at the lights in the ceiling going by as they take you there to freeze your ass off. I always ask, for some reason, what music the doctor listens to when he works, his was classical. After the surgery, the doctor came into my room the next day and was all excited, this case was more complex than he realized. He told me the guy in Pennsylvania did a 'by the book' laminectomy but failed to look on either side to see what would happen when the vertebra dropped, which they do after taking out enough disc material. When it collapsed, a bone spur had nearly severed my main nerve bundle that went down my left leg, more so than the right, though it had been damaged also. He told me that I would always have trouble with my legs and he had tried to restore most of the nerves so that I could walk again. I did have to endure physical therapy to learn how to walk anyway, but it worked and I am not complaining. Except now, my left leg doesn't always tell my brain where its' going; so I fall over things that don't exist. More on this will follow, I must warn you, these medical problems, between the Vietnam damage and the Key West accident, will go on for quite a while before all is said and done on the subject.

After a few weeks I was discharged from the hospital and resumed my studies at the university, one good thing was they allowed me to park much closer to my classes. It was not difficult to catch up, these were 400 level courses and I had a Master's degree, it was just the State making sure their teachers were up to speed.

One of my classes' was at the Fort Lauderdale annex; I had

no choice because that is where it was offered that quarter. It was your standard art education course with me and one other guy in a room filled with women. But to listen to these women speak before the class started would make a man angry and sick at the same time. They had it all worked out, they would teach for a few years until Mr. Right came along; you know straight teeth, blond hair, somewhat passive and a virtual sperm bank. They would then have their 2.5 kids and the dog, and then after several years, when little Johnny was old enough, they would jump back into teaching art, oh my god! It was sooooo simple. Ashley, you are a genius! I had to listen to this tripe every week, and plan my revenge.

Because of my hospital stay and the travel involved I did not spend a lot of time on this course, so when the instructor decided that a 'show and tell' type essay was in order for a high percentage of our final grade, I remembered my slides from the prison in Dallas, PA. It was the last class, and I was the last person to present my final written report and slide presentation. I had requested a slide projector from the A/V department and it was there, my slides where already in a carousel with a typed script to remind me of my place, keep in mind, there were 72 of these grenades.
That is what it was, because we had all been or, were art teachers, the presentation had to do with one of my most creative ideas, or teaching experiences, I just remembered those particulars.
When my turn came, I gave the introduction and the room fell silent, as I mentioned, people react in a strange way to anything having to do with prison.
I went through every slide real slow, allowing the image to burn holes in these air head brains, naturally it was payback time for all of those weeks of listening to the scheme's, if you recall I was a victim of one of these years ago, so I did have a vendetta in my motives. When I was finished, everyone just got up and filed out, quietly, the only person to speak to me was the instructor as I packed up my stuff. He was amazed at what he saw, and admitted that all of those

images were new to him; no one gets to see the entire inside of a large State correctional institution. He asked me how I shot those photos and I just smiled and told him it was illegal and would rather not say, but I used a Nikon 35mm with 1000 asa slide film for available light shooting, I wasn't in a position to have flash bulbs go off. When the grades were posted, I received an A+. And the program was published under an assumed name.

Our VW Rabbit was starting to act up, so I called my friend who owned the car dealership, it was a big place, he sold Mazda's, Lincoln, Mercury, Volkswagens, and his pride was the top end Porsches.' I sent Teresa down to pick out a car, she came back with a Mazda Miata, they had just arrived and it was brand new, she was having fun driving it, but I could barely fit in the car, it was too small and impractical for our needs. She left and a bit of time passed, I was painting in my studio at the time, when I heard a car pull up. Teresa came in and said; "I think I have been driving our next car." It was a Toyota 'Cressida' their top of the line car for that year. When I popped the hood I was staring down at an "Offenhauser" racing engine and that is exactly what it was, the Japanese had bought the rights to the engine design, tweaked it and dropped it in this car. You could be sitting on the hood and not realize that the engine was running, plus it was fast, real fast. This was the car that we used when we returned to Florida. She also scouted out a nice two bedroom apartment in Boynton Beach where I did some very nice artwork. I think the Florida Sun had something to do with it. The funny part about this apartment that she found was her call to me in Pennsylvania, she told me it was going to be very romantic and was a surprise. Once I finished up there I shipped my foot locker studio and booked a flight. After arrival she led me into the back yard, it was nice, citrus trees, an avocado tree and a hedge row, I peeked through it and there were the two sets of very well used railroad tracks, this was the romantic part, except at 3:00am when they started blowing their whistle and roared past us at 50 mph which shook our bed. I had to get used to that romance. Here is a case where I am slightly out of sync with the chronology; again, the car tipped me off. Everything I talked about prior to this, the medical problems, courses at FAU and the rest should come into play now, but somehow I put the horse behind the cart as they say. Later a mule pulling a cart is described in another country, that we will save.

During this time Teresa worked at The Boca Raton Country Club, a nice address for a resume, she was good at what she did, and had quietly completed two Associate degrees in the subject of Small business management and Hotel & Restaurant management, an impressive achievement considering one was in Florida and the other, Pennsylvania.

Allow me to relate a mother-in-law story, with a car thrown in for good measure because it leads to the 'Cressida' mentioned on a previous page.

I bought this non-descript automobile from my friend, it was the type of car you parked in front of your mobile home. Another thing about this car was its color, blue. I have never had good luck with blue autos. Anyway, we decided to drive Teresa s' mother down to West Virginia to see her sister. Her side of the family came from Berkeley Springs, West Virginia. It was hot, and the forecast called for hotter still. The first leg of the journey was all interstate to Winchester, where Patsy Cline is buried; someone placed a long stem rose on her grave every day for over 20 years and no one knew who did it. After 4 hours of I-81, came about one hour into the 'Razor Back' mountains. Well the first few hours went well, then the air conditioning unit just burned itself up, now I have a wife and her aged Mother and its' over 110 degrees outside, the hottest day on record thus far. I stopped in Winchester and bought some ice and a few towels at a truck stop, along with a small pail from some kid's stuff. I told Teresa to ride in the back and keep a cold wet towel on her Mothers neck. Also to keep drinking the bottled water I purchased. I told her to wring the towel out on the floor, it didn't matter because this car was history when we got back; if we got back I should say. We made it, the visit was pleasant, and the temperature dropped while we were there. That was how we ended up in one of the finest automobiles I ever owned; the Cressida. But, what a way to really meet your future mother-in-law!

If I am not mistaken, that was a great loss to the Southern states when West Virginia went with the North during the Civil War; all of that high octane moonshine going to those Yankee dogs. They were not too happy about that at all and there were some major battles fought in West Virginia. The reason West Virginia did that was because of an ongoing feud with Virginia over whiskey, it was an issue that went back a long time. But, if you have a few cannons and a thirst for some 120 proof liquor, you don't have to say please, or how much?

These are another one of those small departures from the given path; but allow me to explain something that was never answered in the text. If you recall I always would ask what music a surgeon preferred while working in the operating room, it turned out that the guy I had in Boca Raton was very particular about his music and it turned out to be 'Wagner's' "Night on Bald Mountain" and, " Flight of the Valkyrie." I found it interesting to note that over the years I had very few surgeries with Hitler's' favorite composer playing in the back ground. Many years later I was reading the Washington Post and ran across an article about this same doctor who won a very prestigious award for developing a technique used in brain surgery, the same guy who saved my legs because I knew a bit about cars. I promise though, this car thing will come to a close, it starts to lose its' glimmer in the pages to come, more important things begin to happen, exciting stuff I may add, plus at this age I have just about lost my obsession with cars anyway, now it is jet planes with someone else behind the wheel, who will fly us to Ireland, Europe and Mexico.

After finishing everything in Florida, before we left we had taken one of those 'you just won a free cruise!' to the Bahamas. It was a gambling boat and what would normally take a few hours to get to Freeport, had taken most of the day. On the island we had a choice of the casino on the beach, or a small one story, seen its day, motel inland; and that was the one we choose.

On the way over we met a couple from New Jersey and struck up a conversation. The husband was a gambler; I think everyone in New Jersey gambles, I can say that because my mother was from that State. He excused himself and went below to what else? Gamble. A few hours later he came back with $6000 dollars freshly won at one of the tables. I was jealous, because we were on a tight budget, not starving, but there wasn't room for gambling either. As mentioned in the Navy, I never gambled and I can tell you why.

My father cured me of gambling at a young age. Once a year we would go to an amusement park, it was the official opening of summer you might say. They would get a nice picnic table under the tree's and had coolers with cold drinks and sandwich's and the rest of the picnic fare. But the most important thing were the rolls of coins, each of us would receive a roll of dimes, nickels and pennies, and back then that was a king's ransom. It was supposed to last all day for the various rides which in the 50's were really cheap. They had a good roller coaster, the Bear Cat, and a Wild Mouse, Tumblebug, Dodgems, plus a host of other death defying rides guaranteed to wet your trousers. But did I do that? No! I, in my infinite wisdom, went straight for the row of rip off joints trying to win that big prize, within an hour all of my rolls of coins were empty wrappers. I then went back for more and was confronted with a battery of questions concerning the whereabouts of the money I was given. My father then told my brothers not to give me a dime for the rest of the day. I was screwed, all day without a nickel for the Bear Cat. It was the longest day of my life, I spent hours looking under rides for lost change, but basically just moped about, jealous and coveting while I watched everyone running from one ride to another, I never gambled again.

We arrived at our port of call and got the bus to our motel; it was old but clean and there was a pool in the center. I went to the supermarket to pick up some snacks and something to read, they wanted nine bucks for a magazine! As I was leaving, there was a kiosk selling encyclopedias, they only had the first one, it was 'A' for .99 cents. I read about everything that started with an 'A' for 3 days and drove Teresa crazy, the other highlight was renting a scooter for the day and exploring the island.
On the ship back, we ran into the same Jersey couple and I asked him how he made out at the casino, his wife just laughed, she said he lost the $6000 dollars, then maxed out both of his credit cards, now he wants mine to win it all back, I told him fat chance. I felt good and vindicated,

Upon our return we packed up and headed for Charleston, South Carolina. I had done a large triptych for a couple there and agreed to hang it for them and receive my last payment. We were in a hurry because we were on our way to West Virginia to get married, the week of May 20th, 1989 is very special. I married the woman of my dreams, Teresa, at her aunt and uncles house in the Razor Back Mountains. Her uncle's son was a preacher in the Church of the Brethren and he performed the service. It was a simple country style wedding under the weeping willow trees. My brother-in-law had just finished a film school and he videotaped the entire ceremony, unknown, or unnoticed by everyone, was a double barreled 12 gauge shotgun blast in the distance, just as my father-in-law was giving away his daughter. When copies of the video surfaced weeks later; "Shotgun Wedding" was written on them.
We were now officially married in the eyes of the Brethren Church and the State of West Virginia, her first and my last.

Afterward, we returned to Pennsylvania and put on a really nice party for all of our friends and relatives. It was completely catered and I had a jazz trio play, plus I hired an old Italian woman to make two large chocolate fudge cakes with a minimum of one half inch of chocolate fudge icing, these cakes weighted a ton and they were fresh for the evening. When it came time for me to have a piece, there wasn't any left. But, everyone was quick to tell me how delicious it was. I never tasted my own wedding cake!

By the end of June 1989, I was back in the hospital ready to undergo surgery number four of the lower back. By this time I was living in constant pain, it was called "Chronic Pain Syndrome." I have it to this very day, 24/7 nothing but pain, every single day and night. Teresa kept a record and found that during that 5 year period, I spent 60 days a year in the hospital, either having surgeries or recuperating from one. It was not an easy time, and it actually got worse.

This one was particularly bad, the doctors in all of their infinite wisdom and experience; which hung over my head like the Sword of Damocles, 'nicked' my spinal cord! You 'nick' yourself shaving, or a guy named 'Nick' makes you a pizza, but you do not take a scalpel and nick someone's spinal cord because that leads to one of two things, or both; a major lawsuit or a bullet in the back of the head. My "nicker's" weren't bad enough; they also told me that a wee bit of spinal fluid 'leaked out,' this is a Dr. Fine, Dr. Howard, Dr. Fine surgery. Spinal fluid is something the body produces very slowly; it surrounds the spinal cord for a reason, one of which is to keep it cool. When you lose a 'wee bit' of spinal fluid, you can expect a mind shattering headache, besides being paralyzed from the neck down. I woke up in the PAC unit strapped to the bed, once I received my wits about me, I knew I was fucked.

My head could only be raised 22 degree's; they had a special device for this. When I was moved up to the 8th floor, they ever so carefully placed me on the Island of Elba, I couldn't help but notice extremely yellow stains on the sheet of my last conveyance, it wasn't urine either.

When the apologies started I just raised my hand and said, please stop. I do not want, nor need to hear these feeble excuses from people whom I had mistakenly considered to be professionals, with the same hand I pointed at the door and said, go away!

During all of this duress my second book of poetry entitled, "Nervous Reader" was published by Radcliffe Press of South Carolina, they had it perfect bound and I submitted four pen and ink drawings done by my ex-friend who refuses to speak to me to this day from the incident involving a "Demon." The book was pleasantly successful and sold out in a few years; which is not bad for poetry in America.

Meanwhile, I spent several weeks strapped to the bed in a hospital in Scranton, PA. One day, I was reaching around for something to read and felt a book, it was a 'Good News' Bible. When I opened it, on the first page was a sentence which read;

"What will you say when you meet God and He asked you the question, 'Did you read My Book?" For some reason it really stopped me cold. Over all of the years and all of the books that I read, I never read THAT book! This began a 5 year exodus that saw me reading three completely different Bibles, the Good News Bible, the N.I.V., and the King James Version. Each one had taken an entire year to read. I also read the Koran and attended Torah classes for a year. Then to top it off, I got involved in a mail order Minster program which I passed and received my diploma as a bona fide minister of some obscure church in Alabama somewhere. I embarked on this venture as literature, I do not profess to be a Bible banger, or authority, that entire experience was prompted by the one sentence in the book while a patient at the hospital. Though I can say this, after all of that reading and study it boiled down to one glowing precept; it is an unconditional trust.

337

After a memorable stay, I was released and walked out of the place. It is interesting to note how we transverse life and experience a horrible nightmare like the 'nick episode, and then something really worthwhile happens. In this case it was my attorney in Miami, I knew there were a number of letters from him, but I was in such a state of despair that I really didn't spend a lot of time on them.

There was one that got my attention. It had a 5 figure number on a check that fell out; this was a partial settlement having to do with my lost wages. The medical portion was also worth money, in fact the insurance company had once sent me a check for $25,000; my tongue was hanging out, and my lawyer said you can sign it, but I would suggest you don't ,consider this, what if you need another surgery, how much will that cost? I sent the check back.

The first thing I did was go to triple A and bought two first class Eurail pass's and made plans to travel all over Europe. Stop to have espresso under the Eiffel Tower, then end up in Portugal to paint for 6 months. Which we did!

We started in Ireland with a rental car and liked what we saw; my only regret was an opportunity to purchase a beautiful property on the Ring of Kerry outside of Killarney. It was a two story hotel with a pub downstairs, rooms upstairs and an apartment in the back. Across the two lane road was a beautiful lake and behind the property there was a million dollar view down the valley into Killarney. But the best part of all was the 'Green Belt' it was in and there weren't any other structures for miles, nor would there ever be. I had the money in the bank and the Irish 'Punt' was low at the time; this was before they went over to the Euro. Yes, I've heard all of the sayings about hindsight, that doesn't mean I have to like them! Our passes went into effect when we boarded a ferry for Cherbourg. I spent the extra few dollars for a berth and upon our arrival in France the entire rail system was ours and all first class.

I had promised that this book wasn't a lot of things and a travel journal it isn't either, if you want Europe on $6.95 a day, forget it, those days are gone forever.

We arrived in Cherbourg with enough time to catch a train into Paris, but I got into a fight with the ticket window, he would not learn English and I refused to learn French, Yiddish yes, not French. The long and short of it was a night in Cherbourg which is actually Normandy, and that made a big difference.

The next morning we trained into Paris, it was Sunday so all of the shops were closed. Teresa was window shopping and looking at a small hair pin while I was doing the conversion into dollars, lots of dollars; I said, yes darling, its' too bad its Sunday, what are you going to do? Shoppe closed! We had to take a cab to another train station, there are four, all the points of the compass. The cab driver was friendly enough, that was until Teresa said we were American, he thought we were from Canada. Then his entire demeanor had changed, he started bitching about us to his dog, a French poodle named "FiFi "I kid you not. When he brought us to the station, he would not even take our bags from the trunk so I shorted him on the fare, its' and old trick I learned in Vietnam where you roll the money around your finger then when the person pulls the roll, the bigger bills stay on your finger.

On the train to Amsterdam, we were seated in a first class cabin with 4 Dutch business men, young guys, and I struck up a conversation, their English was impeccable. Finally I came around to the question of the French and their attitude toward Americans.

What I didn't say was that Americans gave their lives on two occasions to free these bastards from the Germans in two wars, and then they had the audacity to fire on our troops in South Africa because their demented leaders thought Hitler was the best thing since sliced bread, fuckin' Vichy.

They all laughed and went on to say that they had been

doing business in France for over 15 years, primarily Paris, and that they were rude to them as well. One of the group then said that they came to the conclusion that the French hate themselves that is why they didn't like anyone else. This brought on a good round of laughter, so I called in the Porter and ordered drinks for everyone. These men were glad to have decent people to talk with for a change and gave us a lot of helpful information concerning which hotels to stay in, how the tram system worked (it was on the honor system) and other helpful hints with the museums and where not to go, especially at night.

Upon our arrival in Amsterdam, one of these guys must have called ahead for us, they hailed a cab, told us how much the fare should be and told the driver to take us to the Hotel Washington, with this they said so long and enjoy. We arrived at the Hotel, I held out a fist full of bills and the driver only had taken what was a fair price and tip. The Hotel was owned by two gay men and it was spotless. They obliviously knew the guys we travelled with and were happy for the recommendation. When we got into the room I could not believe it, even the tops of the doors were clean, these dudes were anal retentive (no pun intended) and this was my kind of place, spotless. Teresa just told me to take the white gloves off, shut up and come to bed. The next morning we had breakfast with our hosts.

They were a well spring of information, I came here to see the Van Gogh museum and I wasn't interested in the old masters. As far as I was concerned, they were all frustrated photographers, if they had good 2 and a quarter negative cameras they would not have bothered painting at all. Speaking of which, like Andy Warhol, most of these guys had apprentices that did all of the work, then they came along and spent an hour or two, signed it and that was it.

No, art started when crazy guys like Van Gogh kicked reality like a pin ball machine and almost knocked it into tilt. They just pushed it a little out of focus that was when art became a means of expression rather than a race to see who could

340

capture Gods handy work the best. We already had a master in that department. It was that way when I was teaching art, I used to tell my students that we had one Jackson Pollack; we didn't need 14 more, so keep drawing that nose!

Amsterdam is my kind of city; I could live there without a second opinion. Most people spoke English well and I was an artist so I carried a small notebook and would draw a picture of what I needed, hell, I even bought a co-axial converter that way. I spent a lot of time at the Van Gogh, and in the evening our hosts at the hotel would recommend nice restaurants which weren't in the Maxims' bracket in price.

One night I went out to get some reading material from the English bookstore when I stumbled upon the street of windows. If you haven't been there, please be careful. I was walking along trying to take in all 4 floors of the ladies of the night and bumped into a pipe, I almost went right over because it hit me at the certain point of weight vs. gravity, well it was a canal. Imagine explaining that to the Gardaí, or my wife, walking in soaking wet, well dear I was looking at, ah, chrome bar-b-que grills when splash, I was in the canal.

I found the bookstore and haven't really told that story that often, it is rather embarrassing. Maybe I'll stick with artwork for a bit. I appreciate the 'Frick' museum in New York, some of the egg tempuras are incredible, and knowing the technique makes them even more impressive. As you recall I studied under and old master, portraits are some of the hardest paintings to get paid for. I am serious. The artist has to place his subject in the best light possible to achieve the desired effect. Though when you look around you, a higher intelligence provided us with all of the visual art we can digest. One day I was teaching in Florida and I had this girl with a rare sight disorder, she could only see in black and white, I came by and she showed me her painting, I said its' really nice, why not put some blue up here. She looked up at me and said, what is blue?

341

The Post Impressionists were the artists that opened the doors; I would even call them Impressionist transfer artists' because they had one foot in that reality crap, and who really knows what reality actually is? Look at it this way, I don't like Picassos' paintings but his sculpture is terrific, think about the bulls head, an old rusted bicycle seat welded to the handle bars, man, talk about bumping reality out of focus, its' great and doesn't need anything but a wall and a nail. My feelings are this as an artist, and it is something that I endeavor to do.

The image on the canvas speaks to a different part of our conscience mind, the art composition is maybe 75% of a circle, the viewer is the other 25%, when they come together, and you have art, real unadulterated modern art. It is pure art for the sake of having art. I tell my clients, if it doesn't speak to you, don't buy it, you have to look at it on your wall, not me. In fact for the first 2 to 3 years after I finish a composition, I can't stand to look at it, except upside down to correct any small design flaws. But right side up, just take it away. Then years later, I might walk into an old customers house and look at one of my own works and think, you are pretty damn good if I must say so myself, hell I had better be good, after 40 years of doing something, if you aren't any good at it, go buy a pick and shovel and dig a hole in the ground, anyone can appreciate that if you work for a cemetery at least. I am my work, it is a piece of my soul, every painting takes it's' toll on me as it does every other artist. I have to keep traveling, if I don't I end up doing variations of myself.

The entire city of Amsterdam is a PhD program in obsessive/compulsive behavior; it is so neat and clean. Teresa thought that I was slowly losing my mind (which isn't really a revelation) because I kept pointing out things like the tram cars and sidewalks, even the ladies that almost cost me a swim in the canal last night were out there sweeping and throwing sudsy water on their steps. As I spoke to different people and asked about rentals, I was told that you could find a reasonable place, but, here they even take the light bulbs with them when they move. I thought taking the toilet paper was bad!

On the 5th day we left Amsterdam, I wanted to take the train to Copenhagen but my wife thought that it was under an ice sheet with Mammoths and Sabre Tooth Tigers running around on top of it. Ok, it was winter. We ended up in Koblenz, Germany, the cab dropped us off at what appeared to be a dump until we got inside, when the bell hop opened the door, at the other end of the room was a giant castle across the river, all lighted up for our enjoyment. I carried a handful of Kennedy half dollars as tips, it was interesting to see these guys faces light up when they realized what it was. It was the famous Stolzenfels Castle we sat and looked at from our balcony. I ordered coffee for two and a carafe of wine for Teresa, we sat and relaxed, living large. I noticed that there was a Malecon, or Esplanade, take your pick. The next morning I put it to good use, I was up before her so I went for a walk and had some German coffee, afterward, I noticed a boat parked up the way and made a dash for it, as it turned out it was a hydrofoil and the surcharge to my Eurail pass was $25 dollars apiece, I asked about the banana boat and the woman told me there wasn't an extra charge for the aging process, it would take four hours. I booked the Hydrofoil, it was 45 minutes; it was more James Bondish anyway. Teresa was up and dressed. I told her to pack up we had a date in Nuremberg.

It wasn't until we roared away from the dock that the comment came, you Goodman's' always have to have that horsepower fix don't you. I just smiled and said load high speed film; there are a lot of castles. In Nuremberg the cab driver offered us a tour the next day, ending at the train station. He would pick us up at 9:00am. He was there in his Mercedes and showed us things that most tourists never get to see; he had friends everywhere and even got us into the big castle in the old walled part of the city. We got to see the real torture chambers in the bowels of that place; it was Vincent Price in the flesh. Then at a few minutes to nine we were in front of the train station, I tried to give the guy a $5.00 tip and he would not take it, he said I gave you a price and that is it, he was saving money to get his girlfriend out of East Germany. At the time that was no easy task, it was an easy way to get a bullet in your back, and the Stasi were noted for that.

Before we left I spent a lot of time getting visas for these commie countries, one of them wanted a tourist 'bond' of a few thousand dollars, non-refundable, which meant you had to spend it or lose it, I think that was East Germany, I said screw that. The next stop was Budapest with a lot of cheap black leather and greasy hair, plus everyone was drunk, it was a terrible place. We moved on to Zagreb. This was an error on the part of the hotel in Budapest, I wanted to visit Dubrovnik, the famous city made completely from white marble, it was supposed to be beautiful and something to behold. I paid for this fuck up; the girl put us in the hotel called Dubrovnik in Zagreb, Yugoslavia. Even then I had to bribe the guy for a room, its' a good thing I bought a National Geographic about Yugoslavia in Amsterdam, that was the ticket to a hotel room. During the war over there, the Serbs set up large artillery guns and blasted the white marble city into dust just out of pure malice, 2000 years it stood there with no military value what so ever, even Catherine the Great spared this city during her conquest for Russia. It was a sad day when I saw that and recalled the screw up.

Zagreb was interesting in the sense that the people were all dressed to the nines. I recognize expensive suits and clothes when I see them. I sat at a few outdoor cafes and watched people promenade up and down the street. But, in the store, a 5 story department store, complete with escalators, there was hardly anything on the shelves! Strange, the people wore their wealth.

We stayed there two nights and somehow only paid for one night's stay, it could have been the Kennedy half dollar I gave the bell hop there also; he was a god over there.

I had promised that this wasn't going to be a travel log, and I have no intentions of showing you any wedding albums either. I related those stories because they pointed out the sheer stupidity of war and hate. We never made it to the white city and the Serb generals responsible for genocide and the destruction of irreplaceable historic places and objects' like the ridiculous Taliban and their blowing up those huge statues carved into the side of the mountain, for what? Those bastards couldn't fill their pockets fast enough when they had to get out of Kabul; that makes them common thieves, there isn't any religion there. Stealing; hell, they were cutting off hands from people caught stealing a month earlier, did they amputate their own hands when they got back to moms house? They go in and kill everybody in a village for taking American, or should I say the Great Satan's' food, then take the same food and eat it yourself? "War, what is it good for, absolutely nothin'."
Well thanks for letting me get carried away, am I the only one who notices these things? But I'll stop there. On the Italian Rivera I used the town of San Remo as a backdrop for a terrific painting of Teresa with a glass of wine at a small round table, that thing was sold before the paint was dry. Then we trained around into Spain and the town of Figueres, Salvatore Dali's' hometown, it was a real treat. We stayed there a few days, the town was great and the museum was even better. I always liked his work, it was so far ahead. I'll relate a story.

On Fifth Avenue in New York years ago, there was this high end shop that hired Dali to do something, they are the operative words here, with their front window and paid him 5 grand up front. Months went by and the owner's started to call him on a regular basis and started to obliviously piss him off. One day a Rolls Royce Silver Cloud pulls up, Dali jumps out of the back seat dressed in a pink bunny rabbit costume, he ran into the store, turned around and ran and jumped through the window, crashing on the sidewalk, got back into the car and they drove away. This is a true story by the way; I was at the shop on Fifth Avenue. So the owners take Dali to court to get there $5000 dollars back, the judge ruled in his favor because he 'did do something to their front window.'

We then moved on to Barcelona and the Picasso museum, this is where I established an appreciation for his sculpture. I never realized that he was as prolific in that medium as he was in painting. My only problem with Picasso was his reputation; he was known to 'borrow' other people's ideas. Like the concept of 'Cubism' another artist actually developed that, Picasso came by, liked it, did a bunch of things in cubistic style and because of his name and reputation, was first out of the box. There was an old saying, hide anything you are working on if Picasso is coming by, but his metal work and ceramic sculpture impressed me a great deal.

Our final destination was Lisbon, Portugal. This was good because the very next day our Eurail passes expired, 30 days we rode those passes around Europe. On the train across Spain into Lisbon I offered the conductor Escudos, the money of Portugal at the time and the guy didn't even want to touch it. I had to reason with him, sir, where is this train going tonight, he said Lisboa, and I then said what kind of money do they use in Lisboa? And he said the Escudo, then why will you not take this money from me? He didn't answer that because he couldn't, they just didn't like each other, it was that simple. The same thing happened in Portugal only reversed.

Call it luck, or coincidence, or help from a big hand up there in the sky; but things just fell into place for us. I personally attribute it to positive living; but things just happened. We had wanted to stay in Portugal for an extended amount of time; but had not made any kind of prior plans; we just had faith that all would be well. In fact we were not even sure where we would want to stay once we got there. We spent a night in a B&B in Colares; about 45 minutes west of Lisbon, very close to the coast. We met this flamboyant guy named Antonio. His ex-wife managed a villa nearby, that belonged to her brother, while he was back in England; her native country. Antonio offered to drive us by to take a look at the place. It was great; an old villa, on the side of a hill, three levels, with one bedroom, bath with shower and tub, three fireplaces and a small simple kitchen on the bottom floor. The village was Penado, and was in the shadow of the famous Sintra castle, where Beardsley, Blake and Mary Shelly were known to hang out. He then drove us by to talk to the ex-wife. She was eager to rent to us and was quick to furnish it with a new bed, a few chairs and carpets. It also came with a maid; once a week this lady would come and wash the floors, on her hands and knees. The entire time she would be talking to herself, funny; and she did this for five escudos, about $4 dollars.

Penedo was a small village with very narrow and steep cobblestone roads. I had to park on the top of the hill near the church and carry everything to the villa. Lumber, groceries and a weekly trip to get the propane gas tank filled which we needed for the stove and hot water.

Antonio, who had about five other names; that was traditional in Portugal, it showed your long lineage, well he had this old panel truck that he said he would lease to us for $150 dollars a month. I had an international driver's license so all I had to do was get insurance, which was pretty cheap.

I drove the old panel truck to Lisboa; Lisbon, and picked up art supplies and lumber to build an art desk. I placed the desk in front of the window with a view of the mountains and the Atlantic Ocean. I arranged to meet with a woman who worked at the American Embassy in Lisbon. She offered to have a one man show of my work there at the embassy; I had to get to work. They were excited to have an American artist to live here in Portugal and paint; I promised 18 to 20 canvases. It would be good press and a gold star in this woman's portfolio, not to mention mine.

I have always been a disciplined artist, whether it had something to do with my German heritage; it is possible. You had to be disciplined in order to accomplish anything. The idea of sitting in a smoky café, wearing a black beret and discussing the virtues of various artists wasn't real. To be a professional, you had to work, and work like hell. An old professor of mine once said; an artist is someone who is engaged in the act of doing art. If you are just talking about it, call yourself someone who "talks" about art.

I would open the studio; that consisted of turning on the spot lights, at 9am and work until about 5pm. After I completed four paintings, I would rent a decent car and Teresa and I would take a 4 or 5 day junket around the country. All of my compositions are pre-designed. I never stood in front of a blank canvas, and if I may quote Bullwinkle the Moose, "paint what I see". My works were drawn on napkins, bits of paper, anything I could get my hands on. My nude studies were based on Teresa; she had a very good models body. She wouldn't necessarily pose for me, but I'd catch her doing something, like taking a bath or sitting at her vanity and the image was burned into my brain.

I also shot my own photos with a good c.1972 Canon EB 35mm, then work from those compositions. I studied photography in depth at University. Even though I was quite successful in both photography and sculpture, I never cared for multi-media shows. This Portugal show was strictly acrylic on canvas.

During the several months we lived in Portugal the contrast in culture was incredible. For example, one day I was standing at my art desk and on the opposite hillside was a road, one lane, which leads out of the village. I kept hearing this car horn blowing and tooting, and then heard the shouting. There was this huge black Mercedes auto behind an old man in a donkey cart loaded with hay, just moving along like he had all day; which he probably did, and he was completely ignoring the automobile and the shouting occupant. There were a few small pull-offs for the purpose of passing, but this old guy just ignored them; touché.

Another sight to remember happened on a return from one of our jaunts. We were traveling on a four lane highway and in the distance you could see an overpass; as we got closer we could see what was crossing over us; a road full of goats and the man with his 'crook' in his hand.

Something we also found amazing were the sidewalks and some of the roads; they were made of blocks of colored stones, about 4" x 4" in size. The grey, black and white blocks were set by hand. I checked the odometer on a two lane road which we were traveling, and we drove for 22 miles on this unbelievable road. I had to lay stone on a number of occasions and it is back breaking work.

While we were living there it rained constantly for 40 days; sounds biblical but it wasn't. They said they hadn't had that happen for 150 years. The ocean road into Lisbon was closed because a slice of the mountain just slid down trees and all and buried it. I seriously thought about packing up and flying over to Madeira, a place I've always wanted to see, but wasn't practical because I happened to be working on a 30"x40" size canvas for the show.

We met a few Americans while living there; one guy worked for Fed-X, and his wife raised Golden Retrievers. Teresa met his wife while out walking and taking photos for us to work from. I forgot to mention that Teresa did a lot of pen and inks while we were there. I did a canvas from one of these photos; the one Teresa took which was the view from their villa. They ended up purchasing this canvas after my show in Lisbon.

Our circle of friends grew larger after we started visiting a coffee and wine café in the square down the hill a ways. Teresa would walk down there while I painted and met another couple from the mid-west; a Navy guy and his wife. It was a great place for tapas and conversation. We also became friends with the waiter, a very gay waiter; who happen to speak English very well. That would actually work against me in an infamous story I'll tell you about.

She had a small English/Portuguese dictionary which helped her to get by. Teresa would make up the grocery and butcher shop list for me. The language is so difficult to speak, it is a mixture of Spanish and Arabic so instead of me butchering the language at the butchers shop, I handed him the list. He read it and burst out laughing, then handed it to a few other old men who were sitting around having wine; and they burst out laughing. Even the boy and the dog were laughing! The butcher sent the boy across the square to the café to fetch Joaquin; the gay waiter. So he reads the list and the laughing doesn't stop. Finally I need to get in on this joke. He says, in his most effeminate way; "Jason, do you know what you are asking for here"? He puts his hand up and made the motion of someone milking a cow, and said you want "squeezed beef". I looked around and everyone was in tears now while mimicking a 'hand job'. Great; now the whole village knew me.
Teresa thought she had the word for 'ground beef'. I was pissed, but find it pretty funny now. Every time I walked into that butcher shop, I was shown the 'hand job' sign language with lots of laughter.

Our American friends really had their day with that; you know how those artists' can be!
The art show was more successful than any of us of had imagined. Even the 'Gulbenkian' museum sent a representative to purchase a painting for their permanent collection. The Gulbenkian Museum of Modern Art was one of the best in Europe. The man who had en-trusted it made

this country, Portugal, his home after coming here as an orphan when he was very young, he arrived with nothing but the ragged clothes on his back. These types of stories always have a place inside for me because I grew up dirt poor and know what it's like to go hungry. Somehow, he worked hard and got into the oil business and made millions of dollars. The man never married, nor did he have any family, so he turned his attention to of all things, modern art. He was fascinated by it and bought very important pieces for his collection, telling his representatives that there wasn't a ceiling on something he wanted. His men would out bid everyone and nobody knew who the collector was until after his death, he had planned it that way. Upon his passing, he left most of his fortune for a large building to house the collection and plenty of cash for additional acquisitions. His intent was to leave a poor country like Portugal, which helped him make his fortune, with the best modern art collection in the World. He did, and one of my paintings hangs in that collection. I have had great success with my work, former President William Clinton has a piece in his offices in Harlem, among other private and public collections, but this one is one of my crowning achievements.

Only two compositions out of 21 exhibited made it back to America, one was of our village which my lovely wife insisted on having, she must be saving these for a rainy day or something, but she will always pick one of the top earners from a show. The other one went back to the collection of one of my older clients, a person who believed in me in 1970.
It was an impressive feat, and though worn out, I felt good inside, but my other symptoms were making their appearance. I was having problems walking and the pain was really bad. Another couple we met was an Italian doctor who lived below us in the lower portion of the village, he and Antonio, who leased me the vehicle, were Congo exiles. After that war was over, all of the 'colonials' were told to leave with one bag, or be shot. These people were well off in

the Congo and had been there for at least one full generation; everything had to be left behind, their land, homes, furnishings, everything. Because Portugal was the original country that called the place a colony, they allowed everyone to return to that country, but didn't make any provisions for any type of compensation. This man had accepted loans from the government to become a Doctor, but the devils contract called for him to work for $5.00 an hour for 5 years before he could open his own practice, or join a hospital staff at the going rate. He had taken care of Teresa, she had an ear infection and he wrote a prescription. It was a syringe that she had to take to a clinic to have it injected. For me, he would give me a shot once a week of morphine and pills for during the week, I was relatively comfortable until the time came to leave.

I packed my studio into the foot locker and got a deal with Fed-X on the shipping, zero, somehow it just ended up on a plane for the U.S. Antonio suggested that I donate all of my other equipment to a school for special kids, he said it would help them out a lot because the government didn't have money for those programs. I was more than happy to do it; hell, Portugal had taken care of me quite handsomely.

We flew to Ireland, via Heathrow, in London. There was an Atlantic storm with wind gusts and straight line winds of over 180 mph. They announced a final flight to Cork, Ireland and she and I had to run to make the plane, they were pulling the tunnel away when we showed up and jumped across the opening into the plane, it was one of the worse and most dangerous plane trips I ever flew.

Once we got into the air, I could tell that there was a terrific head wind just by the sound of the engines, they were wide open and screaming bloody murder. The Spanish guy next to me grabbed my hand and would not let it go, no words were exchanged, but as the flight progressed my fingers turned blue. Once we lined up for an approach at Cork airport, the plane was all over the sky, to this day I have no idea how those guys put that thing on the ground, you could see the wings dipping about 40 degrees from side to side. We were buffeted by those winds, when the plane hit the runway all of the masks dropped out of the overhead and the Spanish guy flipped right the fuck out, he was praying like there was no tomorrow, maybe he had a point?

Once we got to Ireland, the next morning we were to meet with Teresa's parents at Shannon airport. We still had a way to go. This flight was the last one out of Heathrow, they closed the airport for almost two days, and after we landed, Cork airport closed also, we were the last flight in. As we taxied to the terminal I politely asked the guy if I could have my hand back now that it had to be amputated.

We spent one night in a B & B, then into the rental car and off to Shannon for the in-laws. Her father had to make a trip to the 'old sod' as prescribed by folklore; it was a duty before an Irishman dies. I assumed the posture of a driver and nothing else, wherever he wanted to go, I drove them there. Driving on the left almost came natural to me. I never had a problem in Australia, or Jamaica. I always attributed it to my left handedness, and doing everything left.

Leaving Portugal, the biggest problem that I had was getting my security deposit back from the English babe who 'oversaw' the property for her brother in England, she waited until the last possible minute when we were staying at our friends B & B, and she nicked me money for a few things which was stupid because I actually fixed the place here and there. Antonio warned me about her.

This has happened to me before, if you go into a deal with a British person, it always seems a chore to get any money back from them. It's a rash generalization, I know, but it is based on my own experiences. One guy actually said we were from the 'colonies'.

In a 10 day period I put over 2000 miles on that car, considering the size of Ireland; that is saying a lot. We drove the back roads, some of which were one lane. There were times when Teresa and her dad would have to chase the sheep off the road, they acted like they owned it so they didn't see any reason that they should move. John had me drive him to every place he had heard a story about while growing up, he was re-living his family history, and digging to the roots. He and Teresa did a lot of family research, which will benefit her in the future. I had plans for Ireland, big plans, so I was in no hurry. One night we stayed in a small town called Westport. It is the town Teresa and I have been going to for over 20 years. Yes, John was in his element, he quaffed a few pints with his daughter in more than one pub, and he actually laughed a lot, something that did not come easy to this man.

I dropped the car at Shannon Airport and we all flew back to JFK in New York, another rental car and a few hours later we were home; a very successful adventure all around.

Upon my arrival back, I was exposed to more MRI's, CT scans, and all of the other degrading tests they could fit into my insurance company's pocket. Then came the physical therapy which was a pain in the ass, I never saw the purpose for this before a surgery, except maybe to justify someone's salary. The diagnosis was simple, Jason is fucked again. I have to use that adjective to describe these events. They would beat around bushes, hem and hah, and the answer was always the same. I knew my own body; we all do, we know when something isn't right, so here we go again. If I am not mistaken, it was 1990, late spring, so this must be number 5 back surgery. The night before the operation I had a guy come in to cut my hair, he was as gay as Joaquin.

Naturally the nurse's had to squeal on me because the doctor came in and said, Jason what are you doing to my nurse's this time? So I told him, after these surgery's, unless you 'nick' my spinal cord, I have to go 4 to 5 days before I can take a shower, do you know how that feels, especially the hair? He understood and sent up housekeeping to clean

up the hair on the floor. The funny part was Roger, who preferred to be called 'Roe jay' told the doctor that he could do wonders with his hair and make him look 10 years younger. I could tell by my saw bones body language that this wasn't going to be a nice exchange of hair style commentary. He may have had a bit of that aversion to men in an alternative mode you might say?
He walked out just shaking his head.

The following morning before being wheeled into the house of pain, 'what is the law?, that is from 'The Island of Dr. Moreau', the anesthesiologist approached me, as they always do, but this was a little different. He said, I always thought you guys with your back pain were all just making it up to beat the insurance company, or for a lawsuit, but last Summer I threw my back out bad while golfing; blew a disc out, and I have to apologize, that is the worse pain that I have ever experienced. I feel sorry for you poor bastards now, how many times have you been here? I held up my hand. Five times, how in the hell do you deal with the pain? I just smiled and said, not very well. I was then wheeled in, now slide over and let me see, just count to ten.

I woke up this time wearing a suit of armor. I asked the nurse in the PAC unit what the hell was this thing strapped to my chest, she said its' called a 'Jewette' brace, it's an apparatus designed to keep your back perfectly straight so the fusion can heal. Fusion, what fusion, did I ask for a fusion? Your doctor felt it was the best course of action considering the number of surgeries you have had in that same basic area; it is a piece of your bone inserted between the vertebra that keeps them from collapsing. I could have used this in 1989.

The worse news was that I had to wear this thing for 8 weeks. It was terrible, I could hardly breathe it was so tight; then the doctor told me he usually puts a lock on it, and there was a place for a lock, so that I wouldn't be inclined to take it off. But, the severity of it is this; if that fusion doesn't take then we have to do it all over again, so it would behoove you to keep this on day and night, except in the shower, but you cannot bend over when it isn't on.

I wore this thing for 8 weeks. Years later after having another CT scan I told the doctor that I had a fusion in 1990. He just said, if you did its' not showing up on the scan, we have no evidence at all of a bone fusion having been done on your back. This doctor assumed that he may have placed a small piece of my own vertebrae in there but it was probably pounded into dust by the pressure exerted on the spinal column.

Another medical malfunction at my expense in pain and suffering, they were long weeks, plus the thing had a plate that dug holes in your groin when you sat down, it was a medieval torture device. I kept the brace for close to 9 years, I then ripped off the vinyl parts (which used to stick to my skin) and sold the aluminum at the scrap yard, it is probably part of an engine block by now.

After my recuperation, Teresa and I moved to Charleston South Carolina and found an apartment by the ocean. But before I go into the entire experience, allow me to relate one more hospital story.

After a back surgery, they want you to walk as soon as possible. I would walk the entire outside perimeter of the 8th floor in the hospital. One evening I was shuffling along and came upon an open door, it was a closet with a skeleton in it. I kid you not! It was a full size human one on a set of wheels. I went to the laundry room and got a sheet, covered the skeleton and wheeled it into my room, unnoticed. I put it in my bed with the nurse call button in its' boney hand, then hid the rolling part in the bathroom, pushed the button and ducked into the bathroom myself; when I didn't answer the speaker, four nurses showed up. One of them actually screamed; the others were not amused. Again they called my doctor and squealed on me. A few hours later the doctor showed up and came in, he said, Jason, what in the hell are you doing now to my nurse's? I told him that I just had a protest which centered on the amount of time it takes to get a shot of pain medication around here. I said that the next shift would come on before someone showed up with a needle. He accepted that, what was he going to do, throw me out?

Now, let us go to Charleston. I set up my art desk as usual and started to paint, the store downtown, Tidwell/Slavens sold art supplies, did framing services and they had the best gallery on Duke Street. It was an excellent location, and they had been around for years. I gave them a brochure and a card and asked if they were interested in a selling artist; they were. By this time it was getting on in 1991, after a few moves, Teresa found this old beach house with a closed in front porch that was all windows, overlooking the Atlantic Ocean. It was on the second floor, in fact our apartment occupied the entire second floor; a perfect studio with a view that you could only dream about. My advertising agency started with a simple request, a guy approached me to design a striking business card for him; which I did and it was successful. They then asked me about newspaper ads; that was my cue, I said sure, I do those also. I will design your ads and negotiate a decent price with the paper for you, then just bill you directly.

The idea flew, within a year I was doing advertising almost full time. Teresa would take care of the books. This is when my studio became an S-corporation, the word 'INC' appeared after the name. New stationary, a separate checking account with new business checks and my business grew simply by word of mouth, I never advertised my own company. In that first year I grossed almost $50,000 dollars, added a few more clients and started to do some radio then television advertising; my accounts grew exponentially. I was also lifting weights at a gym with a trainer named, Happy!

There was a multi-part TV show on concerning how they make television commercials. Most of the interesting information dealt with the technical side of the camera and the control room. Much was done on one half inch Beta-Max tape which was a worthy substitute to 35mm film, which was a very expensive way to go. Then there was the control room where all of the pieces came together, it was called the 'Chroma key' a level that was the joystick of a control board. At the 2 year college I went to, the gentlemen I mentioned in that portion of my book; taught me how to draw storyboards with a stopwatch. I planned every square inch of a commercial in advance, by the second everyone on the set knew where the host was supposed to be. I would then hire an entire crew, usually for no money; provided I bought advertising on that network. I would have a camera man, light control person, small railroad tracks for following the subject, and a boom for overhead and sweeping shots. On a few occasions I bought footage shot from a helicopter with one of the advanced high tech cameras that did not move or vibrate. These were sold by the second and used very sparingly. The first time I did a television spot I just kept my mouth shut and acted the part of the tired genius, every now and then I threw in words like 'Chroma key' and this helped produce the desired effect, plus the storyboards. A storyboard is a large piece of Bristol board, a heavy weight drawing paper, either 16 X 22 or, 18 X 24. On the surface, the board was divided into smaller squares with small clock faces drawn alongside each small square. Inside that square was a drawing of the action for that particular point in time. The commercials were either, 15, 30, or 60 second and had to be precise in time, not 59, or 14, they had to be exact. Usually when I had everyone on site, I would make at least one of each for use on more expensive networks, this saved time and money. At my studio I would write the dialogue, draw the storyboards and basically direct and produce the entire event. Some ads required disclaimers, this entailed checking federal guidelines; most people skimp on these, but they, the FCC can levy very steep fines for not following the proper guidelines. They specify the size of the font, or, letters and the message has to be up there for a very specific amount of time also; long enough for a person to be able to read it. The next time your television is on look for the disclaimers at the bottom and the end of the ad.

Two of my biggest accounts were Mortgage Companies. The broker was from Charleston and there was a franchise of the same company in Greenville. It was difficult working for these people because I knew what they were doing, they would put mainly minorities into very expensive mortgages, sell the paper to Fleet Mortgage Co. and then the people, who owned their house for years would be forced to default on their payments and lose their property. Most of the time, these same people didn't need to go to these mortgage companies, they qualified for a bank loan but didn't know that. It was my job to make them go straight to the mortgage broker and forget about the banks, I made it sound so sincere on television but behind the scenes they were all cutthroats, it was all about the money, the fee's they charged, some of which were very questionable, made these guys big money provided they had a line of suckers waiting to get in the door.

There are some small lenders that help a lot of people that have damaged credit, and they are sincere in their dealings; the rates are high because the risks are even higher for them. These were not the people I worked for; I felt I had blood on my hands as well because I made some very creative television ads for them.

When it comes to music, there is what they call canned music. You cannot just take someone's song and put it in an ad unless you like courtrooms.

I decided early on that the canned music sounded all the same and that in turn made the ads sound the same, so I decided to make my own music beds.

I bought time at a professional sound studio, then hired a professional musician, Ted Bird, and told him what I had in

359

mind, he would play a few bars and I would have him tweak it until we had something. Ted played multiple instruments which meant the technician could over dub them on different tracks and make it sound like an entire group was playing. I made a number of these "music beds "and had them copyrighted in the name of Alchemy Studio Inc. Now both my radio and television ads had their own sound, as soon as they came on, you knew what the ad was for. It was quite a coup and won me respect with the people I dealt with.

Another thing I did, which people get paid a lot of money for, is negotiate a monthly schedule of spots on television. In Greenville, I could buy 30 second spots on BET network at 3:00am for $2.00 dollars each. It sounded stupid, but people were up, some worked, some couldn't sleep because of their bills and all it required was one person seeing the right ad at the right time. Advertising on television is a whole game of sparing and ducking, arguing, begging, whatever it takes to get the schedule you want for less than what they want you to pay. My commission was a percentage of the final cost, plus I had all kinds of fees and expenses, per diem. It added up quick, every year I more than doubled the gross income of the business; about 23% of the gross going into our accounts, it worked out really well.

Allow me to say this; Ted Bird was an old friend of mine. I knew him and his wife from grade school. Ted and Jane were school sweethearts, married and had a terrific daughter, Allyson, who we used to baby sit so she wouldn't be a turnkey kid. Ted died at a young age and is really missed; he was a good friend, a good person and a great musician.

Alchemy Studio, Inc. had eight major clients by 1994; it was a very heady time. I was showing close to $500K by 1994 though it came with a lot of stress. In 1990 I had my first cellphone; it was an 'in car' model with a large box in the trunk and a microphone up by the sun visor. Every month I spent a full weekend, sometimes longer if we were shooting an ad, in Greenville. I learned what it was like to live in motels and eat bad food, now I knew what my brother-in-law went through every day as a lobbyist for the Tribune.

But there was a dark side to all of this; under the cushion in the living room I had a .38 caliber snub nose "Pagan" pistol, no numbers, a killing gun. At night after Teresa went to bed I would sit there in the living room and bring out that gun and unload the hollow point bullets, wipe everything off and put it all back together, then lay it on the coffee table and stare at it. My legs were so bad, especially at night, I would get leg spasms that would wake the dead; it felt like someone was turning a cork screw down the marrow of my bones. I was seriously thinking about terminating myself because I didn't see a way out. I was seeing a few doctors at the time, one was for the pain medication (which didn't touch these leg problems) and another who was a pain specialist, it was a father and son team. Every month they would shoot Marcaine into my back along with a few steroids, but nothing was working. Combine this and the stress of maintaining a half million dollar schedule and you have the ingredients for a very sad affair.

I maintained a very busy schedule, working out at the gym 3 days a week, I didn't do any heavy lifting, it was all toning exercises; I had to offset the weight gain of the steroids.

I would rarely sleep with Teresa in bed because when these leg spasms hit they were violent, they would also come on right at that moment during lovemaking; that was frustrating as hell for the both of us. The daytime seemed so successful and normal, but at 3:00am it was a different story, despair and hope draining away, I had been here once before though you never master it, the feelings are always brand new. I knew something had to change.

One day, I worked up the courage to speak candidly with the father doctor; he was the older, wiser one. I told him everything, including the gun and begged him not to mention the 'S' word to anyone, that was an instant 72 hours for observation. Isn't it strange, suicide is against the law, what a ridiculous concept; if you shot and missed, you were in a world of trouble, I never understood that, I always had nothing but respect for some of my heroes' who committed suicide. Let us take Hemmingway for example, his health was failing. His eyesight was going very quickly, so everything that really meant anything in his life would cease, someone would be wiping his rear end and shoveling food into his mouth because he didn't know where it was anymore. So while he still had the strength and the presence of mind, he took his favorite shotgun, walked into the woods a way and sat next to a tree and pulled the trigger. Was this wrong? Not for him it wasn't and it was his life to do what he pleased with. Grief is just selfishness in disguise. We will miss the person, so what, who the fuck are you to decide if a person should stick around just because of her tollhouse cookies? Maybe the person is tired and wants to take a dirt nap, isn't that permissible, or do all of the relatives have to OK it first. We should be happy when someone dies not sad, they achieved the ultimate in life's' journey, they are on the new bus to somewhere, no one knows where because no one comes back with a Polaroid. Jack London was another, his doctor told him if he stopped drinking and living on the edge, he could add 10 years to his life, he didn't, basically told the doctor to fuck off and lived wide open to the very end. What? Did he cheat us out of another book? Did he squander his talents on wine, women and song? No, he put his shift in and decided that enough was enough, maybe he hated writing and only did it because if he didn't his mind would drive him crazy. I know that feeling, I call her 'Mother Art' when she calls its' more like nagging until I can't stand it any longer. I think many artists' have a love/ hate relationship with their work, I do.

After a few days, the doctor in Charleston called me and told me to come in for an injection. He had consulted with a few

362

of his colleagues and came up with a new concoction of medicines to put in that needle of his. Each time I went there I had to stay until I could walk; right after the injection my legs were like rubber, I couldn't walk anywhere. He started this new regime and told me it would be every week until further notice.

I also discussed the problem with my pain doctor and he adjusted my dosage and medication, he went to a stronger level. With pain medication there is a dependency, but one has to weight the effect of the pain on life's quality with the effects of a dependency on a medicine that contains morphine. Personally, I will deal with a dependency any day of the week as opposed to the mind numbing pain that I live in on a daily basis.

Before we really started to look at more powerful compounds he asked me to go into a 21 day program for pain management at the same hospital my needle man worked. Prior to entering this clinic, a small spot of 'hot' pain developed on the left side of my back, I could put my finger on it. As I went through this boy-scout camp, they kept telling me it was all in my head and to use a cup of ice to fix it. I requested a simple black and white x-ray, what was it $50 bucks, I even offered to pay for it. But no, it was a mental thing that I must learn to overcome. The longer I stayed the worse this spot became, plus I just suspected that something wasn't quite right with this outfit, I mean, I have spent a considerable amount of time in hospitals and something didn't ring true here. The food was sent in and looked like leftovers, their approach wasn't medically professional, and my back was really screaming in pain now. They told me the same thing; keep the ice on longer, what, until frostbite sets in? A few days before discharge I had Teresa book me a flight to Scranton; the day I was discharged, I flew to Pennsylvania.

They immediately admitted me and prepped me for surgery. My neurosurgeon must have known what was wrong. Within two days I was in the OR again, this time they removed a tumor the size of a baseball which had grown from the nerve endings in my back, it was benign and the doctor explained to me it wasn't that rare to have this happen, the name for this thing would take up all of my brain power to remember. I had a pretty good cut on my back exactly where I used to put my finger. I had to stick around for a while because they had to put a drain in, that thing left a good size hole back there, I told the doctor to just shove one of his socks in it. He wasn't very amused. This large cyst was the problem all along; just one x-ray would have found it.

After I was discharged I flew back down to Charleston, caught up on my clients' needs then made a special trip to the hospital. It could not have been better if I had planned it. They, the guy that ran the place and his stooge, just received a piece of equipment (something they were lacking in) and it was a modern day 'rack', it had a leather sling that fit around your neck, leather belts that held your ankles in place and a crank for stretching the spinal column, it was all on a table which was the perfect height of my ass. I pulled my shirt off and dropped my pants and shoved this huge still healing scar into the head masters face and said, is this in my head? Should I put ice on a cyst the size of a baseball, well sir, should I? I kept his face almost touching this thing while awaiting an answer. Then added, you made me suffer for 21 days, I begged you to take an X-ray but noooo, put ice on it, that was all of the profound medical advice I heard from either of you. As far as I am concerned, you are the most incompetent individuals that I have had the pleasure of doing business with in a long time. Personally (I was getting dressed now) I feel that you're both frauds and know less than I do about chronic pain, and I live in it. Gentlemen, I'm not in the habit of making idle threats, but in this case I will make an exception, I feel that a report to my insurance company is in order. With that I left, and wrote a report.

One time the doctor tried something different, he went up my spine a few inches from where he would normally put the shot. Afterwards, I would lie in a hospital bed under the care of their nurse. At first everything seemed as usual after the procedure and then I noticed I couldn't feel my arms or mid-section; so I called the nurse over. She went to the doctors and they came running out with all kinds of stuff. They injected me with a few syringes, put in an IV and put on an oxygen mask. I was just a head; that was all I could feel. My head on a pillow, I couldn't feel any other part of my body. Then I got scared; what if this doesn't wear off. This is what a paraplegic with a neck injury goes through. I thought about Christopher Reeves, 'Superman', and all of those poor bastards at the Oakland Naval Hospital.
The Doctor then explained to me what happened. The drug went up the spinal cord instead of down; and if it had not been discovered in time, my breathing would have stopped. I was in that bed for 4 hours that day; and very grateful to walk out to the car where Teresa was waiting.

While all of these medical processes were going on I was still going to the gym and working out with 'Happy', my trainer. At least some of my body was very strong. I had to keep active so as not to blow up like a balloon from the effects of the steroids. It was quite a busy period in my life; I could not say I was bored.

We made a trip up north in the autumn. I decided to get us a different car. So of course I headed to my friends dealership. He said he had the perfect one for us; a Mazda RX-7. It had been some rich guy's toy and his wife, while he was away on business, traded it for a Porsche. It was in mint condition with low mileage. I asked my friend if he thought it was a good investment; he burst out laughing. He said as soon as you drive it off the lot, you've lost about $2000 dollars; no car ever made was a good investment. It was a little muscle car with incredible horsepower, but lousy on fuel. No matter; I bought it.

Driving back to Charleston, I decided to get off Interstate 81 around Roanoke, Va. Right up the road was the entrance to the Blue Ridge Parkway. While I gassed the car, the guy told me that it was closed because of the budget impasse in Washington. I drove up there anyway; there were two saw horses with the closed sign on them across the road. I had Teresa get behind the wheel while I moved them to the side just to let her through, then put them back. I got back behind the wheel and told her we WERE going to make it to our reservations at the Little Switzerland Inn for dinner at 9pm. What else could I ask for; I had a good powerful sports car, the Blue Ridge Parkway for myself on a beautiful autumn day, and my girl. Teresa was hanging out of the sun roof taking photos, while I drove the thing hard, it took corners without tilting and stuck to the road like peanut butter. Needless to say, we pulled in at 10 minutes to 9, just in time for a Trout dinner fresh from a Mountain stream.

This was 1993; the agency was doing really well. I still had my lawsuit going in Miami, but some things were going to change. The guy from the insurance company that I dealt with since 1986 was taken off my case. He was responsible for dragging out every claim, and would tie up my checks. I think he was costing them more money than saving; my attorney got $150 dollars per hour when there was a dispute. The man that was assigned to me seemed like a straight shooter. Our first phone conversation he said he'd pay me whatever I was owed and asked me to think about how much it would cost them to make me go away.

Before I answered that question both Teresa and my lawyer asked me to go to the Mayo Clinic in Minnesota, so I did.

I flew out there, booked a hotel room across the street and checked in with a doctor. I caned my way into his office; he had an audience of interns, so during the question and answer period I told him about the leg cramps and how they were particularly vicious when I was making love.

He said, laughing, we can fix that with a prescription for no sex! I almost hit the guy; instead I stood up and said, I flew 2000 miles, drove for 2 hours just to hear a very bad joke, one I've heard before, but now it comes from a World renown doctor from the Mayo Clinic, It was a huge mistake on my part to come here, I'm greeted with this hackneyed disrespectful trite.

With that I walked out and slammed the door. I was really pissed now and kicking myself for not blasting this guy and his interns. After a few minutes I heard footsteps running towards me at the elevator. It was the doctor and he was full of apologies. When I told him that these had been going on for about 8 years, his face changed. I still wanted to pop him; there was that frozen soul.

I spent 5 days at the Mayo Clinic. When I arrived the pain was not too extreme; but they decided to put me through more tests. They started with EMG's; which are from the inquisition. I had this test a few times before on my legs, but they wanted to do it on my arms as well. The tests went on for hours; these bastards were using me as a test subject for the interns. If you know where the nerves are and hit them with the needle there is hardly any pain, but if you miss, the needle has to be moved around while in there, the patient needs a leather belt or iron girder to bite on.

I pulled out all the wires and the needles myself, cleaned up most of the blood before putting on my clothes and prepared to leave. When I walked out there were more of these children of Frankenstein waiting to draw blood. I hobbled up to the doctor's office and presented one of my better extemporaneous dialogues explaining my disgust with him and the institution. All of these tests had been done previously and were in my records. It was almost criminal what he allowed to happen. My nerves were now awakened and I would suffer for weeks, possibly months. I left the clinic, drove to St. Paul to spend a day with a friend we met in Portugal, dumped the car and flew back to Charleston.

367

Within my record; had the man looked at them, he would have read about a technique that was done on me in 1990. It consisted of implanting a catheter in my coccyx and then injecting a host of 'secret' medicines into my spine. Every month for 5 months I flew up to Scranton and grabbed a cab at the airport to the hospital. These 'experiential' drugs that were administered, one made your entire body itch and the other made you constantly nauseous. So I was injected with another drug to counter act those effects. All this was supposed to rid my back of scar tissue from all the surgeries. They felt all that tissue was pressing on the nerves. After the 5 days, I'd take a cab back to the airport and fly back to Charleston. All those treatments ever did was make me itch and vomit.

My neurosurgeon thought I was taking too many narcotics for chronic pain; which he was partially responsible for. So he decided I needed a subcutaneous morphine pump. This was to be placed in the stomach area under the belt line and had a tube running around to my back where it dripped the morphine into the troubled areas. This idea came from the same doctor who had the secret formula for melting scar tissue. I think they were in cahoots because my insurance paid for everything. They showed me this sleek unit about the size of a woman's compact, but when I woke I had this coal fired lump in my lower stomach. I asked what happened to the sleek one as this one must be four times the size. The old 'bait and switch' routine; the clunker was probably 20K cheaper than the one they showed me. They said they were all out of them at the time of the implant. Fish anyone?

After approximately four months I had them remove the thing. It hurt my leg, left my thigh numb to this day and made me completely impotent.

I do remember after surgery, waking up in my room and experiencing total pathos. It may have been from too much anesthesia, but it was something that I had never experienced in my life. I WAS Pathos; it left an indelible understanding within my mind of complete and total withdrawal from all existence.

SUITABLE FOR FRAMING

(not included)

The year of 1995 marked a time of change. I wrote the insurance company and presented them with a tidy six figure amount to settle my claim and they paid it. I also won an ongoing suit from 1988. Plus on top of all that was the income from the sale of my business with a commission check every month for a year based on a percentage of my clients advertising budgets. Money was not a concern.

If I am not mistaken, May 1st, 1995 was when Teresa and I left Folly Beach, South Carolina for the last time. It is interesting to note here, a few years later we returned on a vacation and stayed with Teresa's' friend who had a horse stable on Wadmalaw Island. We were up that way so we stopped by our old beach house. Someone had bought the vacant lot across the street, which used to house a small amusement park in the 1930's, and built a huge condo block, three stories tall. All you could see from 'my' old studio were their bathroom windows, you could not see the water at all, and the place was so depressing. The town changed also, they modernized it and painted it pink; we left at the right time, as usual.

I sold one of the cars to a friend for his son, and the other one we had driven up to Pennsylvania. Teresa rode up in a mid -size U-Haul truck with me, we looked the part. In South Carolina they are still pissed off about the outcome of the Civil War. So, the 'blue bloods' there do not like Northerner's and they have a saying, Yankees that come to visit and leave are called 'damn Yankees,' whereas Yankees that come to South Carolina and stay are called(I don't care for this word) Goddamn Yankees, we were leaving and we let everyone know. When we arrived in Pennsylvania, I opened up the rest of the rooms in the studio where the ghosts had been living. I built an apartment to last 4 years, no more, while I built Teresa's' dream house on the side of the mountain. She called it the "Tree house" because it was actually very high in the living room and you felt like you were in the trees. Most of the work we did ourselves; I only subcontracted a very small percentage.

The plumbing and heating, central air conditioning, and the electric panel work, I installed all of the wires and box's and ran various circuits to the main panel, once a week my friend, who had taken over my job as general manager of the construction company, came by and 'heated' up that circuit which meant all of the switches and wall plugs etc. We did this every week. Also, I had a tenet living in the old mobile home portion of the property, so we built around him. I first built an octagon shaped 'gazebo' with a Japanese style roof; the end curled up. I did this by buying laminated boards and attaching them on an aluminum ring at the top, the cupola was custom designed and built. I lined the inside with aluminum sheeting then extended the roof line over the main building's roof; the cupola was also an octagon. When it was all finished (I built it entirely on the ground) I'd then slide it up planks to the top. It worked like a charm, during the winter when it was 20 degrees, after removing the insulated cover; the 105 degree hot tub gave off a lot of steam. This in turn created condensation which would have dripped on your head, I know because it happened to me in San Francisco, a big blob of ice cold water would hit you on the head. My cupola would condense the water on the aluminum inside; it would then run down and drip onto the main roof through openings that were covered with brass screening. The cupola came to a sharp point, so I installed a long rod to act as a lightning rod that was fully functional.

Meanwhile, my dealership friend introduced me to a good money manager and I invested a large chunk of cash with this man, he represented Northwestern Mutual Insurance out of Milwaukee, a city I knew quite well, in fact I ravished it as a young man, and yes I had a friend there, the old hippie, his wife hated my guts like the rest of them.

The next building we built was my new studio/ guesthouse. It was a cottage, fully equipped with a kitchen, bath and sitting room. The one end was my studio. I built this on a monolithic concrete slab, poured in two parts, 12 X 28 total feet. All of the sidewalks were poured and the buildings done before I dug the temporary road out. When I started, I rented a bulldozer and an old backhoe from my brothers' you should have heard Teresa about that, she couldn't get over the fact that I had to give my brothers money to use the machines that I grew up on. What can I say; a few of them were begrudgers. They were jealous because of my success, but all they saw was the money, they didn't look at the pain and suffering that went into that blood money.

The house trailer on my land was rented by the same single guy for 13 years; he paid his rent cash every month. When I took over my land I told him he could stay and continue to give my father the rent, my comment to my father was, you can keep the rent money, provided you pay the tax's every year, which was about one month's rent. When I instructed my lawyer to do the deed and title search, it turned out that my father never paid those taxes and now I owed thousands of dollars in interest and penalties. That was my father, a real piece of crap, I want to use the other word but its' gross and unkind to the dead. The worst part was he never told me, I had to find it out from the attorney; that was really low.

A farmer friend that I grew up with on the mountain gave us a stone wall as a gift. I bought an old beat up four wheel drive pickup and used it to haul these stones down to the project. We had to terrace everywhere with laid dry walls; there was a whole technique which I had learned as a kid. If you wanted the wall to stand forever, you had to take certain precautions. Behind the stone, at the lowest point I installed a piece of perforated plastic pipe, and then covered it with crushed stone. As the wall was built, someone had to "chink" it in, this word came from the sound of the hammer, and entailed placing small flat pieces of stone in between the larger stones so that the wall was tight, as weight was placed on it from behind it tightened up even more and the drainage pipe drained away any water from rain or, underground springs. When water freezes it expands and pushes things apart, the Greeks knew that!

Years earlier, we drove by the trailer house and Teresa said who owns that, I said that I did, she asked me to build her dream house there and without thinking I said yes. She was now calling in that promise and I had mixed feelings on the matter.

As you know, you are reading the story of my life, everything that I am writing is 99% truth and accurate to the best of my knowledge. As you have read, I am German and very retentive, I file everything and save information that has a direct impact on my being. This consists of: love letters, photos, hate letters, mediocre letters, diplomas, and certificates, speeding tickets, magistrate hearings and the resulting fines and expense's. Mary T insisted that I keep a journal which I did in Vietnam until someone stole it. But she kept every letter that I sent. Another good source of information I mentioned before, calendars. They are full of notes, doctors' appointments, plane reservations, train tickets and times, and a wealth of additional information. As for my art work, every painting had an invoice attached, these contained more than just price, there were names and addresses which I used for mailing lists for show etc. I have employed every piece of material to provide the most accurate and factual story of my life. This is the guarantee of the authenticity of this autobiography you have elected to become a part of. The introduction of Teresa into my life is an important attribute, and the cessation of the use of alcohol to deal with pain, both physical and mental from the horrors of combat, has placed my life on an even track. Think of it, turning 20 years old in a gun mount on a jungle river under hostile fire, what a gift!

I have been called a " Renaissance Man " on a number of occasions by friends and the press because of my ability to perform so many seemingly unrelated disciplines and professions. You can be the judge of that, its' not something I have ever dwelled upon. I simply live large enjoying every drop of its delicious ingredients; the good, the bad and the ugly.

Before leaving Charleston completely and prior to the really difficult work on the house we built. There is a little history I would like to relate. We flew Mary T. down and after getting her up the steps to the second floor porch. She had some problems with that, it's ironic that I am now in the same position. Mary loved the ocean, everything about it, the sound, the color changes, and the wave action. We set up two rocking chairs on the deck and a small table, she would sit out there all day, Teresa, being a bartender, mixed her favorite martinis, Beefeaters, stirred not shaken. After dinner she and Teresa would retire to the porch/deck and enjoy the Sun set and a few glasses of B & B. Then in her own words, she would tell us it was a joy to fall asleep listening to the waves break. We snatched her from an ugly Pennsylvania Winter and gave her 10 days in a really beautiful place. It didn't cost her a dime. But it is terrible using your own mother as a tax write off!

John and Anna, Teresa's' parents came up from Florida by train, that in itself was a treat for them because it had been decades since they rode a train. Again, they used our bedroom with the view and sound of the sea and everyone enjoyed the deck. One day, John 'helped' me build a ladder to scale the 12 foot seawall in front of our house, just past the vacate lot. It was well used and appreciated because without it you had to walk a few hundred yards to get to the beach. But as with all good things, some smuck busted it, and I did not replace it. John was just starting to get sick at this point. He didn't have his famous energy. It was a good thing that he got to experience so much in a short period of time, because time was running out for him.

He was undergoing radiation and started to get worried about driving; his wife never drove a car in her life. So he called me and asked if I could get away for a few weeks, what could I say to that request. It was winter up there and again I assumed the posture of a professional driver. While he was in the hospital, I would clean the car windows etc. One day I was driving him to the hospital, the radiation wasn't doing a thing and he knew it, but he went anyway, as we rode along I said, you know John, you are pretty relaxed about all of this stuff that is happening to you. He then explained something to me which I never forgot. He was in the hedgerow fighting in France during the second world war and watched his best friend get shot, he himself had been wounded a number of times but rarely, if ever, spoke about it. So John told me that he never expected to get out of France alive during that fight, and he did, he called it his "bonus" time. He told me that he worked a job and retired early, raised four beautiful daughters and basically had a good life. Teresa flew up in April of 94' and spent her last days with her father, Johns 'bonus time' had run out. After his passing I adopted the concept, I didn't think I was coming back from Vietnam and then had the combat of 1987, so it was all 'bonus time' for me also. You don't need a war to have 'bonus time' in your life, simply an attitude.

Another small thing I forgot to mention before we put the tool belt on has to do with my injury in Key West.
After I had settled with the insurance company and it was over. I went to a Ford dealership and bought the 'O' ring kit that the truck had needed when it flipped over and almost killed me. I gift wrapped the box and sent it to the father who was going to replace me with an alien from Krypton at $4.00 per hour. My note was a piece of poignant craft, it described the relative cost of this small kit, a few rubber rings and two paper gaskets, and the amount of suffering, pain and loss of some functions, not even gloat on the amount of money. That was a fairly substantial amount when everything was added up. No, this had to do with the father's stupidity and feeling of superiority over the lowly worker. I mention this now because this same attitude is rampart these days in the workplace. Go out there and risk your life selling a can of soda, or, 10 bucks worth of gasoline and be told that you could be replaced by some immigrant for less money.

My apologies for the tangent, its' getting late, but yes, I did send the package down to Key West with a note in it and I kept a picture of that truck in my manbox as a reminder of what it had done to my life.

Most of the first season was installing the underground utilities. I had to hook up a well that was drilled and never used, I ran 220 amps. Power up to it and then ran the water into a 1000 gallon cistern which after everything was hooked up, I buried under a few feet of soil and planted ground cover on top of it. There was a float device that would activate the pump, which was 200 feet underground; once the water level dropped to a prescribed level. In the back of my head was the idea of survival, here was a considerable amount of drinking water protected underground.

I had made up my mind to never ask my brothers to do anything for me for nothing, if I had a lot of concrete coming and needed help, they all got paid well. In this respect, I owed them nothing. But, they earned most of the money they got from me.

We were building four different buildings on the property, the gazebo, the guest cottage, a small garden shed and enclosure for tools and the main house.

After that season, there were pipes and wires sticking up everywhere with different colored tapes on them which went with a set of plans, this way I could tell what was what the next year. Winter was for painting, at least that first winter, after that I bought a window flower box companies' complete stock of red cedar boards, 3300 board feet for $1000 dollars. These boards were all 1"x 8"and range in length from 16 to 22 feet. After I bought all of this wood it changed the design of the house, I based the design of all of the buildings on the rich peoples 'cabins 'in the Catskill mountains during the 1920's; exposed soffits, low buildings with large overhanging roofs to keep the snow and rain off the main buildings. I put all of the gutters on the ground, in 'French' drains.

Being surrounded by tree's would have made for an ongoing maintenance problem and I didn't picture myself climbing on the roof, a person that suffers from vertigo, cleaning out pipes and gutters with nothing but air too hold on to. So I dug these trenches and lined them with a waterproof fabric, laid down perforated plastic pipe and covered it all with crushed stone. Then set paver bricks on top of everything to break up the splash pattern of the rain and minimize the amount of moisture that hit the house. I had to carefully sculpt the entire property for water runoff; this was the side of a mountain I might add. There were three different levels, the first level was a short driveway that went into the garage under the living room, the second level was the 'courtyard' where all of the life in the house would take place, it was exactly 3" rise into the house, this was for my future if my legs kept going the way they are. The entire courtyard was covered with concrete and surrounded by a stone wall. Then there was the third level, it was in front of the 'barn' and provided a parking space for the guesthouse. Also, after everything was done, I had each of these paved for a few reasons, water runoff and to make it easier to operate a snow blower in the Winter, a paved surface is always preferable to stone, another reason concerned weed control. In front of the 'barn' was a nice garden area shaped like a crescent, I brought in good soil for this, because the soil on the mountain was pretty bad.

As far as snow goes, I have another snow thrower; it is interesting how that came about. When we sold that house and moved here, my one neighbor told me if I buy the machine, he will operate it. You have a deal pal. I have a better idea, here is the key; I have to catch a plane to Puerto Vallarta for a few months, see you in the spring! I liked it so much there I bought a timeshare and found a small 'designer' hotel with a million dollar view.

For 27 years I had escaped the ravages of a full winter in a place like Wilkes-Barre. There were occasional visits with most of the stays measured in days, or even hours.

As it turned out, the years of 1995 and 1996 were the worse snowfall years ever recorded. 1 or 2 inches shy of 100 inches, which is a lot of snow. After a while you don't know where to put it. We were living in the studio and the family business had a huge loader on rubber tires. The bucket could hold a small car. I would get dressed up and tell Teresa that I am going to get my snow shovel. A few minutes later came this roaring sound, I had the snow piled over 25 feet high on a few piles, big gum drops of white crap as far as I am concerned; I hate the stuff. The first time I did that, she came out laughing like crazy and said I like your little snow shovel.   I told her that it was nothing; I kept it for special occasions, like this one.

I used to help out my neighbors and even pull the snow away from their garage door. They used to pay me with Polish food, all homemade. It was a nice rate of exchange. My brother Bill asked me if I would come to work clearing snow, I told him yes, once you're in a family business you are always in the family business. It was a serious emergency; we were loading truckloads and dumping it in the river, which was the only place to get rid of it. The work went on for the entire winter, as soon as we got the streets and parking lots cleared it would snow like hell again and out we would go. When it first arrives everyone thinks it's pretty, and then a few days later it gets dirty and houses burn to the ground because the emergency vehicles could not get to them. Our orders were to make one lane through each street, and damn the cars stuck in the streets, just push them out of the way, screw the damage, if they bitch tell them to call the police chief. OK boss, we're on it. We worked 22 hours at a time, 12 on the dozers and the rest in a truck where we could at least defrost and catch some sleep. If you fell asleep, my brother would take the machine and rock the truck back and forth until you woke up.

I was pushing snow down this street and noticed the lights behind me, I stopped the machine, got off and walked back to each car and asked them where they were going? It was the same answer; for beer!

These guys couldn't go back nor could they go ahead unless I did. It was stupid. And I also had to deal with the irate homeowners who were throwing their snow in the street from their driveways and sidewalks. I would say where the hell are you going? Listen, I have orders from the Mayor and the Police chief, not to mention the Fire chief also. Listen, I am going to push all of that snow up your ass in a minute or two so you better insulate your buttocks! I would then push all of the snow into their driveway just to get rid of it. The cars we tried to be gentle with, you would get a big pile of snow in front of the blade of the dozer, then push the car out of the way trying not to wreck it too much, though accidents will happen, especially when some half drunken slob would call you names from his porch, then his car ended up with a nice large hole in it, while he got quiet and filled his porch with bricks.
As with all really great things (my sarcasm) it ended, the daffodils started to pop up and it was officially spring. During all of this madness I was still engaged in my personal vendetta with the Veterans Administration, I finally did receive a medical card that allowed me health care at their hospital.

When the weather cleared up we made a trip to College Park, Maryland where they keep a lot of military records. After blood samples and DNA sectionals we were given a plastic card and they let us in, there was more security than a Rolling Stones concert. Lo and behold, I found my own handwriting in a deck log with the names of the NCO's; meaning, not the officers. We were allowed to photocopy at .25 cents a pop, so now we had something to work with. Teresa could go on line and track some of these people down. Over a period of two years, Teresa found a number of people from my boat including the big man himself, the Skipper. He wrote a book on the subject, I sent away for it and found that the first half was exactly what we were involved in. I submitted a copy as 'evidence' in my case. Then came the bullet letters; I wrote to three individuals, all officers, and enclosed a copy of the U.S.Navy official record of what our boat did in Vietnam. It boiled down to a case of 'whitewashed' records because we were in Cambodia and Laos while they were telling everyone we didn't go there.

The United States Armed Forces always maintained that we did not actively pursue any military action in either Cambodia or Laos; at least that is what the American public was told. When in fact, almost every trip we made up that river usually ended up in one of these countries to supply firebases. These were called "Black Operations" or, 'Black Ops.' So the official records consisted of about two sentences, painting us out to be 'The Loveboat,' plying cargo about the coast of South Vietnam.' My attachments had the desired effect, these guys were furious because nothing could have been farther from the truth, so consequently, they wrote multiple page letters on my behalf; 'Buddy Letters'. One of the men actually was a lawyer who had retired from the FBI after 25 years; he offered to fly to Washington to defend me at his expense. He was one of the nicer lieutenants I dealt with. They were irate and justifiably so, just as I was. This placed an entirely new perspective on my entire claim. Eventually, I ended up with my DAV representatives in front of one judge in Washington, DC. He told me that he was going to decide my case, and if he ruled against me there was not going to be any recourse on this matter, in other words, my case was closed. I rolled the dice. The judge, who was of Irish descent, questioned me for a long time, my representative, who just happened to be the #2 man in the DAV in Washington acted as my attorney, conferring with me and objecting etc. There was only the judge, myself and Teresa, and of course the DAV representative in the room. On the judges desk was a pile of documents over a foot tall which were my records. After the hearing, he came from around the bench to shake my hand and thank me for my service in Vietnam. This was the first time anyone had ever done this to me and I was speechless, I think Teresa thanked him because I couldn't speak at that moment. When we were out of the courtroom Teresa said that I had won my case. I asked how she could be so sure, she said, well for two reasons; one you were very honest and convincing and two, he was Irish. She figured that was lucky. She also said that the handshake episode at the end really meant something. The judge was sincere and was genuinely moved by your story. She felt confident, I couldn't be so sure.

As for my case with the VA, Teresa was right I had won and this judge gave me a high percentage, 40% to be exact, but that too wasn't over as time will show. The year was 1997 and we poured concrete, a lot of it I may add, by the time we had completely finished I think 52 yards went into our property. That is a lot of concrete. My brothers called me "Ironman" because of the amount of reinforcement rod, or rebar, that I placed in the forms prior to pouring. Listen, I thought that I was building this house for a long time for the two of us and did not scrimp on essential areas, some of these pads were part of our foundation, the concrete in the courtyard could get a stress crack; I had to back trucks down there, it had to be strong. Also I built with the new climate changes in mind; everything was on a bed of stone, like Frank Lloyd Wright did with the Imperial Hotel in Tokyo. In an earthquake, the shaking would right the building above by allowing it to slide back and forth, it worked; the hotel stood for over 30 years and was torn down by hand. Don't laugh, Wilkes-Barre and surrounding areas just experienced a 5.8 quake about a year ago, strange, very strange. Because we were building this place ourselves we could afford the extras and the time they involved, my work went way beyond building codes over normal building practices. All of the structures were bolted to the concrete slabs with one half inch 'J' bolts every 36", these were tied directly to the rebar

384

frame work. I also used rubber connections wherever the plastic piping joined the concrete so that it would not just snap off. All of the roof rafters had "hurricane"" straps nailed on them where they met the wall studs, and the roofing was both glued and 'CC' coated nailed. Teresa installed the hurricane straps and it wasn't an easy task, the nails are slightly bigger than the holes they fit in, 8 nails per strap, there is a reason for the difference in size. When the wind buffets a house it produces an effect called "harmonic vibration", over time, this will rip the roof off, so if the nails were smaller it would occur much quicker. There wasn't much that I did not think about on this house. Every evening before quitting we would make a trip to 'snake ridge' for a load of stone wall, we called it snake ridge because I picked up a rock one day and a 'copperhead' snake came out. These pack a mean bite and they are very aggressive. I started carrying a gun up there, loaded police fashion.

After the decision in Washington by the Veterans judge, a very large check came in the mail, it was prorated compensation, going back quite a few years, so right before Xmas of 1998 we flew to Ireland and rented a brand new four bedroom apartment(they were all ensuite too!) in Killarney. I set up my studio and began to paint. If I make a trip lasting 4 months, I try to complete at least 12 paintings, 2 months I shoot for 4 to 6 depending on the size and complexity. In Killarney I befriended a man who turned out to be a son of one of the richest families in those parts, they owned automobile dealerships and a number of hotels; in fact he offered Teresa a job at one of their better hotels. He was in the process of building a large modern design house for himself and needed some artwork; it was a marriage of minds because he could relate well to my work and bought a serious number of paintings. Out of the 12 I did, 3 were left, one Teresa grabbed and the other two I left with a gallery over there. This turned into a disappointment, a few years later we went back on a visit and the canvas' were rolled and in the back room. I brought them back to Westport, re-

385

stretched them and sold them both. My studio was on the third floor and had a perfect view of the mountains, or, 'Reeks' as they were called. It was a very prolific studio and another resounding success. This visit to Ireland laid the groundwork for citizenship.

If you recall, they had a terrific fire in the " Chunnel " from England to France, I was painting and on the radio in the news was a blurb about the stock being roughly $2.00 a share, I told Teresa to run down to the bank and buy at least 2000 shares. She returned empty handed, it was a European offering only and you had to be an Irish citizen. The last time I looked it was $55.00 a share; I no longer look at it, but the citizenship would be addressed shortly.

We returned to the States and I went to work on the house. I also was seeing doctors at the VA hospital now and they fixed me up with pain medication. It must seem awfully crazy to have a bad back, take loads of pills, and then go and build a house, I agree, its' completely insane, though it had to be.

The new medication was intense. Every day I left a Greek hero, bulging with muscles, and every night I was found floating in the river Styx, face down. At this time Teresa had returned to work as a restaurant manager in a large hotel, one of the better places in Wilkes-Barre. From here on in I worked mainly alone, except for those areas I mentioned that required skill beyond my knowledge. I did have a Vietnam Veteran friend who helped me with the bigger stuff, like installing the windows, putting the roof truss' on, the main house used prefabricated roof truss' whereas the other building were stick built as they call it. Teresa was also spending more time with her mother since John had died, so there were many nights that I didn't see her, it wasn't a problem, I understood, her mother was like a bird in a cage and needed someone around her a lot. My brothers offered to help but never showed up, unless of course there was money involved and it was a Saturday.

I am not sure how far I should go into the building of this house, to some people they would undoubtedly prefer to watch paint dry. I think I will move this whole affair into fast forward a bit.

It was 1999 and I wanted to be living in the house early in the year 2000, hopefully on the 1st. So I picked up the pace. I subcontracted out the sheetrock and spackle work, but I painted the entire interior. I also made, attached and finished all of the trim work inside; none of the red cedar went to waste. I ran the cedar up 4 feet using a 'shiplap' style siding which I made right there, then attached red cedar shingles or, shakes everywhere else, two nails each, remember that.

Heat and ac went in, all of the plumbing was hooked up, lights were installed and then came the wall to wall carpet and a commercial grade of vinyl tile; it was now looking like a proper house. The quest house was finished and could be used, I set up most of my studio, and then finished the bulk of the stone walls; we built almost 390 feet of walls. They sell for $350 a foot, 3 feet tall with the stone and labor.

I did do a lot of landscaping; bought quite a few fruit trees and finally, I installed an underground space and filled it with MRE's, Modern C-rations, good for 30 years at least.

It was January 1st, 2000 that we celebrated the New Year in the guest house. Soon thereafter we moved into our new house; the Tree House, as Teresa calls it, the house of her dreams.

Sometime after we moved in my attorney brought a friend of his to the house. This man owned a lot of commercial real estate and needed a designer. He handed me his card; he was impressed and told me to contact him. Alchemy Studio LLC was reinvented as a pure design studio and attracted a high end clientele. They were good people to work with and didn't argue about money. I was a good designer and was paid for that knowledge. Within a year I was grossing over

$100K and working 12 hour days. I enjoyed the design challenge, a battle of wit and wisdom.

That year I became certified in 'Design' for buildings both residential and commercial. I also went a bit further and received the same for 'Project Management'. What this meant was I could design a building addition and then offer my service to oversee its construction. I arranged everything, the contractors, materials and the payment of all invoices with a monthly report to my client. Most of the clients enjoyed this aspect of my services; I did not add a percentage of profit for me on any materials purchased, I was paid only a flat hourly rate. I could purchase materials at contractor's prices and that savings to the client paid for my services. They basically were having the work done at the same price as if they were doing it themselves; and I could prove it to them with the monthly line item report. This all took place during the Bill Clinton years, (who has one of my paintings in his Harlem office) everyone had money and everyone was making it.

Returning to my hometown was not high on my list of things I had wanted to do in my future, but I was around before Mary T passed away and I am thankful for that. I did my best to make her last years fruitful. While she was still ambulatory I took her to plays and even had her read some of her poetry in front of an audience at a book store. Once a week, Teresa drove her to an antique mall where she sold her collectables. She was a hard one to keep down, was active to the end. I set up the extra bedroom at the bighouse for her with a hospital bed, lift chair and her own TV. She did spend some time in the hospital and a few nursing homes before she passed. Her only regret was never getting to China; and I would like to be able to take her ashes there some day.

Around this time I had what I'll call my last back surgery. I was tripping over things that did not exist and was losing the feelings in my legs. The difference was that this time I went to a really good neurosurgeon; who I know would have done just one surgery on me in1986 and that would have been the last one. The next day I asked the doctor how it all went. He said, "Jason, it was like doing a major surgery at night, in a mine field, with a blindfold on; do not let anyone ever again touch your back. It is a complete mess back there; nothing is where it is supposed to be; the nerves are entwined with a lot of scar tissue. What I thought would take an hour, or an hour and a half, required five hours to accomplish. Be careful Jason, you are almost in a wheelchair".

At one time I had four major projects going at once. My cell phone contract had 2000 minutes per month, and I always went over that. I drove around in my new Ford Ranger pickup truck with my briefcase and the files for each job, making progress notes, taking photographs and arguing with some of the contractors who took it upon themselves to change my design. They received a set of plans that were pertinent to their phase of the project. They didn't have to know about the metal fabricator coming in behind their finished work. If they changed my plans it affected the whole design. My only recourse was to find contractors with vision; perhaps those who had wanted to be an artist at some point in their life. Maybe they made the mistake of getting their girlfriend pregnant, which usually doused a flame of creativity with the need for a steady income to feed and put clothes on little Johnny. Any dreams of being an artist are usually put to rest if this occurred. They'd have to go out and get a job.

My client who owned the commercial real estate asked me to design individual units in the mall he owned. He had an attorney who needed an office and a woman who wanted a 'high end' fashion shop. The Attorneys office had a glass enclosed conference room and a second floor 'loft' for his office. The woman's shop had a loft also; the dressing room was below and the designer dresses on display at the top of the staircase. I had an aluminum countertop fabricated and wooden doors custom made. In one of the bathrooms I covered the walls with 48" diamond plate aluminum.

In the fall of 2005, Teresa and I flew to Ireland and set up a studio in Westport, County Mayo. It is just that, the very western edge of Ireland, about a mile, or a couple of 'klick's, from the ocean. We were to stay for four months. Right after Xmas Teresa received her Irish passport, she was now a citizen of Ireland, little did I know at the time that my bid for the same would require another 6 years.

We rented a two bedroom apartment on the 'Octagon' in the center of town. I did 12 paintings there; sold a few, and the rest went into one of the oldest galleries in town, down at the Quay. Westport is a very nice little town and Teresa and I have been returning just about every year.

While I was living in Killarney I opened an account with an Irish bank, so if the "Waterfront Gallery' made a sale all they had to do was to deposit a check into my account. The sales were quite good for a while, but seemed to just stop. We found out through Teresa's friend that the Gallery owner had given the business to his son and new daughter in law, and they were both artists. So my work was put in the back room. I called my friend Colm and within two days he had all of my canvases in a new gallery, right in the town; that is Irish hospitality. This was around the time that the bottom fell out of the economy; art work doesn't sell in that kind of environment.

During this time my oldest brother and good friend was having his share of heart problems; he had three open heart surgeries. Before I went to Ireland I gave him my truck and placed him on the insurance in case he had to drive to Philadelphia where the last surgery was done. In March when Teresa and I returned from our trip, I drove past his house and there was the truck in the very same spot;

it hadn't been moved. I called and his wife answered. She was never very nice to me, didn't like me as so many other wives. She told me if I wanted to see my brother I had better get to the General Hospital. After my appointment at the VA, I drove over to see Bill. The moment I walked into the room I knew he wasn't going to make it. We talked for a while, I even made him laugh, and then he let it be known that our conversation was over; he was too weak. The next day he died.

He was supposed to have been 'Medevac'd' by helicopter to Philadelphia; hell, he could have flown it himself. I called a good friend of mine who was a doctor and asked him to see what had gone wrong.

Later that night he called me back and said he wasn't sure I'd want to hear what he was about to tell me. I told him to go ahead. It was Bill's health insurance company. He was supposed to have been moved to Philadelphia a week ago, the day after he was admitted. They found bacteria had formed in his artificial heart valve, but they just kept going back and forth about transporting him. I said I knew where this was going. The insurance company had already paid for three open heart surgeries and that was all they wanted to pay for. My friend said he was sorry, but he sees this happen all the time; it is all about the money.

Bill passed away on Saturday, the service was held on Sunday afternoon and Teresa and I had reservations for Mexico in two days. We drove to Teresa's sister's house in Alexandria, and left for Puerto Vallarta, Mexico out of DC. It was somewhat surreal. There I was in 84 degree weather, in a Jacuzzi, sipping coffee watching the sun go down; and grieving for my brother. It was an abstract way of mourning. Of all of my brothers, he was the best. You could set your watch by him he was that dependable. He had a long list of accomplishments of his own. He could fly anything in the sky, was a gourmet chief; he was well read and had very measured opinions of things. He was opened minded about a number of issues; something my family was not known for. His only fault was his devotion to the family business. It was going downhill every year and I begged him to get out. But he wouldn't do it. When I returned home I would find out more about my family and Bill. I'll miss him.

Teresa and I had been to Puerto Vallarta with a few friends on vacation a few years ago and purchased a time share. It is a beautiful resort called Melia. I found out the owner of the place started out as a hotel bellhop, and now was the owner of over 350 properties around the world. I respect a man that works himself up the ladder, as I have; with blood, sweat and tears.

When we returned home, my design work was not holding the interest it had. There were new building codes to be learned, and books to be purchased and I wasn't sure I wanted to continue. This was not a new career for me, I felt more like retiring.

I started to hear some terrible things about my youngest brother. He was giving my brother Bill $200 dollars a week, but expected him to be at the garage every day; a garage without heat.
Bill had called me in Ireland on my birthday in January and sounded good, and he told me he was doing well. I couldn't understand how he went from there to 'no more'. I found out he got sick from being in that stupid garage in February. He kept getting worse until he passed out at the garage and they had to get him to the hospital.
It was so absurd, it didn't make sense. He had just had open heart surgery and was standing around a cold garage 4 hours a day; all week. If I had known any of this, I would have paid Bill every week. My youngest brother was responsible for his own brother's death by insisting that he 'earn' his $200 a week. Bits of information of what had happened that winter were coming to light; although there

was a lot of altering the story being done by my brother and his wife. Bill had been a good friend of the farmer who gave me his stone wall; and he provided a lot of the truth behind this tragedy. My youngest brother was a merchant of Death. He and his greedy fat ass wife assumed the position that they were carrying the needy. Are there not workhouses? On a job the past summer, my youngest brother made a comment to me, as we watched Bill barely walk to the backhoe; that he liked sitting around the house and watching television! I looked at him, astonished that he could even think of something like that and said, look at him you fool, there is a man that just underwent open heart surgery and we are out here busting our asses like we always have done and you make a statement like that, I can't believe that thought is even in your stupid pea brain head! Later, I was placing a chain on an old pipe and he pulled out with the bulldozer almost with my right hand included.

Then in June my father passed away in the VA hospital. I had arraigned for him to get health care at the VA because of his service in the Coast guard during the war. They kept him alive for about 12 years by administering those $1500 cancer shots every few months, no private insurance would have done that. I went to see him and as soon as I got home from the hospital they called to say he had just died. It was strange and interesting. I was the last person that spoke to my mother, my brother and my father before they died. The son that had been blackballed; when I was dying, no one came to see me; it was ironic and bitter.

Since 1989 with our first trip to Ireland, Teresa was active in the pursuit of her family history. Her father had originally started this research and she picked up on it when he became sick. Hours were spent in libraries; including the National Library in Dublin. Records were searched and there were interviews with Parish Priests, in a few cities; and the cemeteries, well there were many of them to be searched. We found her great grandmothers records and place of birth and I actually stood in the remains of the old workhouse where Teresa's grandmother was born. These findings are what allowed Teresa to apply for citizenship. But there were more old burial grounds to be covered. She was still looking for her grandfather's birthplace. There was many a rusted old fence I opened for her. But I am going to relate a story that both Teresa and I were witness to; and it is the truth.

We spent the night at a B&B just north of Ballina in Co. Mayo. During conversation the next morning, the hosts pointed across the bay and told us there was an old cemetery there near the church. I drove a new Audi, rental car, with LED readout in the radio; a rectangular screen that printed out the name of the song and the artist in red letters. We found the church and parked next to a tall stone wall. The cemetery was too new to look promising, but I looked down the hill and through the morning mist I could see the remains of an old structure. I told Teresa we should go down there and check it out. The metal gate was rusted shut but I finally got it to open with a loud screech of the hinges. It was a cemetery and turned out to be the one we had been looking for; for almost 20 years. Well this place must have been over 200 years old. The chapel roof was gone, and there were trees growing inside. The headstones surrounding it were tipped and tilted to all angles. There was still quite a bit of morning mist, but we found the family burial plot and the tombstone.

Teresa wrote down all the information that was on the face of the stone and took photos of it as well. It was a chilly morning so when we finished we headed back to the car to get warm. I carefully closed the gate with another loud screech. We got in the car; I turned the key, and the letters 'FEE' appeared on the LED screen. It stayed there about 15 seconds then the title of the song came on. We both looked at each other. I laid rubber getting out of there. It was an eerie occurrence and there was no logical reason that word should appear on the LED readout. You are no doubt wondering why the word FEE would be so significant; it is Teresa's family name, the same name on the tombstone. We found the right cemetery alright, beyond a shadow of a doubt, and I lost a few years of my life in the process.

As far as that subject is concerned; the occult and the paranormal, I don't disregard it. My feelings are that there is something more to it than the critics would have us believe. But then again I have had several unusual experiences of my own. The one I just described; and some of the events in my house in Australia.

Prior to my father's death, Teresa and I prepared all of his clothes. We got out his black suit and the back of it was covered with mold. That went to the cleaners and I went out and bought him a new white shirt. Teresa was sent on a mission to find a red silk bow tie. The Duke was stuck in a time warp; he owned and rebuilt Model T and Model A Fords. When he'd drive around town he always wore a straw hat. So we dressed him the way he would have wanted.

Then I contacted the Trappist Monks; who hand build coffins. They are located in Idaho, and when they are not praying, they build beautiful coffins from the trees on their own grounds. I ordered a walnut coffin but when the time came there had been a mistake; they sent one made of Pine. My Father would always say, 'just put me in a pine box', well, he got his wish.

I made the arrangements with the funeral director, (as you recall I worked in the profession). I was able to do this because I held the 'Power of Attorney'. Bill had it until he passed away, then I went to an attorney and had it in my name; but power of attorney stops at the time of death.

Our timing was right because my father died two weeks after everything was arraigned. During this entire time my youngest brother did absolutely nothing. The day before the viewing, at the funeral directors office, my youngest brother showed up with his wife.

During this business meeting she slipped me a folded piece of paper which I put in my briefcase. When I returned home I handed it to my wife and told her that my brothers little misses passed it to me like a note in grade school; under the table; and, I should add, underhanded.

I was involved with the business at hand, but I recall thinking why she was even there, she had absolutely nothing to do with these negotiations. When I got back home, I threw the papers on the couch in our 3 season porch. Teresa started to read it.

I was just sitting there having some coffee when she asked me if I read this, I said no, just that tubby passed it to me like a school girl, and said," I didn't know why she was there in the first place". Teresa said to me "I know why, this is a new Will naming your youngest brother as executor of your father's estate". I couldn't believe it until I looked at the dates and the witnesses; this thing was done in March right after Bills death and the witnesses were 'wino' borough workers who my young brother worked with.
I called him and started in on this, "what the hell was going on, plus you never told your other brothers about this? You know as well as I that Mark was the Dukes favorite son, and he was the oldest, after Bill, legally he should have been the executor". The conversation quickly degraded into 'words' and I was in no mood to get into an argument with this lying piece of s___!
I realize that over half of the readers of this book have a story to tell along these lines, so I will not belabor the subject only to make a very serious point.

As time went on that summer I kept hearing atrocious commentary on the way this young brother treated his oldest brother, there was no respect, he was rude and demeaning and all of that lead to his death. They insisted that he make a

4 hour appearance every morning at that godforsaken garage in the middle of a brutal winter. Bill developed pneumonia and that in turn ended up as a bacterial infection in his new heart valve. He passed out while he was at the garage and had to be transported to the hospital by ambulance. The more I uncovered, the deeper I spiraled down into Dante's' recollections the closer I became to that frozen soul which I had buried for so many years.

I owned an assault rifle with a banana clip that held a lot of rounds; slowly I started to formulate a plan of extermination of some insects.

Another affront to my honor was finding out that every time I left the viewing at my father's funeral, he was taking credit for everything Teresa and I had done, including contacting the Trappist Monks for the casket, and the red silk bow tie. My sister-in-law, Bill's wife, who hates me, was sitting in the front row and told me all of this. It was typical of him, he is a thief along with his stupid obese wife, so why not steal the glory of every ones comments about how it was perfect for my father who was stuck in the 1920's anyway that was the reason I did what I did, I placed his remains in the era they belonged.

Another thing chubby and tubby did was have a priest show up at the viewing. I pulled him aside and told him my other brother and I had not been consulted about this arrangement. My father was by no means a catholic, if anything, he worshiped the other guy. He had even sued the church for payment when they refused to pay for work we had done; and he won. I told this Padre to leave or keep his comments brief, and skip the prayers.

It was Mark who saw it, he stopped by a few times and he picked up on my thoughts, he knew. His advice was to sell this place and get the hell out of here so that I wouldn't do something rash, like kill people as I was paid to do in another difference of opinion. Mark was the only one in my family who knew how bad it was because they never asked and I never volunteered any information, they didn't know how frozen I was inside; I listened to my brother Mark and put my house on the market.

Mark knew what that look meant because of an incident that happened in a bar years ago. We were shooting pool and some ass-wipe came in and started shouting and harassing people. At first I was nice and asked him to 'can it', but he persisted. I walked over to where he was sitting at the bar, picking up a heavy glass ashtray on the way, and just smacked this clown upside the head. He fell into a bleeding heap in the floor. I looked at my brother; who had a look on his face like he had just seen a ghost; and said, what? Who's shot is it? He realized then I wasn't crazy, just completely detached from normal social behavior. Jason could kill you and then continue to play pool.

It was a while before he talked to me about it. How casual I was, like swatting a fly. I had talked some about my Vietnam experience one night when we were both drunk, but that was back in 70 when I returned from the war; he hadn't really witnessed the frozen part of me until that night.

Around Thanksgiving of 2006 we were house shopping in the Lititz area. I was looking for a very specific building, an apartment building with a small lot and a garage, preferably two cars. As coincidence would have it, I made a wrong turn on our way to sign a contract with a realtor and stopped in front of this house, a sign said, for sale by owner and gave a phone number. I called the guy and made arrangements to meet him the next morning at 11:00am. We toured the interior, there were two apartments and the second floor had access to a very large attic space, the potential was limitless, I began designing everything in my mind. I told him I would take it and wrote a check for $10,000 dollars as a deposit. Meanwhile, the house in the Wilkes-Barre area was not getting the traffic it needed, so we put it on e-bay.

We made arrangements to close on the Lititz property May 1st, 2007. During the interim, the owner collected the rents until the lease's ran out which was around this date. That was another reason we set the closing ahead, to save on the legality of the current lease's.

We had a problem with the May 1st closing date, it was the bank actually, the woman who was doing our loan up and quit the night before. So I arranged another $27,000 to add to the deposit, I suspected that this guy was offered more money for this house and would love to have us disappear, I wasn't going to allow that to happen. We closed on June 26th of 2007.

I know I may try one's patience, but allow me to regress one more time, it is an important story.

Teresa and I were clearing some saplings from the forest behind our Tree House in the summer of 2006; it was May to be exact. There had been a sustained drought for 5 years and as you walked through the woods the old leaves were not only deep, they sounded like potato chips. I don't know what it was but a fire started behind us, I think it may have been my cigarette ash. We didn't smell it until flames started to show. Then a stiff breeze came out of nowhere. I told Teresa to run to the house and grab every fire extinguisher after calling the fire department. It must have taken about 15 minutes for the fire company to show up, but in that time this fire was really starting to spread. I was on the leading edge, which was a dance, you had to gauge the flames and dive in low, rake back the combustibles then jump back. I had done this before on the side of this mountain. Teresa was on the trailing edge trying to keep the fire away from our guest cottage. When a sudden gust of wind came up it forced a surge of extreme heat towards her and burned her face. At the time she didn't even know it happened; it was a good thing she was wearing her glasses and a hat. My brother, the prick, stood by the fire truck 'BS-ing' with the guys there just watching Teresa battle this fire, he never lifted a finger to help. When it was over and the fire out, she had 3rd and 2nd degree burns on her forehead, it was bad and I felt terrible, I promised her that once it healed a bit we would call a plastic surgeon.

My life was changed completely in February of 2007; I received a large manila envelope from the Veterans Administration in the mail and threw it on the floor of my little pickup truck, I could not open it, and I waited until 11:00pm that night when my Irish honey came home. She opened it and said, Jason, you are now 100% disabled, permanent and total, it also says here, there will be no further testing. And guess what the date of the decision was, my birthday. I called Philadelphia the next day and spoke to the main guy who was working on my case, he actually had taken my file home and found a "clear and unmistakable error "which knocked the door down.

Joe told me that I was set for life now, after 30 years of denial, I had finally won the big 'rat'. These benefits also applied to Teresa, and she had a pension if anything happens to me. I cannot explain the extent of the benefits for a 100% rating as it is called; they are vast and very comprehensive. The VA puts out a veterans catalog every year which has all of the information along with the compensation rates. I came out on top of the heap again, every month that money is automatically deposited. I had the same DAV representative for almost 5 years and we became friends over that period of time. He was younger than me, but had served in the Marine Corps as a lightweight boxer, of all things.

Joe married his 10 year, on and off girlfriend; she was from Trinidad and had a great accent and an even better laugh. As a wedding present, I gave them the guesthouse for a long weekend with the hot tub, and then turned them on to a little restaurant in the country that served two things, steak and lobster. You bought the lobster by the pound, so the sky was the limit. For a human dumpster like Joe, this was right up his alley. The next day he was the only guest that ever blocked up the bathroom in the guesthouse; with I would imagine a 5 lb. lobster and stuffed shrimp and steamed clams and a few other items. His wife just laughed. How could I get mad at someone who just set me up for life? Of course the down side to all of this is my body; I live with chronic pain, numb legs and arms; have been sprayed a few times with Agent Orange (which is causing me some heart issues). But those 5 digit checks for retroactive payments keep coming into my mail slot, so I'm not complaining.

A few months later Joe called me to tell me that he won his 100% disability also. But my friend Joe had a few serious problems, he was into certain substances and he had a thing for gambling. He told me that he lost $6000 in a few hours playing computer poker on the internet. I never realized that was even possible. Pass the Visa card dear!

A few weeks after that, his wife called me to tell me that Joe was gone, it must have been a 'hot shot' as they call it, but it cost him his life, what a waste, he wasn't a bad person and I will always be grateful for what he did for me.

As for the selling of the 'Tree House", for the e-bay presentation, I had taken the photos with my 35mm and wrote the copy. I was selling the house complete, right down to the toothbrushes in the bathrooms. I actually mean that, I had brand new toothbrushes ready. The copy read, just bring some groceries and your clothes, you will not want for anything else. All of the pots and pans, dishes, and most importantly the tools were left. In the garage was an air compressor among other things. The 'barn' had an assortment of power tools, chainsaw, two weed whackers, one was a John Deere with a few attachments, it was all there and it did exactly what was planned, it sold the house for good money, this was right before the bottom fell out of the market. I closed on the place in early October; a guy from Long Island bought it for a getaway, because the Poconos were full of the people he was getting away from. Everyone was happy.

During this entire time I was driving to Lititz every weekend and working on this place, getting it ready for a makeover. When we closed on this house, our bank messed up one piece of paper. At the closing we were using the same lawyer as the seller; in hindsight it was a mistake because we started to get the feeling that they wanted us to fail, and why not? The crumb that owned the place would get to keep our $37,000 and the building, which he could turn around and sell for more money. But that didn't happen.

This wasn't the first time this guy tried to pull something. In December he called me and said that the price went up $5000 because the flat roof portion was leaking. I told him it would when I looked over the roofs with binoculars that I carried in my bag. It was a rolled roof which under the best of circumstances had a life expectancy of 5 years and this was on the house for over 7 when we looked at it. He told me that if I didn't pay it he would send my deposit back. He was still trying to get out of our contract.

After we had been living here for a year or so I ran into a roofer working next door, it turns out he was the guy who installed the new rubber roof and said he was paid $2100 and then told to leave. Later that day I called the guy I bought the house from and told him about the coincidence that occurred that day. I asked him if the other $3000 was for pain and suffering. He told me that I moved the closing date, yes, I said, I did, but I made it worth your while with $27K. Then I told him something I have used before, I said listen, in less than a month I will replace that amount of money, but for all eternity he was always going to be a thief. I also added that $3000 was a cheap price for his lifetime of integrity, I bought him for 3 grand and that was a pretty cheap price, about the same as a questionable used car.

About two weeks later, he fell out of a tree with a chainsaw and broke both his arms. Bad things can happen to bad people, they say. But it wasn't over yet. He mistakenly had left paperwork inside the house, it had to do with the 'Homestead Tax' break; one of the strict rules for signing this document was that it had to be your primary residence. He had filed for this tax break for 7 years claiming it was his primary residence, when I held both apartment leases for about 5 of those years. Just above the place where you sign and date the forms, there is a paragraph about submitting fraudulent forms, 5 years in jail and/or a serious fine.
I spent a week or two thinking about whether to drop this dime on the guy, and after I reviewed all of his underhanded deals, and the input from my tenet downstairs about what a cheap person he was, and how he would just barge in whenever he felt like it, which is against the law in the lease agreement. My mind was made up; he did not deserve a break, so I sent in all of the paperwork to the tax office.

Teresa saw him a few months later and she said there was nothing but hate on his face, so we must have succeeded in preventing a miscarriage of justice from going unpunished.
I have adopted a policy of trying to live a positive life style, I do not knowingly hurt people unless it is a case as related above, and the man was supposedly a 'professional' person also.

ILLUSTRATION ON BOX

My disability rating from the Veterans Administration has affected my life in a number of ways. Yesterday, a bunch of suits converged on my 100 year old brick house. One of these men from the VA office in Philadelphia was connected with a housing grant.   He was the one who approves the design of the new accommodation for a handicapped Veteran, in this case, me. Last year he and I were locked in a battle of words concerning the retrofit of my current residence. It just happens to be on the second floor, where I prefer to be, one major reason had to do with being in that machinegun pit under fire; I was in a hole in the ground, a ready-made grave. After I had survived all of that, I have always strived to be on the second floor anywhere.

My house had one of those old cast iron bath tubs with the shower and controls at the opposite end. I knew over time that this tub was going to kill me; it tried on a few occasions. This was the gist of my conversations with this man who made the decisions. I needed a walk in shower stall and he insisted that it had to be of enormous size, whereas I suggested that it fit in the same space as the bath tub. So a spirited debate started between us. Their housing grant is a carrot attached to a big stick; the U.S. Government's. They always have the final say. So before I ended up in a body cast, I fixed the bath myself; or I should say, paid for it.

My neighbor who is an architect mentioned how slow business was, I brought up the VA Housing Grant but warned him to read the paperwork very carefully which I do not think he did. They submitted architectural drawings on at least 3 or 4 occasions, and the suit in Philadelphia would keep changing the rules, it drove them crazy until one day I found a large envelope in my studio; they never received a cent and got paid in a lot of frustration.

While we sat in Mexico looking for whales in the Bay of Banderas, carpenters, plumbers, tile setters and painters had converged on our house, the last person was our cleaning person. We came home to a shower stall and a clean house. The construction looked like it was supposed to be there all along, I used my own money and some borrowed from my business to accomplish this task. Inside the shower is a 'Rain Forest' shower head 10" wide; and a hand held one on a sliding bar, that one was for my wife. Also, there were stainless steel hand rails on all four walls, so I could wedge myself in there and felt safer, as opposed to a large space which allowed me to waver when my eyes were closed.

Yesterday, when the same VA guy was here, who was quick to point out our running gun battle from a year ago; came up to our second floor home and looked at the shower, his comment was that it was a nice bathroom, Teresa pointed out that Jason had designed everything. Upon hearing that he had to return to the first floor where he decided the renovations would have to be made. My input was not asked for nor listened to even if I said anything so I walked away. If the day comes that I need a wheelchair, I will address that; for now, I have a view and an advantage.

The years of 2008 & 2009 became times of surgeries. The VA doctors had sent me to a famous medical center to have work done on my neck. The reason was quite simple; they did not have a neurosurgeon on staff at the time. I was scheduled to undergo at least two surgeries at the same time. One was to correct the space in which the ulnar nerve is found, usually around the elbow. I had this surgery done once before at the VA hospital on East 28th Street in New York, but they picked the wrong place to cut out, afterward the problem was just as bad. What happens is your last three fingers curl in and left untreated they stay that way and call it 'claw hand.'

The problem with my ulnar nerve was it was my left hand again. While that was being fixed, they were going to find out why I had these electric shocks shooting down my right arm.

408

I went into this place and it was like an assembly line, they performed a total of three surgeries on my neck. The main concern was the total loss of the use of my right arm, it required 10 days of phone calls to get a real person to explain what had happened there. The answer; the nerves to the right arm were "shocked" because of being moved during surgery. That would all return to normal, but it took months. My claw hand was repaired, but now I have a numbness going down my arm, my left arm and into my left hand. It is more than disconcerting; this would go on until my hands were cold as ice. Why am I always having surgeries to repair the surgery I already had?

There are some readers out there that are saying what about this guy, Jason? He is writing, painting, and receiving compensation. What's up with that? The truth of the matter is this. It is difficult to be an artist when your arms and fingers are numb, being an artist is impossible if you have to rely on it to make a living. It is every artist dream to have an annual income so that they are free to paint, this I found is only true if you stop using alcohol completely, but over a period of time it will sneak in, it is insidious remember, and most artists are inclined toward this escape, it is part of the career choice.
In a few weeks Teresa and I will travel to Naples, Florida and then onto Mexico. Last year, the country of Mexico banned any form of morphine or, opiate in their words, and any form of diazepam, or, a psychotropic medication. I am mainly treated with opiates and I take anti-depressants; I have to, but it does not matter if you have a prescription or not, the answer is still no.

At this point in time you are probably wondering if I am just a vindictive, angry and frustrated individual. The answer to that is a resounding no, I am not. In most circles I am considered to be a good decent individual, very generous and thoughtful. The reason I have related a number of these stories regarding thieves, liars and scoundrels is quite simple. Someone has to stop them if they have the opportunity or the same behavior will be repeated, then someone else will fall victim. Some of these people need to be exposed because they live in a certain community and everyone thinks that they are pillars of society; then you find out that the guy likes little boys around. Sometimes you have to stand and dig your heels in and say, enough! You would not care to be taken advantage of in a blatant way, well neither do I; that is when my famous bullet letters go out. I have taken on large corporations over being mistreated or disrespected and it is surprising how often they will listen.

One time I was waiting for a flight in an airport somewhere and I was sitting at the bar, I struck up a conversation with a gentleman who looked the part of being a CEO or, President of something. He told me two things that I never forgot; one was the definition of success; having the integrity to take credit if it is actually yours and to except responsibility for something that does not go to well. The other thing he mentioned was if you want to get anywhere with someone or, some company, get on the elevator and push the button with the 'P' on it; (Penthouse). Please do not misjudge me or my intentions, I do not go around looking for things to hang on people, but, if it happens and the evidence is overwhelming, then I act upon it.

Consider our own country; the current demonstrations on Wall Street. I remember the war demonstrations because I was an organizer, but a demonstration because of greed? That is an interesting concept in these times. But I am getting too old to be bothered with a lot of these issues because they are rampart. It is not going to be an easy task to take a lot of money from people once they are accustomed to having it and the power that goes with it.

Why Lititz? Interesting question, just when we finished our designer house on the mountain side, my brother-in–law had to move into this area due to his position and they had taken Teresa's mother with them. We were in the house about four years and one night Teresa started to say it and I stopped her. I told her that I did not want to hear any of those words. We left Charleston, came up here to this dust bowl, I had taken 20 years off of my life building this house, not to mention the money spent, and all of Teresa's family moves away, isn't that ducky?

Every time we visited the Lititz area, I would always book a room at the General Sutter Inn. This was the same guy who owned "Sutter Mill' in California where the famous gold rush actually started. One of his employees found a nugget of gold in a creek that serviced the saw mill equipment. The General, which is rather a dubious title; many historians feel that he gave it to himself, had asked him to keep it quiet for a few weeks, but once word got out , well you know the rest. From what I gather the Inn was not his, he lived in a house across the street. But his ghost is said to occupy the Inn. When you enter, there is a well-appointed lobby with a large fireplace and a portrait of the 'General' above it. Teresa and I stayed in the Inn for over a period of 10 years, probably staying in each and every guest room. We became friendly with the owners and members of the staff. It is said that whenever the portrait was moved, for painting or cleaning, strange things happened. An example was a c. 1940 radio that was part of the décor; it would start playing when it wasn't plugged in. There were reported sightings of an old man with white hair, in uniform in the halls. This of course piqued my interest. Over the years I narrowed it down to one room on the third floor, room 302. I was convinced that is where the General would be. I picked that room because of a few reasons. One because there was a laundry room right across from it and I managed to get an old window open so I could smoke a cigarette. I had to be careful because the police station was directly below and their cars would come and go at all hours. It is a good thing they didn't check their roof, as it had quite a few butts on it; too many to be all from me.

When we decided to move here, we were aware of the 'historical district' and the flood plain. The house we found was in neither. That meant we didn't have to follow the historical society's guidelines with your homes façade or construction. We also didn't have to buy flood insurance.

Lititz was originally called "Lititz Springs" because the park in the center of town has a natural spring. The stream would often overflow after a heavy rain but never reached our street.

People often speak of the "Pennsylvania Dutch" and the lifestyle they live. A correction is that they are not Dutch, but mostly of German descent, thus "Deutsche". Their farms surround Lititz. They are tidy and organized like all of we Germans. These people migrated to the United States a few centuries ago in pursuit of religious freedom and they are quite stoic in the life they live. The true "Amish" do not use any type of power equipment, either gasoline or electrical. All of their farm work is done with animals; 'Beasts of Burden', as 'Mick Jagger' would say. It is not uncommon to see a boy of about 14 years of age plowing or threshing a field with "8 in hand"; that means he alone could handle 8 mules. These work horses or mules are huge animals. Then there is the horse or horses they use for transportation; the ones that pull the buggies, they are so well disciplined they barely take notice of a sports car or even a bus that may decide to pass them. The roads around here do have pretty wide shoulders so that can happen safely.

In my travels throughout the world it is surprising how many people hear about and would like to see the Amish. I do enjoy seeing them in town and like hearing the sound of the horses as they pass my house. They really do keep to themselves, but support each other beyond any other group I know of. I suppose they are the closest thing to a successful 'commune'.

Back in the 'hey day' of LSD and free love I had many opportunities to join communes where everyone would just ball all day in between hits of acid and smoking joints. I never got involved because I grew up in a place where you had to cut wood for heat, grow food and raise animals to slaughter.
You better not let someone go out into the woods high on LSD with a chainsaw in their hands; not a good combination. I never considered myself a 'hippy'; a bohemian yes, with poetry, bongo music and a black beret.

On Sunday mornings I sit on my front porch, smoking Camel cigarettes (I am in the process of quitting) and drinking very fine coffee that is sent in from a small roaster in Alexandria, Virginia. All of their products are 'estate' and free trade. On Sundays' the buggies clop by, full of kids with hats on their way to church which is down the end of my street. In fact my contractor is a Baptist Preacher, so I watch my language at those meetings.

We are rarely here during the winter months because its' no secret how I feel about that season. That was the only drawback to buying a new home in Lititz, it is still in Pennsylvania, and prone to cold snowy winters, albeit a bit milder I may add in both temperature and snow fall than the mountains.

Puerto Vallarta, Mexico is 84 degrees in February; it is one of those places where the temperature stays between 75 and 85 all year long. The only time there is a change is in August when it is humid and perhaps rainy. This is my way of suffering through winter; in fact, we are leaving in a few weeks for a period of at least two months.

But, I was still talking about Lititz, so I will get back to that subject. This place isn't quite "Leave it to Beaver," but it is close. We have some section 8 housing, and a vigil police force, this isn't a place to be a drug dealer by any means. A number of the officers are Lititz born and raised so they know all of the hiding places. Right up the street is one double block that's' full of kids and babies, with large mothers, and no men around; I don't begrudge their being there at all. I used to have a maple tree that blocked out the view of that house most of the year, but it had been struck by lighting and slowly died over a period of 4 years. I kept cutting pieces off until it became the ugly tree award winner, when it got down to one branch that was it, it had to go.

Some readers may object to my use of certain words to describe people. Well, I do not claim to be a disciple of the 'political correctness' wave in this country. My age is of another generation, it is easier to say exactly what you mean than walk around with a resentment for not speaking out. If a mother is beating her small child, I will interject; I was that kid once and I know what its' like to get your ass kicked, especially in public. I use these phrases in gest or sarcasm because they tell it all; phrases to describe someone as 'physically challenged' or, 'gravity deprived', 'grocery enhanced' or a, 'dinner table magnet'.

In some cultures being pleasingly plump is considered quite beautiful. A thin person is frowned upon as sickly and unable to bear many, many children. But these places the people don't have a little yellow card to use at the supermarket, hell, they don't have a supermarket. They don't have a welfare system to abuse by having more children to receive more money every month. I was grocery shopping in one of the more expensive stores in town, this was in the Wilkes-Barre area, and I went to this store for certain items. In the checkout line was a large woman wearing a full "Burka," the one with just the slit where the eyes are. I waited and sure enough, out came the yellow welfare card; or, 'Access' card as they are referred to. Listen, I don't know about anyone else, but if I stood there with a ski mask on that covered my face, the cops would hand me some nice new jewelry for my arms. This is still America if I am not mistaken, it may be owned by the Chinese, but its' still called America anyway.

Our constitution guarantees freedom of religion, but it does have its' limitations, and there are certain rules of the road you might say. In these trying times, someone covered from head to foot in a black garment with just eye openings would set off alarms, there could be a guy in there with eye makeup on and a sub machinegun. I don't know if those people are cross dresser's or not, but the concept is easy to grasp.

When I first moved to Lititz I told my wife I was going to become the town idiot. When I went down to fill out the paperwork and pay the stipend I found out there was a waiting list! So I am fairly far down on that list and doubt if anything will happen in my lifetime. The current town idiot lives up the street on the back side of our house, he has dogs that bark all night long, when you call the cops, they just sigh over the phone and say, we will look into it sir, thanks for the call. We just turn up our sound machine anymore; it's part of the experience.

I realized what I was going to interject earlier, people treat me like a leper and with very vocal disdain because I smoke a cigarette, as with sex and good food, they go well with a lot of nerve racking pain. I won't go into a diatribe, but I fought for supposed 'freedom' and, 'democracy' yet in my own country I am exiled for a fix.

If you really look at the statistics, obesity is responsible for more health related issues and costs more to treat in the long run than anything else on the list. I am not implying that cigarettes are health food, they aren't, and I am starting to show the effects of 40 years of smoking at this very moment. But my affliction will not cost anywhere near what morbid obesity does. I can't use the term "Fat Bastard "anymore because its' a wine label. Lititz has some obesity, though the term could also apply to their propensity of spending tax money on things that we don't really need, and leaving the important issues unfunded.

At 60 years of age, I am caught between generations, or, I am turning into my father which may be impossible due to the fact that while he was kicking my ass, or beating me with a switch (flexible stick) he was always screaming: " You are just like your mother!"
Let us take an inventory, I am formally trained to educate and manage a classroom of 25 kids four or five times a day, I have my opinions about my nieces and nephews and the fashion in which they are being turned into men and women. But, if I say anything, the first broadside will be the comment you don't have kids, how would you know? I have a degree in the subject; a few degrees' to be exact. That should carry some weight regarding my opinions, you are dealing with one or two of them, I dealt with hundreds every day and each one is an individual.

Maybe I am becoming cognizant of my age and the undeniable fact that old age is slowly and quietly sliding into my life and my realm of conscience thought. I find myself in the bathroom frantically searching for hairs in my ears. I do believe that is the first sign, or indicator of the presence of old age in prelude. Rather than adopting new opinions, I should just not say anything anymore. In all honestly, I do not have an understanding of nieces and nephews anyway, all of that stuff about 1st and 2nd cousins, then throw in 'twice removed,' and I will be ready for a few valium and a rain storm. I effectively stop at aunts and uncles; that I can grasp. There are people that send birthday cards to these myths and legends. That is what this page has been about, my lack of decorum and personal ignorance of these subjects, it wasn't important when you are working at eight years old.

Many years ago, and this will be it for the subject, one of my relations was talking about their troubled son and his tendency to be flippant about his higher education, a very expensive one at that, during a lull in the conversation, I piped in with a perfectly sane idea, send the boy to welding school in Detroit!

As they looked at me with mouths ajar, I went on to say that the world can always use good welders, and this course was not only comprehensive, it was intense. Plus, he could add on a several week program in welding aluminum, and then qualify for a really well-paying job in Groton, CT; where they weld nuclear submarines together. Everyone just looked at me like I fell off of the turnip truck coming in from the field and then proceeded to continue talking about colleges.

Some readers may find this story entertaining; others may question their own sanity for spending hard earned cash for the dubious pleasure of reading it. Maybe it could prove to be an inspiration to some poor kid, male or female, older or still in youth who has or had a controlling mother and an abusive father. A rewarding life can follow this punishment if you really want one. You can make dreams into reality. Just don't give up.

Personally I would not suggest using alcohol to motivate oneself into action, it is just another lie; it will take decades of your life and give you an I.O.U. in return. This substance can only promise a life full of damage and heartbreak, because you come to realize, usually too late, that you cannot stay up there, no matter what you try, a tomorrow will arrive and bring with it all of the same problems plus the new one's made out of fear from the night before.

An old man once told me this in relation to drink; every day you knowingly place a thief in your mouth that is going to rob your brain. It required many years of trial and error to understand what the old man was really saying.

I am not very familiar with computer games or the X-box. What I do understand is a lot of people spend huge portions of their days in front of television monitors playing games, or killing off hundreds of other people with graphic reality. One evening when I was 10 years old I was sitting in the living room watching black & white television. My father was there in his chair and you watched whatever he decided to watch, there was no debate or talking on the subject. You had to actually get up to change the channel. I found out what happens when I disturbed his concentration on the "White Owl" girl, who just happened to be well endowed, during a commercial of the Ernie Kovacs show. That was the night he threw me into the snow bank outside and locked the door. This might explain why I read so many books and continue to do so. On one other occasion, 'Wayne Newton' was singing his song about red roses and blue ladies, out of nowhere my father said look at him, 18 years old and he's on television, you can't do that, you'll never amount to a pile of_____! I hate using that word. On another occasion, he brought out this roll of cash and said; do you see that, its' a measure of a man, you won't ever have something like this. I had time.

Years ago, I studied Zen Buddhism and read the works of Alan Watts and D.T. Suzuki, I ran across a small paperback written by a Chinese guy and translated into English. This was a perfect inroad into the Chinese mind and the Eastern way of looking at something that we in the West would find completely opposite our take on the same subject. The name of this volume was "To Save Face," and its' message stayed with me for a long time. The Chinese do not care how long it takes to settle the score, or setting the record straight. Saving Face is not shallow; it pulls from many points of reference within their culture.

At the time I adopted the Zen philosophy into my life and added the concept of saving face. Throughout the book are examples of dealing with people who disrespect you, or owe money that they refuse to repay, I have used these old time tested concepts to great success. That showing of the wad of cash would be addressed at the right moment.

For my parents I applied the Judeo Christian ideals, in those many years of biblical study there was one thing that stuck, I was expected to honor my father and mother. I showed this, or, better yet, I lived this philosophy, in taking care of my parents in the last years of their lives. One way was by establishing the spare room for my mother and making her life as comfortable as possible. Teresa had a hand in it also; she helped me in this pursuit.

As for my father, the one person that I should probably have very little to do with, I set him up with the VA for both Health insurance and a pension, the last few years of his life he had more money than he had prepared for, that was another loveable part of his selfish personality, he didn't care who paid for his funeral and he had told me that if it was up to him he would have sold everything and basically screwed my brothers out of the entire business, his rational was the fact that his father never left him anything. How could he, he didn't have anything except that Army Jeep. This all fell under the word respect, I came to realize that it was for my own benefit, my soul was transparent; I never forgot that voice in the hospital room in 1987. I had a reason to do right.

Teresa's mother is in better physical condition than I am right now; she has what is called 'expanded dementia' which is the loss of the short term memory. She can't remember what she had for breakfast, and doesn't remember her daughter's names, but her face does light up when they visit; a spark of memory of the past.
It is interesting the way we are wired, at the time of our old age we forget the daily affairs, pee in our pants and smile a lot, it is a total regression to our earliest possible time on Earth, our birth. Who cares when you ate anyway, if you aren't hungry, so what. Is there anything wrong with returning to an early time when deals were made with a handshake, when a nickel, .5 cents could buy a bag of candies that would last all day if you hid them; chewy

fedoras, sugar watermelon slices not to mention the long twisted black licorice.

I had to use my 'Franklin' to look up the word 'licorice' and it went on to say; "...dried root of a European leguminous plant or candy flavored with an extract from it." I would wager that our licorice candy was not an artificially favored stick, how many people had the job of stacking those black sticks into that jar with the glass lid.

While driving through the Alentejo region in Portugal, Teresa and I stumbled on a cork plantation. We walked through it with the rows of tree's some of them over150 years old. We picked up some pieces of cork, it was the bark of the tree and would take about 8 years before it was thick enough to harvest for wine corks. They would then punch out millions and millions (In memory of Carl Sagan) of wine corks. Now, due to greed, they are made of plastic, and even more disconcerting is the return of the screw top bottle on an $18 dollar bottle of wine. The only screw top I remember was Pisano $3.99 a gallon, Italian red table wine. Now, the cork trees and the licorice tuber are sharing the same fate, the bottom line.

Having been a surgical patient many times removed, I feel that there may be a good analogy to dealing with the dead. Picture yourself lying on a cold hard, stainless steel surface with tubes sticking out of every orifice of your body and few that are new, then at 7:00am a group of people walk in dressed in blue and wearing hats and masks and one asks you: " How are you doing?"

"Well, if I had my vinyl, LP copy of "Staying Alive" and my white, wide lapel leisure suit, I'd be dancing down the corridors". What kind of question is that anyway? The same one they use at a funeral parlor, "he looks good." No I don't you ass, I am dead and worse yet my lips are glued together so I can't smoke a cigarette.

Trust me; I have spent a lot of time in hospitals and besides the gowns that allow your ass to be judged 1 to 10 by the nurse's, and a piece of fish the size of a postage stamp with the same amount of salt. You find yourself looking forward to certain things, a good action movie, or anything with Sir David Attenborough in it about Giraffes. Then it happens, the 'well meaning' guests arrive. They pile in and sit under the television, and ask, "How are you doing?" Oh I am in this hospital bed full of tubes because the local Red Roof Inn was full due to a Velcro medical closure convention. They then sit there waiting for the next question to come along, so you throw in; "I have decided to become a woman while I am here." By this time all of the good shows are over; then they announce that visiting hours are over. Then a nurse walks in and asks," How are you doing?"

My point is this, when someone close dies, it is the memory that we cherish. True grief in some cases may be the most honest thing that a person has ever done. We can't keep clutching onto the person's shell, if you are busy clutching on to something your hands aren't ready to receive new gifts. Give peace a chance!

Do you remember the crystal radio? I had one at that same period in time of my life. You had to have a really good antenna at least 12 feet long for it to work well. You used one piece of wire with insulators on both ends so that the wire wasn't grounded. Crystal radios always had one earpiece, these radios did not use any batteries or exterior source of power except for the 'crystal,' in all honesty, I had no idea how it worked. On top was a small plastic ball attached to a rod of steel that would slide up and down to tune in an AM station. A device of this nature usually came from the back pages of a pulp magazine like "Fate." I used to wait every day for the mailman to come bouncing down the road and deliver that brown box. I'll bet they had a special room where they parked boxes like this just to drive guys like me crazy. I could guarantee some station was playing "Volarie."

My father rarely paid out money to anyone; it was always a barter of some sort. The quality of the work performed was always predicated by what they were receiving in return from the Duke, it was either liberated coal, or later, on some bulldozer dozing. But he paid his bills with our backs. And all of the while he would have a wad of cash in his pocket and he liked to pull it out and show it. One day he shoved it at me and said, do you see that, it's the measure of a real man; you will never see this .Here is the entire irony of this story and why I had to go back in such a roundabout way, except for the crystal radio set, anyway.

A few years ago, the 3rd of the month was a scared day, for my father; no one ever parked next to the mailbox, it was check day. So I waited until the 15th when his tongue would be hanging out and he would be broke.

I went to the bank and withdrew a pile of money, 20,s 50,s & 100 dollar bills and rolled the whole thing into a wad with a rubber band around it, it looked just like the one he used to shove in my face. I personally never carried that kind of money around, I use my AMEX card.

I stopped at the bighouse and as usual I'd have to listen to him rant and rave (as he usually did) and in a matter of time, he'd start to sing the 'no money' blues. At the perfect moment I pulled out the wad; it was 'To Save Face'. I peeled off a few $100 dollar bills for him, and then I shoved the wad over and said: "Do you see that, it's the measure of a man, yes sir, this is it." I noticed that Mary T. had a weird smile on her face, she knew! I then said well I'll see you and left. A few hours later my brother Bill stopped at my house and said, what in the hell did you do at the bighouse after lunch? I told him the story and then summed it up by saying, its' payback time.

That was the entire reason for all of those tales, from the guy with the Chinese title, to the wad of cash. It was all designed to show that all it takes are a few mental notes and the fuel to melt steel in ones' own personal furnace; I would never give up.

In a previous chapter I mentioned the Design and Management business which was in the period of late 2000 and running into mid- 2007 a few months prior to selling the house. One of the secrets to my stellar success was the fact that I did not use any form of computer generated design work, commonly referred to as a CAD drawing. There were two reasons for this, one I did not have a CAD unit and two if I did it would be Greek to me anyway. All of my work was hand drawn plans, from a kitchen make over to and entire house. A little dirty secret is the fact that most architects cannot draw. I used to do the 'artist renderings' that appeared in the newspapers for a few firms. These required pen and ink and a set of two dimensional plans, it is interesting to note that they all wanted me to 'enhance these prints, turning a $285K spec. house into a $685K finished drawing. I did this a number of times.

All of my designs in turn were 'one off,' so if a discriminating client, which most of them were, wanted something unique they would call me. Usually all of my clients were high end. If I met with someone and they mentioned a budget, I would pack up my briefcase and walk out.

I hung a boathouse over a lake just to beat the ordinance against building it. No part of the structure touched the water. That did not endear me with council members, some of whom were WASP and my client happened to be Jewish. Most of my clients were of the Jewish persuasion. I saw it and hated it, so, just for spite, I told my client, let's do it just to make them sweat. He loved the idea. This work went on from 2000 to 2007, roughly half of the first year, and the same for the last year. They changed all of the codes in 2006 and it was a mess, they were International Building Codes, which meant going back to school, after I received that 100% from the VA; everything changed. I never loved money, per se, its' a means to an end, but as an entity it can't stand alone in my mind. I love Teresa, but, I don't love money and that made it easy to walk away again from a high earning business, I didn't waste money, but I'll be damned if someone is going to stand over me with a clock, or a magnifying glass and say you missed a spot!

Those damn 'Sisters of Mercy' never mentioned, or said a word about the Mayan Calendar, they talked about the Roman calendar, and the Gregorian calendar, but never a pagan designed device that predated them all by 5000 years.
Well, how could they endorse such a thing, being married to the big guys son and all, so the pope who had a direct line with unlimited long distance, tweaked it a little and named it after himself. The fact that the Mayans were accurate to within 10,000 years didn't matter, have Cortez kill them all, it won't make the headlines because the Sisters of Mercy patrolled the streets and beat anybody with a newspaper.

I really must stop watching these Nostradamus reruns on television, they are causing a lot of stress about where to be when the bottom falls out completely, I mean eating out of a dirt pile with rocks as minerals. We talked about being in Ireland, they can say the Our Father in 3.6 seconds flat, then we thought about Pennsylvania because the Amish have been doing without power for hundreds of years and they aren't starving. We would be surrounded by food and farms but the big cities aren't too far away; that means guys with guns and a bad attitude; could come up this way. I am too old to be Rambo again, I played that part once but I was younger then; sounds like a song, doesn't it?

What it boils down to is simple, if you have a handful of soybeans, while staring at the barrel of a hungry gun, you either don't eat that day, or, you'll never have to worry about eating again.
The orthopedic clinic called and informed me that there was a cancellation and my surgery date was being moved up, actually this was good because we had a date in Ireland. Before the knee surgery I flew over to go in front of the judge

to swear my allegiance to the country in order to get my citizenship; this was the last part of a 6 and a half year saga. A judges' signature on a green piece of paper and I had dual citizenship, I still have Australian citizenship, but that is one hell of a ride for a cup of coffee and the morning paper.

At the hospital I swagger and act tough, I told them I am going to safety pin the gown closed, so, bite it baby! I ain't scared, yeah; wait till they ask me to roll over on the operating table. There won't be any ass there to make fun of, or maybe I should think of some catchy slogan, U.S. Grade-A Beef, butt cut. No seriously, this wasn't really a laughing matter, it was an entire knee replacement, plus it was complicated by my congested arteries from the Agent Orange, something about the full anesthesia. They mentioned a local and I said no way is that going to happen. I did that once for a nose repair. I was in Australia at my boss's house and there was this father of a student there, who was not invited, and he was drunk, and we got into a fight and I pounded him quite well until his son jumped me. Anyway, I had seen an old Lee Marvin movie where he fixes his broken nose with a mirror and a band aid, so I asked the hostess for a mirror and a band aid and, crack, I put my nose back. What I had forgotten, because Lee Marvin didn't do it, was pack the nose for several weeks, and I had to have it re-fixed, so there is the whole story, except for the part where I had to pay for a piece of furniture I smashed across this idiots head.

I've been up all night, no choice really, an entire week has been lobbed off my schedule. It is really my own fault, I was the one who asked to take any cancellation, and I did. We were scheduled to go back to Ireland for two months; December and January.

Today I was released from the hospital. I spent seven days in there with a lot of pain in the PT department. I couldn't leave until my leg was straight, no bends at all by the knee, and that hurt. You hear these stories about Auntie Tilly having a knee surgery and danced naked that night at her club for the elders, then there is Uncle Oscar who had his knee redone and got out of the hospital to go skydiving in Alaska. Don't believe a word, I had a lot of surgeries and this one hurts bad, trust me, it is difficult to walk without a walker. I feel like all of the muscles in my leg shrank 3" in all directions around the knee. Listen, most people have at least 38 hospital stories, I have told my share haven't I but there is one more that I would like to relate.

About a day before our discharge (my roommate and I) I got up around 2am to go into the bathroom. I used the walker to get to the door and reached out to grab the handle. I glanced down and noticed both feet were in the walker. Because my left leg doesn't tell my brain where it is (it should have been behind me) and I hadn't yet reached the door handle, I fell backwards and landed on top of my roommate's new knee. His shouts woke up the entire floor. Fortunately no one was hurt and there was no new damage. After a while our pain levels returned to their unbearable levels. He was a fellow Vietnam Veteran and we got along well, but I sure felt badly about falling on the guy's knee. My punishment is waiting to go in again; there is something wrong with my new knee.

This book has forced me to undress my past and really examine its content. More importantly it has to be a complete examination, not just the hero dressed in white saving Earth from an alien horde. But also the fallacies and less flattering moments I've described. This is a journey of puzzle pieces being used as rafts on the sea of humanity. Some are more sea faring than others by virtue of size and shape; others are mere airplane seat cushion floatation devices. The sea surface texture also changes; there are the slick and polished horizons that have the 'come hither' look. While some surfaces look solid, they may be miles of rusted and burning trash, small smoldering piles of worn out tires and empty refrigerators. Each of these interlocking segments were designed and built during a phase of my life. I could then 'wind surf' it onto another piece that was almost finished, then jump ship and start the process all over again never bothering to look back until a sea of plastic flotsam formed; that has constituted the major content of this tome; my life, as lived and seen with all of my senses.

Speaking of life, while lying in the hospital bed a few days after the screaming banshee, Teresa came in with an envelope and handed it to me. There was a fully laminated sheet with my picture on it. It was completely written in Gaelic or 'Irish'; it was my official citizenship document. Six years of forms and a considerable investment of money; and there it was in my hands. Another future adventure was on the horizon.

Over the decades I have had many opportunities to swerve off my path of choice and take the one well-trodden. It is tempting at times, the only thing that stopped me were the 'ruts'. The nice shiny path looked good as far as you could see and looked as if it was smooth going, but once you started on it the ruts formed. At first you could ignore them and they were just a bit of a nuisance. Then they would keep getting deeper until you could only see a patch of sky. It is then I remembered an old saying; "A rut is a coffin with both ends missing".

In my case, it started with the family business; I could have stayed. Stayed and dealt with the stubborn fears of taking too many monetary risks where we might have made a real success out of all our years of working. Stayed until the day I would watch as they pried the Duke's fingers off it; when it was too late, when the business was tired, rusted iron.

Then there was Australia. I was approached with another contract down there and spent hours debating whether to stay or not. It was just another 'rut' with an accent.

Now the Prison job was a peach as they say. A real milk run of steady salary increases, bonus' and job security. Hell, I was a civil servant, have you ever heard of one being fired? After working there for just a few months, I found a small farm for sale, so I went to the bank. When they saw where I worked, the only question they asked was "How much do you want"? My job title was golden, but the implication was that I wouldn't be going anywhere; a definite rut to fall into.

There were so many opportunities after the removal of alcohol from my itinerary; making my fortune was achievable. But there is a hidden clause in the contract; if you want to be a millionaire. Just dust off the deed to your integrity, values and freedoms, then throw a piece of your soul in with it, you won't need that either. It is just another subtle, gradual decline, which can eventually leave you with a small rectangular view of the world. But your stone will be the largest in the cemetery.

I cannot take credit for my salvation from this carrion while dying of hunger. It wasn't fear of success that was driving me; it was the fear of the results. I would dive into uncharted waters and wrestle demons until I satisfied my curiosity and success, then swim to shore and walk away. During periods of depression, that only hindsight can conjure up, I would have to convince myself that it was all an illusion anyway. Reality is the inability to realize how humorous one's life can be.

After we sold our 'Tree House', we bought a pile of plastic tubs with locking lids and filled them with our treasured objects. If something didn't have a history to us, it was just that; history. We left that house with only the things that mattered, on our back; the rest was left for the next guy. So we started anew (once again). After we made the Lititz house our home, I turned my attention to building a studio. There was a two car garage in the back and I turned half of it into my new workspace. The other side was for our only car, and a scooter.

When the studio was finished, I pulled out all the files dealing with diplomas, certificates and various other letters from big shots. There were thank you letters from Presidents of the U.S. for my service in Vietnam; I even have one from Donald Rumsfeld for my service in the Cold War. Don, where I was cold wasn't an issue, hot lead and steel yes, but cold? So there was a pile of glory and only so much wall space.

Now all it would require is a sum of money for matching frames and mattes for these certificates, some with ribbons and gold stars on them, and the cuneiform signatures. The people that signed these all had impressive titles, most honorable, his best socks, esquire, secretary of defense, a reverend Horace Von Godlike and the YMCA. The list goes on but what had been lacking were my fancy titles, so I call myself, president and CEO when it comes to the Alchemy Studio.

With all of the right tools, it was just a matter of time before my glory wall became a reality. I even placed a spotlight on it in case someone has to read the accolades; though people rarely go into my studio, for any number of reasons, the least of which is insurance and the city of Lititz.
For about a week I used to peek at it and admire it with pride as long as no one was looking, I tried different angles, adjustments, moving things around until it was perfect. Now, after a year or two has passed, I rarely look at it unless I bump into it with something.

When you go to a doctor or dentist you expect to see a glory wall, if you notice diplomas that have a line and under it reads: 'Fill in name here,' I may suggest another doctor if its' a plastic surgeon. Now when you go into your local artists studio you will see a lighted 'glory wall'. I should have built in one of those secret bookcases like Peter Cushing had, you pushed on the right breast of the statue and, pop, the door swings open with all of the diplomas and certificates hidden back there.

Volumes have been written about the many elixirs and magic oils sold to women to help with the dreaded, 'change.' All of this time, us men have been ignored except when we say something totally stupid, which some women would say is all of the time! Men go through their change also I'll have you know. One of the early symptoms is the "belly suck and hold."
This is usually a technique used at the beach, or pool. Another outward manifestation is the refusal to drive a mini-van under any circumstances, even to the Home Depot store, which in itself is a man change indicator.

The man, who has not the slightest idea of what he is doing, goes to the 'Depot' as he now calls it, and purchases all of the lumber for a rear deck, even if you have one, he intends to add on to it. He transports all of this wood and lumber back to the house in the used 'Le Baron' convertible he bought when you were away. The yard is excavated like an anthropological dig site with yellow and orange string lines going in every direction. He has a 4 foot level but can't see the bubble because those peeper glasses are just not cool and must be avoided at all costs.

As for the hair, if various hair clubs don't work, there is always your local barber shop and 'super glue' to rely on. If you have some hair, then travel to the next State over and go to a salon and have it turned from grey to blond over a period of time. Stop buying clothes at Eddie Bauer, or the back of the VFW magazine, and hit Old Navy, and the Gap. Don't forget the 'Harley Davidson' belt buckle that is the size of a dinner plate and has "scratch and sniff ", etched into it. Empty the basement and buy every bow flex machine there is on television, don't worry about the money, just stop paying the kids college tuition and rent their rooms out to young girls who are going to be actress's someday, that's why they work in a 'G' string joint. Then always walk around the house in your speedo.

If your wife hasn't left yet, give it time, she will. This will cover the basic information for the "man change."

During England's 'empire period 'there was nothing they could not do in their frame of mind. The entire World was on their "To Do List." With all of the wars and human rights put to rest, they had a very active, and white, club in London that dealt with geographic exploration; there were two frozen places that needed a look, and the other big adventures had to do with rivers, very big rivers.

It was important to put together expeditions to go find these things that were not really lost to the people who lived there! The search was on for the famous 'head waters' of any great river, this one was the Nile, and in the process they discovered two Niles, one of which had the moniker 'Blue Nile.' As time passed all of this effort and sacrifice came down to a slang expression stating that: denial is not a river in Egypt; Hence my elaborate introduction to one word, denial.

According to my "Franklin 3000 Language Master," Oh Frank, your mother called…it contains the entire contents of the Merriam-Webster dictionary and thesaurus, the word 'denial' used as a noun means: rejection of a request, or the validity of a statement. And the verb version is: declare untrue, disavow, refuse to grant, so now we have the reasoning for what is to follow; I do not deny I cannot spell.

My academic education was placed in the hands of the Sisters of Mercy, a total contradiction of the definition of good words. I could not spell, I still cannot spell and that is why I have my Franklin 3000, 'Oh Frank, I wish you wouldn't do that', is right here on my desk. Just think how many beatings I could have avoided, or detentions filling in blackboards with the sentence: Jason can't spell worth a fuck! And it didn't end there, I would then be late for work and that would demand an explanation to the highest authority. Then, to top it all off, Mary T would agree with everyone about my spelling, including those starched sisters of doom. Now, here I am years later, holding on to those memories of sheer brutality with a machine the size of a good rib eye steak that tells me I never did have to know how to spell anyway.

ACTION FIGURES INCLUDED

After I had been given the 'all clear' on my knee we were ready to leave for Ireland. Everything had been arranged and paid for in advance. Teresa found a three bedroom apartment on top of " Tubor Hill " which is a hard walk straight up from the ' Octagon ' as it is called; in the center of Westport. Our flight left on March 15th, 2011. A few days prior to this while at the hospital, the Vascular Department had called for a CT scan with contrast, I have been having these and MRI's for almost 12 years checking up on supposedly two aneurysms; an aortic and a thoracic. All of this time they kept going all over the map with the sizes, which is important, because anything over 5cm is considered to be an operation of considerable risk. On the 14th, at 4:00pm some Chinese vascular doctor who I never heard of told me that I could not go to Ireland, it was too dangerous. I had an abdominal aortic aneurysm that was 7.6cm and very deadly. I ignored the guy explaining that I have been hearing this stuff for years and to call me the night before I am scheduled to fly to Dublin was a really bad time. I had already shipped my art studio equipment, at considerable expense, to Ireland weeks in advance so it would be through customs once I arrived.

Once in Westport, I went to see my Irish GP and he looked at the disc of test results and almost fell out of his chair. He said, Jason you have a hand grenade in your stomach with no pin. He then set me up with a very sophisticated clinic in Galway, a few hours' drive down the coast. I was to see a World renowned surgeon in vascular medicine; he was a young man from Egypt. He wanted to schedule me for surgery; in fact they did while I was there by moving some schedules around. He also sent me to a cardiologist for a heart work up and a serious look at my vascular system. Little did I know that the effects of Agent Orange were going to play a part in all of this; the doctor found considerable blockage, calcification of the coronary arteries, this was not good. My 100% rating comes with a foreign medical program that pays for this stuff. So Teresa contacted them.

435

After weeks of e-mails, they denied me compensation because it wasn't listed as "service connected" in my official records. We tried the US Military hospital in Germany, again it was a wash; they didn't have a vascular surgeon. We tried to get help from the American Embassy in Dublin, they were useless, but they closed the e-mail by telling me to have a nice day! Here, have a nice this! As a last resort I filled out the paperwork for the Irish social medicine scheme and tried to get it approved ASAP. That worked, and both Teresa and I were issued our identification numbers. These allowed us complete medical care, free, including all of our medications, goose egg, nada, zero; now you know why we go to Ireland a lot. So I said fuck it, Teresa was worried sick but I told her that I didn't feel close to dying, it was as if I knew my days were not over here on Earth. In two months I never even opened my art studio, I just re-addressed the boxes and sent them back at even more expense because the Euro was trading at close to $1.50 USD, and that hurts.

We flew back to the U.S., if the airline knew about this, I would not have stepped foot on any aircraft. We arrived in the States in the middle of May. Within a few days I was on a train to Philadelphia to go into the VA hospital there for tests. They found what they were looking for and more, a surgery date was set. As it turns out, the vascular people and the respiratory people were arguing about my general anesthesia; was it going to be twilight or all the way? It was 7am when they wheeled me down to the operating room. The same people mentioned above showed up and I looked at the clock, it was almost 8:30am. I was lying there freezing my ass off, my teeth were chattering, everyone was standing around until this 7 foot tall Egyptian anesthesiologist came in, he was pissed, he leaned over and asked me, I told him no freakin' way; I wanted to be completely under for this. I never had problems in the past, having had two major surgeries not even a year ago. He was fine with that, and then he went nuts.

This guy looked like a Pharaoh from ancient Egypt, honest to God. He started shouting out orders, cover this man up, look at him you fools, his teeth, I can hear them from over here. He then turned to the vascular and respiratory people and told them to get out of his operating theater, now; and he chased them all out. He shouted orders to nurse's standing around; do this, you do that, get those tools in here. And finally he came over to me with a needle, no 'count backwards' or recite War and Peace, nothing except: "You go to sleep, now!" With that he rammed that plunger down and bang, I was gone. It just so happened that my charmed life kicked in again, the surgeon who was doing my surgery studied for 3 years in Edinburgh, Scotland under Dr. Scofield who invented the procedure of stints. My surgeon was cutting me then leaving that afternoon for Scotland. After the surgery, I was in the PAC unit and well awake when he came in, the doctor told me that my aortic vein looked like a summer sausage. He said it was transparent; it was stretched out that far. He was amazed that I was still alive any second could have been my last. I told him that I owed God too much money, so He didn't want me until I paid down my debt. It was true, but it wasn't money that I owed. I paid in souls by helping other veterans get over the tough spots before they blew their brains out. My friend Doug and I attend and run two meetings a week for military people. He was in the service for over 8 years, 4 of those spent in the Marines. That is my payback time; and a pleasure for me to be a part of it. Look at what just transpired, I had been spared a certain death again, flying at 39,000 feet for 6 hours isn't an exercise for aneurysms. I am not immortal, I am not lucky, I was Mr. Lucky a long time ago in the stock car days, but that does not apply here, it's not a question of luck at all, I am to live and try to make this world just a tidbit better.

Once I received a strange commission, the client wanted an exact copy of Van Gogh's' painting, "Cypress by Moonlight." Most people think it's called "Starry Night."

To prepare for that painting I deprived myself of sleep, sex and a big diet. I drank Pernod because it was close to his favorite Absente, which you can't buy in the U.S. I went to New York a few times to study his brush stroke and use of color. I then stretched a canvas the exact size after having made my own bars, and proceeded to paint. Out of all of this, the two months of deprivation and pain, I somehow started to contemplate immortality.

Because man is an animal, there will never be immortality, as long as we have to eliminate waste products every day we can never be immortal; but being an artist and a writer; as long as someone, somewhere looks at my artwork or even reads this book, 50 years after I am dead, I shall be immortal, I will be alive for that individual for a short period of time.

Years ago I studied meditation with the Swami Rama at the Himalayan Institute in Honesdale, Pa. He is the guru that could control the blood flow to his heart and for 16 seconds had no pulse. He did this while being monitored by a bunch of scientists He did it with his mind; that is the part that will live on. In one of his books he address's someone's desire to own a Mercedes, his comment was by the time you have attained that, someone else will be driving it, taking you to the airport to fly out to your next business meeting. Was your desire fulfilled? Or wanting a million dollars, he said that it is very easy to do if you devote your entire being to the acquisition of wealth; you will achieve it, but at what cost? And that is where he left it, for the reader to answer.

My body is the mortal part with all of its failing's, but my mind is a different matter. I may be quite content with a large percentage of my life, but it does not cover the small regrets.

One unrealized goal was to become a bass player in a famous rock and roll band. A few incidentals flew in the face of that bid for success, one, that you must know how to play a bass guitar, another was the 'fifth column' at home; Mary T.

438

She made a comment to me one day when I told her of my aspirations, she said: "You will be playing in a dark, smoke filled bar with a cigarette butt stuck on the guitar neck under one of the strings." I never forgot that because it was too graphic, it had too much information, she knew something!

No, at the age of 60 I won't be that cool, expressionless guy off to one side of the stage. This is one piece of the puzzle that didn't come in the box, in fact, there are a lot of piece's missing by virtue of never being meant to be there. This book tells the story of my life and completes the puzzle to the age of 60. It is not to say my life has just stopped, even though there are a lot of health issues that are presently apparent; mostly from my involvement in war. There will be room for what the future has in store for me. But this is the only story I will put all the pieces into, there isn't space for another finished illustration.

I lived my life with the pedal to the metal, as they used to say in racing circles. I lived as large as possible during an interesting generation, from flowers, love, peace and tree's to ammo with full metal jackets and then back again. My regrets are few, even though I allowed opportunity and individuals to remain adrift on a storm filled sea, every accomplishment is tempered with at least two failure's, the bent nails or broken puzzle piece's I tried to make fit, knowing too well that they, like me, didn't belong there.

I sincerely hope you enjoyed this endeavor, if it made you laugh then I have succeeded, if there are things you can relate to, then I don't walk alone. If by chance I wrote things that made you angry, then I can relate having been an angry man for so many wasted years. If I earned some respect, then I have fulfilled my purpose and was awarded the highest compliment to my life, something to truly cherish in these waning years.

Allow me to thank you for your precious time and consideration, you have placed the final piece into my puzzle, it is now complete.

COLORS WILL NOT FADE.

1950   TO   2010

ACKNOWLEDGEMENTS

Many people, some faceless, others nameless must be thanked for their unwitting involvement in this adventure. I would like to extend my deepest appreciation to my wife Teresa, for her help and motivation is without doubt. She also commands an important position in my life and has for many, many years.

Without my Brother-in-Law, Sloan Winters, and his vast knowledge of these electronic devices and his wife Kathleen with her editing expertise this book would have probably remained simply an idea.

I would like to also thank Professor William Irwin, for taking the time to read my raw manuscript and then to provide his input and personal publishing experience.

Teresa Marie Fee, an accomplished writer and artist in her own right was kind enough to become the most objective voice for me to listen to; she has read the entire manuscript, as did Dr. Irwin before they penned their Introductions.

Please allow me to thank those musicians from the 1960's & 70's, along with their record labels, for the few words I quoted from their songs found in the text, they were essential in providing a pivot to swing on while making a point on a few occasions.

There are some individuals mentioned here that I will not thank at all, and others that have my full appreciation. I hope that thousands of art lovers and clients who helped make my career a success for 40 years have access to this text and realize what a crucial role they all played in my professional life. As for personal, I am not sure the reception would be festive under certain circumstances.

Finally, let me thank the person who is currently reading this book, I thank you for investing time and compensation in my life story, and hope that it proved to be a worthy endeavor that will leave you satisfied, as any good book should.

Sincerely

Jason

TABLE OF CONTENTS

12923665R00243

Made in the USA
Charleston, SC
06 June 2012